Unsigned

Unscene

John Winstanley

ISBN 978-1-78222-192-0

Book design, layout and production management by Into Print
www.intoprint.net
+44 (0)1604 832149
Printed and bound in UK and USA by Lightning Source

Contents

Front and back cover concept by John Winstanley with layout and technical support provided by Michael Guy. Font cover digger photograph reproduced by kind permission of David Gilmour.

Sound Bites

"A biographical whistle-stop tour of the Lancashire music scene as told through the eyes of band manager John Winstanley and the acts he has worked with over the years"
Laura Simms-Luddington (Monkeys In Love)

Chapter 2. "Pogo'til I Die"
"This particular chapter is very evocative of a Proustian 'Madeline Punk Rock Cake'! This will appeal to those who experienced this first hand as well as the younger people who have heard all about it. This is a vital document; I also like how it fades in an out of chronological time events."
Stephen Dobson author of "The Man Who Killed The Hamsters"

Chapter 4 Chorley FM
"An honest and reflective account of life in Chorley and an exciting read with lots of anecdotes to add flavour to the tale! Back then there was a focus on fun over format. With increasing competition in the radio environment, community radio stations are now seen as a training ground for young people hoping for a career in broadcasting. From John's words I get the feeling that back then it was rawer and more experimental - essentially what community radio is supposed to be."
Catherine Wilkinson BA, MSc and currently working towards a PhD with "Connecting Communities through Youth-led Radio"

Chapter 5 "Let's Not Lose mars To the Commies".
"Their live performances were infectious...as a parent of a teenager you are always proud of them but you also are naturally anxious! The band was very successful fairly quickly and sometimes had to travel great distances to achieve their dream. These are hard times for a parent ... feeling very proud when they made their first recording and when they played in Glasgow with Farse...All steps towards independence and confidence, which often only music can bring.... I don't think any of the Commies will ever forget the impact of the band at that time in their young lives."
David Wright – father of Liam

Chapter 8 The Penniless Playboy (Shaun Maxwell)

"Shaun is incapable of writing a bad tune. He is a big teddy bear of a man, who looks pretty tough but is a real sweetie. You'd better have a sense of humour and don't take yourself too seriously because he will prick that pomposity. He is one of the funniest and wittiest men I know and frequently has me in stitches. John has managed to capture the essence of what it is to meet Shaun and describe the complex personality that captivates and educates.
Stephen Dobson author or "The Man Who Killed The Hamsters"

Chapter 11 The Digger Movement.

"Charting his personal journey across the borderlands of the northern music scene, John Winstanley's book records the vibrancy and tenacity of all those involved in a grass-roots activist project, The Diggers' Movement. Drawing on the lessons of the 17th century socialist-radical Gerrard Winstanley and the original Diggers' movement, John attempted to regenerate a spirit of the 'commons' – and a voice of dissent – against the profit-focused machinery of mainstream music production and dissemination. This book contributes to the cultural zeitgeist of Digger' revivalism; here, in the context of digging into, and unearthing, the life of music subculture and participatory politics. A stirring read."
Dr Penny Rivlin, Research academic at the University of Sheffield

Foreword

This is a book for anyone who wants to understand the unsigned music scene and the appeal it has in many communities. It is an autobiographical account of the discovery, promotion and management of some of those involved in and around Chorley, Lancashire (2002-2007). The author reveals the personal highs and lows that many musicians experience by providing a detailed analysis of the musicians he helped and some that he stills retains an interest in today. It is a must read for the fans, friends and relatives of those associated with local music in the towns throughout the North West of England that he encountered. Interwoven is the personal journey of a married man bringing up a young family during his early forties balancing his passion for music against the changing world of his full time job in finance. This story is at times fascinating, hilarious and heart breaking as we ride the road and dreams of anyone moved by the power of Rock and Roll.

The author wishes to give the following special thanks:

Glenys Lilian Winstanley (mother), Bernard Stanley Jones (uncle) and Irene McGarry (aunt), now all deceased, who are a constant guide. Hannah and Holly Winstanley (Daughters) George Rawlinson (father-in-law) and Glyn Winstanley (brother) who are continual reminders of the old saying "you are a short time young and a long time old"! All of you who have contributed directly or indirectly to this book, past and present that are not mentioned in the pages. Finally, my wife Helen without whose support none of this would be possible.

To you the reader

Someone told me about an assumed contract between the writer and the reader -which takes for granted that grammar and spelling will be perfect. This book is a self-published endeavour and I am ultimately responsible for its shortcomings, not the publisher, who has helped me beyond what I can reasonably expect in terms of technical accuracy- thank you Mark Webb at Into Print. As for factual details, some will differ to others' version of events. I have taken what I can from the main sources that have approved of what I have written. The result may provoke debate in both what is covered and what is not. I welcome others to correct me and fill in the gaps in their own book. I consider literature like some of the purest music that moves me - its uniqueness exists despite its imperfections. Thank you for your patience and perseverance.

01 My Musical Journey

(Dedicated to the memory of Elizabeth Voskamp and Andrew Bennet. R.I.P)

Music is in my DNA thanks to my parents. My mother was Glenys Winstanley and she loved to listen to the radio and dance. If I heard music in the womb then I would have been jiggling about to pop songs of the day like *Bobby's Girl* by Susan Maughan. Mum told me that I was nearly called Robert on the strength of this number three hit from the October of 1962 – a few months before I was born. My father was Frank Winstanley and he was a car mechanic by trade. He taught the piano in his spare time and played the organ semi professionally at weekends in pubs and clubs throughout his life. I cannot remember a time or a place when music was not present.

For the first few months of my life I was a gypsy of sorts living in a caravan parked on a piece of land owned by sympathetic friends. This was in Okehampton, Devon and my arrival had halted my parents' plans to emigrate to Ghana. Dad was working for a local tractor manufacturer who was negotiating an export contract at the time. He was expected to fly out in advance and prepare for the cargo arriving, check the deliveries and stay there to show the locals how to operate and maintain them. As it turned out, my untimely birth was a blessing in disguise. The deal fell through but they could have been stranded there. A short time later, we left our tin can for a detached bungalow on the steep hill heading east out of the village. My father always had a desire to better himself and he often had things that we could not afford. Throughout my mum's life with him, she had to work to cover the debts that he ran up. The jobs she took on were varied: a telephone exchange operator, egg packer, and occasionally she chalked the betting odds on the boards in bookmakers. She did what she could to keep our small family together and solvent. When I was two and a half we moved to Southfield Close, Woolavington, near Bridgewater, Somerset. It was a brand new three bedroom detached bungalow with gardens all the way round it in a small cul-de-sac. It is here that I have my first memories and where I can recall the impact of music.

My dad was born in Wigan and his father was the pub landlord at The Grimshaw Inn in Upholland. My grandfather was called John and played the piano for his customers who knew him as Jack. Frank was sent to piano lessons from an early age and his talent reached to concert standard. But he chose to be a motor mechanic and have a part time income playing keyboards. After moving to Somerset he formed a duo with the next door neighbour called Mike who was a drummer in his spare time. They played dance music and accompanied touring vocalists. Amongst my early recollections is one of my dad recording songs from the radio on a reel to reel tape recorder which was before the smaller cassettes had been invented. He played them back and would write down the chords to the songs just by hearing the tunes. This saved money on manuscripts even though he had a lot of these too. His note books were filled with song titles and their unique code sequences which I later learned to decipher. Back then, the first tune I remember hearing was *Water Melonman* by Herbie Hancock. Dad recorded me singing it one day and I was loved; happy and very settled in our expensive home.

My very first memory was sitting on the kitchen floor hitting pots and pans with wooden spoons. Mum had laid them out for me to play with so she could hear me while busy with cleaning and other house work. As long as I was making a noise on them she knew where I was and I *loved* making a racket. This may have been why I eventually became a drummer and not a guitarist or keyboard player.

I had lots of friends at the village school and took part in every activity going. I remember playground kick abouts, war games, kiss catch, chain tag and racing Corgi, Dinky and Matchbox cars on a slope by the climbing fame. We swapped football cards that came in chewing gum packets for the 1966 Football World Cup. At the age of four, mum put me into a children's ballroom dance class in town, while she went shopping on Saturday mornings. I took to it like bubble and gum. The teachers demonstrated the dance while we watched –the boys on one side of the dance floor and the girls on the other. Then the boys had to walk across the floor, bow in front of the girl lined up opposite, put your right hand out and ask if they would dance with you. All very civilised and in keeping with the etiquette of the dance hall culture of earlier decades. This was at the same time the swinging sixties flourished and changed all those old fashioned ways. I learned the intricacies of the Waltz and Quick Step but had more fun swapping partners in the Mod Rock Barn dance. At an end of term exam I got a silver IDTA pin for my Cha-Cha -Cha and I enjoyed the other South American dances too such as the Samba, Rumba and Tango. Dancing made me under-stand rhythm, tempos and variations of styles. I associated music with move-ment, an awareness of space and meeting people. We danced to the current pop tunes like – *The Last Waltz* (Engelbert Humperdinck), *Michelle* (Overlanders) and *Puppet on a String* (Sandie Shaw).

I absorbed music actively and semi consciously. I liked to sing the hymns in assembly or at Sunday school in the church across the road to our school. Dad bought loads of records and I remember an album of Glen Miller's greatest hits and a compilation of famous songs from musicals including the tune *Zipa-de-doodah*. My Christmas present one year included a 7 inch copy of the Jungle Book and Sparkie's Magic Piano - I wore them both out. There was plenty of diversity but it was Pop and Rock'n roll that registered most!

I have always had good health but I remember not feeling well one day at school - a tummy upset. Some senior girls had to look after me in a class room over the lunch break. One of them played piano as the others sang *King of the Road* by Roger Miller, clicking their fingers just before the hook line. It's my standby karaoke song today as it has a strolling tempo and a spoken delivery. It's the earliest form of rap in my collection - the vocal tune shuffles along in a matter of fact style. There's mention of: trailers for sale or rent, rooms to let at 60 cents, the price does not include a telephone or food and pets are not allowed. To top it all, poor Roger is out of cigarettes! He's sweeping floors and has a keen interest in keeping up to date with who's who on the railway. He knows all the engineers names and those of their kids and every lock that's not locked when no one's looking i.e. he has a side line in stolen goods! Gangster rap it isn't but I bet Public Enemy or Eminem tilt their caps to the song's subtle observations which I have learned to savour as I got older.

Occasionally, my dad took me with him to visit music shops in Bristol. These were splendid palaces where the instruments fascinated me. The lights dazzled as they danced on the brashy chrome and gold of the trumpets, saxophones and drum kits in contrast to the richly aromatic varnished woods of the refined violins, pianos and acoustic guitars. Ah! The guitars - arranged in rows on the floor like soldiers on parade or suspended, God like, from the ceiling. The electric ones were magnificent – an array of ruby reds, deep blues, darkest blacks and others with a mottled turtle shell effect in shades of grey and blood browns. They were unlike the other instruments - something supernatural. They had to be connected to a box with knobs on it which brought them to life! I did not need to be told "not to touch" as I had a respect for everything in these spectacular emporiums – where everything was magical because of the sounds they created. Recognising my attraction to the guitars dad bought me a ukulele and showed me some tunes, but holding the strings down hurt my small fingers and I lost interest too quickly preferring to play out instead. Dad also tried to teach me piano but he didn't have the patience he was paid to have for his private pupils who came to our home for lessons.

The third bedroom in our house was a music room. It contained Dad's Kemble Modern upright with a glockenspiel on the top of the lid, his white Hammond organ, huge Leslie speaker cabinet and boxes of sheet music and neatly organised note books. Sometimes he had other musicians round for auditions or rehearsals and the sounds filled the whole house and made the walls come alive. It moved me inside, shook my brain and made me want to tap my feet and clap my hands. He and Mike got a residency at a hotel restaurant in Brent Knoll. It was owned by a Greek family headed by Max the cheery father and grandfather to several kids. Dad would take me over there when Max invited him for meals or to discuss work. I'd play with the other children but one day Max showed us his party piece. This was an incredible feat of skill and strength. He took us into the dining room where he stood next to a table. It was set out for a meal for four - all the plates, cutlery and a selection of glasses. Before he knelt down at one corner he encouraged us to clap our hands like they do in *Fiddler on the Roof* – slow at first then steadily faster. He opened his huge mouth and griped the table in his jaws. He stretched his arms along the sides as he pulled the table leg between his thighs. Then he started to get up, the glasses rattled and the clapping got louder. When he was upright he raised his arms above his head and started to click is fingers as he walk across the dance floor and back again supporting the whole weight with only his teeth. Absolutely amazing showman ship and something I have never seen anyone else do. This, and the Bridgewater carnivals, was my first experiences of how music and performance could be an incredible form of entertainment.

At the end of the sixties we moved to Conniston Avenue, Euxton in Chorley. One of the reasons we had come up north was because there were more clubs and cabaret lounges for my dad to work in than down south. I expect the cost of the property was a factor too. We downsized into a two bedroom semi detached on a housing estate built on a former WWII camp site for American soldiers and air crew. I went to the newly built Primrose Hill school at the other end of the village. Here I met Peter Hardman and we shared a love of music. The Beatles had split up and we decided to form a kid's version with me as Ringo and Peter as Paul. We imagined that we were reading fan mail during art and craft classes – time wasting but in a creative way. We discussed songs we made up and thought up ways of avoiding the fans (other kids) during break times. It was an excuse to run around and fantasise that we were being chased by girls like the real Beatles in *Hard Day's Night* which was shown on the TV every Christmas back then. At Peter's we would play records. Amongst his family's collection were The Carpenters and Queen but for most of the time we listened to whatever was on the radio.

My friendship with Peter had music at the heart of it – unlike those with neighbourhood friends – Mick Mason, the Jones's and the Morgan brothers Alistair and Gareth who all lived in the same avenue. With them it was all about war games, making dens and cap bombs from large nuts and bolts, fighting and lighting fires on the building site at the back where the rest of the estate was still being built. At lunch times in the holidays the local chip shop was packed with builders and the radio would be on. All these labourers with large dirty hands, wearing rough clothing and huge boots would whistle or sing along to the likes of *Chirpy Chirpy Cheap Cheap* (Middle of the Road) or *Brand New Key* (Melanie) - reducing them to something less threatening. Music was an equaliser and no matter how old you were or what you looked like it crossed the divides by its ability to be shared and appreciated by anyone.

Our home had a long lounge and, on the main wall facing the open plan wooden stair case, my dad had set up the record player. He built his own speakers and placed them at precisely six feet apart either side of the turntable. The day he was ready to test them out he called me in and sat me down at exactly the midpoint between the black facia of the pine wood cabinets.

"Now then son, stay there and listen to this" he said in a restrained but childishly excited voice as he lowered the needle onto the vinyl. He turned round fixed a stare into my eyes and declared "Stereo!"At which point a man's voice came out from the centre of the room,

"This is a journey into sound, the sound of stereo..." or something like that. It spoke in a deep and authorative tone. It went on to explain that a steam train was about to leave a railway station. From one speaker I heard the locomotive hissing away, passenger voices and the slamming of carriage doors came out of the other, the whistle blew and its shrill pinched my ears. The engine chuffed and chugged speeding up as the volume rose. Before long it was building to a roar and just as I felt it would crash into me it passed through my head from the right speaker to the left one, rattling the ornaments on the mantel piece as it thundered through the house. I looked out of the window at the houses opposite and thought it was on its way to smash the building site to bits and crush all those labourers!

"What about that then eh kid!" my dad beamed – I had never seen him as ecstatic as that before or since. I was in awe of the experience too and a little scared in that way when I went too high on a swing or too fast on the roundabout – scarily enjoyable!

"Stereo......." He sighed with rapturous contentment and shook his head slowly from side to side, temporarily mesmerised by the other sounds on the rest of the record. We shared, for one of the very few times in my life, a father and son bonding moment- an appreciation of sound. Mono was dead. He bought records that showed off this stereo effect. Big band orchestras and *The Wonderful World of* ...so and so series and lots of albums featuring organs and great vocalists like Tony Bennet and Matt Monroe. But I liked the ones my mum played - the Top of The Pops sounds like collection that Pickwick Records put out. They had busty models scantily dressed in the latest fashion on the front cover and the songs were cover versions of what was in the charts. For years I preferred some of these versions to the originals like *Tokoloshe Man (John Kongos)*, *Mother of Mine (Neil Reid)* and *I Just Can't Help Believing (Elvis Presley)*. I mimed once to the latter in front of my parents on or about the time I met my half brother, Glyn for the first time.

My father had been married before he met my mum. He had two sons by his first wife Betty – Glyn and David who were, respectively, thirteen and ten years older than me and mum explained that Glyn had wanted to get to know us. Glyn lived in Wigan and mum was originally from Birkenhead so it seemed that Mum had moved closer to her family as had dad to his other family. Glyn would visit and it was like having an elder brother for a while. He liked music too and went to the Isle of Wight festival to watch Hendrix perform. When Hendrix finished and the drummer was walking off stage he threw his drum sticks into the crowd and Glyn caught one of them. Glyn gave me a cassette tape of rock music at some point. It was called "Axe Attack" and had loads of bands on that I'd never heard of before like Aerosmith, UFO and Ted Nugent. I didn't take to it as much as did when I heard *Jeepster* by Marc Boland for the first time on the radio or saw Rod Stewart perform *Maggie May* on TV. Glam Rock had started and the Thursday night Top of the Pops show on the telly was required viewing for playground debates on the Friday morning.

"Did you see Rod Stewart on telly last night kicking that microphone stand into the air and twirling it above his head!" and we would all step back and do an impression of it.

"Or Boland doing that pose (demonstrating the Electric Warrior stance) and shouting that "......and I'm gonna suuuuuukkkkkk yaaaa!" line (we all shouted the same line too with total innocence about what it really meant). The collective consensus was rites of passage for awkward pre pubescent boys. To be "cool" you had to agree on what was fashionable to listen to, pose to and shout about.

Boarding School 1971-1976

Just before my ninth birthday I was sent to an all boys Preparatory Boarding School called Lawrence House in St Anne-on-sea. It once stood proudly at the end of the first fairway north of the club house to the Royal Golf Links before it was knocked down in the 1990s to make way for a posh housing estate. But it was my "home" from home for five years. My dad had been moved to consider this form of education when I brought home my class photo from School. He was enraged to discover that I wore the playing out clothes he usually saw me in when he got home from work. He left in the morning before I got dressed and the photo showed me wearing T shirts, demins and he took exception to the long hair on the other boys and the fashions worn by the teachers. Mum supported the idea of private education as I was not doing very well academically and I was getting into fights. My southern accent was literally kicked out of me as I learned the harsh northern one and I'd just about managed that adjustment when I arrived amongst a load of tofts for the Michalmus term in the autumn of 1971.

There were many rules to obey and one of them was that you were not allowed radios or cassette players in your dormitories. You had to keep them in your tuck boxes in your classroom and only play them at break time – even then it was frowned on by the teachers. This explains why I was starved of music other than the one music lesson we had each week with Mr Garrett and the hymns at assembly or choir practices. I did have private piano lessons with the grey haired and wrinkly old Mrs Saunders but that was like the other music lesson; full of the classical composers like Tchaikovsky, Brahms and Rossini. I excelled at music but compared to the other kids, I was crap at the rest of the curriculum. The very first history home work was to write a short story of a historical figure we admired. I chose Robin Hood as I loved the theme music to the TV series starring Richard Greene. I was singled out by the History teacher to read my work out to the rest of the class. Thinking I was being held up as an example of good work, no sooner had I began with "Once upon a time in Sherwood Forest..." the rest of the class burst into uncontrolled laugher. I was stunned, embarrassed and on the brink of shedding tears. In time I understood, what the other boys knew, that he could be wickedly cruel, cunning and without favourites. He had marked me out as he did with all of us at some point, but when he did I, like all his victims, instantly won over friends. In my case the friends I gained were attracted to my "ordinariness" and tainted northern accent – which I lost in time as I adapted to the "social upper middleclass peer group" tone if you can imagine that. My mum even paid for Elocution lessons at the school given by the Headmaster's mother – a kindly and genteel old lady. This and music lessons were an extra cost to her but she wanted me to integrate and not be singled out for the way I spoke in the same way she had made a point of not speaking in a scouse accent which she always felt had helped her get work with telephone exchanges. I was entered into public speaking and music theory examinations which I passed and won school awards for. I was also very good at sport too especially football and made a lot of friends through this, Rugby and Cricket.

When things settled down I started to figure out where my place was in this hierarchy. I suppose being good at sports made up for being in the lower end of the classes throughout the time I was there. Music wise – I could play piano but was not naturally talented like one lad who could play from hearing a tune– like my dad. He was younger than me and could play *This Town ain't big enough for the both of us* by Sparks which impressed everyone over my best tune *Concerto Theme in B Flat*. The choir master got us to learn traditional songs like *Dirty Old Town* and a song about Jessie James and another about the Titanic. From these sessions he would select those good enough to perform in the choir or just make up the numbers at the back, for the end of year Carol concert. I remember one Christmas when *Merry Christmas* by Slade was number one and he let one of his favourites sing it at the concert and again in the end of term assembly. It was a welcome relief from the traditional tunes and I don't hate it as some do. We also did a production of "Oliver" the musical and I loved every song in that as it takes me back to the gym and a time when I was happy and innocent.

I came home every half term and mum took me dancing to the Labour Club which was on Friday Street, Chorley. She pushed me round the dance floor and before long I was able to lead her and dance with the other regulars. I became popular with everyone as the young boy who could dance and was smartly dressed – mum saw to that. I was eleven and my dad had left us to be with a woman called Molly, who he'd met when he was in his late teens before he had married Betty. I picked up the dance steps from where I had left off half my age earlier, and I enjoyed the modern and old time sequences. This club and others that we use to go to were full of adults and not like the dancing lessons in Somerset. The old people were good to me. I got on with them but, over the next ten years or so, I spent less time with my own age group when not in school or college. I found that their stories and advice more relevant in the absence of my dad. Hence my aunt (Irene McGarry) and uncle (Bernard "Pidge" Jones) in Birkenhead became very important as surrogate grandparent figures as my real ones were all dead. They came to watch me dance and said I should do it professionally.

14

Working men's clubs in the seventies was, for some, a place to drink cheap beer and try your luck at Bingo. For others, it was where you socialised, danced and enjoyed live entertainment. If they had a *Now That's what I call working men's club hits* it would have included the likes of *Hi Ho Silver Lining, Is This The Way to Amarillo, Sweet Caroline,* and the instrumental dance classic *The Birdie Song*. One holiday in 1975 I went to my first disco. It was at the Methodist church hall in the dip on the A49 leading out of Euxton towards Charnock Richard. This hall had a badminton court lines painted on the wooden flooring, but that night it doubled as the perimeter of the dance floor. The Bay City Rollers had a number one hit at the time called *Bye Bye Baby* and all the girls screamed when this song got played (several times). Like Beatle mania it was called Roller mania and girls shouted the names of the band members which had the negative effect on lads who didn't look like Eric or Woody. Not that I was that fussed about girls even though I'd had a few fumbles with some. They were curiosities, dance partners and not as much fun as sport or building dens.

It wasn't until I was thirteen and in my last year at Lawrence House when "proper" music re-entered my life. As seniors, we had old arm chairs in a bay window area in our classroom where we would congregate in our spare time. My friends Sam Woodcock and Martin Harrop had cassette players and two tapes I remember listening to were *Venus and Mars* (Wings) and *Crime of the Century* (Super tramp) – which were not in the same league as The Rock Follies! Someone else had their first album from the TV series of the same name. The show followed the fortunes of three women singers trying to make it in the music business. I loved that first album and the track called *Glen Miller is Missing*. For weeks we would ask each other "guess what?" "What?" "(Singing) Glen Miller is missing...." We did not have debates about music, it didn't matter what you liked but there was a teacher who hung around and brought in copies the New Musical Express. This would be at weekends and he tried to get us interested in music in his own way and I picked up on the reports of people called Mods and Rockers who met for fights at the seaside over bank holidays. That was in another world to where we lived and there were plenty of games we could play outside during that summer heat wave of our last term in 1976. But, one day he said that it would all be different now that punk had started. This meant nothing to us but I do remember looking up the word when, at the end of an episode of The Rock Follies, the voiceover mentioned "....and next week the little ladies meet a punk band..." I didn't get to see that episode so I did not know what these punk people looked like or how they behaved. That would become clearer when I left boarding school to go to Balshaws High School in Leyland in the autumn. But, before I started that school I got invited to spend the summer holiday with Robin Goodwin at his house in Cheltenham. "Rob" became my best mate and we maintain our friendship to this day. Again, music was something we both shared an interest in and that summer we listened to his record collection which contained *Pet Sounds* by the Beach Boys and other middle of the road pop stuff.

Balshaws High School 1976-1979 and punk initiations

Starting in the third year at any new school is awkward. There are plenty of films on the subject now and my experience was reasonably smooth compared to those in Hollywood land, thanks to my interest in sports and music. My reception group included Mick Robinson who would eventually become the Head Boy. He and his friends played football at break times and I joined in and got on with them. Mick's elder brother had been to watch The Jam on their first tour and Mick came into school one day singing *In The City*. I said I liked it and he did me a cassette of the LP. I played it and shared a common interest in the band with him. He copied *This Is the Modern World* when that was released too. These LPs became the sound track to my life for the next two years. The lyrics spoke to me about teenage angst and most songs had a driving beat that I responded to. They looked smart too. I could identify with their dress code as it was nearly the same as the school uniform- black blazers, black trousers, black shoes, white shirts and the tie was black with a silver twist. Occasionally I went the out for the full Jam look by wearing white socks too! I didn't consider them a "punk" band even though this is how the press referred to them as I was still unclear as to what Punk was.

I cover most of my initial awareness of Punk Rock in Chapter two – but the first Punk record I remember hearing was in 1977. I played for the Chorley Cricket Club's under 18s team and we won the Sutcliffe trophy that year. To celebrate our success there was a party and a disco in the club house on Windsor Park. It was a hot evening and started very predictably: cheese and pineapple on cocktail sticks, ham sandwiches and chart music of the day. One of the older lads was called "Bisch" – and one of the coolest characters I had met up to that point – the first being David Bamber at Lawrence House. Bamber's coolness was excelling at French so, as he explained to me one day, he could chat up French birds as everyone one knows they are better than other girls! That knowledge of the "...better than..." was mysterious and in my books cool. But that balmy evening Bisch was about to top David Bamber in my league table of who's who of cool.

16

He arrived later than the rest of us, a cool thing to do and who cares if all the food and most of the orange squash had gone – he was leaning on the bar and able to buy a "shandy" with the other cool team members and their girlfriends. I sat down on my own and blended into the wall paper as best as I could as I didn't know these people outside practices and match games – none of them went to my school. At some point, Bisch slid through his entourage and sauntered over to the middle aged Disc Jockey. He pulled out a seven inch single he had tucked into his jeans and, in a slow, purposeful semi circular movement he leaned over and mouthed something to the DJ as he placed the disc in his hand. Bisch turned, stretched his neck out, his shoulders back and wore a devilish smirk as he strode confidently back to the bar. The music up to that point had the dance floor full of kids and adults shuffling to the likes of Tina Charles and Showadddywaddy as the blue, green and red lights blinked on their faces. Unnoticed by most, I saw the DJ nonchalantly take the record Bisch had given him out of its sleeve. His flow was suddenly interrupted as he noticed the vinyl was a lime green colour. I'd never seen records in any colour other than black – neither had he it seemed as he examined it under the tiny spot light attached to his decks. He scratched his head and stared out to see if Bisch was watching, I sensed he was having second thoughts. His gaze located Bisch who nodded back to him in a way that suggested everything was "cool" and, as if to reassure the doubting DJ further, he discreetly pinched his first finger and thumb in the "OK" sign. He wiped his forehead with an overused handkerchief and finally set the needle down. What followed stays in my memory as happening in slow motion. The sound explodes with a screech of searing guitars and sneering vocals. Those on the dance floor froze like rabbits and starred at the DJ who just gawped meekly at having unleashed a beast upon them. Those at the bar with Bisch were equally shocked. They were caught in the confusion of trying to understand how to react and what they needed to do next. How would their coolness be classified if they did not react correctly and would they all still be welcomed in the club house or would they be expelled for knowing Bisch who had spilled this venom amongst them!

The line: "What the hell is wrong with youuuuuuu uuu uuu!" from this master piece, thumped my stomach and tore the breath out of me. The bar staff had stopped serving, stunned by the same audio ray gun as everyone else. It was one of those rare moments, and very few times in my life, when a song had the literal and figurative effect of shaking my world. The record was *Nasty Nasty* by 999 and it is only two minutes long but that time frame has wedged itself in my brain to a fixed moment and place for the rest of my life. I am sure we all have had similar experiences but that was my Punk baptism and it was euphoric! Thank you Bisch whoever you are/were and wherever you are now mate as you opened a Pandora's Box that I have never wanted to close since.

On hearing a Punk song like that, as an early aged teenager, it set off a reaction of hormones in me and for lots of others of my generation. This is not unique as the mixture has been shared by teenagers for decades. In the 50's they had it with Elvis, Gene Vincent and Bill Hayley. The 60's kids got it with the Velvet Underground, early Beatles, Stones, Small Faces and the Kinks and in the early 70's it was probably Bowie, Roxy Music or Pink Floyd and Led Zep that did it. But in 1977 for me it was this song by 999 that "shook me up", "blew my mind" and "really got me going". Steve Carter, Stuart Place, Michael Robinson and Mark "Champers" Chamberlain and some girls like Judith Bainbridge and Tracy Barnes were tuned onto music beyond Radio One. We met at the back of the 6th form blocks and listened to the radio during break and lunch times. There were debates on what was Punk or the New Wave and then we got confused by "peach" (our substitute a word for "cool") tunes like *Lido Shuffle* (Bozscaggs), *Road Runner* (Jonathan Richmond and the Modern Lovers) and "Romeo" (Mr Big). However, we were united when we heard, *Psycho Killer* (Talking Heads) after Stuart raved about their appearance on The Old Grey Whistle Test. These conversations seemed to put Ian Nelson's obsession with Abba into perspective but we forgave him as he was a tough lad, brilliant at sports and, after all, the blonde one had been voted as having best backside in the world at that time!

Northern Soul

I was too young to go to the All nighters at the Casino in Wigan even if I had wanted to. No one mentioned this style of music in school. The local discos at that time were held at the Parish or Meths (short for Methodists) which were organised in their respective Church social clubs. I went to one of them, not sure which, and like those at West Paddock, there would be sections of music played amongst the run of the mill chart stuff. This was a way of appeasing kids who wanted the DJ to play a particular style. Hence, there would be three or four, Mod, Rock or Punk records and something called "Northern". When it was time for Northern on the first occasion I heard it, the dance area cleared and up popped some girls dressed in long skirts that were tight at the waist but widened out at the shins. They had flat shoes on and white ankle socks. Their blouses were tight but the collars were loose. The record I remember most was *Interplay* by Derek and Ray – no lyrics just a harpsichord lead floor stomper of a tune. It has a break for two beats after the first five notes to which the dancers responded to by raising one hand above their heads and slapping down on the other held out at a right angle to their stomach. Done in unison the Clap! Clap! Was loud and you felt that all those on the floor were sharing some secret bond. The girls glided about the floor in a marching shuffle step with a sideways motion, changing direction at the end of the line they moved along. Some older lads were in the centre doing high kicks, into the splits to jump up and then fall back, flipping over to rise up into a fast spin before going back into a sliding shuffle step in perfect timing. The songs had a bouncing bass, xylophone and driving snare drum with a syncopated rhythm. It was the most exciting dancing I had ever seen and I had to get into this.

I found out that there was Soul club at the old civic centre in Leyland. I convinced my mum to let me go and, as I didn't know anyone who liked the style, I went on my own. Northern Soul was an underground scene and I was out of my depth. The dance floor was packed with older teenagers and, having studied the dancing I got up to have a go. I was absolutely rubbish. There is a type of code to certain dances. Those into the scene know which they are and, more importantly, when to clap. Furthermore, this dancing is not for amateurs, it has to be practiced. The centre of balance was different to what I was use to. It strained your back, pressurised the calves, thighs and was unrelenting on every muscle in your feet. I was not use to dancing on my own. As a couple you had each other to support your movement in a more upright position, without constant and abrupt changes of direction. Apart from the Jive, there were very few jumps, flips, splits or spins. After a couple of songs I left and got an early bus home, deflated, I never went back. However, over time I did have another try and grasped the basic steps and got reasonable at it. I collected compilation CDs to practice to after I was married and living in Hindley Green (Wigan). Every now and then I still have to get a fix of Northern Soul and the best dances I've been to so far have been held at King George's Hall, Blackburn. For anyone who hasn't got a clue about Northern Soul – there is a film called *Soul Boy* which I recommend or the Granada TV documentary Tony Wilson did in the Casino before it got closed. Glyn went to school with Russ Winstanley who use to DJ at the casino and is probably the most famous Winstanley from Wigan since Gerrard (chapter 11). I recommend *"Soul Survivors- The Wigan Casino Story"*- to you, which he co wrote with David Nowell, and his local radio shows which are always packed with classic tracks. *Do I Love You* (Frank Wilson) and *Time Will Pass You By* (Tobi Legend) are in my top thirty all time tunes. I never told anyone at school about my early encounter with the soul club but I was about to make up for it after we left school and signed on for A levels at Runshaw 6th form college.

19

1978 and the Reading Festival

The summer holiday of 1978 at Rob's was another one of those rare moments when things changed and I was never quite the same again thanks to Punk Rock. Unbeknown to me before I arrived, Rob had asked his parents if we could go to Reading for the annual Rock music festival held in a field not far from the railway station. His mum had Okayed it with mine and on the Friday morning we were on the train all giggly with excitement. Aged 15 we were allowed to go to Reading, by train and back, all on our own – brill! We arrived in Reading late morning, walked to the ground and queued for ages to buy tickets. When we got in, the field was a mass of all ages and we soaked up the relaxed atmosphere under a sun that shone all day. We took sandwiches and our only concern, apart from losing each other going to the toilets, was to be away in time for the last train home.

The day was glorious and the bands were all memorable. Amongst the highlights was Penetration – with a girl singer (Pauline Murray) who put up with the gobbing from the crowd and had a piercingly beautiful voice. Radio Stars lead singer was mental climbing up the scaffolding crossing one side of the stage to the other. He got pelted with cans and then the crowd gave a huge cheer for not falling down when he got back to the microphone. Throwing cans went all day and in the centre, between the two stages, was a DJ deck where John Peel played records. He had to endure chants of "John Peel's a cunt" before a Watney's red label family keg got wazzed and hit him square on. Just as it was about to get dark Sham 69 came on and there was a riot of the fans pogoing mad in a Punk rock version of a mosh pit. Fights broke out and Jimmy Pursey had to make an announcement from the stage to calm it down. I think Ultravox were on next and they had a light show – wow – all blues and greens as their singer stood motionless and sang songs with weird titles *Slow Motion, Hiroshima Mon Amor and Quiet Men* -all very moody and relaxing after the Sham army onslaught. The Pirates were on just before The Jam - old men dressed in striped "pirate" trousers, bit tame but hard core old style Rock'n roll, so fair dues and their original but dead lead singer Johnny Kidd, left us with the classic *Please Don't Touch*. The moment Paul Weller walked on stage he had to dodge a can that whizzed by his head - I thought The Jam, as headline band, would have commanded a bit more respect. But this was Punk Rock and no one worshiped idols remember! The stage was a blaze of white light and the trio wore sharp light grey mod suites. I shouted the lines to every song even as we started to leave to get to the station. It had been the best musical day of my life and has never been topped. Not that I have ever been to any of these types of festivals since as that one day did it for me. Anything else would not be the same – even if it was Glastonbury, T in the Park or Download.

Rob went onto Dentstone College, after leaving Lawrence House where he got into the contemporary and cutting edge punk bands and was soon far ahead of me. Future summer holidays were musical feasts on Rob's vinyl collection. He introduced me to Wire, Stiff Little Fingers, Gang of Four, The Vibrators, Joy Division, The Cure and early U2.His brother, Jonny, was into Suzie Sioux and the Banshees, Killing Joke and played drums in local bands in Cheltenham. We only went to one more gig together which was at Cheltenham Town hall featured Attila The Stockbroker and Fuzzbox who had the aptly named minor classic "We've got a fuzz box and we're gonna use it".

The Dancer returns

Dancing got brought up to date in the mid seventies by John Travolta. *Saturday Night Fever* and *Grease* were massively successful films and both showed off his brilliant dance moves. *Saturday Night Fever* showcased disco to the world and his dancing electrified me. Overnight there were dance classes to learn the steps to the songs in this film. The Bus Stop was the name of the one I learnt to the title track and the rest I have forgotten now but they all had names too. I enrolled for some classes at the Ambulance Hall in Chorley. A middle aged bloke and his girl partner taught us once a week and I also went to a few at "Dancers" in Preston. I got good at it and some girls at school asked me to help them choreograph steps to *I Will Survive* for the end of term disco that year. I entered the UK Disco Dancing championship competition heats that were held at Romeo & Juliet's in Blackburn. I didn't get anywhere but I did think seriously about what my Aunt and Uncle had urged me to consider – a career in dancing. When I looked into it you were expected to have certificates in Ballet, Modern and Tap –which I hadn't. Within a few years though, films like Fame, Flash Dance and Footloose had characters in it that showed the formal dance establishment that all you needed was talent. That precedent came too late for me and I was in a different career. Had I pushed myself would I have made it? I'll never know now! After the disco heats at Romeo & Juliet's there was a band playing in the main lounge room. I saw Jigsaw (*Sky High*), Kenny (*The Bump*) and Sweet Sensation (*Sad Sweet Dreamer*). They were one hit wonders on the pop ladder but it was better than anything I'd seen in working men's clubs and a taste of cabaret that I had not had up to then. Sort of sad for the "has beens" but it was an inspirational training ground for those trying to make their way up.

I had a house party for my sixteenth birthday. It was very tame as my mum and her work friend Gronwyn Bennet stayed in the kitchen and made sure "nothing got out of hand". *YMCA* by Village people was number one and mum insisted I and all my guests did the dance to it – very embarrassing! I wanted to be older - much older and independent! By the time the end of 5th form came round to the leaving concert I had a girlfriend called Julie who invited me to her ballroom dancing classes at St Ambrose Church. I learned some new sequences and we entered a few competitions. I found the lessons very strict and all the kids were very serious about doing the steps correctly. I was use to free styling off the basic steps to the Jive and the Latin American dances and when I did my thing in the dance classes I got frowns from everyone, especially Julie who couldn't understand. I tried to explain how I'd been brought up to have fun and not be confined by the rudiments. It came to a head when we were in a competition at Belle Vue. On the way there I convinced her to follow my lead and not fight against my free styling. Reluctantly she agreed and we won a bronze in the Waltz and Gold in the Cha Cha Cha. I had the widest smile on the coach home but I never got invited to anymore classes or competitions. I guess I'd upset the order that the school teachers and senior students conformed to. That's why I disliked the ballroom TV shows back then and those today. They are too rigid and more like gymnastics and a world away from the spirit of freedom dancing is supposed to embrace. Maybe I wouldn't have made a professional dancer after all.

College 1979-1981- the drumming and acting years

The standard of education at boarding school put me about two years ahead of my peers in high school. This meant that by the time I sat my O Levels I demonstrated a reasonable intelligence to get seven passes and a place at Runshaw Six Form College in Leyland. In my last years at school and, through those two years at college, I worked every weekend as a drummer in working men's clubs. The organist at the Labour Club was a true gentleman and friend to me. His name was Bert Hill, he lived in Farnworth and he asked me if I'd be interested in playing drums as the resident drummer was about to leave. He took a chance on me that paid off for both of us.

I'd been banging on kits for years and could keep time for dances as I knew most of the tempos and tunes the "turns" would ask us to play. "Turns" were the singers or entertainers who needed organ and drum accompaniment to their "spots". They played two "spots" – usually thirty or forty five minutes each, a selection of classic pop standard songs in one and a "free and easy" mix of tunes in the other one. The first catered for those who wanted to listen to popular songs – mainly ballads- that they could sing along to. The second one was for the dancers to get up and jive or shake their legs to. I spent about six years on the club circuit and enjoyed every bit of it. The money was better than working in other part time jobs. At one point I had two drum kits – one (a Pearl, black mixed wood fibre glass) permanently on the stage of the club I was resident at and a smaller kit (black wood Leedy, customised by Eddie Ryan) for mid week gigs. The Leedy came via Fred Kelly who did a bit of drumming with Rarebird – an American band who wrote fine soft rock tunes including *Sympathy* which Marillion covered. I got to buy the kit via Fred's brother John Kelly who was the best drummer I ever watched during those days. He was resident at The Tiger a sort of Pub/Cabaret Bar which was at the bottom of Golden Hill, Leyland and mum and I would go at Sunday lunch time to see the acts that were appearing during the week. It was a sort of warm up performance to showcase what they were like if you wanted to go and see a full performance the following week. John had an orange Premier kit with a rack of Rota Toms and cymbals. He used every piece of equipment unlike some drummers who just had them for show. I learned a lot by studying him play and when he got into his groove he was like Buddy Rich whipping the tunes at the head of a cavalry charge.

Mid week gigs were popular during the Falkland's war. There were plenty of benefit events and, while the money raised went to good causes, they always covered the musicians' expenses generously. I got approached by the father of a guitarist who came to one of these gigs. He asked if I'd be interested in forming a band with his son, who was called Ricky. His mum, as it turned out, worked with my mum at the Royal Ordnance Force (R.O.F) factory Soon we were rehearsing in a shed on the grounds of Chorley Football Club. We formed a Shadows tribute band and called ourselves **The Blueprints**. Ricky played the lead and another older lad called Neal played rhythm guitar. Our debut gig was at The Football Club – one song -"Apache" with a full gig of our own, soon after at The Toby Jug which was a small pub on the road to Aldington between Fredrick's Ice Cream shop and the traffic lights heading south. The third, and final gig, was at a club near Wymott Prison (Leyland). We didn't get round to finding a bass player so the sound was very hollow and we split up through indifference. I'd also been asked to rehearse with a few people from college but that never got anywhere near a live gig. I did help out **The Perfect Strangers** from Preston whose drummer had to work away for a few months. They were very good and went on to appear on local radio. They used to support a bigger band called **Ritzi** who were popular at that time. But, bands and endless rehearsing that never paid any money, made me limit my playing to the clubs. I had a good run after the Labour Club, doing a stint at Chorley Football Club before pairing up with a Jazz organist, Alan Loat, at The Trades Hall, Bamber Bridge and then a series of organists at my final residency at St Mary's Catholic Club in Euxton.

Alongside the drumming, I was introduced to amateur dramatics thanks to my English Literature lecturer, Helen Tozer. She took classes in Drama as well and asked for volunteers to make up the numbers for the college plays. My first character, Patrice Bombelles (Ring Round the Moon, by Jean Anouilh) fitted me as his first entrance has a dance sequence. After one performance of this play I was approached by Jean Robinson to join St Ambrose players based at the church of the same name in Leyland. From there I got asked to do plays and musicals for other groups over the next five years. My dancing skills got used in shows like *Fiddler on the Roof*, and *Sweet Charity*. In that way I did get the opportunity to see what theatre life was like and I am richer for all of the experiences that went with it. On reflection, music and dancing did develop my self confidence, voice projection and an appreciation of space and body language. This proved useful in my future career. I stopped playing semi professionally when I moved to Barrow-in-Furness in the autumn of 1986 and sold off my drum kits as time went on.

The eighties and going to gigs

When the Jam played Blackburn (King George's Hall), on their Setting Sons tour there was group of us from college who went. The support band was The Vapours and when they came on we all rushed to the front and erupted with energetic pogoing. They were electrifying and I'd never been that close to a band or large speakers before. I was sweltering in my thick brown (brown? with bright orange quilt effect lining), Simon Snorkel "parker" and I lost my hearing temporarily. I had to make my way to the back to recover but I was bitten by the gig bug. It's a pity that the Vapours are regarded as one hit wonders for *Turning Japanese* when other songs like *Gallery for Guns, News at Ten* and *Jimmie Jones* deserve to be better known. This started a period of going out to watch bands about the same time I started to work for one of the main banks in Preston in August 1981. Clouds Nite Club was at the top of Church Street in Preston town centre and it had "alternative" nights on Thursdays. Here, apart from the DJ's selection of the best in alternative music, the venue put on bands. Amongst the diverse range I saw there were Nico and The Faction, Sigue Sigue Sputnik, and John Cooper Clarke. The best though was a little known band called **Mercenary Skank** for the fact that I knew nothing about them, bit like The Vapours, and that made their impact all the more impressive.

During lunch times I'd run up Church Street and over the other side to Action Records. I was still reliant on what Rob told me was worth checking out and I wanted to develop my own taste. We had a friendly rivalry and I was now trying to find bands he didn't know. I had to get out more and be more adventurous in my choices. I searched the bargain bins in Laskys and other shops in the St George precinct. I invested in vinyl – and went through phases of buying LPs by bands I knew nothing about like **Pink Industry** and I filled a box with one off singles by the likes of **Tango Brigade, The Passage, Epileptics**, and one of Rob's recommendations the Young Marble Giants. At Action Records I would listen to what was being played on the sound system as they were always good tunes. I also ear wigged the conversation between the store owner (Gordon Gibson) and customers and scanning any posters they put up advertising local gigs. I didn't know the owner at that time or his brother who played in local band **The Genocides**. In time, however, that would change but I never forgot how Gordon's and other independent Record shops were back then -vital sources of information on music and bands outside the mainstream. For this reason I recommend Graham Jones book "Last Shop Standing" which features Action Records and another shop I still buy music from called Townsend records in Chorley.

Blackpool Rock

At the end of 1982 I accepted promotion to be a cashier, working in the South Shore (Blackpool) branch and I lodged at the other end of town at Mrs Bridges' B&B (in, Cliff Place, Bispham). The other lads I met there were into music to varying degrees and the early eighties encouraged diversity. One night I'd be dancing to chart disco fodder like Wham or Michael Jackson at Bunters, the next I'd be drinking and smoking something in someone's flat listening to Crosby Stills Nash and Young or Bob Dylan. One night at a club called Bananas, Julian Ormiston and I saw a band called "**Dog Food**" who's lead singer introduced themselves as "We're Dog Food, because today's dog food is tomorrow's dog shite, 1-2-3-4" and a second generation punk onslaught pelted us. I bought my vinyl at Melody House, which was close to the branch just off Waterloo Road. I spent many lunch hours "thumbing" the racks and listening to whatever was being played or requested by other shoppers. They sold tickets for gigs too and some that I went to were held at the Bier Keller where I got to see bands on like the Armoury Show and Icicle Works. But The Smiths were the most important band I became fanatical about next.

As the baboon buffoonery of the New Romantics reached its peak these four lads from Manchester brought music back to ground zero, in the same way the

Sex Pistols had the decade before. I had seen a concert "Live at Gold Diggers, Chippenham" on TV and was hooked instantly. Morrissey was the anti hero, wearing beads; loose fitting shirts and the back pocket of his demins were stuffed with gladioli. He commanded that stage, cavorting in twisted stances as he sang about Moors Murder victims, Handsome Devils and posing questions about whether the body rules the mind or does the mind rule the body. The other three bands members stood like statues casually laying down the jingly jangly pop brilliance that defined that style of "Indie" music. I think I was the first person in Chorley to buy *The Smiths* (first) LP and I played it until I knew every word. I took to wearing the same clothes as Morrissey and gyrated on the dance floors when *What Difference Does it Make* or *This Charming Man* got played. 1984 was my year of obsession with everything Smiths. I recited Morrissey's lyrics and bought into the cutting wit and subtle obscurity of his own life laid bare. The climax was seeing them at the Winter Gardens just as the single *William It Was Really Nothing* was in the charts. Then, just as instantly as I fell in love with them, by the time the LP *Meat Is Murder* came out I'd moved on to other bands like R.E.M, Echo and the Bunnymen, Simple Minds and Big Country. About this time I listened to tapes sent to me by a lad called Pete Buttle who lived in London and recorded gigs secretly.

I got to know Pete through Chris Dewhurst whose then girlfriend I fancied. I thought my luck was in one night when I was drinking with her at the Gynn (a pub mid way between Bispham and town). I was about to ask her out when in walked Chris and she said, a little flustered;

"Hey John, you've not met my *boyfriend* Chris before have you...!"

Chris was taller and squinted menacingly down at me. I thought he was about to punch me but instead he put his hand out and apologised for staring as he was trying to adjust to his new contact lenses. Phew! We talked music for the rest of the night and he told me about The Alarm who he'd got to know when they played Manchester, where Chris was at University. His enthusiasm led to me going to watch them the following year. By then I'd met my girl-friend (Barbara) who was a student at Liverpool University where the gig was. I was impressed by the band and met Pete, who was there to record the gig. I got stopped by police after the gig while we were waiting for a bus back to Barbara's flat in Aigburth. They thought the large rolled up *Chant* Tour poster was a baton and I was up to no good! We laughed about it back at the flat but I felt the strong arm of Thatcher's police state and I started to take a closer inter-est in politics as the government were forcing through changes and Liverpool was a target for Tory policies of privatisation that caused mass unemployment in that fine city.

On Tour with The Alarm and Wire Train

Pete knew loads of bands I'd never heard of and I bought a stack of tapes from him over the next few years and amongst them were The Stone Roses, The Sundays, the Mighty Lemon Drops and lesser known bands like **Dislocation Dance** from Manchester. In February 1986 Pete organised a trip to Europe to watch The Alarm on their *Strength* tour and invited me to go. This was the coldest holiday I have ever been on when not up a mountain on a skiing trip. We had Transanpino Rail tickets which gave you unlimited travel through the countries the band played in: France, Belgium, and Holland. I nearly fell out with Pete while getting ready for the first gig at the Salle De La City, Rennes. We were sharing a room and as I came out of the bathroom he was injecting one of his arms. He noticed my shocked look but we didn't say anything and carried on getting ready to go out. I'd never been involved with hard drugs and seeing it for the first time scared me. I was thinking how it may impact on me if he was caught in possession of whatever he was shooting up. I could get arrested too by association – shit! What had I let myself in for!

"It's not drugs, John" he told me as we were walked in silence to the venue.

I was about to say "look Pete, it's got nothing to do with me but....." when he interrupted me.

"I'm diabetic and have to have a shot of insulin every so often, I should have told you in case I went hyper, which can happen if I don't eat right and. (pauses)......you OK?" He said noticing my open mouth. Suddenly, I bear hugged him with a rush of relief, pinning him to the wall of the street we were on. I was so relieved and felt a total pratt for...well jumping to conclusions without checking my facts. We creased up in stitches, laughing loudly. At that moment a couple of uniformed thugs came over and pushed us both up against the wall. In my pigeon French and their broken English, they wanted to know where we were going and why we were so noisy. They asked us to turn out our pockets – I think they were looking for drugs or alcohol. Luckily Pete had left his syringe kit back at the hotel. Then they got interrupted by a senior look-ing thug. They turned away and we ran off in the opposite direction. Later on we got to talking to The Alarm's roadies at the theatre. They told us Le Penn, a French Fascist, was having a rally in the town. Some of his security people were known for confronting anyone who looked or acted suspicious and we fitted that. I was wearing a three quarter length, royal blue Italian trench coat that had shinning buttons on the front and gold braiding on the shoulders and cuffs. Underneath I had a scarlet grenadier jacket and with my grey para-trooper pants, pixy boots and John Lennon cap I must have seemed "odd". It was an incident I reflected upon back in England and at any time when I hear or read debates about the far right or left wings of any political party. It made me question a lot of what I had been taught and I concluded that I believed in what I'd read about The Digger Movement when it came to politics.

Meanwhile, back in France and the tour, we met up with four friends of Pete's who joined us in Paris for the rest of the tour. One of them, Dave, played drums in a London based Mod/Rock band which was either called **The Gift or All the Mad Men** who I went to watch play at a reunion after the tour. The Alarm had a day off before their gig in the city so we thought we'd blagg our way into a Lloyd Cole and the Commotions gig that night. Waiting in the alley, having failed at the main entrance, we hoped to meet the band arriving. We were at the point of giving up as it was bitterly cold, when a car pulled up and Lloyd Cole got out. He bought our story about coming all the way for the gig only to find out that that it was a sell out and no tickets were available. Inside we caught the tail end of support band, Del Amitri's set relieved to be defrosting. I got talking to some Americans who told me about The Violent Femmes. When I got back home I bought their first album and the next two. I got Chris into them as well and wish now I had got to see them live – but, like a lot of bands I never saw in their prime, I prefer to keep my interest in them preserved. Sometimes I got so into a band or musician but when I saw them live and it was a disappointment – like Ocean Colour Scene in the nineties, it tainted my affection for them. However, it worked in the opposite way with unknown bands I discovered later on.

When the tour arrived in Rotterdam I met up with Lesley Craig (see later) who was visiting her friend Elizabeth Voskamp who was Dutch and a student there. Lesley and Liz met on the Tall Ship Race and Liz was planning her move to study or work in London. We all went to the gig that night which was memorable as another encounter with drugs. During the gig I went to the gents and was shocked to see so many people taking stuff. Deals were happening in the cubicles and some punters were injecting themselves openly. The floor was flooded with urine and several kids were sitting in the corners with glazed expressions. One lad had fallen asleep with the needle still in his arm. It was horrific and put into perspective our earlier, sightseeing "trip" round the pot cafes in and amongst the red light district. It was enough to put me off hard drugs and nothing since has convinced me that taking them is cool. Some years later Liz went on a Safari trip in Africa. One day she was riding in the back of an open truck. It went over a rock throwing her out. She cracked her head in the fall and died instantly. Whenever I think of Liz, I remember that first meeting, the gig and that desperate and degrading scene of humanity in the toilet. Liz had an enthusiastic smile – brimming with confidence-and it was a tragedy her life was snuffed out in an instance. I contrast the voluntary death of those involved with drugs to the cruel act of fate that took away Liz and her positive life force.

The last gig of the European stage of the tour was at The Paradiso Club in Amsterdam and we got invited to the Alarm's after show party. I remember talking to the band's front man (Mike Peters) and he told me why he introduced the flinging of a deck of cards in to the audience during *Where were you hiding when the storm broke.* He did this to the line "...all cards are marked and all fates will collide" In a live performance when the deck showers the crowd it is in the sense of life is a gamble rather than being taken as meaning all our destiny's are set down and cannot be altered – which is the tarot cards intention I felt when I first heard the line. Looking back now, I am reminded of Liz again and her fate and where I am now compared to then. The way fate and destiny have conspired and the choices I have made and opportunities I grasped or let go. I think of other people I met and other adventures we got up to in those seven days on that tour. I felt I would do the same type of holiday again as time seemed endless and I had no ties. How quickly I realised too late that life happens and I didn't do it again and now feel I'm too old to.

That tour did change my life. I got a feel of what it is like for a musician on the road as we spent a lot of our time with the members of both bands. Kevin Hunter (**Wire Train** front man) was engaging and loved to hear what we'd all been up to, how we were getting to the next show and we became fans of the band introducing the "DoDaDo DaDodaDo etc" melody break as he meanders into a rendition of *Walk on the Wild Side* during the live sets. Both bands did not have a huge commercial success but I did tell Mike Peters, some years later, that the experiences of being around the band and their song lyrics did influence me in a positive way. My love of live music was cemented on that tour. I loved to watch live music and seek out my own interpretation of what has been put into a lyric by a stranger. The live experience of how the song is presented can bend, twist and enlighten what you have heard up to that point.

Poems and song writing

I had started to understand hidden meanings and interpretations in literature through my studies at college and this made me think about the messages in songs which I had not fully appreciated up to my late teens. Like most teenagers I was content to sing along to a good chorus and fist the air with the rest of the crowd. One of the poems we were given to appraise was *When I'm 64* by the Beatles. Having to critique it, break down each line and try to put the melody out of your head, made me aware of a deeper sadness to the song. I started to listen to other records I had, especially Joy Division. Ian Curtis has been acknowledged as a genius by many writers and fans after his death. Even the band's bassist, Peter Hook in his book, did not realise how closely his songs mirrored his life, his depression and his eventual suicide. I played both Joy Division LPs repeatedly, lying on my bed in the dark and felt a connection in a way that I had never done before. I began to write my own poetry from sixteen and carried it on for a few years. Perhaps the best one I wrote was after my Aunt Irene died (June 1981). It was based on the Joy Division's song *Isolation* as my words do fit as a substitute lyric.

I was on my own a lot and retreated into my bedroom like most teenagers do at some point. Hearing someone more depressed than I had any right to be, had the effect of cheering me up. I read that Leonard Cohen had the monopoly on depressive songs but found them to be brilliantly imaginative and spiritually uplifting. The Smiths got criticised for being a miserable band because of the contents of their songs, but not to me. I thought their choice of morbid subjects was a conscious way of reflecting the life they, and most of the people in their home towns, had experienced – a drab, grey and suppressive one. The effect was to be grateful for what you had and what you did not have to put up with. From that point on I did task myself to ask "what does it stand for?" and "does it stir an emotion in me?" I applied this to Roy Harper who played Longridge Civic Centre one night when I stopped over at Chris's. His parents lived in this village Nr Preston and Harper was in his most fertile and accessible writing period. I soon bought up everything I could find of his as he had a cutting and informative way with words and no subject was off limits. He courted controversy all his life and played himself in a film called *Made* in which he sings my favourite song of his *Little Lady*. I went to watch him a couple of times and recommend him to anyone who is open minded and an English patriot.

London and weekends away

In 1984 I got a four week holiday to take part in the Tall Ships race. I was one of a twelve man crew selected for the Bank's twin mast schooner on the Denmark to Liverpool leg of the race organised by the Sail Training Association. This started in Fredrickshaven, out into the North Sea, round the top of Scotland and into Greenock before a parade of sail in Liverpool. At the training weekend in Portsmouth I met someone who has become a lifelong friend - Lesley Craig, I mentioned her earlier. We hit it off straight away as soul mates and she welcomed me back to her tiny one bed flat in Highams Park, London en route to Blackpool. From then I took up her invites down as often as I could and she showed me all the sights of London while sharing our taste in music. She is a few years older than me and had an unhealthy affection for Phil Collins and the Alan Parson Project at that time. However, we discovered some song writers together like Tom Robinson and bands like Frankie Goes to Hollywood, Soft Cell and Latin Quarter. One day we went into stitches as I was fixing a drink, she said,

"Change the tape wilya, John?"

"What's that Les?" I asked, a bit pissed on beer or wine.

"I want some Latin Quarter on!" She muffled.

Due to her southern accent and me, not hearing her right, thought she said "I want a glass of water John", so when I walked in with one in my hand and we had worked out the confusion we were in hysterics. Odd what you remember when you think of a band or a song isn't it!

The Tall Ship Race of 1984 changed my life too. At the disco the night before we set sail I chatted to a Danish girl and she invited me back to her flat where I lost my virginity to the sound of *I won't let the sun go down on me* (Nick Kershaw) and nearly missed the boat setting sail the following day. When we arrived in Liverpool, Lesley, I and a few others went to The State disco. This is where Frankie Goes to Hollywood had shot their first video to *Relax,* a song which Lesley and I loved and it got the band onto the Channel 4 music show The Tube. It kick started their phenomenal rise to fame and it was a TV programme that I watched every Friday tea time. All the best bands played on it including, Echo and the Bunnymen, Spear of Destiny, The Alarm and I saw U2 on it for the first time – highlights from their Under a Blood Red Sky concert at Red Rocks somewhere in an American desert. It also had one offs like Foffo Spear Jig a north east comedian, videos for bands like **Die Haut** (*Die Karaibische Western*) and **Bourgie Bourgie** (*Breaking Point*) which I have never seen again or know anyone who knows either band. There was a ground breaking moment when they showed the video to *Small Town Boy* by Bronski Beat. Jimmy Summerville's distinctive falsetto, which, coupled with an electro beat and his role in the film, pushed the life of gays and society's closeting of them into the open. That trio's popularity, Queen/Freddie Mercury, Soft Cell and Frankie Goes to Hollywood's too, made me aware of gay rights and the freedom of expression of all sexual preferences. The decade stands out like the sixties had done for free love and the liberation of women in the seventies. Up to that point I was naive about gay people. I knew a few from my amateur dramatics but did not know Freddie Mercury was gay until it was talked about as he was dying. I knew some members of FGTH were gay but I wasn't sure about Marc Almond –like I say – naive.

Meanwhile, back in Liverpool and the end of the Tall Ships race in the summer I had my hair styled for the first and only time and bought the latest fashions – encouraged by Lesley. I got army grey trousers, grey pixy boots and some shirts I'd picked off the peg at "Sexy Rexy's". It was the time of Ultravox with Midge Ure's colourless look and the start of Stadium Rock. More importantly I had met some great friends on that voyage which was more about my own of self discovery than a demanding introduction to seamanship. I was in love with life, free will and the future seemed like a giant oyster. I spent the next two years seeking out new experiences and bands to follow.

I'd met Barbara during the Tall Ship Race. It was at a beach BBQ on a small island off the coast of Scotland and I was one of the few people who had a bottle opener and she was serving food.

"How do you like your burger – with or without sand?" Was her first line to me that got us talking. When the race was over we dated for a few months as her parents lived in Poulton and she shared a flat with some student friends in, Liverpool during term time. We had an intense relationship and I spent weekends in Liverpool going out a lot to clubs and parties. At someone's house I met there a student, who went to Hull University, told me about Ben Watt and Tracy Thorn. This got me into Everything But The Girl and others on the Cherry Red label. 1984 was also significant for the year Thatcher took on the miners and the battle of Orgrave was shown on the six o'clock news. I'd started to listen intently to Billy Bragg having seen him on TV doing benefit gigs for the Miners who were fighting Thatcher's injustices.

Barrow-in-Furness and the Bluebird Club (1986-1988)

Barrow is where my real love of the unsigned local music scene blossomed. I got transferred to that 27 mile cul-de-sac, on the edge of the Lake District, at the end of the summer of 1986. I shared a two up two down back street terrace on Rodney Street with a draughtsman at the Ship Yard. Giselle Norman was one of my new work colleagues and her partner Kim had played guitar in a Barrowvian band called **Lets Active**. She invited me to go to a disco at a club called Scorpio where **Perfect Circle** and **The Valley Forge** were playing. That was it - I was hooked, as both were excellent and I bought as much vinyl as I could by these and any other local band that I got to see like **Tier Garden.** That night at Scorpio's I got talking to Paul McCauley who went to watch bands too and he introduced me to a diverse range of music – Sonic Youth, Jesus and the Marry Chain, Wedding Present and The Mission. He told me about Thursday alternative nights at the Bluebird club. This was the members bar attached to Barrow Football Club on the fringe of town. A couple of students called Mike and Michelle had convinced some bands to play to the 50-70 regulars who came for about six months of its existence in 1986. The night Pop Will Eat Itself played support to Primal Scream Paul and I became die hard Poppy fans on the spot. PWEI played 15 songs in about as many minutes. They were blisteringly unrelenting and their twee outbursts and the "real dumb bitch she's a waste of good skin" line became our catch phrase put down on anything we disliked for months afterwards. The club's Xmas party that year had Pauline Murray as headlined act - how the circle had turned since 1978. She was supported by **Gone To Earth** and **The Waltones** and I had a party back at mine organised with my girlfriend (and future wife) Helen.

Helen and I went to watch bands as a sort of dare and day out trip. She wound me up by booking tickets to see Ah Ha (Birmingham NEC) as a counter point to my obsession with bands no one had ever heard of outside Barrow like **The Cotton Scourge** who did gigs in tiny rooms in pubs like The Queens, on Rawlinson Street. She compounded this by dragging me along to watch Genesis and Paul Young at Round Hay Park, Leeds – where she lost a wellington boot in the mud – ha! Revenge! Her friend, Cath Whatley was seeing a bloke called Alan Biggins who introduced me to Folk music. He gave me a copy of *Drag down the Moon* by **The Tansads** who I fell in love with instantly – one of the best live LPs I have ever heard and a good introduction to this under rated band from St Helens/Wigan. Alan told me about USA band the **Shoulders** who played a one off gig at Eddisons in Barrow while on tour with the Pogues – another band that I am yet to find anyone else has heard of other than Cath, Helen and Alan.

On a trip to New Zealand in 1987 to visit Lesley who had moved back there, where she was born, I discovered a native band called The Chills and began to listen to Aussie bands like The Triffids, Dave Dobbyn and the Herbs and the Hoodugurus. In 1987 Paul, Helen, Cath and I went to see U2's on The Joshua Tree Tour at Wembley Stadium. It was a day of differences. I'd seen Queen on their Works Tour at Birmingham NEC a few years previously and thought the highlight *Radio Ga Ga* and standing up with everyone else in the crowd doing the clapping hand held high thing could not be topped. I felt U2 could top it but they didn't – the large stadium thing didn't do it for me-too impersonal and full of dick heads who were not music fans. Even the support acts, Lone Justice, The Pogues and Lou Reed failed to make an impact for the same reason. I preferred the smaller venues and clubs and I sought out any gigs in such places from then on. During this time I met up with Chris and Pete in Leeds to see Wire Train who were touring with The Waterboys. We went bonkers to their songs with a few others at the front, but the life of an unknown, foreign support band is a lonely one and we stood out but we didn't care as Wire Train were tremendous despite being yet another band I have still to meet anyone else who has heard of them.

1989 - Settling down

Two years later Helen and I got married and moved into a modest two bed dormer bungalow on an estate near Wigan. During our courting days we listened to albums that became classics like Gracelands (Paul Simon), On the Beach (Chris Rea), Green (R.E.M) and Hull 4 London 0 (the Housemartins). We continued our very predictable tastes as we settled into married life and started to have kids. Hannah was born at Billinge Hospital (since knocked down) in March 1993. In the delivery room a radio was on and *Come as you are* (Nirvanna) was playing as she was being delivered. The following year, Holly was born at Chorley hospital there was no radio just a TV and Match of the Day was on. Both kids got exposure to Punk, the Stone Roses and Northern Soul music which I use to play loudly in the car. They have both grown up to like their own styles too. Holly prefers club/dance orientated tunes and has been to see artists she has admired (Cascarda, Neo, Pussy Cat Dolls, Calvin Harris and Rihanna) and, for a while she took guitar lessons from Martin Simm (Pretendgirlfriend, Chapter 8). Hannah's tastes are more varied and through her part time work she has been to Leeds Music Festival and has seen a wide range of artists from Glee, Muse, Dizzy Rascal, The Vaccines and Bastille). The later and Imagine Dragons are two bands Hannah has introduced me to – so the circle has turned 360 degrees! For the most part, when they were younger, family life and my career as a Financial Adviser was in full swing.

Otley Folk Festivals

In 1998 Alan Biggins and I went to Otley for the Folk Festival. I enjoyed it so much I went to the next four festivals. I knew one of the organisers – Steve Fairholme and his wife Mona who I'd met on a skiing trip to Andorra in 1985 which Lesley organised. They told me who to see and what was going on as sometimes I only went over for one or two days rather than the full Friday to Sunday. The range of entertainment was wide and varied. Traditional dancing by Morris Men and their modern day counter parts like the crow men (with blacked faces) occupied the streets and cobbled alley ways of the village. Small pubs would come alive with impromptu jamming amongst musicians.

Sea shanties and traditional folk songs would be sung by anyone who wanted to have a go. There were workshops in handicrafts and loads of stalls to buy joss sticks, whacky clothes and silly hats. During the last time I went in 2002, it was shortly after I started to get involved with music and I interviewed **Les Barker** who read his humorous poetry while comparing some of the shows. **Joseph Porter (Blyth Power)** and Aussie duo **Cath Mundy and Jay Turner (Mundy & Turner)** agreed to be interviewed too as I wanted to do a piece on the parallel between Folk and Punk for the fanzine I started to write for ("Pogo'til I Die" –see Chapter 2). I ended up submitting it to a Folk magazine but never got to know whether they published it as I got swept up by other things and have only just remembered it as I wrote this down! I put forward the contention that both genres have similarities. They are marginalised by the music business and have a core following of society miss fits that wear odd clothing but shared a communal interest in the politics of life and the environment. Furthermore, I have seen how a performance will impact on the meaning of the song to the writer in both styles. This will have the effect of a crowd reacting to a line or word in the same way even though the delivery can be extremely different in passion and volume. I do not have the same deep interest in Folk or Punk now. Both were of their time to me. I like to think I know what I am talking about when in conversation on either subject. I confuse the purist punks as some believe that Punk was a reaction to Folk music's "hippies" and cannot understand when I say that I put both on equal par. Then I explain the similarities and convert some of them. It's not a mission but I hope it shows my open mind to give anything a go and see what mark it leaves on me.

The Naughties

Helen heard *You Stole the Sun from my Heart* (Manic Street Preachers) and asked me if I had a copy. A few years previously I had been introduced to the Manics by Tony Jones who was on a course with me at the Bank's training centre in Hindehead (Surrey). He lived near Cardiff and I was into Catatonia at the time. We got on as we chatted about Welsh bands and other music he was into. After the course we stayed in touch and he sent me a tape of bands including the Manics, 60ft Dolls and The Flaming Lips. One side had a copy of the whole of *Holy Bible* which he assured me would change my perception of the Manics, which up to that point was one of them being Punk revivalists. He was right, that album moved me in the same was as Joy Division's had. It's a master class of lyrics by Richie James and JD Bradfield's singing dexterity with colossal tunes you have to endure rather than enjoy, as befits the subject matter. But, their recent material was more accessible and we booked to watch them at the Millennium Stadium in Wales on 31ˢᵗ December 1999. We stayed in a sea view hotel in Penarth, smuggled in some spirits and had a memorable night. Super Fury Animals, Shack and Feeder were the support bands before the Manics opened up with *You Stole the Sun from my heart*. I had Helen on my shoulders and at some point in their set she can be seen on the official video amongst the 60,000 other revellers that night– fame at last! The following year Helen won tickets on a Radio One phone in competition to see them at the Coal Exchange, Cardiff with 1000 others. We toyed with the idea of seeing them in Cuba but we couldn't afford it and settled for doing a homage visit to their home town of Blackwood when we went to the Coal Exchange gig. For the next few years we went to watch them whenever they played locally and even watched JDB when he did a solo tour – which shows how into them we got. It's worn off now but she has a knack of introducing some great bands to me like Feeder before the millennium gig, with The Vaccines and Jake Bugg being more recent ones.

And now for the rest of the journey....

In many ways I was a "well adjusted" member of society by the time I hit forty and it amazes me how each incident or experience, in either a small or big way, gave me the confidence to take on and do what I did. I became a music jour-nalist, radio presenter, gig promoter, band manager and loads of other titles besides, all by accident rather than plan. My credentials were limited and not what I consider to be adequate. However, my integrity and enthusiasm shone through, illuminating my way into the unknown.

Before I got into the following five years from 2002 if someone asked me what my favourite lyric was it would be: "I tried to kiss you through the bars of a rhyme" from *Romeo & Juliet* by Dire Straits.

It is clever- simple and direct. It captures the frustration of communicat-ing emotions despite the barriers created by the lovers' respective family feuds which forbid their courtship. The imagery is one of imprisonment. The "bars" conjure up those on a jail cell to stress how their love is confined. The singer uses the bars of music to express his feelings and frustration. But, music tran-scends barriers and the words touch this listener with an audible sensation rather than a physical one they both yearn for.

Over a decade later the one song that sums up the five years that followed is *"Sweeping the Nation"* by Spearmint which I first heard on a Rough Trade compilation during that period. The track has the Dobie Gray's *Out on the*

Floor back beat and it is a tale of unsigned bands that no one got to hear about and how, despite the knock backs, you need to keep beleiving as one day you will realise your dreams. I like to think that what follows gives you an insight to why this is and how the people involved in that world inspire each other and some never stop because they are driven from within or have not found anything better to replace what to others is a beautiful distraction.

02 Pogo'til I Die

Accidents will happen

When, as the Elvis (Costello) song goes, accidents do happen it is how we react and the perspective of time that determines what significance they have been. This happened to me when I noticed a poster in the window of The North Bar, Town Hall Street, in Blackburn at the end of May 2002. I was sitting in the Kentucky Fried Chicken outlet opposite it with Hannah & Holly, gazing in the direction of the building while they were finger licking away, and, as the saying goes – I was happily minding my own business. The place wasn't busy and I was at a stage in my life when a quiet five minutes to vegetate on the day's events and those ahead was a welcome break. Anyone who has kids at the ages of nine and seven knows that it is a constant drain on your senses. If you are not taxiing them about you are trying to keep them busy. You wish they were older so they would be more independent. When you do get time to rest, you need to take stock of what's on the "to do list". I had money on my mind, pre-occupied with the mental balancing of debits and credits and wondering which bill was due next. My day job had progressed swiftly when I arrived in Manchester in 1988 and a year later I was promoted to a Financial Consultant. By 2002 I had a constant eye on what sales prospects I had lined up for the week ahead as you are only as good as your last set of commission figures. It seemed to be a life of wishing time away – looking forward without really appreciating what was in front of me. And, what was in front of me at that moment was a sign that both puzzled and beguiled me.

You know that sensation you get when you think you hear a tune you sort of recognise but can't get your ears full of it? Well this was happening to my eyes – apart from being short sighted, I could make out something... "Sex"...which is always pricks your senses - but followed by "Pistols" meant only one thing to me and anyone of my generation –PUNK! But, in that window on this street in 2002 it didn't compute. The rest was....something... The Ramones in black on white.... my curiosity was making me stand up and squint even more. I walked over to the far side of the room to focus on the words. "Anarchy in the UK revisited tour 2002. 25 years of punk" insert Queen Elizabeth's head with safety pin and flanked on both sides with the anarchist "A" symbol. "Tribute by the Sus-Sex Pistols...& The Marones" was followed by "31st May doors open" and costs details. I must have blinked and done a double take while I processed the words again.

I had a flash back to 1976 – and the first time The Sex Pistols came to my attention. It was in the play ground at Balshaws High School, Leyland and I was nearly fourteen years old at the start of that autumn term. John Dean or "Deano" had brought a magazine into school and he was showing it to a select few he thought would be interested. At first I thought it was a mucky mag– all glossy pictures of fleshy close ups as the pages flashed by. He stopped on a feature headed up "The Sex Pistols". The pictures of the members of the band underneath it were crude, distorted posturing wearing shabby, garish clothes stitched together with safety pins – it was ugly and made me feel like I was peaking into a world of the obscene. Some in the audience had coloured hair in shades of blue or red. Most of them didn't seem to be much older than a fifth former. One lad had rage in his eyes and a safety pin in his ear lobe – ooohhh that must have hurt I thought. He was sweating and in mid air, spitting at the stage. It was all very absurd, violent and disgusting. "It's not for me, mate", I summed it up to Deano - shaking my head. Deano thought it was brilliant saying how it was wild, different and exciting. What they sounded like did not cross my mind and I dismissed it as a publicity stunt for a fringe group of art students and nothing I'd be pursuing with further interest. Little did I know how, within the next twelve months all that changed – along with the rest of the lives of others who heard and actually saw the Sex Pistols play live. In a way, society was never the same again, no matter how some tried to ignore it.

By the time I understood what this band were about they had fallen apart. Sid Vicious was dead, John Lydon had moved on to form Public Image Ltd and other less deserving bands had grabbed the headlines. I didn't understand what the word Punk meant. I looked the word up in my Collins pocket dictionary and I took and active interest in any conversation amongst my friends when Punk was mentioned. Talking about Punk, what it stood for and how punks dressed became the subject of debate as the end of year disco approached. What you wore at this disco became a very important statement. Jeans and a shirt didn't cut it anymore as we had become fashion conscious over night. What you wore defined who you were. Flares meant you were a rocker or a hippy/glam follower and yesterday. Drain pipes, Doc Martins and a Ben Sherman or Fred Perry top and you were a boot boy/girl. Add in short hair and you were a skin head or if styled slightly, maybe suede head. I was none of that and, with a very narrow choice in clothes , I wore a light grey checkered pair of parallels, brown shoes and a wide collar beige shirt with a canvas chocolate brown jacket. That was bad enough but my mum had sown "Elvis" in white rope threat on the back. A surprise present for the disco! I greeted her generosity with a forced smile and wore it rather than upset her. But Deano topped us all. He had a wrangler jacket and had painted a pair of white crossed pistols and the word "SEX" at the top – he was _in_ the moment and his credibility was sealed for ever as another one on my cool list!

Unless you were close to what was happening, you only found out what was going on after the event. I don't remember seeing anyone fully dressed as a Punk in Leyland or Chorley. I do know that when I did see my first Punk I was shocked. It was a girl about a year or so older than me at Wigan town centre bus station. She was wearing a short black leather skirt decorated with studs, safety pins and a chain belt. Tantalizing fish net stockings stretched down her slim legs to stiletto heeled short boots –wow! She must have taken ages to put her make up on – it was immaculate – porcelain white contrasted with her ruby red lips and the coal black eyeliner made her look like a pander bear. Her hair was black, sticking up and out at odd angles. What made it all the more spectacular was what she was holding - a twelve inch record with the news paper ransom cut out words "Sex Pistols" printed on it that seemed to be shouting out to me. I was in awe - she was magnificent and I felt less than mediocre. I imagined she was going to a party somewhere, on her own, while I was with my mum on our way home. I was dressed in a light blue anorak and bell bottom corduroy trousers, bottle green to the knees and fire orange to my boring brown shoes. Just the words Sex Pistols and the way she was leaning against the bus stand, detached but outstanding gave me a glimpse of another universe – one where girls were very different to those on the planet where I lived. In my world girls didn't present themselves as confrontational and the ones that did were dressed up for fun at Halloween. The girl glanced at me and noticed me staring at her. She put a cigarette to her lips, sucked in while looking me up and down. She exhaled, tutted and look in the other direction. She destroyed me. I was defenseless and wanted to crawl into a deep hole.

I didn't tell anyone how insignificant she made me feel. I knew I had been taught a lesson in youth culture. I was in my mid teens and less than ordinary. I did change in time just as my life was about to change in 2002 by an equally graphic jolt in much the same way that girl and that record sleeve had made an impact on me when I was a snooty and insignificant kid. Twenty-five years later and with a lot of growing up in between, unlike those early encounters, this time I was going to grasp the moment Punk came back into my life. That poster, those words: "Sex Pistols" and the sequence of events that followed the weekend of the Queens' Golden Jubilee sealed my own date with fate that would lead me all the way to meeting and promoting one of the members of the band.

On the brink of middle aged

By the end of May 2002, keeping the kids occupied from the moment they rise to their bed time was very tiring. Like most parents you do what you have to do to entertain them. After school our brilliant child minder (Sandra Aspinall) took care of them until five thirty when either Helen or I collected them. During the week I spent one night watching them learn to swim at Brinscal baths and, for a while, they both took piano lessons on different nights at Blackburn School of Music. The weekend was a nonstop "Mummy Daddy 'athon" in how to keep them busy from eight in the morning. Hannah and Holly were in a world of their own and Helen and I had to revolve ours around theirs. Above all, you make do with pushing your own interests to one side in favour of keeping your commitments to theirs. They had Saturday morning lessons in ballet, tap and modern dance at the Community Centre in Eaves Green with a Miss Rachel then, when she got pregnant we enrolled them at Christine Murray's school at the Ambulance Hall, Chorley. Later, they progressed to gymnastics at Coppull and did a few terms with Stage Coach at Parklands School in Chorley. Apart from working to a time table and driving them to and from these activities, I had to sit through the hours and hours of watching them learn and enjoy themselves. God, it was bloody boring at times!

It was all very new to me at first. Aside from the fact that I was in an alien world of girl related activities, I was charmed by their fledgling attempts to glide like swans in their sweet and fluffy two toos. I suspect every parent secretly hopes that their little darlings will have a natural talent. The escalating cost of lessons, equipment and occasional costumes are insignificant if the teacher takes you to one side after a session to express the opinion that your child has a rare talent and the potential to reach the very top. Each time they enrolled for a different discipline I hoped this would happen for my two but it didn't. And with equal relief, I was not disappointed. Far from it as I could see how other parents who were got affected. It seemed to me that some of them had given up their lives to funnel their own aspirations into their kids'. *Pushy parents*-making a point of telling the teachers how "excellent" their child had performed in the lesson and how they were ready for their next exam, "don't you think?" and "shouldn't they be move up to a higher level?" as they were "doing *so* well". Their children were usually, in contrast to their parents, slim, petite and innocent. I often wondered if these mums and some dads had wasted their youth – unfulfilled in their own attempts to be successful at some sport or other pursuit. Perhaps, they may not have been given what they wanted, maybe their parents could not afford lessons or if they could, had they squandered the opportunities?

In the 1980s there was a sense of all things being accessible to everyone. We got sucked into the consumerism too. Jetting off on summer or winter holidays on budget airlines and putting more and more gadgets in our designer homes. Lenders offered us larger loans than we could afford to buy bigger and more luxurious cars in the age of the people carrier. Hollywood told us *greed was good*, and it was time to grab our share of anything that could make us richer than we had any sensible right to expect. Thatcher's government sold off our national assets, making fortunes for those able to invest and sell at the right time. Carpet baggers were plundering the building societies scooping up shares as they privatized. The credit boom caused an explosion in house prices that rewarded the *loads of money* culture of lads and ladettes.

Whereas the followers of Punk had dictated fashion in the late seventies, by the eighties the celebrities had taken over and their trends spanndexed the generation gap thanks to Lady Di, Dallas and even Margaret Thatcher herself. The Smiths and the shoe gazing, rain coated bands like Jesus and the Mary Chain, Echo and The Bunnymen and Joy Division/New Oder had temporarily rescued pop music form the frills and bloated egos of Duran Duran, Spandau Ballet and the rest of the New Romantics. But stadium bands took over and we got to worship in our thousands to the God like U2, Simple Minds and Queen. Quaint festivals like Glastonbury became big business that catered for every music genre. This was the age of technology that changed the way we communicated with each other. Little did we know it then but the brick sized mobile phone of the yuppie city slickers would become the palm size tablet or ipads we all take for granted today. Computer games like Space Invaders which we played in pubs and amusement arcades went on to inspire a world that sucked in anyone who wanted to become a cyberspace super hero. The supersize me, VDU hypnotized couch loungers played shoot them up games, won races and solved riddles to reach levels of perceived glory they could not achieve in the world outside their front door.

In the nineties, it became affordable for our children to have the opportunity to realize their dreams. My parents were not wasteful but they did try and give me what they had never had. For me it was music lessons at boarding school and Helen's dad had a small boat and taught her how to sail. We did make the best attempts at mastering both for a while but we knew we would never become professional at either. In 2002 I studied the parents I swapped small talk with and wondered whether it was their dreams or their kids' that was being encouraged? I categorized them into types. Those who had taken comfort in saturated food, washed down with sugary fizzy drinks, molding arse shaped hollows on their sofas where they expanded their knowledge of multiple satellite channels and the introspective cyber worlds mentioned above. The other category was those whose sense of personal style had become disheveled and frumpily dowdy. Their conversation was all about time tables, school events and observations of other children in order to make some exemplary point about their own. If they had thrown away their chances they were as sure as freebies with bargain bucket orders, to shove their kids into doing what they did not. In addition to all this *me me me* craze, the television had started to provide a generation of non achievers the opportunity to exorcize their own frustrations at being useless by becoming a judge on talent shows from the comfort of their own reclining chairs. This was a stroke of genius by television programmers as the market was increasingly competitive for a growing stay-at home audience.

The Punk Wars

I had grown up watching Opportunity Knocks, New Faces and the revamped version of Juke Box Jury. They were entertaining and provided future stars of the day – Mary Hopkins, Lena Zavaroni, Lenny Henry, Canon & Ball and the first hearings of future singles did sometimes become "hits" and not "misses". But the viewers' participation was limited and not the immediate one we have today thanks to text or the red button. Back then you could only post in your vote, if you could be bothered to, with a letter or card and then you had to wait a whole seven days to see the result in the following week's programme. By the naughties you could do it at the push of a few buttons and you knew by the end of that show who had got through or been voted off. It was instant gratification; self belief in what you felt was good or bad and totally callous for the losers.

2002 was the time of the early versions of Britain's Got Talent and X Factor which were called Fame Academy and Pop Idol. They were the thin edge of what became the dumb down of the manufactured Pop and Light Entertainment we have today. These series of shows reduced the process of becoming a star to a two minute audition. While it has its place, I doubt anyone of my generation thought it would become the dominant form of the decade and allow the likes of Simon Cowell, Louis Walsh, Piers Morgan and Amanda Burton to become spokes persons for the CHAV generation and other disciples who have put them on some God like pedestal – the celebrity era had arrived complete with Big Brother, WAGS and the 24/7 visual garbage we have today. The Christmas number one has now become a foregone conclusion and the winners get thrust into a life that is both beyond their capabilities and an insult to anyone who has to graft to make a living wage. By the turn of the twenty first century, apart from a brief hiccup that was The Sex Pistols and punk, the industry had become tightly controlled by record companies, corporate franchises and a media obsessed with their own image of perfection. Those that spent years touring the circuits of nicotene encrusted working men's clubs, beer stained pubs and sleazy cabaret lounges found their trade demeaned by Tracey Nobody and Jimmy Dipstick who, in a matter of weeks, became a "sensation", instant celebrity stautus guaranteed, backed up with a lucrative record deal, playing to large audiences on National TV.

I am immensely proud of that generation of teenagers who inspired and supported Punk. The bands and musicians that immerged out of the Pub Rock venues and garage lands with protest and attitude had a message and vitriol unseen before and they refused to be tamed. Along with the non conformity of the protagonists, came a new breed of managers, promoters and entrepreneurs who made Do It Yourself a rallying call to arms. They formed their own record companies and set up distribution net works into the growing number of independent shops that successfully challenged the corporate stranglehold. Their communication was in fanzines, media stunts and word of mouth. Their icons were visually unattractive and non-commercial. It was acceptable to make our own fashion and style choices in makeup, hair do's and clothing rather than copying magazine images. For a brief period in the mid 70's the musicians and their followers were going back to basics after the excessive years of the frivolous and the plain daft. Uncomplicated three chord guitars drove less than three minute songs to replaced banks of keyboards, lighting and stage craft that had, like the drugs, become "far out man" – beyound the relaity of what was happening at street level. The Prog Rock songs of tales of wizards, goblins and an alternative world had nothing in common with unemptied bins, grave digger stikes and the rising cost of a gallon of petrol. Up to that point Pink Floyd, YES and Emerson Lake & Palmer composed mammoth solos for those inhabiting cloud cuckoo land. This was not for the new age sons and daughters from ground zero. Punks spat out songs about their broken society by championing the down trodden and ordinary. They did it with day glow colours, a dash of tartan and, above all, a common sense worth of fun - taking the piss out of themselves and those who tried to stifle them. For a glorious moment the music was in control of the business and it felt like those of us who followed it were too.

That all happened when I was in my early teens and another world away from where I ended up in my late thirties and on the brink of my fortieth birthday. My day job was at the height of its twenty year career. I was a successful manager of a team of Financial Advisers operating from offices in Liverpool, St Helens and Warrington. The job was well paid. I had a company car, share options and the respect of my peers. I had nothing to grumble about but I was also bored stiff and I didn't know it. I developed an interest in self defense after being beaten up by two muggers on a street in Manchester one night after work, a few months before Hannah was born, and Judo was the only activity that I had any interest in. I trained under Tommy Hudson at Mill Hill, Blackburn. It kept me fit and I enjoyed the friendship of those who took part like Bill Chew, Pete, Jim, Rolf, Kevin and Tommy's son Mark. I had said farewell to playing the drums at twenty-one as well as the Amateur Dramatics/Musicals which I left behind when I moved to Barrow in Furness. I listened to what music caught my ear but I no longer sought out the cutting edge or new. My record collection lay dormant and unplayed after ten years of settling down. My adventures to venues in search of new bands had gone the same way – boring by comparison to the excitement of a new discovery. I had mellowed and my only indulgence into anything on the so called fringes of music was an annual trip over to Otley Folk Festival every September. This is where I was at and what filled my head was the acceptable and bland. I was heading for a mid life of the same in terms of being a husband, parent and good citizen. In short, I was not planning to do anything over that weekend other than relaxing as best I could

Pogo 'til I Die - issues one/two: (early-mid 2002)

On the evening of that fateful day when I spotted the poster in The North Bar window, I wrestled with the notion of going to the gig. Why? Well, curiosity certainly – how close to the originals could they be? Nostalgia – yeah I'd have to accept that was in my mind – not that I'd seen either the Sex Pistols or the Ramones live but I'd always had a copy of their tunes in the car and, thankfully, the kids enjoyed hearing them too! But, what else was playing on my mind? What was making me mull over the thought of going to a bar I'd never been to before and on my own as I did not know anyone else who'd be interested – certainly not Helen. I doubted any friends would be able to join me on the spur of the moment. Going out with friends had to be planned in advance and the availability of baby sitters. I'd not done solo nights out since being on the pull in the mid eighties and then it was at Clouds or pubs in Preston- never Blackburn other than for the odd touring band date at King George's Hall. I asked Helen what she thought and I was expecting her to be dismissive and tell me that there was something good on the telly. But, she told me to go as I'd added in that I might bump into some people who use to watch bands

I'd gone to see before I'd met her. It was a way of justifying it to myself too as I was thinking that it should attract my own age group and I'd have a lot in common with anyone who had a passing interest in Punk and New Wave – well, at least sufficient to start a conversation with. Finally, I had no fear of going to concerts or gigs on my own and, as Helen reminded me when I was typing this chapter, "...you liked that sort of thing" so what was to stop me!

It was a hot summer's evening and I'd left home at the point when Brian May started playing the National Anthem from the top of Buckingham Palace during a tribute concert being stage in the grounds. No offence to the band Queen, but Brian May and everything since Freddie Mercury's death has been a travesty to all he stood for in terms of style, originality and impact. I wanted to hear a different version of *God Save the Queen* and any tentative link to what had excited me most in music circa '76/77 had to be better than what was on the box. I was soon striding into the entrance of the main doorway of the North Bar. I handed over the entrance fee and walked directly ahead and up to the bar on the right. One of the band's technicians was sound checking instruments and songs from the era were playing over the PA system. There was a lot of sunlight piecing the window behind the stage which was adjacent to the entrance and the blackout didn't quite cover the large frame. Cigarette smoke clouded the atmosphere, pinching my nostrils and eyes. I could not see how many people I was sharing the space with. However, the sounds and the damp smell of split larger and sticky floor boards made the place feel alive. I was back in the mid eighties and had the same tingling sensations I'd get in anticipation of the band coming on stage at Clouds or during my Barrow days at the Blue Bird club, The Queens or Healey's. A bloke slouched at the bar had a long sleeved shirt on with The Vibrators printed on the right arm from the top of the shoulder to the cuff. He saw me looking at it and, as he caught my stare, I nodded and said:

"Great band in their day – whatever happened to them, eh?"

Pause and cue the opening music from the "Good, Bad and the Ugly". He just stared back. Silence.... cue tumble weed. My feet had sunk into the floor. What had I said? There was a pause in the music too as the record changed. At first I thought I'd upset him as he had the look of someone considering whether I've just taken the piss or made an interesting observation. Not knowing which way this would go "Shot by Both Sides" came on, I kid you not!

"There you go mate" the bar person said as he slide my pint glass over and handed me the change momentarily crossing the space between me and my adversary. Thank God for a distraction to this increasingly puzzled looking and much taller person that was slowly standing up straight and facing down at me.

"Oh Shit! " I thought. I was about to get decked and I summoned up my Judo training and my mind pulsed with options on how best to get out of the place as I gripped my right fist around the pint glass. Then he spoke,

"What d'you mean, what happened to them!" Vibrator Man said in a slow but forceful tone tinged with a smattering of ironic pity as he sniffed his next line,

"Played a cracking gig here a few months back – that's what happened to them!" and he burst into a rasping laugh, pulled a deep drag on his cigarette and breathed the blue cloud into the ceiling. I wouldn't have blamed him or anyone else around if he had added "Wanker" as he exhaled– but thankfully he didn't and I nodded like a penguin that's finally been shown the way to the sea. I took a deep gulp of my shandy and felt a right idiot trying to give the impression I could see the funny side as I looked about for somewhere to hide.

"I'm obviously out of date from watching a few of the greats first time round" I added by way of excusing myself with the intention of heading over to the opposite side of the room. Before I made a step the person in front of me turned round and said,

"That's why I started this." He thrust a black and white booklet into my chest. I stopped and looked down and took it in my left hand and held it up to the light. He saw my lips mouth the title....

"Pogo'til I Die" he said and added, matter-of- factly, "All the original punk bands are touring again but no one is advertising the gigs or wanting to do any sorta write up for them so I started this fanzine – have that copy ...."

I put my drink down fingered my pocket for some change, which was his cue to start introducing himself,

"My name's Roy (extending his hand he gave mine a generous shaking) – been doing this myself since the end of last year and this is my second issue. It features 999, The Damned, UK Subs and **Pike** – who are a local band and mates of mine. There's information on up and coming gigs and reviews of some other local bands like **The Hyperjax** and Slutch in there."

His name was Roy Hesketh and our conversation that evening began my friendship with him and an adventure into all things Punk related. Whilst chatting that night, he dropped one nugget amongst many that set me on the rest of my five year love affair with local music.

"You know if you want to send me anything I can see that it gets into the next issue. If you go to a gig, get to talk to a band or just review some new stuff etc I'll consider anything?" He told me his contact details were in the "zine" and wrote his mobile number on a scrap of paper.

Interviews with bands....I mused and remembered how I had got backstage to a New Model Army gig in 1985 at a King George's Hall (KGH)– co-inci-dentally just across the road from where I was now chatting to Roy. Back then it was a case of asking one of the roadies if I could meet the band which I did as I had with The Alarm and Wire Train the following year. So I had some experience but as a fan not some kind of journalist. That was seventeen years ago and I was a lot younger, the band members were use to it but I suspected it would be different to be coming from the angle of an interviewer, aged late thirties, surely they would be guarded and less willing?

"How do you get to interview the bands Roy?" I asked.

"Well, here (nodding toward the bar), see that bloke to the left (I saw a tall ginger haired stocky bloke), that's Ronnie Brown – he owns this place and if you ask him he'll see what he can fix up for you. He's really helpful and loves the Punk so it shouldn't be a problem – just mention my name" and almost as an endorsement he and Ronnie seems to catch each other's eyes and held up their glasses to one another and mouthed "alright". Ronnie noticed me too and I mimicked the glass raising and I suspect that he was making a mental note that I was a "mate" of Roy's which came in handy a few nights later.

Short time young, long time old

The next day I read the zine from cover to cover. I spotted that Roy had done an interview with Let's Not Lose Mars to the Commies (aka The Commies), a "punk rock band from Chorley". It stood out because it mentioned Chorley and I made a mental note to make enquiries when next in town. In another of Roy's articles called the Final Edition he referenced a two page feature in the Lancashire Evening Post on 29/10/2001 written by Alan Burrows entitled "The Punk Generation". This was a summary of the highlights from the Sex Pistols' gig at The Lodestar, Ribchester on 16/09/76 through to what happened or didn't happen next on their infamous Anarchy Tour –i.e. cancelled dates at Preston Charter Theatre and Lancaster University. In between, venues and bands are name checked; like the Revillos and Bethnal playing The Duck Inn, which was opposite the Railway Station. Half way through I noticed the sentence "Chorley punks **Hangman** also played the Moonraker". Only now, having met that band's instigator, Shaun Maxwell and re -reading this article do I see a circle being completed (see chapter 9). This is why I am so glad to my younger self for keeping all he crates of material I accumulated over those five years.

That was a night of firsts in many respects. Apart from Roy, a nod to Ronnie and the sense of feeling part of what was going on I saw my first punk tribute bands. The gig itself was what I think you'd expect from a tribute band. The main songs were played adequately and the audience joined in appreciatively. It was "Okay" in that they did not try and pass themselves off as the individuals themselves - be it Joey or Johnny but it did not inspire me. What did impress me was the fact that I was amongst a smattering of my own peer group. We were all different shapes, sizes but roughly the same age group- mid to late thirties/early forties. I got the distinct impression, which Roy confirmed later on, that we were fed up with what passed for chart music and wanted to return to the sort of music that had got us excited twenty five years ago. By turning our backs on the TV and choosing to watch a live band I felt we were all making a statement. Rejecting the Pop Idol/ Fame game bull shit that we were being fed. "No thank you!" we are the Punk War warriors who have been pushed too far and are about to do something about it! If that meant watching a tribute band or the remnants of the originals whenever they came to town - then so be it – it *had* to be better.....right?

Roy had given me a copy of his second issue – he had sold out of issue one so I have no copy to relay the contents. Issue two has a picture of a 1950's women leaning backwards over a snooker table. She's taking a behind the back shot, smiling and displaying her suspenders as she poses. By the way, if anyone has a copy of issue one please copy it and send it to me so I can complete my set!

Issue 3 (Late 2002)

That evening I wrestled with the notion of going back to see if I could review the next gig at The North Bar. Roy and his fanzine had set me alight. Maybe I could interview The Jamm- another tribute band on that night. I thought that I could do as good a job at writing something and there didn't seem to be many other contributors to Roy's zine. After the 999 gig review Roy's last sentence was:

"So sweat soaked into the Blackburn night we went, up in five hours for work but it was worth it".

This comment made me think that I could do my writing part time while enjoying a night out. After all, what was the worst that could happen if I submitted something he didn't like – I didn't get published – so what! I'd have done something that I'd never done before and could leave it at that.

Thoughts and ideas I got at that time came out of nowhere. Time and time again over the next five years they would pop into my head without warning. I am sure this is the nature of divine inspiration for anyone moved by the unexplained. These moments came with "what if scenarios" and equally unprompted. It usually happen to me in the shower or as I was about to drop off to sleep or just before I woke. Wallop! "How about this for an idea!" That is how I ended up with some of my finest moments of inspiration and it happened that very evening for the first time. But, I did not know or recognize it as such until a few months later when I had set my senses on a compass baring in the direction of music and all things around it. There again what about those moments of self doubt? What was positive could be balanced against the negative. Well, on those very rare days when I used Helen as a sounding board it seemed only respectful to explain why I was going out without her. I discussed what had happened the night before, meeting Roy, showing her the fanzine and seeing what she thought about me interviewing the Jamm. Helen said that I knew more about The Jam than anyone she knew and it was obvious that I would enjoy it so why not? Why not indeed!

The events of the gig are capture in my review, interview and two black & white photos of the band I took while they were on stage. It is spread over four pages which Roy printed in his next issue. The main points that capture my attention now are the same that did when I first saw them in print - pride and the sense of achievement that the words I had written enthused into me. The night was the catalyst to many more gigs and interviews but for that one night I indulged in the nostalgia:

"...close your eyes and believe you're back at the Red Cow, 100 Club or Hope and Anchor and you will feel what it was that stirred up and excited fans of the day, making the Jam the finest English trio the initial punk upsurge produced.... The Jamm are the essence of the original, a highly professional unit delivering with integrity a tribute in every sense of the word".

My piece set a tribute band into context and their show was close to the original. I had seen The Jam live twice, so I had firsthand experience to judge them against. My interview with The Jamm was easy once Ronnie had introduced me to them after I'd told him that I was doing a feature for Roy. That weekend had left me on a high. The Jamm lads had integrity about what they were doing – I had no issue with them or the circuit they played. The only disappointment was the support band. Young lads from Darwen called **Rocket Dog**. I concluded my gig review of their set as being "....unmoved beyond the instant". I wanted to see the current generation as hungry and prolific as those who had made me fist the air in appreciation for the songs during my youth. **Rocket Dog** let me down and not just in their performance or their songs but in what it said for the whole of their generation if they were representative of it – bland – but it wasn't long before others changed my mind on that!

50

Issue 4: "Believe today I die or do something...." (John Robb)

At some point during that weekend Ronnie or Roy had told me about the North Bar gig with Goldbalde, The Iinviisiibles and Pretendgirlfriend. Whoever it was must have stressed to be early as the former were a local band worth seeing. "Why not video it?" another shower moment! I had seen people taking photos but no one had a video camera. Apart from that, I had struggled to write down the Jamm interview in long hand. Being able to play back a recording meant I could transcribe the comments precisely. On arrival I asked Ronnie if he would introduce me to the main bands. The result was an interview with the Iinviisiibles before their set and a hand written interview with John Robb on the stairs, before his set.

John Robb is the bass player with one of the original punk bands from Blackpool called The Membranes. He has also made career as a music journalist amongst those he interviewed has been Nirvana before they were famous. He was the author of a biography of The Stones Roses but my favorite book of his to date is "Punk"- a definitive version of the events in the mid seventies by way of a series of short interviews with the main protagonists involved. By 2002 he was a regular face on TV programs that did retrospectives of the previous three decades while he and other guests critiqued the highs and lows of fashion, music, TV, news and celebrities of the day. He politely declined my request to be interviewed on video but did agree to answer questions. It took ages for me to decipher my pathetic attempt at short hand and I went out the next day and bought a Dictaphone – the best investment I made – thanks John! He puts a charm on every word he uses like an infectious gift that makes you want to listen to every syllable. While you are mulling over them he's racing off on another tack. He told me that he wants to break down barriers and would stage dive into an empty space to do so concluding;

".....this is what I am. I always wanted to play music...to kick ass whatever the numbers in the audience....most people don't find anything in their life! For some the answer is not in a '77 way or any kind of forms that followed the early wave-just in something with an edge....and if all else fails you could have the best hair styles!"

His band at that gig consisted of two drummers, four guitars playing a mix of psycho/ rockabilly/punk. John's cyber punk crew cut hair was as impressive as his six pack abs as he performed naked from the waste up. Their song "Power of Rock'n Roll" was the opening track I played on my first radio broadcast (see Chapter 4) as it captures the spirit of how I relate to music in the hook line "....do you believe in the power of rock 'n roll".

A lot had happened for me by the time the third issue came out at the end of that October, beginning of November. In July, Roy and I had interviewed The Dickies together and their support that night - Darwen skate punks- **The Reserved**. I did a one page interview with The Reserved and review of the demos they gave me along with a flyer for their support gig to Capdown at KGH in August. There were reviews on **Seven Years Dead** (Stockport), **The Commies** and **Onset** (Chorley) at The Marque club Preston in September and a feature on **Rebekah** (Chorley) who supported **Duckhunt** at The Abyss Club and the Community Centre, in Chorley. I did a review of Goldblade's LP "Do You Believe in the Power of Rock 'n'Roll" and an 18 track compilation of local bands called Jambeezi "Are you ready for your close up?" All the above and these were printed with photos. Roy and I agreed to go 50/50 on the costs of printing up 100 copies and the glossy cover was in colour with pictures of The Dickies, and DEMOB on the front, Mark E Smith on the back with an over lay of the Sus-Sex Pistols and Marones poster I'd seen a life time ago! The reverse side of the cover was in colour too with photos of **Pike**, Captain Sensible, The Vibrators and various ticket stubs from the gigs Roy and I had been to. It was 32 pages long and I evenly matched Roy's input in terms of photos and words. The Dickies interview ran to 9 pages. It was a privilege to spend time with one of the Punk originals – Leonard Graves Phillips. I didn't know what happened to The Dickies after the *Banana Split* song and I went out and bought their greatest hits compilation along with their last two LPs from Action Records. I read what I could on their website and I knew that if I was to do this properly I had to do the my homework as the people you want to interview respect you for it and, as with Leonard, they are more likely to open up and reveal more than you could reasonably expect.

Roy filled the last page with every forthcoming gig of any punk description. It started with Wed 13th Nov Joe Strummer & The Mescaleros, Arena, Winter Gardens, Blackpool through Thursday 5th December -Vice Squad, **Sick 56, Flamingo 50**, Iron Door, Birkenhead to Sat 5th July, **Pink Torpedoes,** Old Bull Preston. When I took delivery of my share of the copies I felt I had a copy of the Ten Commandments. "This is my truth show me yours…" sort of thing. I felt unbelievable pride and wanted to share my experiences and opinions with everyone who I thought would welcome them. I did sell a few copies at Chorley Community Centre but, in the main, I gave them away. I used them as evidence of my credentials as a journalist when approaching people I wanted to interview. Any I had left at Christmas found their way to friends in seasonal cards. I was on a high and my writing had been vindicated in print. I was on my way!

Issue 5: Parental Advisory, Explicit Language (May 2003)

This came out in time for Holidays In the Sun (H.I.T.S) at Morecambe. By now I had gone full throttle into writing and Roy gave me equal billing on the editorial page "issue 5 put together by Roy Hesketh and John Winstanley with help from Lee G and Paul G". I was impressed by the way Roy had assembled the issue. He had to trawl through my rambling emails and word documents. It was 52 pages long excluding the colour cover with pictures of 999 and Faye Fife (Revillos) on the front, UK Subs, **Sick 56** on the inside and an advert for **Sick 56**'s LP *Recipe for Disaster* and Northern Records.Co.Uk on the back. The price went up from £1 to £1.50 to cover the additional costs. It has my interview with Glen Matlock (see Chapter 3) and twelve pages of gigs and CD/DVD/zine reviews.

The opening interview is with Danny Peyronel from the Heavy Metal Kids, one of the first bands Roy went to see in December 1975. As a fan talking to a hero, Roy always had a knack of keeping a balance between the facts and his personal admirations. This band featured the late Gary Holton who became more famous as his *Auf Wiedersehen, Pet* character (the one with coloured highlights in his hair in the series). Roy inserted a newspaper cutting that describes how the band had to play their entire three hour act in front of censors before their concert in Madrid. Gary was banned after police arrested him, objecting to the red stripe in is hair misbelieving he had something to do with the Devil. The conversation talks up the 4th album *Hit the Right Button* due out that June with tour dates in the UK and plans for more in Europe. I never heard of them again but I could say the same of so many bands!

There was an air of optimism for a Punk revival twenty five years on which comes out in many interviews we did. Lee and Roy met the Revillos after their North Bar gig in February: Roy asks Eugene Reynolds:

"Many of the 76/77 punk bands have reformed and plenty have just never stopped. Judging by tonight's turnout (a record crowd at the North Bar up to that point) *The Revillos are high on any fan of that era's list of must see again bands. Did you sense a demand?"*

"Not so much a demand but a feeling we just had some more to offer. We consider ourselves still relevant. And we still want to play live and record stuff." He replied.

In the piece, Roy expresses his frustration with the main stream media and TV:

"I recently contacted the BBC and complained at the lack of any of the '70's punk bands appearing on the "Later" music show (hosted by Joolz Holland). Although they always seem to find room for the new bands who have copied them.

The only era that the show ignores is the early punk, yet radio 2 is fuckin built round it!"

I cannot remember if I met Lee G and there are only a few articles by him throughout the PTID's issues. One that caught my eye was his one page recollection of the Clash White Riot Tour gig at the Electric Circus, Manchester on 8th May 1977. He describes Jo Strummer as *"...the thinking man's switchblade"* and there is a blurred photo of the band on stage. Lee says it was the best gig he ever attended and how he felt everyone there considered the songs as *"our music"* and how *"...we could change the world"*. As teenagers you believe that sort of thing, whether its music, peace protests or anything you feel passionate about. That never diminishes - it only gets tarnished as you get older and understand how the world really works and your place in it. Unless you are a Bono, Bob Geldoff or Bill Gates you have no influence other than from the age of eighteen when you tick a ballot paper. However, I felt, and still do, that Punk Rock and what Roy and I were doing, was a sort of mission to inform what the message was that we all took inspiration from. In Roy's interview with UK Nige (vocals and guitar in **Sick 56**) Nige sums up what Punk Rock means to him:

"(It) ...was always about having your say about things you thought were not right. Most people in the UK do have their own thoughts and opinions about the way things are run by the system or the problems of the world. Go down the pub, in the office or on the factory floor, you hear it everywhere, politics are a part of us whether we like it or not...You got something to say-say it! You got something to do-do it! You go something to be-be it!"

Similarly, in my interview with Joseph Porter (Blyth Power) I got his take on the historical context. I'd met Joseph at Otley the year before and had bought a lot of Blythe Power LPs from him over the years. Alnwick & Tyne (1990) captures the essence of Punk in the music and Joseph's vocals are Lydon inspired. Tagged as "Medieval Punk Rock", his songs are tales of Olde England, of lords and ladies, masters and squires gallantry and rogues. They are testament to how mankind does not learn the lessons of history. I ask his thoughts on my opinion that:

(Me) *"The marginalisation of Folk music is in parallel to Punk Rock. The interview I do with musicians from both genres has lead me to the conclusion that you could print the whole interview and take out the names and you have both sets saying the same thing – hidden from the main stream, commercially ignored and abandoned by the youth. Why is that! Why has it happened?"*

(Joseph) *"Folk music happened as people picked up whatever instruments came to hand and played without influence, what they were able to work out for themselves which is essentially what Punk Rock is-the 1970's version of Folk music....History started just now! It's all history...you can write songs today for the people of tomorrow. Everything is so meticulously recorded and registered now that there's going to be no more mystery in the future but a song about the Cod Wars 800 years in the future will make people wonder what went on!"*

We go on to debate heritage and conservation. He hates the fact that the relic of the Mary Rose has been dragged out of the Solvent and put on display in an expensive chemical environment which prevents you from seeing it properly. It should have been left to rot on the sea bed. Why, he expounds, do we spend a fortune on such rubbish and fail to record events and places which time will fragment. We conclude that people will one day stand in the ruins of buildings like Blyth Power Station and say *"who worshipped here?"* On the eve of the Band's twentieth anniversary he was still enjoying it and had no incentive to stop. He struck me as one of those few people who still hold the ideals they embraced growing up. He has done so without losing the integrity of the initial inspiration Punk and other influences had and despite how hard that is to do along the way.

Politics in Punk

Support for Blyth Power that night at the North Bar, was Southport based four piece **Pike**. I did an interview with front man Mick Pike. They were promoting their *Living the Dream* CD – a compilation of their material spanning the thirteen years of the band's existence. Mick's reason for starting the band was because there was very little music that he liked in the mid eighties and the main reason for continuing was:

"The fact that I want to keep moving on and I object to the way this country is run and the way the working class people are treated like idiots. I object to the way democracy fails everybody in the fact that we are going to war and nobody seems to have a say!"

This was at the time when the USA had given the United Nations a twenty one day ultimatum to tackle Iraq or they would invade. The influence of politics in Punk that I got was in the social commentary of songs. Early on it was Paul Weller's lyrics when he was in The Jam. *Down in The Tube Station* mentions right wing meetings" *Brick and Mortar* is about government corruption and *Little Boy Soldiers* makes the point that wars are started by politicians but it is their electorate who has to go and fight them. Sham 69 used humor and laddish camaraderie (*Hersham Boys*) to suggest that united we stood/ divided we fall (*If the Kids are United*). But Stiff Little Fingers were one of the few bands with something relevant to say and did it so brilliantly. The

Clash made some observation that I could relate to (*Bored with the USA*) and refused to open letter bombs (*Career Opportunities*). The later was relevant to when I was leaving school and how the government Youth Training Scheme (Y.T.S) kept the unemployment figures down. There were plenty of things to get worked up about and loads of protests and demos to go on in the 70's and 80's. They attracted anyone who wanted to shout out or be shouted at. The closest I ever got to any of it was buying a Campaign for Nuclear Disarmament (CND) badge. I didn't go to any of the Anti this or that rallies. Some bands played benefit gigs but I never attended them. In Leyland and Chorley me and my mates were not fired up on anything political and never had heated debates about what bands were pro this or that. I remember Paul Weller getting slagged off in the press for saying he would vote Tory and Joe Strummer was always being asked questions on his politics. But, for many Punk politics was the Do It Yourself manifesto.

Post Punk, I was hooked into the interpersonal observations of the Gang of Four. That band made me think about stereo types in relationships, the power of advertising and how to hide condoms discreetly. In the eighties I liked Billy Bragg who was direct at putting his opinions across. He became popular during the Miners' Strike and made me think about what was happening to the Trade Unions and the effect it was having on communities in songs like *Which side are you on*, *Between the Wars* and *New England*. I never got into the second wave of Punk so I cannot say what they stood for as I couldn't decipher the lyrics and there are other sources that will inform you better. I talk more about politics in Chapter 11, but for now, I wasn't aware of any local or unsigned band that were, what I considered to be, hard core when it came to social unrest in a direct way. For the majority, Punk was about being your own person, making your own mind up on what you believed in and everything else in your life – even down to how you dressed. Mick Pike put this very neatly at the end of our chat:

"Most new bands are Me Me Me! It's Thatcher's bloody Britain! Self-Self Self! I grew up through the Punk era and to me it wasn't about green haircuts and tartan trousers – That's Bollocks! To me the Undertones were Punk and they had donkey jackets on. It's always been what's up top, what you think! It's a way of life, the way you live and what you do."

continuing with issue 5.....

I was managing The Commies by this stage and unashamedly I got them as much exposure in PTID as I could. I did a half page summary of what they had done so far in 2003 and thanked readers for their continued support, inviting them to visit the band's website. Their gig at the Cellar Bar on 8th March and "The Long & the Winding" EP make it on to the review pages too. John Robb submitted a two page diary of Goldblade's "No War" tour in Ireland and a third of another page advertises the dates or the rest of the year. There is an interview with Blackpool's **Pink Torpedoes** and a short feature on new Preston band **Dumb-Down.** Finally, my interview with Justin Sullivan (at Bury Met) is just over two pages long and completed a circle for me. I first became aware of the band he fronts (New Model Army) when I saw them on TV singing *Small Town England.* Five years later in November 1985 I reminded Justin of that time when I first met him and asked him what has kept him going since then.

"I am proud of the fact that in 160 songs we never repeated ourselves – everything's different –hard, soft, political/non-political –we never got stuck in post punk or folk rock. No big egos. I turned away and wrote acoustic stuff - very different (subject matter) I wanted to create something beautiful, romantic and angstless. I am very proud of the 2003 New Model Army tour – the world keeps changing which means there are more things to write about."

The gig that night was Justin solo with occasional accompaniment from Dean White (Keyboards/Guitars) and Michael Dean (percussion). Over twenty four songs that night he covered new material from his recently release (solo) CD *Navigation by the Stars* as well as NMA classics like *Ballard of Bodmin Pill, The Attack* and (my all time favorite) *225.* He was very hospitable and softly spoken on both meetings and looked like he had taken good care of himself over the interim. He explained how he had done this,

"I pay people to take care of the business side...above all it is to motivate myself by always pleasing myself. We never let the audience dictate. Some of the songs don't get played, as I can't reach the keys. If we do we change them around....we are not keen on bitter people! Some people's anger turns over and over inside and they can't see any joys in life. My favourite country is Brazil. It has the worst and the best aspects in life rather like our philosophy."

Issue 6 (December 2003)

This is sixty four pages long; Beki Bondage is on the front and Penetration on the back. The inside cover has coloured photos of **Pike**, Dead Pets, UK Subs and Emergency taken at The Witchwood (Ashton-under-Lyne) festivals in the August and October. It is an example of how focused the zine's content had become. Musically it had the older elements of those mentioned above, but also the younger bands like **Kid Conspiracy** and Kinesis in contrast with elder statesmen like those in super group Dead Men Walking and, my personal favourite, John Foxx (founder and original singer in Ultravox). Geographically, Roy and I had stretched ourselves. There were the bands to see at our usual haunts in and around Lancashire, The Fylde coast and Manchester. But Roy went up to Kendal's IBIS clubs for the **Hyperjax, Pike, AK Riot, Dog Toffee and Gunpowder Plot** and I did my interview with Beki/Vice Squad and The Dangerfields (from Ireland) in Wakefield at The Snooty Fox.. Furthermore the issue had interviews with Crashed Out (Jarrow, Tyne and Wear), The Peacocks (from Switzerland) and Crucified Venus (from Australia). Punk was a global movement and we were doing our bit to reflect that.

I retrospect, the hardest part of documenting the rest of this issue and the other two that followed it, is not what to include but what to leave out. Having re-read every page I have a biased towards the stuff I penned but some of the best bits are written by Roy. He had a knack of being direct and that sense of urgency in his words is what characterised him and is what I liked about him most. I have to be selective too as I am trying to tell a story. You would get bored with a regurgitation of details of who played what, where and when and I have done this in a couple of other chapters which demand a documentary approach. I like to think that what Roy and I did cover was of its time and, like the founding principle of Punk, it burned bright for a short while and then it was gone – we both moved on. I began to understand this feeling during issue six as the articles I wrote were done while I was busy doing a mass of other things – like managing The Commies.

The year started with me organising a residency for The Commies at The North Bar in a series of weekly gigs in the build up to my gig for Glen Matlock. Apart from over forty gigs with The Commies I put together my own one day 20 band Punk Festival "It's Not Cricket" in June (chapter 6). I was still involved with the radio station (chapter 4) and most things orientated around Chorley Community Centre (chapter 7). From what started out as exciting, new and fun, writing for PTID had begun to get predicable and hard work. I did not see it as a viable business, so forgive me if I pick out what I feel highlights the variety and links in with my story.

Interview with Beki Bondage

Stu Taylor was a promoter I'd met at the August Punk Picnic festival at The Witchwood and I liked him instantly. He and his wife were die hard music fans and Stu was further on in his promotions business than I was. He had a network of quality acts he was putting on at his own successful gigs and was moving into making CD compilations as well as managing a few bands. He invited me over to Yorkshire to cover the Vice Squad gig he was running at The Snooty Fox in

Wakefield. In PTID he recognised the work Roy and I were doing and I was that side of the Pennines for the Otley Folk Festival so the drive wasn't that far. The venue was very busy and noisy, so after a brief introduction from Stu, to lead singer, Beki, she agreed to do the interview in my car.

What struck me most about her was how elegantly good looking she was. There weren't that many females in Punk, but Beki, stood out as one of the most glamorous in a very different way to the others. Dressed in a leather bodice, short skirt and fish net stockings her blond hair and perfect make up was a pleasing sight on a wet and cold September night. Her personality and passionate beliefs attracted me to her too. She told me that she started back on the road again with her current band after an invitation to play the H.I.T.S festival. That, and gigs in Europe, especially one in Slovenia, made her fall in love with it again:

"...kids of 16 with this war going on around them and they were into animal rights and it kind of reminded me why I got into it in the first place...a lot of people think of us as old gits – we are totally immature (laughs with an infectious deep rasp)*...Me and Paul* (Rooney, current guitarist in the band and who was with her in The Bombshells)*, write and have a fresh approach to do things. We stuck the Ska stuff in for a laugh and people really liked it* (their latest LP Rich and Famous)*...some people think we've got some mega deal – we haven't. We licence the album to EMI – we paid for it all, they put it out and a lot of people complain as it's not in their local HMV and you've got to go and order it. We're not Kylie – they're not gonna cram the front shelves with our product. They're waiting to see what happens- i.e. we sell it for them...we're still poor in other words!"*

I asked her what her attitude was to the music industry compared to twenty years ago when she set out with the original band?

"I'm slightly suspicious of a lot of the people...good and bad on both sides – great promoters who do a good job like Stuart (and his wife) who really work their butts off – other places we go they couldn't give a shit...and the same throughout the industry now as it was back then – human nature doesn't change!....I always liked bands like The Clash – Joe Strummer in particular was the complete diamond geezer who so stuck up for the working class people and the underdog and I admired that in people like him...respect to all the bands who have kept going- they deserve to go out and earn a living. It annoys me when people say they shouldn't be there – why shouldn't they! They're professional musicians – that's what they do. You don't say to a plumber – you can't plumb anymore mate – you're 35 give it up. That's stupid he's probably a better plumber than when he was 25 so why not! As for the American stuff – we've been swapping across the Atlantic for hundreds of years...it doesn't bother me if it rocks and is sincere music, who cares what the accent is – it's irrelevant isn't it!"

I ask what she thinks about the old punk bands that aren't moving forward which is contrary to punk's ethos.

"We all know why - coz a lot of the audience doesn't like you doing new stuff! It's taken us 5 years to turn it around and be accepted for doing new stuff...My favourite band at the moment is The Darkness.... brilliant musicians, write really good songs and (they) are funny! ... they took a Rock art form that had the piss taken out of it...everyone takes the piss out of guys in makeup – they did it the Punk Rock way and it's brilliant that they are doing well and they are moving forward. To move forward you have to steal from the past – there is nothing new it has all been done before. That's why a lot of bands don't move forward – maybe they can't... I've seen bands like the Exploited today who are a lot better than they were in the '80s...an aggressive speed-metal band, but I bet they get people saying (mock accent) "Do Dead Cities!" so they can't win!"

The rest of the interview is about the album, touring and ends with me asking what the band stands for now?

".... Don't know what the band would say what they stand for but I still stand for a love of music and fairness for everybody and that's probably never gonna happen is it! And fairness for animals as well – can't see me dying particularly happy because they can't get fox hunting banned, it's been through Parliament three times and they still haven't banned it, so for all the other stuff...that's just the tip of a very big ice-berg!"

We had an advert for the album inserted with a few photos I'd taken during their set to go with the feature. Stu was pleased with the copy and I sent one down to Beki but have not heard from her since. That was the case with many things I did in the zine. The moment was everything and when it had been put into print it was done - full stop. And that is how it should be.

While going over the PTID material I have a pang of disappointment in realising that there are some that I never read before! I suppose it must be the same for anyone who is part of any print run or serial. You know what your part is and what you have to deliver. When the end product is done you get on with the next one. In that sense, when the issues came out after this one I would check my material and scan read Roy's and the others. It's like a lot of the CDs I had at the time. If I heard it once and it did not stand out or was relevant to what I was doing then or in the future – it got parked and I know now that most never got played again! This is true of Roy's interview with Chris Wright from **Crashed Out**. Reading it now there is a humorous section I know I did not read before.

After a series of standard questions Roy asks him about the North v South divide. After pointing out the obvious Chris throws in another contrast to lighten the tone:

60

"...and another thing we say giz a canny bottle of Broon will yi pet....and they say Can I have a nice bottle of your finest Ale please my Dear"

[Roy] I noticed a photo on your website "Jarra Elvis" – who is he...and looking at the lyric on "Freak Show" is there a connection?

[Chris] *Fuck me!!!...you haven't heard of the King of Cock n Dole?? Jarra Elvis is a living Leg End or is it legend around these parts. He lives in his Palace "Disgrace Lands" and he performs Elvis Presley impersonations around the pubs and clubs. Yeah we did a piss take song called Freak Show all about Jarra Elvis cos when you see one it really is a freak show. As well as Elvis there are others: Pelaw Pitney, Hebburn Cliff, Simonside La Bon, Prat King Cole and Maltloaf (they) cannot sing a note and are either pissed of just idiots.*

My interview with **The Peacocks** (Switzerland) is brief due to the language limitations on their part (my English was perfect but theirs wasn't!). The gig was a disaster due to a faulty microphone and an PA tech who was not use to the equipment – it wasn't her fault as she was thrown in at the last minute (weren't you Liz you know who you are!). Anyway the best line of mine came at the end: *the Peacocks splendour lures the curious in and can ruffle the feathers of many pallid imitators.* I cannot remember writing that! Similarly, I do not recall the closing paragraph of the interview with Mike Peter's/Dead Men Walking gig at Darwen Library: *The fact remains that it was a cracking show with everyone on their feet in standing applause both sides of the single encore. This is not a "take the money and run" tour of has beens but a genuine wallow in our past with a timely reminder to "our" generation and others that the spirit of '76 still lives on and there's life in the dead men who are able to keep walking the path of integrity.*

Despite knowing that Stiff Little Fingers may be available for an interview, through a loose connection to journalist Alan Parker, it didn't materialise. I did catch a quick word with Bruce Foxton (ex Jam and their bassist for a number of years) while he and the others were walking about Blackburn in search of a drinking hole. A "see what we can do afterwards" did not get taken up as I was double booked that night (10/10/03), wanting to catch **Fi-Lo Radio** and **Kinesis** in Preston. That was how busy things got and it made my piece all the better for not getting an interview. I knew when I wrote the introduction that it was the best I had written. I was annoyed with the disconnection between fact and fiction when people refer to Punk. Who had the birth right to be aggressive when it came to playing punk? I was vitriolic towards those who wore punk as a designer label like they do today. All those who wear Ramones T Shirts, without knowing a single song that band recorded!

"I regard Stiff Little Fingers as an attitude rather than a band. Out of the

Punk explosion they had more reason to light the fuse than a bunch of adolescent arty misfits. They lived in a war zone and breathed the stench of religious persecution, listening to the sounds of riots and bombing was a way of life not something you heard as an intro on a record. This was a time when wearing the wrong colour on any day of the week in the wrong place could get you knee capped compared to tartan bum flaps being the latest fashion accessory. Their world was another one compared to the UK mainland that thought a three day week and rubbish on the streets was equally outrageous as London's middle class kids adorning safety pins and spiky hair. As Punk's forefathers bathed in the images and music of radical guitars these kids from Belfast dodged bullets and water cannons. Being Pretty Vacant, In The City, with your New Rose or just Bored with the USA never convinced me that a diplomat's son and Art students had anything to be genuinely angry about. Punk was void of any real political edge until these four street wise Irish lads adopted the Vibrators' song title for a name and Hiroshima'd the fucking lot. Inflammable Material sparked my political awareness and did more to capture Punk's cry for change than anything The Bollocks (LP) could lay claim to. SLFs first LP is what legends are made of- each song on it and most of the follow up Nobody's Heroes, helped build the altar at which many a true Punk worships".

When I hit the send button on my email to Roy I knew that I was changing my attitude towards what I was writing. I was waking up to the fact that Punk and all things of my generation had had its time and I needed to focus on the new. The Commies helped me see this and I could read it in the PTID articles we were producing. I had made the choice that night to see two of the current bands rather than push for an interview with the old guard. I'd cross the line and, in many respects, I never went back.

This change of direction started with this issue. The seeds were sown when I caught up with **Kid Conspiracy** at the Witchwood, Ashton in mid August. The band was the nearest comparison to The Commies and I wanted to check out the competition as the latter's manager. Their set showcased their professionally produced *December Fall* 4 track EP released late 2002. It was by far the best Nu-Metal, Emo/Punk CD I'd heard up to The Commies *Time Won't Tell* 4 track EP. Both bands were attracting the same attention but I felt Kid Conspiracy were ahead of The Commies in that they had a larger fan base and were able to pull them to gigs further away from home. They also had been Radio 1 play listed and had professional management via their Access to Music course lecturer in London. I had got into a misguided mindset that these young Punk bands should have an appreciation of the original bands and my question to band member James set us on a collision course.

"....we don't take much from the old Punk – yeah it's loud and raw but we want to touch people as well"

I challenge their appreciation of all things Punk by asking *"were you ever influenced by Joy Division – a band that really touched people?"*

(James) *"Not been into them...rather Radiohead and Cold Play – bands who've got a melody and can rock out as well".* (eh! What's fuckin go 'in on here...Ed).

I was wound up as I doubted they'd ever listened to *Unknown Pleasures* or how could they be so clouded by these two bands who stole from what Joy Division and other bands had templated. I tried another tack by sighting a contemporary band who was tipping their hats to Joy Division. *"But, a band like Thursday, have the balance between old and new –they even wrote a song about Ian Curtis?"*

However, the answer was not forthcoming. Sensibly James could see that I was getting wound up and tactfully digressed onto trivial matters. I reflected on this moment and begrudgingly agreed with James' assertion that you do not have to know everything that went before to be entitled to write your own material. I had tried to do this with The Commies and even played a copy of *Unknown Pleasured* to them in the car when we went to scout out a recording studio in Ormskirk one day early on in our relationship. It was a mistake then just as it was for me to peruse my misguided contention with James.

Youth will take what they need and do their own thing. They should not be caged in or told to pay homage to the past. They are the here and now and everything that they do should be about the future. I titled the article "Old Versus New!" and knew that I was pushing an agenda which I was formulating as I typed it. I ended the piece with:

"Looking back now I do not regret pushing the old versus new Punk ideology/inspiration as it was my first interview with a band that I feel will make an impact in the next 12 months – just as Kinesis are doing currently. These are punk's descendents and have 25 years of other influences since year zero. All I can hope to gain is their understanding as well as trying to prise open the treasures that seem to have been lost to the current generation....Radiohead for Christ sake! Yes, Pablo Honey but the rest is just the reincarnation of Pink Floyd and we all know why we have ended up back to Prog Rock and all its worst excesses that Punk tore down. How soon we forget!"

If that was the start of my epiphany then it was confirmed the evening I met with Bolton rising stars **Kinesis** after their gig at The Mill, Preston. The interview was done on their tour bus as I arrived too late to see their set.

I swapped a copy of my *It's Not Cricket!* DVD (see chapter 6) for their LP *Handshakes for Bullets* (Independe Records).

(Me) *"I read an interview with the band earlier this year and it indicated that you had certain axes to grind or that there were things you hated or were annoyed about and I wondered what they were?"*

Michael Bromley (guitar vocals) responds: *"Any thinking person who looks at the state of the world would or should have an axe to grind and should be annoyed at the way things are. We do find things wrong when we look around. In one sense we've only just woken up as people because we're still quite young. We've started to take a step back and are taking a look at the wider world. That's reflected in the songs- the lyrics- there's a lot of confusion and frustration...the music industry is just that – it's an industry like any other...it will be geared towards profit... That is definitely something that sucks the soul out of it for all music fans. As to what can be done...its this* (picking up a copy of *It's Not Cricket!* DVD*) –a perfect example of what people can do to take it upon themselves to by-pass the mainstream, corporate avenues. Pop Idol! It's a TV show – it's not the same world as going out and playing little gigs. Totally different!"*

The Dangerfield's Andrew Griswood had a similar understanding of how the music industry worked. A former mortgage adviser for a bank in Northern Ireland, he confirmed what I said above about the significance of SLF and their first LP:

"Coming from Belfast, which is obviously a rough city, we have our opinions about what's going on there and what has gone on there in the past and I've every respect for bands who want to sing about that but I favour The Undertones approach which was if you've grown up with this shit round you 24 hours a day 7 days a week – the music is an escape from it. So I don't feel any inclination or obligation to sing about politics or anything like that. Although I will say Inflammable Material is one of the most inspirational albums – it is probably the only album about Belfast, about Ireland that has ever spoken to me because it is written from an objective stand point-whereas a lot of others are informed with a bit of bigotry – even if it is subliminal. I think the subliminal sectarianism is a big problem at home. People think they are not bigoted but they are because it is conditioned into us from child hood! So we stick to Rock'n Roll politics...driving about, touring-write about what we do and not fuck anyone over!"

The implications inherent in my writing for this issue stand out to me now as I know how my relationship with Roy started to change in the latter part of the year. He also made an astute observation in his review of *It's Not Cricket!* *"...an excellent record of the day in DVD format should not make financial sense so all credit to John for putting his neck on the block and giving local talent a chance. I'm sure its appreciated by all featured".* I knew I was using PTID for my own agendas and Roy never challenged me on this but in his own subtle way his comment here is a warning shot – do the bands really appreciate what you are doing John! Fair comment and even if he had been more vocal I doubt I would have changed what I was doing. I was on a mission and *It's Not Cricket!* had a hidden objective for The Commies and my wider goals for A3H's future ,which Roy was not privy to – respect to you though, Roy.

Issue 7 (May 2004)

The first 50 copies came with a free Noize Anoize sampler CD. Tracks included **Boredom, The Bobby Dazzlers, Riot to US, Hope, The Runs** (who had just split) and **The Icemen.** Roy's editorial was done just after watching the UK Subs in Blackburn (24th May) which was a Charlie Harper's unofficial 60th Birthday celebration. He mentions how he had been asked to fill in on bass for **Pike** as Jez Pike had chopped off part of his fingers at work which meant Roy got to see the "other side of the fence", as he put it during a support slots with Anti Nowhere League, Menace and Broken Bones. The latter one I saw and he fitted in very well and played competently. The front and back cover is a colour picture of Oddy from Menace with Slutch, **Dumb-Down**, and **The Runs.** It's 60 pages long and the centre fold has photos of The Meteors, Drongos for Europe, The Undertones and The Beat at the Academy in The UK All-dayer at Birmingham on 2nd May. It also had several interviews I had done which was double the number from Roy. During this period I had seen the end of The Commies and I adapted the "year in the life of managing a band" article (see Chapter 5) and photos in this issue. I was now managing **Pretendgirlfriend** (an "Indie" band- chapter 8) and I could see that I had changed my perspective on Punk which I use this issue exorcise.

My interviews start with **4 Past Midnight** and their gig with **III On Speed, Spitting Dummies** and **X-Rippers**. I'd been attracted to the gig for a few reasons. It was a venue I'd not been to before (The Thatched House, Stockport) and I was curious to see if it was suitable for Pretendgirlfriend to play. Stu Taylor was there and he had sent me a biog and sampler CD of 4PMs material back in the spring of 2003. I had liked it and was on the lookout for out of town older bands to play the Chorley Community Centre. It also made sense to feature all the bands for PTID as it was exactly what the zine was set up to do.

4PM were from Scotland and had been going for fourteen years when I spoke to them. Pete (Drums and vocalist) reminded me of how English bands playing the Emo/Skate version of Punk wanted to sound like the American bands that had inspired them – *"...Green Day and Off Spring – they are taking it to a whole different level and you ask kids of today and they will say Off Spring is a punk band. But, it's not a Punk band in my book. The Exploited, Sex Pistols, The Clash, Ramones – that's Punk Rock..."*

Oh dear! I thought here we go the old versus new and I correctly predicted that most of this interview went the way I expected it to. However, I did agree with Wullie's (bass player) contention that Green Day *"...is responsible for keeping some sort of punk recognition in the mainstream. So, all that comes from America is not bad!"* When we debate 4PM's songs and the political messages they expound (sex abuse, Bush's war smoke screen, Tony Blair's mistake *"...you don't go to war without knowing all the fact!"*) we wonder whether there is a lack of common focus in punk in 2004? We agree that the major record labels are not interested in signing bands like 4PM in preference to the Busteds of the day. A summary of what we cover is: if you sing about controversial subjects like paedophilia and the Iraq war you will stay under ground as the majors are about profit and they find that in the rubbish that the kids, who are the main consumers of music, are buying into. I have to remind myself that the rebellion in 76/77 was in the presentation not the substance. I use the end of the interview to lay down the gauntlet to PTID readers to challenge themselves:

"I reflect on the fact that there doesn't seem to be the labels today like Stiff records and Two Tone who set a trend in developing new bands that had a sound and talent which couldn't help but be pushed to the forefront. Scratch the surface and you will find the likes of Deck Cheese, Household Names, Kung Fu, Fat Wreck, BYO and many more record companies who all have their interpretation of Punk spewing out a stream of new hopefuls. However, the failure of most of their bands lies in their lack of writing songs that appeal to the mainstream. The reason why they all sound the same is they generally are, and, in the banality of their tunes. They put more energy into their hair gel, jeans that fall around their arses to reveal designer boxers, and ensure their leaps and fistings are timed to perfection but they do not pay attention to crafting a catchy tune that you'll be trying to get out of your head the following day....but with 4PMs Little Sid or Victim you'll come away humming the chorus or admire the harmony changes in Majors on The Street or just smirk at the simplicity of Get A Life or Fuck off. We take Punk too seriously, yearning for a return to what we think are the misguided values of 76/77 when there was a lot of crap in the charts (there always will be!) or the bands don't take the music seriously enough to deliver a CDs worth of memorable material. 4PM do not disappoint as they have the experience and treasure chest of songs for the old and the young, traditionalist or modernist – you'll have to catch them to decide which category you fit into."

My interview with Jeremy (bass) and Mark (Guitar & Vocals) from the Levellers covers fours pages but the intro and end reads like an advertisement for David Kay and his film company Red Brick Productions (Chapter 11) but I submitted it for PTID as the band promoted the punk ethics of DIY and were the acceptable side of the anarchists in the UK for the last twenty odd years. Elsewhere in this issue are my interviews with **III on Speed** (trio from Gloucester) **Howard's Alias** (12 Bar Preston 19th December 2003) and Roy's with young Fylde trio **Enima** and Rochdale's **Suspicious Stains** – but they have little to record here as the bands were relatively new to the scene and the pieces are background, influences, who does what in the band and what they are doing next. However, I used my interview with **Adequate 7** to push the youth agenda. This band from Cardiff had signed to Household Records and I spoke to them after their gig at the Attic, Leicester. I was aware of Adequate 7 as their name and the record label were on my radar while managing The Commies. I caught most of their impressive set. The interview in a kitchen with Gavin (trumpet), Kazz (guitar) and Jonny (bass) is much like those mentioned above. The only sound bite that stands out now is in Kazz's response to my question on what were the messages the band were projecting?

"Don't take things for granted – think things through and educate yourself rather than react to things and jump on the band wagon...you can't assume you know everything"

I end with the challenge to:

"...anyone who terms him/herself as a punk in the 21st Century...if you are stuck in 76/77 then get out more – to watch the younger end of the age scale and understand what the kids are about. It is true that some are happily clueless; some are on the band wagon or are all sound and no substance. But, Adequate 7 are a fine punk band for the modern era..... Their album Songs of Innocence and of Experience is a land mark UK Punk CD as was Douglas' on Gravity records but how many of you have listened to them or have any idea what I am talking about – go out more and open your minds and ears! Adequate 7 are the natural descendant for today's youth from the original UK Punk lineage in sound, substance and fury".

I was pleased with the final line and knew the last three words would conjure up the same headline the Sex pistols got the day after their infamous interview on the Grundy TV show. I have played their LP frequently over the years since so it says something about my assertion as to how I ranked its significance. Similar to **Duckhunt** in style Adequate 7's songs are more enjoyable as they are catchier whereas Duckhunt's *Vodka* and *Dass Reg* are the only ones that have longevity for me now. Sorry guys it must be an age thing on my part!

I don't show my gratitude to the American's for much but my interview Grant from LA hip-hop Punks Pistol Grip in January (Royal Oak, Poulton) did allow me to vent my anger. The interview confirmed what I had suspected about them and I used the last page to let it all out:

The yanks have nothing to teach us and we should stand proud of the fact that Punk Rock was born in England.... They envy this fact and will never forgive us for not taking The Dead Kennedy's to our hearts as the Sex Pistols heirs.

They send over their ambassador relics who claim the Ramones and New York Dolls gave us Punk Rock. Bollocks mate! Our leaders maybe seduced by your quest for world domination of your so-called culture but the mass majority aren't and don't that suck! It is like a lot of things the Yanks will not have – a history of Democracy that wasn't at the expense of their native culture, a monarchy with our rich tapestry of kings and queens, an appreciation of irony and how big is not always beautiful.

*I am told that this is the largest turnout here tonight –so don't tell me it is co-incidence that a yank band is headlining. For the record I was there for **Sick56** and kick myself for letting the interview make me miss the start of their set. I am saddened that if it is a fact that the majority of those who came did so because a yank band was in town...were of my generation -shame on you! Punk is about being independent and moving forward – to think for yourself and not be taken in by the hype. I see it in the youth of Chorley, Blackburn and Preston who wear hoodies and T Shirts of Designer USA which is as repugnant as the clowns who run our music industry churning out Busted who have the insolence and hypoc-risy to manipulate a punk anthem like Teenage Kicks to number one but denied the founders of Punk rock their number one in 1977.*

I have asked bands about their politics and no one at the youth end seems to have a clue what I am getting at. Where are your balls and if you are Punk then stand for something even if it's to say we are a band from Leyland who sounds like a band from Leyland. I have been fortunate to have interviewed bands who have got something to say but recently I have found fewer and fewer as the qual-ity of this issue may reflect. Punk happened because the music industry forgot the simple fact that music is not a product but an art form and should not be manipulated like a Barbie Doll or hamburger. The Sex Pistols, The Clash and The Damned came from garage land and gave us the DIY ethos to have fun with a sense of purpose – that's politics with real power. For the man in the street or the kid in the bedroom dreaming and making those dreams happen because they could see it happening. Then the music industry had to react to save itself when they had a stranglehold it imploded as it was meant to. It is time for another reac-tion. The retro band of glam/pomp rockers The Darkness are award winners in

2004. This is evidence that originality is on its knees. Do not get sucked into the corporate hype and especially the majority of crap we take from America. Please make your own minds up and support local music –in the words of Jimmy Pursey "...stick America up your arse!"

The last eleven pages are gig and CD/zine reviews and all but a few are done by Roy – he even reviewed his own gig playing bass in **Pike** at their gig at the retro Bar (Manchester) with **Stunt Face**, **One Man Stand** and Broken Bones. I was at that gig and don't know why I didn't review it for Roy but by that stage my attention was drifting away from punk and towards Indie. I had done *It's Not Cricket II!* Festival in February which was a disaster on a few fronts (see chapter 10) and I was full throttle into managing Pretendgirlfriend. It was inevitable that, two years on from when I first met Roy, our relationship had come to a natural end. I was thinking differently about my reasons for writing and, as indicated above, I was becoming a critic and not a reporter. Expressing my views was on the borderline of alienating our audience and I felt that I was becoming fed up with it all. It was time to leave while I was on a high and Roy and I were still on speaking terms.

Issue 8 (Jan 2005)

At 22 pages long it is nearly all Roy's own work. Fittingly, as it was the last issue, Roy ended where he had started out – one man and his typing fired up with enthusiasm but with a sense of things being extinguished that once burnt brightly. The colour cover photos are of 3CR (front), Crashed Out (reverse) and UK Subs, Parkinsons and Jimmy Pursey on the inside. Centre fold is a live shot of Mick Jones and Tony James at the North Bar gig (22/10/04) as their new project Carbon Silicon "This one's for John Peel" is handwritten on the front – the great music fan and radio one DJ having died recently. Roy's editorial is an uncompromising torrent of everything I liked about Roy:

"This will be the last issue of the zine for a while, in yuppie speak "I'm taking time out"....(and this issues is dedicated to John Peel)...without him punk rock would never have broken in the UK as quickly as it did. Simple as that! (It's) Also dedicated.... to those who reckon this mag is too safe and takes no risks. By that I take it they mean there's no politics or sport. Bollocks! Go read Loaded or some other fuckin' corporate rag sheep. You don't know me and I haven't time or patience to piss around with idle chat. I've also, on the advice of my muckers, upped the price to £2. This just about covers the cost of producing it and like many of the bands who've featured in the zine over the last 3 years the time and effort still come free. Who's inside "the best toilet read then"? I'll never forget that Rob Phlegm. Special thanks to Andy Gibson for sorting The Genocides

article, the loveable Manc Drunk Punx 3CR are here, cheers to Dave Coops for that. Beano chipped in at the death with a great Blood or Whiskey interview. Thanks to John for sorting the **Sadie Hawkins Dance** *interview. I chewed the fat in a Preston boozer with Ersy and Dani from Blackburn's finest-* **Boredom***. Staying local there's a great new Preston band the* **Phlegm Fatales** *look out for them in 2005. More familiar faces, well US 77 style punx The Briefs played The Oak Poulton –Le –Fylde recently and onetime Special Roddy Radiation's band the Skabilly Rebels in Blackburn late last year, both bands feature inside. Cheers Roy H.*

My sole contribution on **Sadie Hawkins Dance** is a condensed version of the two occasions I'd interviewed them. In an odd twist of fate, band members: Nick Chatterton (bass) and Pete Wilson (guitar) played in bands I use to watch in Barrow back in the mid/late 1980's. Lead singer Carol Hodge and I did keep in touch for a while and I put her side project **Synko** on at the Cellar Bar, Blackburn and she invited Pretendgirlfriend to play a gig with that band in Barrow. SHD also played the CCC with Pretendgirlfriend too. A few years latter Pete got a temporary job working at the same offices as me in Manchester and a "Carol Hodge" had her own show on Salford City Radio which I listened to one night in 2013. At some point the Carol I knew adopted the stage persona of "Crystal Grenade" and described the sound of SHD as *"Karen O meets PJ Harvey...with the look of Betty Page!....people seem to like it from Emo and metal kids to older people into rock – there's something for everyone."* It was my last link with Stu Taylor who had sent me SHD material since 2003. There were a few circles being completed in an odd series of co-incidences in this article.

Roy and I did a joint interview with the **Phlegm Fatales** at the North Bar. How appropriate, now that I think about it that we ended it together in the same place where it had all started for me. The Phlegms at that gig consisted of Rob Clarke (vocalist/guitar), James Gardner (bass) and Chas Hartley (drums) and their performance was incendiary or as Rob describes their style *"...we are trying to mix Oi! Punk with '77 Punk New Punk and '82 Hardcore then coming back to standard fucking Hard Rock with some fucking face melting riffs.."*- You get the drift.

The zine ends with ten pages of gig reviews Roy had been to and two pages of updates on new releases and plugs for other fanzines. Blackburn zine "Burn Out" (issue 2) gets a positive *review "...with the Bobby Dazzlers interview. It costs 50p, put together well in a DIY style and in the main features the Blackburn scene, but enough variety to keep people from outside the area happy too".* It was written by Kerry McGregor who I got to know

70

and had a lot of respect for. She was at a lot of gigs I went to – often with boy friend Alex Martindale and the pair did a lot to promote the unsigned scene during and beyond my involvement. Lovely people with a diehard passion for music and always fair in their assessment of what they liked or disliked. "Burnout" enjoyed a long run, as my copies which run into 2007, testify. I'd like to think that it picked up from where PTID left off and it couldn't have been a better tribute if that is the case. Its Xerox, handwritten, no colour presentation was closer to the original ground breaker "Sniffin Glue" than what PTID became.

Final words and its legacy

There were other zines in the North West too – I have a copy of issue 6 of Blackpool Rox II 22/10/03 which was Andy Higgins "Minister of Order and Reason" and part of his www.jsntgm.com (Just Say No To Government Music) on line presence. I met Andy a few times and he helped plug what each of us were doing and through him Litterbug's *Laugh Out Loud* appeared on A3H's *Vibes from the Attic* CD compilation (chapter 10).

PTID did attract wider recognition too:

"...this magazine just got fatter, and it is quality and quantity" (Rebecca). - www.punkoiuk.co.uk July 20, 2000.

"....this is really worth your hard earned" Big Cheese issue 40 April/May 2003 which included a picture of the front cover of issue 4.

Nihilism on the Prowl's website did a review of issue 6. In it, and typical of Roy, he says *"Pogo seems regarded as the best thing around at moment; although I was unaware it was meant to be a competition!"*

Roy also built www.onefinfulwood to plug the zine and some fans took the trouble to write to us. I met one, Christian Roberts from Flint, in Action records and he wrote of issue 5 *"...the best one I've seen in ages. Keep up the good work"* enclosing a £4 cheque to cover the next two issues.

If I had not met Roy I know that the events over the following five years, and this book, would not have happened the way that they did. PTID captured elements of the Punk Rock scene in the North West for the 3/4 years of its existence. Thank you, Roy and everyone who contributed to or bought a copy. Even today I still prefer the tangible print of the zine in my hands than using the internet. It must be an age thing!

The final word is Roy's interviewing Arturo Bassick (bassist in Lurkers, 999) (issue 7 2004);

(Roy) *"Where do you see punk rock in 10 years? Will the passion die with the older bands or is it in safe hands with newer bands?"*

(Arturo) *"The passion will go on if we live that long, but there's always gonna be somebody playing a loud fast guitar with a vision and heart to live the life and try to change the world even if it's only their own they change".*

Inside:
Menace
The Lurkers
EniMa
Ill On Speed
Pistol Grip
4 Past Midnight
Howard's Alias
Suspicious Stains
Dave Sharp
Adequate 7

PARENTAL ADVISORY
EXPLICIT CONTENT

Issue No.7
£1.50

pogo 'till die!

FATE
SFFG
TURN AWAY
HEADLIGHTS
HEROES
DRUMMY B
BODMIN PILL
NO SENSE
SNELSMORE
YWT
SOLO
TREES IN WINTER
THE ATTACK
LONG GOODBYE
IF U CAN'T SAVE
LOVESONGS
DEADEYE
R&R

north live

mon july1

the DICKIES

tickets £12
doors open 7.30

STANDING   41   7

SOLID ENTS. PRESENT
STIFF LITTLE FINGERS
+GUESTS
KING GEORGES HALL
NORTHGATE. BLACKBURN
FRI 10-OCT-03 20:00

BLACKBURN
DARWEN

ticketmaster
0870 6063 409
ticketmaster.co.uk

£14.00

£14.00   10   - 0413I

NORTHRECORDS.CO.UK PRESENTS BACK BY
DEMAND 1977 PUNK ROCK LEGENDS!

AS 8502

999

The
Hyperjax

Wednesday 3rd March 2004

The Royal Oak Hotel
Breck Road, Poulton-Le-Fylde, Nr.Blackpool

7:30pm

Entrance Fee: £6
Unemployed/Punk Kids (16-21 yrs) £4 (proof of ID/age required)

(COME EARLY! SELL OUT EXPECTED!)

FOR INFO 07774 333311, northrecords@hotmail.com/ ACCOM* @ Venue 01253 883199
www.northrecords.co.uk/www.ninetninenine.cjb.net/www.thehyperjax.idns.co.uk/
www.punkcluk.co.uk

CD & CLOTHES STALL

UNRESERVED   14   3
STANDING

RONNIE BROWN PRESENTS
THE FALL
PLUS SUPPORT
KING GEORGE'S HALL
NORTHGATE, BLACKBURN
SUN 22-SEP-02 19:30

£14.00

noize anoize music / North Bar
proudly present

SHAM 69 AFTER SHOW PARTY
11pm till Late
featuring live music from the
"truly obnoxious punk bastards" (11.15pm)

3CR

+
The best thing to come out of Preston since Tom Finney

THE PHLEGM
FATALES   (12.15am)

+Noize Anoize Punk Disco before, during and after bands

FRIDAY 5TH NOVEMBER 04

Free Entry strictly by Flyer
ONLY

03 Glen Matlock, Redundancy and Success

"Seven months ago I watched The Sus-Sex Pistols at this venue and it began a sequence of events that culminated in bringing one of the original members of the Sex Pistols to perform on the same stage".

This is how I started my interview with Glen Matlock for issue 5 of Pogo'til I Die. And another circle got completed that night I promoted Glen's gig. I feel very privileged to have had the opportunity to meet Glen and other famous people. But Glen, I expect, will be the one person that most people will know because of the Sex Pistols place in history. If the circle started in the playground of Balshaws High School when I was fourteen, it reached 360 degrees when, at forty years of age, I wished him all the best for the future after the gig at The North Bar on Friday January 24th 2003.

"Roy Hesketh and I worked together to make this gig a success and I would like to thank Ronnie Brown and all the fans that turned up for the event". I wrote that in the interview too and repeat it again now as a continued "thank you" to all of them and Bruce McKenzie in particular. I know that it could have turned out very differently without that support and it is something I do not take for granted. The passage of time has shown me how it made a profound impact on my life since then that it deserves a chapter of its own.

The start to my career in the music industry
Bruce McKenzie and I had had several conversations about what I had planned to do with my musical "career". I had kept him informed of what I was doing ever since we first met at Townsend Records, Market Street Chorley, where he was working at that time. His name had been given to me by my friend Karl Stanley who knew someone who knew someone else who knew Bruce as a potential contact for established bands and musicians.

Roy and I had kicked the idea of a one off gig or mini punk festival but didn't know how to go about contacting better know bands. We had been thinking of the old bands like 999 supported by newer and local ones but at a larger venue like the Marquee Club on Aqueduct Street, Preston, which could take 800. The North Bar was a squeeze at 150 and, without wishing to step on Ronnie Brown's toes, we felt a bigger venue away from Blackburn able to hold more punters too, would cover hire, bands fees and other expenses to leave us an acceptable profit. At first Bruce listened to me talk about the zine copies I had brought into the shop in the hope he'd agree to taking a few to sell. I told him about what I had done since meeting Roy and asked him whether he could help introduce me to famous bands for Roy and I to promote. In due course, he put some names to me; which included Glen Matlock. Glen was beyond my expectations. I had no idea what he'd been up to after The Rich Kids (the group he formed with Midge Ure after leaving The Sex Pistols). Furthermore, I wondered if Roy would want to put him on as either a soloist or in any new band he was with now as we had only discussed bands and not soloists. What would it involve, when would he be available and how much he would expect as a fee - were other considerations that we needed answers to. Bruce said he would get back to me. This was in the October and I had some major personal matters to attend to.

Work and redundancy

I had known for some months that my employer wanted to change the terms and conditions of my contract and I had been given papers which included the option of Voluntary Redundancy (VR). Having got to the second run on the managerial ladder at the end of 1999 I had been caught in the cross fire of a merger between two factions in our organisation and I ended up on the wrong side. Let's just say my face didn't fit and since then I had moved from dealing with personal customer to looking after the Small and Medium Enterprise (S.M.Es) customers of the bank. I was still in my Financial Consultant role selling insurance, pension and investment products but the proposed change in my contract meant working on a commission basis and I knew that I would struggle with this aspect on moral grounds. Selling on commission brought the uncertainty of knowing what you would earn. I had worked with, and managed, commission only insurance sales people and they had an entirely different set of ethics to what I had grown up with as a Banker. After twenty years of working one way and seeing how they operated I knew I had to go back into the more traditional banking career I had deviated from ten years previously.

I had settled into selling products to business customers from a call centre in Preston above the main branch I had started out from in 1981. However, these contract changes, turning forty and facing a cross roads in my career forced a load of decisions on me all at once.

What did I really want to do and what did I want in the future for my family and myself? This was another reason why putting on gigs and making this music thing into a new or alternative career appealed to me. I knew that if I went for redundancy I would need to start working with professional bands to make money and a reliable income stream. Helen was brilliant in her support for me. She said that if I did not take the chance to do something now I may regret it for the rest of my life. I would get a year's salary when I left the job and I had a reasonable inheritance from my mum, who had passed away at the end of August. Helen had a solid career and was earning more than me at that time, hence, it all added up to giving us a safety net. Furthermore, she was in favour of my plan which was to do the music thing for a year and write a book about it. If it was successful I could get into journalism but, if not, I could return to Insurance or Banking as I had recognised qualifications in both.

I signed the VR letter on Friday 1st November writing in my diary "....this is the day I made the final decision to change my working life after 21 years. I will leave employment on 31/12/2002. I have struggled with this for five weeks...." and on the Sunday I wrote "spent morning playing Mouse Trap with the kids – I'm so more relaxed now after weeks of indecision, I vow to myself to get the balance right". It was a simultaneously thrilling and frightening moment in my life. Working for a bank back then came with a lot of guarantees. You worked a seven hour day, Monday to Friday, in return for a reasonable wage but one that was guaranteed every month. You could join a final salary pension scheme which had a death in service provision for four times your basic pay, spouse and dependent child arrangements if you died while still working. The sickness package provided six months full pay, six months half pay and the probability of being pensioned off if you were unable to return to work after twelve months. Paid holidays and other generous perks came to you depending on your grade and how long you had worked in the organisation. You had a defined path to follow if you wanted to progress which went hand in hand with getting older and coping with the responsibilities that went with it. However, the pace of change had accelerated in the eighties and alternative faster tracks to management levels had appeared. This didn't suite some but it did open up possibilities to others. Moving employer to gain position, experience and more money was en vogue which meant that loyalty and the culture in banking I had known was disappearing. The decision I had made meant I was walking away from all that was certain, stable and secure.

Working for one employer since the age of eighteen had the effect of making me institutionalised. Like a long term prisoner I had absorbed the rules and regulations to the point that I was settled and had no reason to change this world, my personality or behaviours. Signing that VR letter gave me a tremendous feeling of taking control of my life that I had never felt before. It was exhilarating and I understood why people choose to be self employed. The thrill was in the new; the potential of what was on the outside and the freedom that other possibilities could bring. The cotton padded environment of branches and offices was gone and a vast universe had appeared for me to explore. I did not think in terms of risks only challenges and it gave me an entirely different focus on what happened next.

The plan

I telephoned Roy to update him after Bruce got back to me with his thoughts on two scenarios. Bruce would speak to Glen and say something along the lines of:

Plan A - there is a Punk thing happening in Chorley and would he be interested in a phone in to the local radio station to review some demos of local bands. In return the station would run a competition for a signed copy of his book (*I was a teenage Sex Pistol*).

Plan B - there is a big interest in Punk in the area and would he be interested in a gig as either a band, or doing an "audience with" chat and playing a few songs on an acoustic guitar type of thing?

Bruce said he would present both and let me know the logistics – if Glen wanted to do either. I was happy with that and got busy with other things.

I was deep into the last minute arrangements for the A3H launch party gig (Chapter 10) as well as telling everyone at work that I had accepted redundancy. That night Helen and I had a meal at The Coach House, Restaurant, in Chorley and we thought it would make an ideal place to have my fortieth birthday and a leaving work "celebration" using the upstairs area. The weekend came and went and Bruce had no news and agreed to leave it for another seven days.

Then Bruce got back with and outline of what appealed to Glen. He preferred plan B as a solo acoustic audience with gig. It would have to wait until January at the earliest and Bruce gave me Glen's mobile number as he said I'd have to speak to him directly to agree terms. Bruce did give me a ball park figure for costs and I explained this to Roy. He said that he could not support it at that level, financially but I was cash rich due to my inheritance. Roy said he would help in any other way he could and I respected him for that. He advised me to ask if Ronnie if I could do the gig at The North Bar which made sense -its size was ideal- as small was now good, it was intimate and I could charge more for punters being that much closer to the stage.

Ronnie had built a reputation at the North Bar and was warm and encouraging when I told him how I visualised the gig. We discussed dates and logistics (i.e. door fee, bar split, PA hire, security etc) and then it was time to speak to Glen himself. Bruce told me the best times to call him which was during the working day and I remember the moment I came off the phone after our first conversation. I went back into the office and took a deep breath and told one of my colleagues about who I had just spoken to. It had been conducive to making the call during a break while still in the office. It was very matter of fact and Bruce had done an excellent job in preparing the ground work so Glen knew who I was and why I was calling him. We talked the deal through and the date was confirmed which was less than ten weeks away.

The gig

I had to pinch myself. I had set up a deal to put on a gig for one of the most famous people I knew at that point. All I had to do now was complete the paper work and make sure I took care of the rest as professionally as I could. The training I had, thanks to the bank, gave me skills I could use in my new career. I had been doing this music thing for five months and marvelled at how much I had done to get to this position. It seemed that moving to this level was the next logical step to take but it felt like I'd gone from jumping off the edge of a swimming pool to facing the water from the highest diving board! I had not done my first gig yet– it was organised and booked -but I still had to get through the night. What if it was a disaster and it got back to Bruce and the deal with Glen got pulled. My career could be over before it started, shit! What had I got myself into......!

I took a deep breath, and told myself that I could manage this. I had to take sole responsibility for the money side of it but I had the good will and technical help from Bruce, Ronnie and Roy. I convinced myself that I would be in a better position to do more of the same if I pulled it off. To do it well and to succeed meant I would gain new experiences to provide me with more variety to go on my CV for future job prospects in this industry where it seemed reputation was everything. The positives outweighed the negatives and fundamentally I was driven by the fact that I may never get the opportunity to do this again and it could lead to a whole lot more. I had better get use to this work and be good at it as the future security of my family could depend on it. Suddenly I was faced with the magnitude of what I had taken on for November. The launch party/gig for A3H (6th) with four bands and a set of challenges I had not dealt with before; I had committed to delivering thirty six hours of radio programming and broadcasting (20th Nov– 10th December for Local Radio); preparation, promotion and hosting a gig with Glen Matlock and sorting out my own birthday, farewell do and Christmas in between. No half measures then and no turning back now.

I sent an email to Glen to summarise our agreement and he left the rest to me. I did not need to trouble him again until a week or two before the gig. I had done my research on what he had done since leaving the Rich Kids and

I back tracked all the key events covered in his book and what was available from other sources. Roy came up with some ideas for posters, leaflets, tickets and support acts. I needed a PA and a band or two -ideally, a band with its own PA. **Pike** had their own PA and would be perfect, if available and willing to do it. I don't remember if Roy or I approached Mick Pike about this but the result was that Pike did agree and **Duckhunt** was mentioned as another support band. I could see this working very well especially after the A3H launch party when Duckhunt head lined and delivered on every level. Their fans would draw in younger ages than those that would turn out for Pike and Glen appealed to all ages – notoriety and nostalgia – I'd take both. Soon everyone was on board and excited about the whole thing. The rest quickly fell into place but it was mid December when I realised that Ronnie had nothing booked between the New Year and the gig on the 24th January. That was almost four weeks and I had a fear of momentum being lost if the North Bar had no live entertainment on during this period. The solution came from an unexpected source.

I had been asked by Matt and Steve from The Commies to be their manager after their radio interview at the start of December – which I accepted a few days later (see chapter 5). This and the popularity of radio sessions I had been part of meant my profile had mushroomed in size – making me a big fish in a very small pond. I was on top of it all and called in a few favours. I asked Ronnie if I could book every Friday night at the North Bar to put on The Commies and a few guests support bands. He agreed as I paid for the PA hire (I contracted Phil Baker) and would not charge an entrance fee. In essence it was loss for me and a bar take for Ronnie on whatever came in – less costs for his staff, electrics etc. I saw it as publicity for Glen's gig and a chance to get The Commies a residency during which they got exposure in Blackburn. I wanted to see what they were made of to plan what I would do next after January.

Count down to the door

Meanwhile, my prospects of getting a job outside the Bank before the New Year were poor. I had been for an interview at Rock FM as a sales consultant but, after an all day assessment, a job offer was not forthcoming. However, something extraordinary did happen following a chance comment to a trainer for the bank. I told him that I did not want to leave and would prefer to stay and become a business manager. Word got back to the right people and on the eve of my last day I got a phone call from the centre manager in Preston offering me the job I wanted as one of the current managers was about to leave for a position in Lancaster. I was back in and on the same grade, pay etc. I had to rescind my VR application, but that was a formality. Phew! Helen was ecstatic when I broke the news just before Christmas which was magnificent that year!

During the weeks in between signing the VR letter and getting this offer to stay in the bank I had a glimpse of what was on the outside of the "prison" in that vast universe I had imagined. It was frightening, cold and I was/am grateful to have been able to wrap the familiar cotton wool around me again. I regard those weeks as a valuable life lesson. Since then I no longer take for granted what my employer does provide for me. Before I got back into the bank, I reached a point one day as I was walking down Fishergate in Preston when I imagined that I was seeing, and was seen, in a very different way than before I signed the VR letter. I looked at passersby and felt differently about who I was as if I had a label round my neck with "unemployed" on it. I thought I could detect them looking into my soul and labelling me as "prospect zero".

24th January 2013 - Day of the gig

I met Glen and his friend on the bridge at junction 8 of the M61 sometime in the afternoon of 24th. I had taken the day off work and after handshakes and introductions they followed me to the Fernhurst Hotel, Ewood, where I had booked him into. When we arrived Glen asked me if I could get some skiing brochures. I drove into town and grabbed an arm full of glossy mags from Lunn Poly. Back in Ewood, Glen and I exchanged notes on ski resorts and I knew some resorts and hotels that catered for kids. It was a good ice breaker; Glen made notes and thanked me. I briefed him on what the agenda was for the rest of the night and left him to settle in. I returned at the appointed time and conducted the following interview in the car as I drove him and his friend to the North Bar.

[Me] *"What are your expectations for tonight?"*

[Glen] "I've got a song called *Suck it and see!* And I think that is a good maxim for life. Like when you called me up and asked me if I fancied doing this – I thought yeah all right might as well put the guitar in the boot of the car...."

[Me] *"Do you think you might make a habit of it?"*

[Glen] "Well, I've been doing a few things like this in Europe-not many-and the thing with Dead Men Walking, which is myself, Kirk Brandon (Ex Theatre of Hate, Spear of Destiny), Mike Peters (The Alarm) and Pete Wylie (The Mighty Wah!). We might be doing another tour – which is a grandeur version of this where everybody does their 4 or 5 best known songs acoustically. So that kind of gave me a taste for it".

Glen explained how he'd been speaking to Pete Wylie about solo work he'd been doing and how it put hairs on the back of his neck. This had given Glen the encouragement and confidence to have a go himself. That said there still remains the challenge: to walk on stage with no backing band: little in the way of theatrics and give an hour's worth of your old and new material in front of a mixed crowd – some of whom weren't born when "God Save the Queen" was released.

[Me] *"What's been the reception to the Dead Men Walking project?"*

[Glen] "Gone down really well wherever we've played and we might do another tour later this year....we did clubs, theatres and the Guildford festival. I did a CD which is available via the DMW site – it's kinda the sum of the parts plus a bit more!"

[Me] *"What new material have you been recording?"*

[Glen] "I'm on the final third of recording a new Philistines record – my other Rock' n'Roll band! It's Steve New (ex Rich Kids on guitar), myself, Chris Musto (drums) and Terry Edwards (Keyboards) - started doing it last March, got a bit side tracked during the summer with The Sex Pistols. I will be doing some acoustic versions of a couple of the songs tonight so it will be a first for some of them".

[Me] *"Is this the first time you've done a full solo acoustic set-other than the book fairs?"*

[Glen - pause] "Yeah, pretty much so. I did a show a year ago, small one. David Johansen (New York Dolls) had this Blues project called Harry Smiths, were he covers old 1930's blues songs. I kinda wandered in on this Country Blues stage – he's got these guys- really good musicians who play in pit orchestras on 42nd Street in New York. ....I love playing acoustically. The main thing I am is a songwriter. I'm no Luddite when it comes to computers but this dance music! People like it (with sarcasm) – it's great! Like when I was at Art school the most disturbing thing that any one could say about somebody's art was the medium was the message, meaning that there's no fucking content! When you get machines that sound great, when it comes out of a box, you're tempted to think, "That's it!" But, it ain't! You've got to have a song! I think a song is not a song unless it hangs together on acoustic guitars. Music is about communication. Trying to get what's going through your head on a one to one basis across to an audience".

[Me] *"Inevitably people will ask about events 25 years ago. What do you remember about playing near Blackburn (Lodestar, Ribchester 15/09/76)?"*

[Glen] "I remember we stayed in these digs, kinda theatrical ones – B&B for the travelling actors doing repertoire. ......if (the cook) liked you, you got an extra fried egg... (proudly)... I got the fried egg! So, I got ribbed. Some woman ran it – she liked us but no one else in the building did...it was one of our first ventures up North!"

I put the question, later raised during the audience questions part of the gig, which surrounded the very brief and unsatisfactory dismissal of Bernie Rhodes' and his influence on the band. Glen mentions this in his book and I wanted to know why they did not dump McLaren for him?

[Glen] "Why didn't we change managers? [Pause] Because it was a team [Pause] it's just the way it was. It weren't like a normal band "band" who chose the management company. It was a different thing entirely. Bernie Rhodes had certain foibles that made him very hard to work with – the devil and the deep blue sea. I don't know –why didn't we? Didn't even cross our minds!"

[Me] *At forty odd – how do you manage to keep a family and income coming in and still maintain the pace of a Rock' n'Roll life style?"*

[Glen] "I'm just going to keep doing what I am doing. I'm trying to carve out a niche. I'm associated with The Sex Pistols but I have a whole set of influences...on my song writing and, if you dig where I'm coming from perhaps you'll dig what I'm doing now. I'm not interested in world domination but I think I'm as good as, if not better, than a hell of a lot of people out there. I have lived through a lot and think I bring that to my music and write some pretty good lyrics these days. Don't be too blinkered about things and be questioning all the time. You know I wouldn't say I was the bloke who was sailing at the top of the charts every time I put a record out. But, one of the things that's in my favour is that whatever I have done; I've always stuck out like a sore thumb. Everyone has to be pigeon "holeable" these days and I don't know what pigeon hole I fit into – which I think is a good thing. But, if I had tried to fit into one with the other guys from The Sex Pistols way back in '74-'76 who would have heard of us! We'd have sounded like a jazz-rock outfit. So stick that in your pipe and smoke it!"

We had arrived, I parked up and we wandered into the North Bar. Ronnie showed Glen upstairs and I checked he was settled in and the rider was to his liking. **Pike** had the PA set up and the members of **Duckhunt** were a buzz of nerves and shuffling about. A friend of mine from the Judo club, Jim, turned up to take the tickets on the door. Glen's friend set up the merchandise in the booth at the back and I mingled with the audience who'd started to arrive. Glen had arranged to meet some friends at Tiggis restaurant which was a short walk away and he headed over for his meal. It was a dry evening, cold but not freezing and I went outside for fresh air as the place started to fill up. Simmy and Smit from Pretendgirlfriend came and a load of others I knew including pint size Marcus Barnett and his Dad Steve. I was grateful to him for posting a comment of Glen's official website as soon as word got out about the gig. I had spent weeks handing out the flyers Roy had designed and printed up for me. I stood at the bottom end of Church Street near Action Records which was close to where I parked for work during the week. This corner was a popular short cut for Students going from the bus station and up towards Newman College. I'd discovered it when doing the street walking for the A3H launch party. But, Marcus's website posting was the one that probably got the biggest Matlock audience possible. The local papers had the gig listed and John Anson wrote an article after Glen agreed for me to pass his number to him for a phone interview. I had posters up in as many places as I could and I know everyone else connected with the night did their bit. I could do no more I started to relax as best I could.

I went to Tiggis to accompany Glen back to the venue. He'd had a good meal I asked if he had any last minute requirements. He said he did not need a full sound check as he saw the stage set up and would plug in and let the sound tech do the rest. We went up stairs where I had set up my video recorder and I asked him if OK was for me to record him warming up. This footage is my favourite of all in my collection. Glen sat on the couch, tuning up and then letting rip with some of his songs. The best moment was "Pretty Vacant" – one of the finest songs The Pistols recorded and one I'd heard countless times and in numerous versions played by others too. However, here I was, on my own, just Glen Matlock and me. One-on-one with the writer, of some of the classic songs that inspired so many of my generation – wow it was a very special moment and it doesn't get much cooler than that! It was a privilege I will never forget. Mick Pike came up for a drink and some of the Duckhunt lads wandered in and out. Soon the latter were about to go on for their set and I headed down stairs. The place seemed to be heaving and I'll let Roy describe the rest from his gig review, under a picture of Glen performing his set:

Up to this piece being written it was the biggest turnout I'd seen in the North Bar. I've been told the Fall hold the attendance record! Having seen most of the 70's "punk" bands over the last two years or so it was pleasing to see such a good crowd come out for one of punk "year zero's" prime movers. If Rotten, Jones, Matlock and Cook hadn't given everything a big stir first it's debatable as to whether any of those bands would have even existed. Listen to the other pistols talk today and they'll say when Sid Vicious replaced Glen Matlock it was the end of the road from a creative viewpoint. Good on them for admitting that.

Rather strange arriving at the North Bar early on and seeing the Sex Pistol bassist wandering around. The same guy who'd played a gig in front of 50,000 Pistols fans stateside last summer. Perhaps he too was wondering whether this "Audience with" night thing would work.

By the time young ska/punks Duckhunt took to the stage the place had filled up and the punters were still queuing at the door. No better way for the kids to show off their talent than in front of an appreciative audience. Warming up for a Sex Pistol they'd nothing to lose and everything to gain. The guitars were choppy and their songs full of energy and enthusiasm. On goes the brass section and this is skaville. Duckhunt could have played all night: they left the stage to great applause and looked like they'd fully enjoyed their night. They'd finally got to play with Pike too.

The majority of the crowd had come to pay homage to Glen Matlock and the guy was given plenty of respect as he made his way through the audience to the stage. There was nostalgia in the air tonight. The untimely death of Joe Strummer contributed to that and although Matlock's set reflected this he still left room to showcase some new stuff. Bit of a tune up (insert picture of Glen squatting as he checks his monitor levels) and he kicked off with "Who's Side Are You On", new song for the audience yet it received great applause. An early indication that this was going to be a good night, "A Different World" followed and again the crowd loved it. As Glen got into his stuff it was then I began to realise tonight was real value for money. Considering you'd have paid forty quid to see the full line-up play the less intimate Crystal Palace Sports Arena last year. I drew the line at Finsbury Park. From the Rich Kids "Burning Sounds" he could do no wrong. "Stepping Stone" had everyone singing along and "Sad Meal for One" got on the subject of who does their shopping where. Matlock's an M&S man. At least he fucking admits it. It all got a bit weepy then as he shared early memories of Joe Strummer, The Clash and Bernie Rhodes. Glen was at Joe Strummer's funeral and told us "Wandering Star" had been played as the coffin moved off. He then went on to play a cracking version of Sonny Curtis's "I Fought the Law" with maximum audience participation.... with "God Save The Queen" (performed solo by Glen for the very first time) and cue "sing along" at the North Bar. Glen's set was interspersed with questions, from the audience, compared by Promoter, John Winstanley. Eh up he even plugged the fanzine! Matlock then gave us the Rich Kids "Ghosts of Princes in Towers", The Philistines "Idiot" and "On Something". There could only be one song left and "Pretty Vacant" got the biggest cheer of the night. Time then for one more question from Promoter to Glen "who was responsible for reforming the Sex Pistols?" Glen to promoter (with a knowing wink) - "The Bank Manager".

84

Next up were Pike. That's Mick, Shaun, Rob and Jez Pike. Loud, dark and uncompromising. Guitar hero's no more heroes. Your reality factor. They played a blinder and included some new material in their all original set. Not easy following a Sex Pistol. They did it and won over the North Bar. Rock Punk! When you thought it was all over Pike stayed on for a cover of "Pretty Vacant". The cheers went up as Glen Matlock got back on stage joining in on backing vocals. If that wasn't reward enough, Jez Pike then handed over his bass to Matlock for full on Pike Pistols versions of "Anarchy in the UK" and "Holidays' In The Sun". The crowd went wild! Glen Matlock left the stage to much applause for a second time. Pike fittingly closed the proceedings with their own tribute to Joe Strummer, a blistering version of "White man in Hammersmith Palais". Four bands for the price of three, now there's a treat".

Thanks again Roy!

The gig was a huge success on a lot of levels. Ronnie was happy as there were plenty in and he let me do a few more gigs there while I was finding my way and trying to discover fresh talent. Roy and I never did a joint gig but we went to a fair few and made his fanzine into a local chronicle of everything Punk for the next few years.

Those at the gig, who I have met since, have told me what a memorable night it was and I have many photos of my mates who showed up to support what I was doing. The fact that I pulled it off did help enhance my reputation as a local promoter. Bruce was pleased for my success and introduced me to a few people he went onto help. One of my favourite moments was when Glen asked Jez Pike if he could borrow his bass to play with the band while Jez was still on stage. Jez told me later how humbled he felt – that Glen had asked him "....as if I was going to refuse!"

For me Glen's was a true professional – I could not fault anything about him. He stayed around to sign books and chat to fans much longer than I expected – which I took as a signed that he enjoyed the event. Before we parted company we talked loosely about doing it again sometime. The thought crossed my mind for a while afterwards but I did not peruse it as it may not have been as good second time round.

Thanks again Glen.

'A3H Promotions Ltd' in association with 'pogo 'til I die' fanzine
present an audience with the

Sex Pistols legendary Bassist, ex of Rich Kids and Iggy Pop

Glen Matlock

an acoustic set/one night only

at North Bar, Town Hall Street, Blackburn

plus special guests

pike

and Chorley's premier Ska/punks

-Duckhunt-

on Friday, 24th January, 2003
first band on at 9pm

Tickets £6 or on the door

(subject to availability from venue/bands
or from Action Records, Church Street, Preston)
Further information on www.a3hpromotion.com
A3H: 07812 577987 · **pogo:** 07703 829165

Designed by Clarke Design 01772 456660

Below: Glen, Smit (Pretendgirlfriend) and my mate Karl Stanley, at North Bar.

04 Chorley FM and guests

Chorley, a small town in Lancashire…is not noted for being adventurous unlike some people associated with it.

Geographically, it lays South East of Preston and South West of Blackburn with Wigan and Bolton a little further down the M61 west and east, respectively. Nuzzling up to the Pennines are the villages of Withnell and Brinscal, further south is Rivington Adlington and Horwich. To the west, sandwiched between Leyland and Chorley, is Euxton. During the Second World War the Royal Ordinance Factory (R.O.F) site in Euxton spread out touching the boundaries of Chorley, Leyland and Whittle. Most of it is now part of Buckshaw Village housing estate and Business Park. Leyland was home to the vehicle manufacturer British Leyland, whose factory produced cars, trucks and the Transit van before going bust. These two industries were the main employers that touched my life. While I was at school their production lines provided manual trades for school leavers not academically gifted or inclined to venture into further education and my mum spent the last ten years of her working life at the R.O.F.

The decline of manufacturing in the area by the naughties has left its mark on Chorley and, like the industrial mills that once dominated the landscape of many Lancashire towns, the mass employers have long since gone. Chorley was cuttingly described as a "fodder factory" town by Dennis Leigh who was born and raised in Chorley. I did a telephone interview with him for *Pogo'til I Die* as I sat in my car parked up at St Michael's school in Chorley one day in 2003 when the kids were rehearsing there for a dance show. He told me that he remembered how exhilarating the acoustics were in the Railway Road Community Centre. In Manchester he discovered the power of Hi and Low Fi electronic music in basement parties before moving to London. In time he changed his name to John Foxx and emerged as the lead singer in mid seventies band Ultravox. Their "Systems of Romance" LP nailed a sound and style that became the template that the electro pop bands of the eighties adopted. Not many people in Chorley know of Foxx who I rate as the most important musician to have been born here after Shaun Maxwell (chapter 9), but I digress to make my opening line more emphatic. Oh, by the way before anyone asks about the significance of Jamie Walsh and Starsailor no, I don't know him and

I am sure there is plenty written about him and his band elsewhere.

I like Chorley for many reasons, but primarily for its modest aspirations. When it has modernised it has done so with reserved taste and functionality. The new bus station, built opposite the railway station, and the Market Walks shopping arcade are examples of this. The main street is a pedestrian friendly place for shopping during the day and many of its pubs in the centre are still open for trade! My youngest daughter informs me that Apple Jax is the only true night club in Chorley, which caters for the eighteen to early twenty year olds. The Sir Henry Tate adjoins Booths on the site of the old bus station, which caters for young and old drinkers and is named after one of the founders of the Tate and Lyle sugar empire who had family roots in the area. Opposite is the Imperial pub that looks after the needs of the younger student aged drinkers by providing a regular platform for live music thanks to Landlord Ivan. The Railway pub does the same for the more mature of life's students and is literally on the other side of the rail tracks. The Community Centre is between the two and occasionally hosts live music. Back in 2002 The Community Centre played a huge part in promoting local music (see chapter 7) and through my involvement with it I got invited to help with what became Chorley FM.

A good family friend, Julie Hamer, said she felt I had a voice that was suited to the radio. This was about two years before I got invited to a meeting at Tatton Community Centre to begin my short stint as a radio presenter. I had no prior inclination to be one but when I got the opportunity to be part of the Restrictive Service Licence (R.S.L) for Chorley's "Live and Let Live Radio" I seized it like a trophy. My name had been put forward by Ben Greenaway (see index) and, as I sat listening to the chairman - Christian Moss (AKA "Fish") and the rest of the committee, I wondered where it would lead.

We had to explain what we wanted to do as volunteers. This ranged from making cups of tea and handing out leaflets, to helping with sponsorship, the technical side of producing the shows and the administration with Offcom. The purpose of an R.S.L is to demonstrate the capability of those running a radio station over the test period as part of the application for a five year broadcast licence. Hence the administration was as equally important as the content of what was aired. All I wanted to do was help promote local music. I told the rest of the 20-30 people there what I had done in the last few months and felt that I could continue this passion by helping the station. Also at that meeting were Cliff de Carteret and Stephanie Chlond who were Sixth Form students. They wanted to be part of the local music scene show which was referred to as "Local Alternative Music". We were put into the same group to discuss ideas; we gelled with mutual enthusiasm. By the end of that meeting we had committed to working as a team to put together 36 hours of programming. This was split into four hour shows on a Tuesday, Thursday and Saturdays over three weeks starting on 21st November. Eventually this, and those other RSL's that followed, did lead to the successful formation of the radio station Chorley FM which started officially in June 2006.

I did not have a lot to do with the other shows, being too busy and focused on our own. I know that they were varied and one was one run by a team representing the Lesbian, Bi, Gay and Transvestite community. I thought this was very progressive for Chorley as I did not know of anything else at that time which catered for this audience. Their team and those on the other shows were, like Cliff, Steph and me, very keen volunteers, which made the planning sessions run smoothly. The test days soon came when we got to use to the equipment and the facilities housed in a couple of rooms above a Pizza shop at the top end of Market Street in the town centre.

We were expected to arrive some thirty minutes before out slots to be ready for the handover from the previous show and it took the same time at the end to tidy up. In between broadcast days we had to invite and make our own arrangements for our guests, agree play lists, sort and vet news items and listener requests. Steph volunteered to handle the internet/web cam, the phone calls and texts, while Cliff and I agreed to do the presenting and sorting out the logistics to push the variety and diversity of the shows. None of us had any experience of working on radio before so there was no wrong way as none of us knew what the right way of going about things was. There were no egos even amongst those who had worked on previous R.S.Ls. We had hours of air time to do what we wanted. This was liberating as we could play whatever we wanted. Everyone we knew wanted to appear on the show and it was a case of how do we cater for them all rather than will we has enough to fill the time. Launch day arrived and my diary records:

*It was brilliant. Can't wait to do more! Anxious at start – the equipment, personalities, timing, issues etc need to relax prior to leaving home – too rushed. First hour quite exhilarating! Couple of errors – played Pink Torpedoes instead of Pike, jammed a CD in the loader and my video camera tape broke, didn't get any of the Anamosa interview or set! But things went smoothly overall. The two Louise's (from **Anamosa**) were natural, easy going, professional and appreciative. Played plenty of local music and let Steph and Cliff take on some air time when they felt confident to do so. Learning points – need to have a copy* (audio) *of the show so I can play back my performance.*

After first one I made recordings of all of our shows on a radio cassette player I set up in the green room. Initially the idea was to help me hear what changes we may need to do to improve. I am very proud of how "profession-ally" the shows sounded and I laugh out loud at the mayhem from the videos that reveal what could not be heard. Cliff and Steph were happy for me to lead the first few shows with Cliff, in particular, chipping in comments and then taking over longer sections as his confidence grew. We encouraged Steph to do the same but she felt more comfortable off mic and did a great job in that vital, if unsung role, taking care of the administration. Our shows were full of our music mates and the true "guests" were usually from local community groups or anyone we didn't know who sounded interesting. When possible, we invited anyone playing at Chorley Community Centre on the Saturday nights like **David R Black**. I came up with the "5 before I Die!" which was a morbid slant on Radio 4's Desert Island Discs for visitors to bring the songs they would want to hear before they popped their clogs. It was a standby to fill in time during the interviews when interviewee's dried up. It was, for most of them, the first time they had appeared on radio or been interviewed formally. We mixed the playlist to include what Cliff liked (nineties and current), Steph (Modern Punk and Ska) and I would play everything in between that ranged from Northern Soul to what was current from the local bands. My "ones that fell through the cracks" was a way of introducing obscure tracks from the less famous or total unknown. For example: Tobi Legend (*Time Will Pass You By),* The Living End *(Pictures in the Mirror),* **The Tansads** (a signed band from the Wigan/St Helens area who had a cracking track on their final LP called Reason to Be) *Hello* and Preston band **Marwood's** EP track - *Rope.*

All my memories of the Live and Let Live Radio sessions are good ones, never hard work or dull. The Saturday shows were probably the ones we looked forward to the most but the crack and buzz off all of them fuelled me with adrenalin wiping out any feelings of tiredness. The experience also taught me new skills and how many I didn't realise I had –especially when it came to handling interviews. I learned how to appreciate the allure and power of radio by all the positive ripples we were creating for a lot of musicians and the community. It was a spiritual vibe affecting my own evaluation of self worth. Perhaps the best was of relaying some of those moments, is to highlight those that stuck out rather than trail through each one verbatim.

Fighting talk and tales of the unexpected.

The management encouraged us to stress the community aspect of the station to broaden the appeal of the listeners rather than to focus purely on those specifically involved with music. This was a tall stretch for a show that was supposed to be about "Local Alternative Music". Anyway one idea was a martial arts show. I set up an interview with my mate Peter Noblet from Mill Hill Judo club. To "spar" against Peter I asked Barry Holden (a black belt instructor) from the Ju Jitsu club, based in Eaves Green Community centre, Chorley. All three of us had been to the other's club to learn from each other's skills. The show was about what we had learned from the exercise as well as encouraging the people of Chorley take up this form of exercise. Others shows featured Brinscal Swimming club with Mike Cawood and another one had Rachel Cleverly from Anita Murrays dance school. This drew on what I had been involved with through my kids. All manner of songs with cheesy titles got used in the build up to them.

Perhaps the biggest lesson I learnt was my failure to predict what my guests would want to talk about and the selection of songs they brought with them to play. I thought Ronnie Brown would talk about Punk - wrong! He came armed with Northern Soul and talked about what The North Bar was doing to promote that genre. Steve Henderson was on the same evening and I had got to know him through his "Mr Kite Presents..." events. His gigs that I had attended promoted singer songwriters in the "folk" tradition. Hence, I expected an airing of that genre and not the Punk and New Wave tracks he requested. Unbeknown to me, Steve was involved with booking bands at Leeds University in the mid seventies and was instrumental in the "Northern Triangle"- a series of gigs for touring bands at the Universities in Lancaster, Leeds and Manchester. During his tenure the likes of Ian Durry and The Blockheads, Sioux and The Banshee and The Jam were booked. Furthermore, his involvement with local bands from that city lead him to know the members of the Gang of Four very well - a much underrated band that I really like. The conversation and material he and Ronnie played was a surprise and the most interesting for me as both knew far more than I did about the old as well as the new. The team and production crew that night all agreed it was all the better for it too.

The most bizarre show featured Peter Savage and Robert Byrne who were Uilleann pipe players. Uilleann pipes are a sort of bag pipe that is played by depressing an elbow on a wooden part of the instrument – the sound is rather like the Northumberland pipes popularised by Katherine Tickle and in the Lord of the Dance music. "Robbie" was from Walney Island (Cumbria), an Ex Scot Guards piper who formed a band called Shebeen to perform at various folk festivals at that time. I contacted him as a result of talking to Peter (who was our local post office manager in Withnell) who was a player too. Both agreed to perform together in what I felt could be a moment of either total disaster or something amazing either way is would be "alternative" for the listeners. The crew did a lot of head scratching when they got their pipes out and stuck up. But it was the most imaginatively diverse genre I featured for the radio - performing on an instrument I had never heard before or since!

Lessons learned from the talented.

Hollis Brown was a solo acoustic guitar songwriter I invited in after discovering he worked for the same employer as me in Preston. He also played at my fortieth Birthday celebration at the Coach House in Chorley. I felt he had a talent but the radio session and the live performance made him think differently about what he wanted and we parted amicably. It taught me to appreciate that some musicians only need to do what they do to a select few and bigger ambitions do not figure in their plans. Each to their own, I surmised at the time but now, with the benefit of hindsight, I feel that he was far more mature in his decision than I gave him credit for. I have since learnt that it is better to recognise your limitations early on than be disillusioned by the disappointment of unrealistic expectations!

The most listened to show was for the Chorley Battle of the Bands winners **Dumpstar**. I was at the final and no one in the other bands (The Commies, **Onset** and **Boddah**) or their fans I talked to about the result, had expressed anything but respect for Dumpstar. I lead the interview and Ben did his best to remain unbiased in providing the content to cover as he was, co-incidentally, managing the band. He had also asked me to help him plan a tour for Dump Star. His idea was to hire a bus and sell tickets to fans to travel with the band to each gig to fulfil the minimum attendance. I presented the costing and my assessment of the tour – great in theory but who would rough it on a bus with limited washing facilities, pay up the £100 for the ticket to ride and then the £3/4 entry fee to the gigs as well being available for the 4/5 weeks. Dump Star are perhaps one of those bands who "....could have been a contender" so to speak. They had it all, musically current in their influences (Incubus) yet unique in their interpretation, Rob Foster was a good looking and confident front man and the rest of the band were excellent musicians. They had a strong following but, like so many bands formed during their mid to late teens, further education and job considerations were stronger factors leading to their beak up. Here's to what might have been and the memory of being able to participate in what was a magnificent moment in time!

The most significant event for me was after the interview with Steve and Matt from The Commies They asked if I would be interested in managing their band. Ben and Russ Carlton (see index) told me that it was only a matter of time before some band asked me to manage them. Being asked was the stamp of approval on what I was doing for local music. Also, the listening figures for our shows were the highest throughout the RSL- a tribute to the joint effort between the three of us and everyone in the production team. It was a brilliant time despite the long nights and fly by the seat of your pants moments. I loved every second and will always be grateful to everyone involved.

2003 and my final broadcast

The following year, I was invited by Phil Baker to help with the RSL which began at the end of November running through to 18th December. I knew that I would not be able to give the time I had first time round. I put a plan to the committee, which they accepted, which offered local bands the chance to host their own shows. Phil did the Tuesday evening shows, while I saw to the Thursday and Saturday night's running order. Those who took up the call included **Idiom Lifeline, King Genius (Daniel Rossall)** , **The Reserved** , **Geoffrey Bungle** (including **Jake Maxwell**) and **The Hyperjax.** The only show I hosted myself was the 6th December as I knew it would be a date I could bring in The Commies as part of their end of year tour I had organised. The station was housed in a corner of an undeveloped floor space above Iceland Food store in Chorley Walks precinct. It was empty; all cement and concrete with a makeshift cabin/room at one end. There were no luxuries at all; I cannot remember even a kettle being available! It was a very different atmosphere to the last one and I did my best to warm to the austere surroundings. I invited my friend Karl Stanley to co host with me. Karl and I had similar musical interests and he was great at filling in with anecdotes and witty asides.

Echo Freddy was a Manchester based band and gigging buddies to both **Duckhunt** and The Commies. So after their session Duckhunt came in as a full band and were bubbling with enthusiasm for their recent gigs with signed bands and had plenty of prestigious gigs lined up. Next in was Steve Hodson (from The Commies) who came in on his own. The contrast could not have been more acute. My heart went out to Steve who was inconsolable at the prospect of the demise of the band he had founded. For me, the breakup of The Commies was the end of a roller coaster ride that was exactly 12 months long. It ended where it started – on airwave of Chorley– perhaps one of the little known facts in the history of Chorley FM!

I kept in touch with what the station was doing but I could not give it the attention it demanded and in the end I had become too remote from those who eventually took up the reigns and made the station into what it is today.

05 Let's Not Lose Mars To the Commies

"Let's Not Lose Mars to the Commies" was the name of the first band I managed. However, the significance of *The Commies* is not so much as part of my story but for the impact they made on the local unsigned scene base around Chorley. Over four years and because rather than in spite of its changing line up, the members consistently inspired many other bands to form in the wake of their prolific performances. Below is, in the main, an article I wrote for the press when the band split up after their last gig in December 2003.

A year in the life of managing a band – an obituary of:
"Let's Not Lose Mars To The Commies"

"What follows may be typical for anyone who has ever tried his or her hand at band management. The high is watching their performance and soaking up the adulation the audience feels for the group you have poured your soul into. The low is the blow to your stomach when they decide to split and the awkward motions of the demise compounds the pain. I was given the opportunity to manage "Let's Not Lose Mars to the Commies" - the Emo/Skate/Punk band from Chorley at forty years of age and helping them gave me opportunities I never expected. "The Commies", as they were known to their loyal fans, had a huge impact on the teen-agers of Chorley and inspired a surge in the underground scene throughout the rest of Lancashire. All that is their legacy –this is their story.

The nucleus of the band formed on Bonfire night 1999 as friends Liam Wright, Steve Hodson, and Bruno Booth pulled an "A" tribute band idea together with a "Tim, Tom and Jennie" in a changing line up which eventually played their one and only gig as **Blind Inside** *in March 2000 at the R'n R Bar in Chorley. The next event was the writing of* **Forget It** *in the early part of 2001. Liam told me "....this was the first proper Commies song but it wasn't called that at that time as we referred to it as "that cool one". We also wrote "that fast one" (**Leaving Me Behind**). The cell was completed when Steve's other band,* **Starkey's Walk,** *played a gig with Matthew Gogley who was providing an acoustic support slot. Matt's singing impressed Steve and Bruno enough for them to invite him to rehearsals and on to their first gig at The Cellar Bar, Blackburn in May. From that point they became regulars at the "Punk Revival "all ages nights at Chorley Labour club during which they recorded "...**are shaved apes**" -featuring the endearing* **Whys, Lies 'n' Pies**. *They gained wider recognition after coming runners up (to* **Modus**) *in the Lancashire Evening Post's 2002 Battle of the Bands. Being second place left a bitter taste and they titled their next four track CD* **2nd Rate Music.**

Their tight sound and professional attitude got them invited to play the Golden Jubilee Festival in Chorley. The Commies performance that day is regarded by many as the event that sparked many bands to form over night.

My interest in The Commies happened, as is often the case, as a result of a series of co-incidences. After meeting Roy Hesketh (editor of Preston Punk fanzine **Pogo'til I Die**) he mentioned a feature that the 'zine had done on The Commies and said he would be interested in anything I wanted to send in about them and what was going on in Chorley. I met and interviewed Matt and Liam on 20th July. Matt did most of the talking and for an eighteen year old, he had more of an idea of where he wanted the band to go and what they were about than I expected. I got my first glimpse of the band as a trio –Matt (G & V), Steve (B) and Liam (D) in the final of the Battle of The Bands competition at Chorley Community Centre on 17th August (Bruno was away on holiday at the time).

At this time my involvement in the unsigned scene had meant my spare time had become a twilight zone of nightclubs and hours spent surfing the internet for information and contacts in this underground world I had dived into. My involvement with local radio allowed me to invite The Commies in for a session on air and Matt's side project, at the time, **Duckhunt** (for whom he played trumpet and backing vocals). I had interviewed Duckhunt at the end of August at a gig that marked the debut of **Rebekah** – a Commies inspired trio from Chorley. Impressed by Duckhunt's explosive mix of Ska and '90's Punk, I booked them for my company's first showcase gig at The Marquee Club (later known as The Mill, Preston) in November and I gave them a support slot for the Glen Matlock gig I promoted (see chapter 3). Duckhunt would have also played my one-day festival "It's Not Cricket!" (Chapter 6) later that year in June had they been available. I mention all this to clarify how these bands and I were all inter-linked with a lot of what I was doing at that time. Furthermore, Matt and Rob Catlowe (drummer in Duckhunt) were best of mates and Duckhunt was Rob's passion, which, as it turned out, was a fact I failed to fully appreciate and one that would lead to The Commies eventual demise.

It was after the radio interview with Steve & Matt that they asked if I would manage The Commies. The third CD **"...the long and the winding"** appeared and we put its final track-**Better Days** on a Sampler CD along with **Why's, Lies & Pies** and **Enough Confrontations** to highlight the band's output to date. I dispatched these to the media, other bands and anyone I could think of to try and get publicity and, vitally, more gigs.

About three weeks into all this Matt and Steve came round to my house with the news that Liam wanted to quit the band. Great start to my career in band management, I thought with my first band splitting within a month!

*Furthermore, Matt expressed the opinion that he wanted to just be a singer and was attracted to what Rob was doing in his own side project (**Days End**) as their front man. Steve thought they should ditch the band name and come out as another sort of prospect. I stressed that the name was worth keeping as it had taken 3 years to build and the band would still have a problem of finding a drummer. Steve could play drums – so we needed a bass player –broad as it is long! In the end it boiled down to Liam wanting to get a job and save for a year travelling the world –which he felt was a lack of commitment to the band and it would be better if they got someone else sooner rather than later. I thought this incredibly brave and mature – rather than drift on and go through a series of turning up late for rehearsals, not wanting to hang about before or after gigs and becoming less involved in the song writing – the downward decent that leads to the band sacking you. Once we'd acknowledged his direction it was like a weight being lifted from him. Consequently, he stayed and we all got down to business.*

In retrospect every month of 2003 was a series of steps that built to an incredible climax:-

January *- As if to re-affirm our confidence the sampler CD got reviewed by Conrad Murray –a respected journalist who's positive critique in The Big Issue in the North referred to the band as "...displaying a rougher and more credible underground edge than a lot of noveau punk bands currently dancing like it's 1977, these boys mean business. Enjoy a close encounter"*

February*. (Unbeknown to me at the time), the band had sent a CD to Kerrang music magazine, who ran a competition is association with Moonska Records. One of their bands on this label was called Farce a five piece who played Speed Reggae Emo Ska Punk. They were based in Birmingham, had a song on the "PRock" satellite channel and were finalising a 35 date UK tour in the spring. The competition allowed the band to choose the local support acts for several dates. This in turn resulted in loads of demos flooding into their mail box including the Commies'. One day Matt got a telephone call from Farse's management to advise him that The Commies had been chosen from hundreds to support them on 6 of dates of the tour.*

March *– first gig on the Farse tour was at King Tut's (Glasgow) and we travelled in three cars, as we were told to bring all our own kit. Meeting up at Liam's parents' house in Wheelton we set off on a sunny afternoon just after one o'clock. Bruno had to sandwich himself and his brother, Randolph, between Matt's car (with Liam and the girlfriend's at the rear) and me and Steve in my car at the front. Bruno, we discovered, did not like to drive above 67.5 mph so we arrived in M8 rush hour traffic and parked up at the venue at quarter to six. We received a friendly welcome from George Ibbertson (venue promoter), members of Farse and* *fellow tour support band Schism. Oli Patterson (lead singer with Farse) I liked instantly as he told the Commies how he and the rest of the band had to plough through 120 odd demos, whittling them down to the half dozen that made the cut and they were in total agreement that The Commies were the one band they especially wanted watch on their tour! The gig was a success playing to 75/80 people who rushed in when the doors opened at 8pm. Steve was a man with a mission, using every bit of available space on stage, he moved about like someone possessed and Bruno was equally manic putting Matt somewhat in the shade. Matt was probably overwhelmed by the fact that there were monitors on stage that worked properly and, for the first time in his career, he could hear himself properly. I supplied water and towels and the merchandise sales came in at 3 T shirts sold at £7 each, 5 CDs and I exchanged one copy for one from local support band* **In Car Stereo** *having engaged in a long conversation with pleasant front man Jordan Yates. We leave the venue at twenty to midnight and I dropped Steve off at his home at two thirty in the morning. Later that day I find out that Matt fell asleep at the wheel while driving and wrote his mum's car off. Luckily no one was hurt but I insist that I drive the band around in future, given that they are exhausted after their energetic shows.*

April –averages two gigs a week and Adam Hartley (ex Starkey's Walk) makes his debut on lead guitar at Stockton Georgian Theatre – freeing Matt of his guitar to emerge as an even more enigmatic front man.

May – time off to write material for **The 1000ᵗʰ Story** *EP (Liam's last recoding with the band).*

June – "It's Not Cricket!" (A one day festival of 20 bands I organised and recorded at Strettles in Preston) is filmed for DVD release showcasing The Commies as supreme amongst the bands that appear on it.

July- Rob Catlowe debuts on drums at an all day gig at The Star & Garter (Manchester).

August – We set up an informal agreement with booking agent Independent Sounds, for gigs in Sheffield Wigan and Leicester.

September – support slot with Preston heroes **Fi-Lo Radio** *at the Life Café (Manchester). Duckhunt recruit a new singer and keyboard player as they start to pick up more gigs than ever before.*

October – The Commies record their final EP **Time Won't Tell** *at Prism Studios (Stoke). This marks both the zenith of their output as well as the start of friction with Duckhunt. The release of the EP was scheduled with a full UK tour. As I began to book them into venues their gigs began to conflict with Duckhunt's putting Matt and Rob under increasing time pressures. Gigging and rehearsing between both bands meant they had to decide which to commit to. Hence the*

EP's release was delayed and in the end never got to exist other than, as with the others, as a homemade CDR pressing. However, Red Brick Productions filmed their last Roadhouse gig in Manchester on 22nd and offered to produce a promo DVD at Red Bridge Studios in Bolton. This footage is fantastic and everything I had been working towards as a piece promotional material. I was sure I could use to catapult them to the next level of fame & fortune.

November – Bruno plays his last gig at The Dudley Arms (Rhyl) leaving the band to concentrate on his University studies in Lancaster. His departure settles the band in terms of their sound but this departure meant Steve was the only original member. Meanwhile, Duckhunt secure support slots with No Comply, book their own gig for **Howards Alias** at the 12 Bar in Preston and their revised line up and sound breaks new ground. I have long conversations with Matt and Rob as we journey to gigs at the Attic (Leicester) and Victoria Arms (Derby) – venues they'd only dreamed about playing 12 months previously. An offer of a gig at The Moles Club in Bath has to be declined due to a Duckhunt commitment – the band is divided as to how to deal with this happening again.

9th November I send an open email to members of both bands suggesting that the next release is done as a joint/split CD to benefit from the economies of scale and I put a case for both bands as to what could happen next for either of them. Scott (original bass player with Duckhunt) and I have an agreeable email conversation on the pros and cons for both bands he says "...I think we have pretty similar goals, but it just isn't possible for both bands to achieve them as things stand....I don't think we are less capable or have any less potential than The Commies yet, in terms of exposure, we are way behind".

I am torn between my loyalties to The Commies as their manager and know that they have the popular upper hand but have to balance this with the central issue of Matt and Rob's friendship, a bond that is pulling them between both bands. At their ages of eighteen I can sense that it is heading towards a breaking point. I take comfort form one of Dave Horrocks' (Independent Sound) emails "....it looks like The Commies are on the move...", he talks about his strategy to "break them" adding a personal recognition of my efforts in "...John you are one hell of a good manager, who does the work and puts in the hours with a band who you believe in. I feel honoured to work with such a professional person". Wow! What do I do now?

December – I want the band to fulfil their promise and release **Time Wont' Tell** as a split CD and DVD. The Commies are riding high on the back of support slots with **Douglas, Captain Everything** and **Yumi Yumi**. In the New Year I plan similar prestigious support slots. But, I knew that there was little point doing all this if Matt and Rob tried to balance being in two bands at once. In the end *it came down where it all started – Chorley's local radio. I had been so busy that I only had time to do one show on the 6ᵗʰ and invited both The Commies and Duckhunt to appear on the same night. The contrast in the two camps could not have been more dramatic. Steve was the sole Commies representative and struggled to talk positively about the band's plans. While, Matt & Rob bounced in with most of the rest of Duckhunt brimming with confidence and chatted like a gang on a high. I knew it was the end and the following day, at what was to be the last rehearsal in Coppull, Matt announced he and Rob wanted to take Duckhunt forward and not The Commies.*

The Commies played their final gig at a packed Chorley Community Centre on 20ᵗʰ December – it was the 46ᵗʰ gig of 2003. Those who witnessed it know what the potential of the band was..... people were actually queuing up to get in! Now, I look back and console myself with the ironic thought that "Time Won't Tell" as I know all four have gone on to other projects that may prove more successful than The Commies could ever have been. Duckhunt have been "discovered" and signed to Deck Cheese records changing their name to Fail Safe in the process with their first album released in the spring of 2005. Steve switched to drums and, with Adam, formed Capulet with Gaz Canny and Pat Crosby (ex Rebekah) – wowing audiences with a mix they describe as "somewhere between Mono, At the Drive In and Biffy Clyro". I wished them all every success and would like to take this opportunity to thank all those fans and everyone who helped them along their way.

For those of you who haven't got a clue about any of the above but crave the thrill of live music- then get out more and watch/support the unsigned scene that is all around you. It's not just one type of music- you'll find all styles catered for somewhere in every town in Lancashire. There are bands like The Commies everywhere who are the natural descendants of the DIY Punk Rock ethics that The Sex Pistols '76/77 started and The Smiths/ Stone Roses/ Manics/Nirvana etc carried on. It is the public who make legends out of bands not the Music Business. So help create the next one and discover the talent that is in your town tonight. The Commies inspired me to revisit my generation's music and appreciate theirs. If you are a parent like me it's a great way of staying in touch with your kids' youth as well as you own. Have fun and don't accept the fakes".

That was the end of the piece and I was surprised, at the time, how quickly the lads moved on. Leaving The Commies at its height was the best thing to do. In part of the press release I sent as my last duty as their manager I said:

For myself, it has been a privilege to be part of this band for the twelve months as their manager and it has been a labour of love. The band commanded total respect both locally and in numerous venues around the country to which they brought their unique style and dynamic performance. They attained their professionalism by understanding how to get the best out of each other and being sensitive to the comments of other musicians they valued. They have...... reached audiences as far as Glasgow, Newcastle, Rhyl and Leicester. They leave a legacy of recorded material on CD and DVD/video which in years to come will be treasured by those who witnessed them first hand. As they will pass into cult status I have only to thank the band, their supporters in the media and above all their fans over the four years of the band's life.

They parted as friends and thanked me for all that I had done for them. In true punk tradition they shone brightly and called it a day before they faded away. I was immensely proud to have been the manager and what they all achieved as part of the band. It taught me how to deal with a whole set of new challenges and gave me a fantastic experience that was vital for what I did next. However, I wanted to have a separate chapter on The Commies because the band deserves to stand out and I feel I need to explain how important they were to my development too.

To return to the beginning

It was Roy Hesketh's article in *Pogo 'til I Die* fanzine that brought The Commies to my attention. It mentions how they were;

" *...just one of a number of young punk bands from the Preston area. Duckhunt, **Hit & Run Holiday** and **Numpti** are some of the others: a number of these bands took part in the Skafest at Strettles, Preston back in June....The Commies influences vary but the band give a nod to the likes of The Hives, A, Blink 182, NOFX, Less Than Jake, Green Day, Mad Caddies and [spunge]. "....* **Are Shaved Apes**" *was released on The Commies own Mush Mush Baby record label. Tracks are **Why's, Lies & Pies, Move On, Passed out on the Floor** and **Forgotten Call**... the band describe their new stuff as darker and heavier than their earlier usual happy songs. I have been listening to their stuff and impressive it is. The early recordings like the excellent **The Way I Used to be, Orgasmatron, Leaving Me Behind, Short Song** and **Up the Ass (kick me)** are all good enough and the playing is well up to the mark. Then it all moves on a step for the later songs from* "*...Are Shaved Apes*" *which has a lot more bite to it. Chorley today, tomorrow the world*".

At the side of the page is 6 photo's of the band playing live at what looks like the stage at Labour Club, which use to be on Friday Street, Chorley – where I started my drumming. I took this as a good omen.

Roy's comments had inspired me to take a closer look at this band from my home town. From July 2002 I dived head first into everything that was happening on the unsigned scene. As detailed elsewhere in the book, I went from month to month picking up any offers to help out and seized any free time to watch bands in and around Chorley, Blackburn and Preston – especially at the Community Centre in Chorley (CCC) on Railway Road. I had asked about The Commies there and at Townsend Records on Market St, Chorley, where Adrian (the shop assistant at that time) showed me the CD that they stocked for the band. I bought copies and he took my details and said that he would pass my number onto the band next time one of them came in with more CDs. This lead to a call and an interview at the CCC I referred to above.

In August I filmed the Battle of the Bands Final at the CCC on my own camcorder and I remember visiting my dying mum in Chorley hospital afterwards. Sensing how enthralled I was in what I had witnessed; interviewing the bands and making connections with the promoters – she told me to carry on. In a way, her blessing of sorts, before she died on the 27th August, was a green light to launch my business A3H Promotion Ltd. A great deal of the excitement I had expressed to her was as a result of seeing The Commies performance that night. The footage is one of my favorites of those early gigs especially the shots of the crowd jumping up and down in unison. I filmed part of it standing alongside the revellers and getting jostled about as part of the surging mass of bodies lunging forward and backwards was one of the moments when you felt at one with everyone else. Steve, Matt and Liam had a knack of whipping up a frenzied excitement and they were a strong runner up that night to **Dumpstar**. It was in meeting Matt and Liam and the band's performances I witnessed that fanned the flames of my interest in them.

I know that Pretendgirlfriend inspired me to get involved with the unsigned bands from day one but The Commies were a totally different experience on first sighting. They played with intensity and energy that was explosive in the way Punk was and Indie was not. Wild abandonment, teenage lyrics and frantic jumping about using the whole of the stage is what set the Commies apart from the other bands I had seen up to that point. Their local rivals that night – **Onset** and **Dumpstar,** had the same characteristics but The Commies stood out for me because they personified what was Punk to me. Not in a '76/77 tribute style but how that spark was inspiring something fresh in the youth of 2002. The Commies absorbed their surroundings and shared experiences, just as the originators of Punk had done, but crucially they related it to what the teenagers of the naughties had grabbed for themselves. The Commies were the spear head to what **Hangman** had pioneered in Chorley in 1977. The Commies had taken up their mantle and were breathing new life into Chorley and the rest of the North West just as Hangman and **The Sinister Chuckles** (chapter 9) had done back in the seventies. All this hit me as I stared down the lens of my camcorder that night and I felt an immediate connection to them as a fan.

The next sequence of events was a mash up of all things surrounding The Commies, CCC and Duckhunt. The next gig I saw The Commies play was at the Mill, Preston (11th September). I covered the gig for PTID which got printed in issue 4:

The Commies had to contend with the overzealous smoke effect but the hard core of fans making the trip – despite the train strike – had no trouble hearing their set off ten 21st Century songs about teenage angst and love. **Classic Rock, New Song** *and* **Enough Confrontations** *benefited from the return of guitarist Bruno –back from a "world tour" – to complete the original line up of four.*

Not a massive feature but it gave them profile and there was a half page photo of them playing live in the same issue just before the new CD & DVD releases section. I had picked up from were Roy had started and we had a meeting of minds on what they represented locally. I cannot remember why I chose Duckhunt and not The Commies to head line my launch party for A3H in the November. One of the band members may not have been available perhaps or they may have had another gig that night. Anyway, I don't regret the choice as Duckhunt were just as inspiring to me as The Commies and it could have gone either way. I am sure that the way I went about that gig and the reputation I had got by that time fuelled The Commies decision to ask me to manage them. Again Duckhunt could have asked me to manage them as I had invited both bands onto the radio doing successful interviews with both during the Chorley radio sessions. Had Duckhunt asked me to manage them I wonder now who I would have chosen? But, it was Steve and Matt who popped the question as I walked outside with them after their interview. I was flattered, pleasantly surprised and equally aware of the unknown that this would entail. I thanked them and said I'd get back to them.

Band manager and who the fuck are Farce?

Band manager – wow, what did that mean, how do I go about doing that and what did the title involve? I asked the band to a meeting at my house a few days after they had asked me. It was the first time I met all of them at the same time. It was the first time I met Bruno too. I confirmed I wanted to manage them but I said that I was going into this with no experience. I pointed out that, rather like they were learning how to become "rock stars", I had to teach myself what I had to do or ask them and others what I was expected to do as their manager. When I said this they all agreed that all I had to do was to do my best for them. I conducted that meeting, and many others, with an agenda typing up minutes explaining that the structures and format I applied was how I did what I did in my day job as a "manager". They never complained about the formalities or the amount of notes I took and the length of the emails I copied them in on. I did need educating in what bands they wanted to emulate or support and the venues they wanted to play. Matt visited me on his own a few times to do this and Adam gave me a compilation CD of bands on small record labels for me to focus on. I needed this when Matt called me on my mobile to tell me this news about winning the Farce support slots. I was in the middle of judging a band competition heat at the Aquellenium night club, (Preston). I took his call between a band changes and, having no idea who Farce were, I remember saying to Matt "Yeah.... wow! Ah...Matt... hey that's brilliant news..... Wow......got to go.... we'll talk tomorrow – say well done to the rest of the lads....wow....!" all the time I was thinking.... *who the fuck are Farce!*

Well, Farce were a top set of lads. All of them were a few years older- late teens early twenties, and the first night we met them in Glasgow they couldn't have been friendlier. For the rest of the dates they would always talk to us and check we had everything we needed. At that first gig, **In Car Stereo** impressed us all and I made a point of keeping in touch with them (see Chapter 8). The tour was very well organised and I'd been sent a booklet for all the tour dates and it became a bible as to how I set up my own gigs from then on. Each date had a check list: times for loading in, sound check, stage performance and load out. Contact details for every band, their management team, what the stage specifications were for all the different support bands and a set of principles/behaviours that every band should abide by. It was comprehensive and every gig we played was professionally managed to the schedule and we never had cause to raise any complaints. The drink and food, when provided, was satisfactory – albeit that all the bands usually shared each others around and we never had a problem getting paid £25-£50 a gig depending on how far we had to travel. Some of the dates were filled with supports from **Schism** and **The Not Katies** too who were equally pleasant lads to work with.

I made up a merchandise stand. It consisted of two large cork boards and a black table cloth. I pinned T shirts and gig flyers to the boards. I laid out more of the same on a table. I had ordered plenty of stock for the T shirts - all sizes and colours including "skinny fit" which was a first for me! I placed the order with the same girl who did the T Shirts for my A3H launch gig at the Marquee Club. She was so delighted with the business that she included a green hoody for me for free which I still ware occasionally today. The T shirts had the Commies name in full across the front and back, written in Steve's handwriting which appears on most of their CD art work too. I sold them at cost plus 50p and the highest number of sales was at The Bar Fly (Liverpool) the scousers really liked the name "it's dead whacky mate!" is how one lad explain his purchase and that was before he saw the band play! What's in a name eh! Oh, and by the way the name of the band was taken from the Harmony Korine novel "A Crack-up at the Race Riots" – it appeared in a list of films titles one of the character wanted to make - which is explained by Bruno during the band's interview on the "It's Not Cricket! " DVD.

The unsigned and unseen

When I went to the office at the Bar Fly, Liverpool, at the end of the gig to collect the expenses, the manager asked me how I was finding the role of band manager. I said it was great and my enthusiasm for the job and the other promotional projects I was involved with, seemed to impress him. He made a point (which I will never forget) by nodding over to a long sofa in one corner of the room and asked in a rhetorical tone *"How do you decide who to promote or offer a gig to amongst that lot eh!"* At that point I saw that the sofa was packed full of parcels and padded letters. He added *"...but somewhere amongst it could be the next Oasis or Cold Play!"* In an instant I realised what any band was up against when it came to promoting themselves by post. The sight of all the shapes and sizes representing the hopes and dreams of others, spilling onto the floor is burned into my memory even now! There must have been hundreds – you didn't stand a chance! It was a boomerang lesson I took away both as a manager and promoter.... think about the poor sod that has the job to wade through the mass to find the diamonds in the rough..... In time that poor sod was me!

Other stand out moments included the gig at Stockton (Georgian Theatre) as Whalley came to watch. He was a die had Commies fan and hats off to him making that trip. I met up with him in 2013 as he was doing the sound at The Imperial and helped Shaun Maxwell with his band recordings in a studio situated on the Rivington road out of town. The proudest occasion I had from the fans was when I turned a corner to the Roadhouse (Manchester) and saw a row of Commies fans greeting us, complete with a banner held by Pat and Gaz (from **Rebekah**). Helen and Mick came to that gig and I met Kris Reid (venue promoter) for the first time too. The last gig on the tour was at The Cluny (Newcastle) and I met a member of **Hug Lorenzo** who was doing sound. Later on I invited that band to headline the *It's Not Cricket!* Festival as well as putting them on at the CCC and North Bar to add to their journey over here. When our part of the tour came to an end some members of The Commies stayed in touch with Farce and got invited down to an end of tour party in the Midlands. I think it was Matt who told me it was a real Rock'n Roll event and "an eye opener" – he didn't elaborate but I thought it was a nice touch for the lads in Farce to invite them as they had sort of taking them under their wing.

After that I did as much as I could to promote the Commies. I touch on some gigs and incidents in other chapters but I feel I need to record here some moments that stand out for very different reasons. Healey's at Barrow-in-Furness was a gig I set up with the venue who recommended **Nana's Revenge** as support band. We also got a good advanced publicity from Pete Mossop in the local press who referred to my previous association with the town. It was a full circle moment having been inspired by unsigned bands I'd watched in that town in the eighties I was the one organising unsigned bands to play at my own gig nearly twenty years later!

The Beer Keller, Manchester was one of the last few out of town gigs and it was the only one of the entire Commies gigs I didn't like. It was freezing cold for the whole time I was there. It was winter and there was no heating on that night in that basement venue. The crowd was thin and everyone seemed in awe of some piss poor American band that were headlining and had nothing to recommend them by. Shit songs, shit stage craft and shit image. I hated them and The Commies blew them away but because they were on early hardly anyone was there to bear witness to this fact!

Conclusions

I had grown into the role of Manager with The Commies. However, it was only during their last few months that I woke up to what my limitations were in that capacity. I was absolutely certain, from my time with them, that I did not want to give anyone the impression that I knew anymore about the music business than I did. I know that The Commies were the definitive Chorley youth band of the naughties. No one came close in terms of fan loyalty and influence on those that came after them. On reflection would I do things differently if I could go back ....?"No!" I have since met with all the band members over the years that followed and there are no regrets or recriminations. That says a lot about what the band meant to everyone concerned and how the break up was managed with a maturity way beyond their ages.

Where are they now....? Well you can seek them out on the internet and I know via those I have spoken to directly or indirectly (through parents or friends) since, that they are all in a place where they are content. For all the fans I leave you with the original instructions I sent out for The Commies last ever gig:

Only legitimate guests will be approved and any bands thought to be abusing this system will not play.

I have absolutely no idea why I put that last line in or how the hell I thought it would be implemented! The gig was packed out and people were queuing to get in throughout The Commies set....

Thanks and well done to everyone involved their history!

'Let's Not Lose MARS to the Commies'

...the long and the winding

LET'S NOT LOSE MARS TO THE COMMIES

...are shaved apes.

Let's Not Lose MARS to the Commies

JANUARY TOUR DATES 2003.

3RD NORTH BAR, BLACKBURN
(TOWN HALL ST. NEXT TO THE CENTRAL LIBRARY)
PLUS
"HIT & RUN HOLIDAY" & "STARKEY'S WALK"
[FREE ENTRY]

9TH AQUALENIUM, PRESTON
(CHURCH ST. PRESTON)
IN THE SEMI FINALS OF:
L.E.P. "BATTLE OF THE BANDS"

10TH NORTH BAR, BLACKBURN
PLUS
"REBEKAH" & "DAYS END"
[FREE ENTRY]

17TH NORTH BAR BLACKBURN
PLUS
"PAIL"
[FREE ENTRY]

28TH LIFE CAFÉ, MANCHESTER.

31ST THE CASTLE, OLDHAM.
PLUS
"10 DAYS"

PLEASE CHECK WITH THE VENUE BEFORE TRAVELLING TO
THE GIGS OR CONTACT BAND MANAGEMENT 07812 577 987.

WWW.LETSNOTLOSEMARS
TOTHECOMMIES.CO.UK

'Let's Not Lose MARS to the Commies'   'Let's Not Lose MARS to the Commies'

The
Dates
We Play
Songs...

Let's Not Lose
Mars to the Commies

9th March, Blackburn, Cellar Bar
17th March, Glasgow, King Tuts, Farse Tour
21st March, Blackburn, North Bar, 99fis, Hyperja X
25th March, Manchester, Roadhouse, Farse Tour
27th March, Liverpool, BarFly, Farse Tour
1st April, Newcastle, The Cluny, Farse Tour
4th April, Manchester, Life Cafe, Eile Radio
11th April, Huddersfield, Abrahams, Farse Tour
12th April, Preston, Golden Cross, Days End
16th April, Stockton-on-Tees Georgian Theatre, Farse Tour
19th April, Oldham, Oldham Castle, This Product
LOOK
at www.letsnotlosemarstothecommies.co.uk

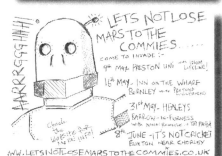

LETS NOT LOSE
MARS TO THE
COMMIES.....

COME TO INVADE :-
9th MAY, PRESTON UNI with Idiom LIFELINE!

16th May, INN ON THE WHARF
BURNLEY with PRETEND GIRLFRIEND

31st MAY- HEALEYS
BARROW-IN-FURNESS
with Nolan Romance + UR PARA

8th JUNE -ITS NOT CRICKET
EUXTON NEAR CHORLEY

Check
the
website for
more info!

WW.LETSNOTLOSEMARSTOTHECOMMIES.CO.UK

"LET AIRPLANES
CIRCLE OVER-HEAD"
+
"CAPULET"
the adelphi, Preston
Thursday 29th December
three pounds
http://www.motivesounds.com

06 It's Not Cricket!

Field work

During the short time I knew Ben Greenaway he gave me many opportunities. I didn't appreciate the long term impact these would have on my story and I would like to acknowledge this now by saying "thank you, Ben" wherever you are. The positives came from his encouragement of my involvement with Chorley Community Centre, Chorley FM and Chorley's own Music Festival. Ben was a few years younger than me and, back then, he was a charismatic individual who would hold court in after show gatherings at the Community Centre on Saturday nights or at the Chorley FM offices at the end of broadcasts. His rants enthralled me with his vision of the bigger picture, not limiting your options and seeking out every chance to do rather than think or talk about any matter that required tangible action. But, some of his ideas I got into did not pay dividends – The Dumpstar Tour, Hype Nights at the North Bar and the original plan for an open air Chorley Festival at Euxton Cricket Club. The later is what this chapter is about and, in fairness to Ben it was his original concept that led, indirectly, to one of my most enduring achievements in the DVD *It's Not Cricket!*

Late summer in 2002 Ben asked me if I would join a syndicate of entrepreneurs he was putting together which required a minimum of £5,000 to join. This was to back an open air weekend music festival to be held somewhere around Chorley. The list of bands he reeled off were credible crowd pleasers doing the big festivals at that time. He said that the money was to cover the set up costs and I would make this back from a percentage of the profits made on the event. It all looked good in theory and I sent in my carefully worded letter of ".... agreement in principle", but no money was asked for up front. Things went quiet for a while and one day in early March 2003 Ben invited me to a meeting at Euxton Cricket Club. This was with representatives from the cricket club and other interested people. We discussed the technical issues: from the PA system, down to the size/type of fencing and the ratio of portable loos per hundred festival goers – thrilling stuff! On the steps of the pavilion, Ben made a short speech about what was planned and then turned to face the cricket field. He raised his hands and declared something along the lines of ".....imagine ten thousand people watching music on that glorious field!" The cricket officials frowned at the prospect of their delicate square being trampled over: those with money in

108

mind licked their lips and the Council representative scratched his head. I, as usual, was Mr Enthusiastic about it all – buying the vision, the challenge of something new and it would all take place a stone's throw from where I use to live which I took to be a good sign.

My role was to supply a collection of local support bands to the headline acts. I set to work drawing up a list of who I thought would be interested and a date of the 8th of June was pencilled in. A series of progress meetings were held at the cricket club in the lead up to the weekend. Gary O'Neil was my contact at the club; a pleasant young bloke who I felt had to push the idea to his (elder) fellow committee members. If the event paid off, the club would see substantial financial income rather than rely on smaller fund raising events throughout the year – this way it all came in one big dollop! From the start he assured me that he would arrange the costs for the publicity material – posters, flyers etc all I had to do was supply the art work. I used Roy' Hesketh's mate (Clarke Design) who put together the fanzine for us. Then I got busy with managing The Commies and left the rest to Ben and the others.

During one of my judging appearances at BOTB heats organised by Russ Carlton at Aquellenium, Preston, I noticed two lads filming the bands. They had a commercial looking video camera and I got chatting to them out of curiosity. When they told me about their company, Seal Films, based in Wheelton, I said we were neighbours and invited them round for a coffee. They brought a show reel DVD of their output and were at the Aquellenium testing out a new camera, toying with the idea of doing live band videos. This lit up my head with the possibility of using them to film The Commies. A music video spoke louder than music in a pure audio format CD or local radio play listing. The video of a live performance had the capacity to expose a band as a complete package. P Rock satellite channel was very popular at that time (which was a few years before U Tube) and I wanted The Commies to have the same impact Farse's video had had for them on that show. I needed to know the cost and how I could get a useable product. The lads wanted business, assured me that they could provide what I out lined to them and we cut a deal. They would supply a two camera shoot of a live set from The Commies which would include an interview with the band. Seal Films would format a master DVD disc which I could reproduce and A3H would own the material completely. The cost was reasonable and I had the festival in mind for a live set of about 20-25 minutes – the average for any support band. The thinking was to have the local bands on early in the day and The Commies would be scheduled to perform just before the bigger names came on when the audience would be at its maximum and the sun would be setting allowing for the best use of stage lighting. I had a vision in my head of U2's performance of *Sunday Blood Sunday* at Red Rocks. My commitment to The Commies meant that I saw the costs as an investment in their future as well as another feather in A3H's cap and it could launch us all onto another level – perhaps even TV in the same way U2's video from that concert catapulted them into the big time. The Commies were excited when I told them and they suggested some bands to put on the festival including **Fi Lo Radio** who they knew. All was fitting into place and I invited everyone I had asked to perform to meet me at the cricket club. After an explanation of the festival details, I lead everyone out onto the field and did a Ben like "big picture" speech to an appreciative ripple of applause.

Change of venue but keep the name!

The next steps were to put the running order together, drum up interest amongst my contacts and arrange publicity and press releases. The art work had to reflect the imagination of what we all felt would be the first of many such festivals. The concept had to capture the fact that, although it was being held on a cricket pitch it was not about cricket, in the same way that Glastonbury music festival is held on working farm land but is not an agricultural show. This got shortened to "It's Not Cricket!" and I supplied a list of a dozen or so bands that were available to appear. However, the initial promises of big named acts appearing as headliners did not materialise. This was left to others who supposedly had contacts but it became apparent that no one had secured any confirmations. With no one famous, the whole proposition changed. Meetings were held and the appetite for an open air concert was still on the menu but instead of any named acts appearing it would be full of local unsigned bands and musicians. The cricket club committee agreed and confirmed that they would continue to work with the council on the logistics. Now that my income would be less certain from this watered down event I needed to work out how A3H would pay Seal Films for the video. I came up with the idea of offering all those who play the festival a video of one of the songs in their set and a short interview. This meant they got a professional video in return for a small fee which was a fraction of the cost of hiring Seal Films for the day. For their part, Seal Films wanted to film more bands anyway and agreed to the change. The Commies set would still be filmed in full and there was a slight risk to A3H in covering any shortfall, but I reckoned that would be negligible as I'd still get a larger percentage from the lower priced ticket sales over what was to be a one instead of a two day event.

"One Day, 20 bands, 10 Hours of Unsigned Music"

What was a confident declaration became a frantic nightmare for me to make a reality. The posters and leaflets were ordered with the title "A3H Promotion Ltd presents, in association with Euxton Cricket Club: It's Not Cricket! One day, 20 bands, 10 hours of unsigned music at Sunday 8th June at Euxton Cricket Club, Southport Road". I liked the title for the implicit commentary on the nature of the event – it being a showcase for unsigned bands and my DVD would be an exclusive of the highlights. Thereafter the DVD and festival gained momentum as a unique happening for our local scene, the age ranges and niche styles. It was not what anyone would expect, it did not fit with the accepted norms and no one had had the audacity to undertake such a venture in the past as far as I was aware. In short – it was simply not cricket! I liked that intensely and poured my energy into it. However, the countdown meetings stumbled over getting things done. The essential bit of administration was to secure the public entertainments licence which was left to others to arrange. I had an uneasy feeling about the delays and time running out. I had to consider the repercussions if the thing did not go ahead due to a technical matter. Visualising this I assessed the impact on me and my reputation amongst those I'd invited to play. I started to sound out alternative arrangements. I could still put on an event and have it filmed but it would not be outdoors. I wised up from my involvement up to that point, that a festival in a field was fraught with too many variables. Furthermore, even if you dealt with all of them, you could not guarantee the weather!

I needed somewhere that could accommodate all the bands, equipment and have a PA and stage with sufficient space for an audience and the film crew. It had to have a single entrance for door security and facilities for alcohol and food (as both appeared on the publicity!). The bar would attract the older bands, their fans and you do not put on a music festival without alcohol – hence the CCC was ruled out. I also wanted to be in a larger town or city that would have a predominantly student population close to the venue. I visited Strettles in Preston as this was opposite Preston University campus on Fylde road. Fortunately, Terry and Ryan (the people involved with running it at the time) were instantly receptive to me hiring the upstairs concert room and setting up a small acoustic stage area down stairs too. I paid a small deposit to reserve it and said I'd be back to confirm as soon as I knew the outcome from a "do or die" meeting at the cricket club later that week. My scouting proved to be a wise move as the decision to abandon the cricket club ground was made when the dead line passed to submit the paper work for the Public Entertainment Licence!

I took a deep breath and made some decisions of my own. "The location had altered to Strettles but the date is unchanged - are you still in?" was the message I communicated out and everyone involved. I had to tell them that their stage time was cut, there was no time for a sound check and they would all share the same back line. This meant that their set had to be limited to three songs – nominating the one song in advance that they wanted filming. The space available at Strettles could not accommodate a back stage area that would allow storage for separate band equipment hence, getting on stage, doing a quick line check, playing and getting off had to take place inside thirty minutes max. They had to check in no later than an hour before their time slot and their interview would take place half an hour later. It was tight but on paper, with discipline and co-operation, sit could work.

Thousands of coloured leaflets and hundreds of posters printed in advance with the wrong venue were destined for the bin. They also listed Fi-Lo Radio (T.B.C), Duckhunt, "Phil Baker (Pulse –echoes of Pink Floyd) and guests" as well as "3 of the best bands from Runshaw College". During the change of location and up to the day itself, while I knew that the majority of those advertised would play, experience had taught me that there would be inevitable cancelations. Sod it! I could not afford to replace them so I got a load of thin labels printed (at my own expense) and Helen and I spent hours cutting them off sheets and sticking them on the material to make the amendments with only a few weeks to go.

The ticket price on the publicity was "£3 advance or £5 on the day subject to capacity" – no one, as I recall, paid for any tickets in advance as I don't think any were ever printed! I adjusted the price in the little time I had left and in the final press release. It was advertised as "It's Not Cricket- a festival" and appeared, for example, in Phil Widdows' article on the Friday 6th June edition of The Lancashire Evening Post, as £3 for either the afternoon or evening session or "....there are day tickets available" which I kept to £5. Back then most gigs that had an entry fee were usually a couple of quid to see 3 or 4 bands so £3 to see 10 or a fiver for 20 was good value. There was a break half way through to let the equipment cool down- hence the two sessions. This also allowed me to use the acoustic stage down stairs where Anamosa were timed to play at five thirty. Their set kept the momentum going and the need to chill out for a while suited the style of this delicate guitar duo perfectly.

My finest day

Sunday 8th of June arrived and I was fortunate to have the support from some great people. For a reasonable fee, Phil Baker agreed to mix the sound, provide the PA, stands, microphones, lighting rig and he built a small stage out of boxes. He even offered to play an acoustic set if anyone failed to show up. Russ Carlton helped out on the door, and got cover while he performed with **Digby**. Cliff de Carteret provided vital back stage assistance to the bands. To help him distinguish the members of the band from the fans Cliff issued them with blue badges as a sort of back stage pass in case any of you who own a copy of the DVD wondered what they were.

The publicity material had "gates open at 12 noon – first band on at 12.30pm". I met Phil at Strettles as early as we could gain access to the building in the morning. I helped him load in and we set up the stage to the right of the bar. The guys from Seal Films were there on time and soon the place started to fill up.

I knew that once it began there was not going to be any let up until the last band had completed their set at 11.30pm. Sorting out 20 bands demanded the detailed schedule of who was expected to do what and when. I typed this on the back of a 20 page programme I self printed in black and white for sale on the day at 50p. It featured my write ups of all the bands that appeared on the day except for **The Message** and **Blood or Whisky** as I did not obtain any of their material and, in the case of the later, the band got included at the last minute. My reviews included others who did not appear such as: **Jack In The Green, This Product, Vinyls, Reemer, Rocket Dog, 3CR, Doublethink, Tin Gods, Joe's Steakhouse, Scary Billy Bob, David R Black, Wasted Earth, The Reserved, Maybees? Fresh Dropped Mites, Hello Mother Fucker, Kraul, Blue Tile Lounge, Effigy, Shorn, Tessem, More Than Here, Efferescent, If All Else Fails, The Sell Out Flaw, The Relatives, Pail** and compilations from **1000 Watt Records** (Volume 1) and **Eyesore Records'** *What's Across the Pond*. It was done to showcase my talent as a music journalist and encourage more material to be given to me to review in the future.

The DVD it captured everything that followed and was all I hoped for. The filming of the band interviews varied from inside the venue and on the tables outside or on a bit of grass by the University opposite. The weather was good and it did not rain after all.

Bowled over by brilliant performances.

The day did go, in the main, to plan which, considering the scale and the majority of young and relatively inexperienced people involved are triumphs in themselves. The bass amp packed up early on which lost us twenty minutes to replace. All the bands shared equipment supplied by **Digby** and **Faultline** – hence no one brought any spares Dohhhh! The DVD reflects the material everyone was putting out at that time and is testament to the quality of Phil's sound balance which is the best I could expect. I regret that **Fi-Lo Radio** could not do the date but their presence was always going to be a bonus. The gap got filled by **Blood or Whisky** after a last minute request from their manager. The band had been let down over some dates on their way to an appearance at the H.I.T.S festival in Morecambe later in the month. They are an Irish Punk/Folk band formed in the mid 1990s and I agreed to pay them some expenses in return for being forth on if they could get there for 1pm. On the day **Blood or Whisky** did show up, played and moved on to their next gig. Unfortunately they declined to appear on the DVD as they felt their footage needed improvements that both time and my budget could not meet-hence, they, and, as with some other bands, did not appear on any pre festival publicity and there is a blank space on the DVD. **Duckhunt** had recently changed their lead vocalist but were not ready for live dates and **Doublethink** (formerly known as **Boddah**) had to pull out too. Those that did play and were satisfied with the results are in the running order that follows with snippets from the programme which I hope gives a feel of what occurred for those who were not there or have not seen the DVD:

1. **Geoffrey Bungle** (Chorley) – *The Future.* This trio were Saturday regulars at the CCC and made a confident start to the day. *"**Pump up the Punk** has been the most enjoyable discovery in my post bag for a long while. **3rd Wheel** has '77/'78 stamped all over it-fast, uncensored fun in the same mode as any of the best Buzzcock songs – G string tight guitars and sardonic suspended supports. **Being Away** shows the producer's credentials (Steve Hodson of The Commies) with lovingly cooked bass and beefy cymbals teasing the sluggish vocals appetite to keep pace in this classic three chord dish. **The Future** has head nodding bass intro to a song of doom and gloom politics racing along to Oi! Oi! Oi! Chorus. **Virtual Reality** – vocally would not be out of place on Monochrome Set's Strange Boutique and gives a hyper dosed Howard Devoto (Magazine) a run for his money. **Imaginary Toilets** the fastest of a Wire inspired song... a sweeping generalisation for this output? Naughties punk rock at its most hopeful".*

2. **Crazytalk** (Leyland) – *Relief.* Cliff had the idea to run a BOTB competition at Runshaw College to draw out three acts to appear at the festival. It was a vote for your favourite local unsigned band type of thing. Out of this **Crazy Talk** came third.

3. **Faultline** (Chorley) – *No Way Out.* This trio were managed by Cliff and had appeared on the Live and Let Live radio show. Liam was one of the most pleasant drummers around at that time and the bass player

(Janie) stood out for two reasons a) she was a girl, and there were very few females in bands at that time, and her voice was light and a little giggly on the interview. However, on stage she did a gruff, deep Emo roar that made my eyes widen at the shock of the transformation. My review drew attention to this too *"...the vocal interplay between Quinney (Guitar & lead vocals) and Janie is unique on the local circuit as these unassuming people off stage are transformed into the neighbours from hell – thunderous screams from Satan's sentinels it seems everyone has gone barking mad. **Defiance** prolongs the dispute and **Change (yourself)** offers no relief either on CD or seeing them live - you endure the perform-ance rather than enjoy but aren't all the best rides at the adventure park like that too!"*

4. Was suppose to be **Blood or Whisky** but for the reasons above a blank appears to explain "...why there is no live footage for those who were there".

5. **Didgy** (Preston) *-13th Floor Elevator.* This featured musicians who went on to appear in lots of different bands on the Preston scene. These included Paddy Green (Guitar) and Ian Bullard (bass) who had put together the Jambeezi 18 track CD compilation *Are You Ready for Your Close Up.* This was a land mark product both locally and in my own development. I had bought a copy when I met the pair selling them at the first **Duckhunt** gig I went to in the downstairs room under The Royal Oak nearly twelve months previously. The CD was in a DVD case with a colour cover and a 12 page black and white booklet insert. The opening page declared *"This CD is a document of what's happening in our local music network running the gamut of genres evident in the local scene, be it punk, metal, indie, pop, acoustic...whatever. It represents music in its most pure form, before the evil forces of marketing get their grubby mitts on it. This is raw, direct and unfiltered – any one of these acts has the potential to go all the way. Hunt these bands down.....most importantly go and see them live, check out their music- look at it this way, imagine having Radiohead's first demo, or a boot leg of Smashing Pumpkin's first ever live gig. In short, if this disc was a meal it be a Chinese banquet with more courses than you can shake a chopstick at, each one seriously tasty. Fuck the napkin, let's get greasy".* The back cover lists the 18 tracks featured on it by: **Hit n Run Holiday, Atonal, Perkie, Anamosa, Hyper-Value, Amy Costello, Cadium, Duckhunt, Ianio, Seven Years Dead, Terza-Rimar, Birdman, HMF, the Hamiltons, Digby, the Remedies** and **Chompo-Pompo.** Finally, below is the declaration: *Jambeezi is a non*

*profit organisation dedicated to recording the best new local music in the North West area and releasing it to you, the listing public...*The fact that the CD was packaged in a DVD case meant I had taken their format and inspiration to the next level in producing the "It's Not Cricket!" DVD.

6.   **In Car Stereo** – (Glasgow) – *Out of Appreciation.* This was Jordan Yates and his three mates who got invited down because The Commies and I liked them after meeting them at the King Tut's gig on the Farse Tour and it added to the diversity of the unsigned choice along with other non locals.

7.   **Pike** (Preston) – *Ghost Story.* Without doubt one of the most respected bands at that time. This song is a mellow ballad and one of my personal highlights on the DVD....*they are the only local band to have the integrity that 13 years of doing what they do under the Punk flag warrants.... their influences range from The Clash, New Model Army to Mowtown and everything that lies in between... to sum Pike up in a word...."Diversity" as Mike Pike wrote me recently.*

8.   **Slick Fifty** (Blackrod, Bolton) – *Pit Pony.* I held auditions at the CCC in the run up to selecting bands for the festival and this trio turned up and impressed me enough to warrant offering them a slot...*with an average age of 14 they have a lot of talent and gave a performance way in advance of their years....a no nonsense set of songs that blended elements of the bands they listed as their favourites – Blink 182, Foo Fighters and Rancid. Tight little combo who are exactly what A3H is looking for in a local band who needs help securing those crucial early gigs amongst a discerning audience.*

9.   **Cornerstone** (Whitehaven, Cumbria) - *Sickly Sweet.* I had a lot of affection for this quartet and put them on as often as I could. Four lads who appreciated everything I did for them. It was a pleasure to capture a terrific performance on film....*a torrent of relentless edgy guitar barrage and Shaun McLaughlin's distinctive vocal range. Let them take you on a roller-coaster ride with their own slow down trademark as you climb to the next peak.*

10. **The Message** (Leyland) – *All My Thoughts.* **The Message** was runners up to **Friend of Foe** in the Runshaw College BOTBs referred to above. **The Message** morphed into **Supernova** to emerge finally as **The Underdogs** and became firm favourites at The Mad Ferret (previously known as Time Square, below Strettles) and elsewhere on the Preston scene.

11. **Anamosa** (Southport) – *Nothing's Ideal*. I had a lot of time for the two Louises and this song in particular. It was the stand out track on the Jambeezi compilation. However, the harmonies are not as strong at the festival recording. The girls were nervous as everyone crowded in front of them at the bar down stairs from the main concert room during the break. But their vulnerability adds an edge to the feel for the lyric that the live performance nails.

12. **Rhythmic Intent** (Darwen, Lancashire) – *Julie*. This 5 piece featured another female (backing vocalist) and their set added a different genre to the line up. I'd seen them play at The Cavendish (Dalton-In-Furness) and an open mic session at the Hare & Hounds (Abbey Village) playing *"Fresh and light Folk Rock blending along the modern line with mandolin and delicate harmonies adding interest beyond the Arran sweater squatters."*

13. **Pretendgirlfriend** (Burnley) – *Limbo*. See Chapter 8.

14. **Helico** (Chorley) - *Day of The Sun*. Starsailor contemporaries and similar in sound. Featured guitarist Chris Unsworth who went onto form the trio **Green Quarter** with Curtis McKenna (previously in Blackburn based trio **Hope**) and "Buster" (David Kay's younger brother) and who featured on *Vibes from the Attic* compilation (see chapter 10). Helico were a band who should have been signed up in another life time. They had a rich batch of MOR songs that deserved to more widely known. How often could I write that line....!

15. **Idiom Lifeline** (Chorley) – *Oliver's Pardon*. This is an unrelenting performance of power and emotion on a scale that singled them out as one of the most dynamic bands to see live at that time. *"....no one comes within the same universe for shear raw unstoppable power of glacier proportions. The three guitars cut through everything at Nature's disposal and their drums were forged long before man spat on the dust of time. Vocalist Diggy sacrifices his throat for every audience I have seen him literally throw himself into. No one on the local scene is pushing the boundaries of their instruments or imaginations like these five. You experience this band and should not have the stupidity of innocence to assume to merely listen or watch them"*

16. **Friend of Foe** (Leyland) – *Spartial*. I had a tape of heir material and - *no listing but plenty to seize the ear. ...track 2 is like listening to **Birdman** and **Freaky Kojack** doing a duet that Mark E Smith breaks in on. The rest is as if the guitars are swapped for angle grinders and buzz saws at a Strokes party for **"Pushy Man"**. **"My Generation"** gets their controlled*

chaos treatment – love it absolutely love it. They know exactly what they are doing. Not for the sensitive but a tonic for the hard of hearing. They are the crop of the Runshaw Bands having pooled the most votes amongst their fellow students. They will give you their fullest attention. The lead singer had a natural stage presence and I invited them to play The Cellar Bar, Blackburn shortly afterwards on the strength of their set that day.

17. **Rebekah** (Chorley) – *Empty.* This band feature elsewhere in the book but I am always touched by their mention of what I was doing for the local scene during their introduction.

18. **Bed** (Preston) – *Good to Go. "A small name for a band with big hope....as Paddy Green said to me (while we watched them in May at the Adelphi, Preston)...why are this band not signed up yet! Beth (Swain)'s smouldering articulation flanked by Pete and Andy's cool detachment...."* is what impressed me when I first saw their heat at the Chorley BOTBs competition twelve months previously. Their inclusion on the DVD is an end of a circle in many ways as they were the first band I captured at the CCC. Beth went onto form **Stolen Pony** and we worked in the same office for a while in Manchester. She played a solo set for my final gig in September 2007,and I got her on to the Accrington Oxjam line up before the end of the same year.

19. **Let's Not Lose Mars to the Commies** (Chorley) – *1000ᵗʰ Story.*

20. **Hug Lorenzo** (Newcastle-Upon-Tyne) – *Problematic."* I had met the lead singer (Pablo) at The Cluny in Newcastle, during the Commies tour with Farce. This Latino /Ska/Salsa inspired band were named in memory of a man they admired (1936-1973).I gave them two other gigs while here for the festival: The CCC and they headlined the final Hype night at the North Bar, Blackburn on the Monday before heading home. They headlined because they appeared on the Suka-Punch compilation CD which featured other leading signed bands at that time. Their shows were, as I predicted a *"...real treat of whip it up guitars and sassy bass. Low down passion that you won't want to stop".*

During the week after the festival I remember saying to Helen that I had done enough and would stop my musical journey – some twelve months after I had started out. I knew that the DVD would be the pinnacle of what I had done. I was shattered and for that brief moment I felt it was over. To my surprise her reaction was to encourage me to carry on. She said The Commies still needed me and who knows where they would go and me with them. Well, with that endorsement I carried on and the next few months were a stop start challenge to produce the DVD itself.

Making the edit

I had a series of meetings with Seal Films at their studio and they were very patient with my demands on how the first edit looked. Armed with several copies on a VHS video tape I posted one and a contract to any bands I could not visit personally. I needed everyone's confirmation that they were happy with both the interview and performance footage. At the local viewings, which I usually did at one of the band member's houses, I took the £50 fee and their signatures on the contract to reproduce 200 copies of the DVD. This was in good faith that I would have the end product and five copies for them as soon as I could. I estimated this would take me a month or two. Next I had to post a rough copy of the next edit to people who I hoped would provide complementary comments I could use on the cover. However this caused a complication of its own making and I had to send out an email to clarify the position on 24th August:

"Contrary to press releases the DVD is not available and will not be until mid September..... The advanced copy of the video that most of you have seen by now was sent.... with a letter explaining that I wanted them to review the material and give me something as a sound bite for the dust cover on the DVD case..... I will follow these up next week when I have calmed down..... I will send details to the graphic designer who did the posters shortly and, bar a little adjustment, the end product will be available for collection in 2/3 weeks.

I have used Digital Reproductions in Bradford to produce the discs and they have suggested.

I use background bands* for the Menu selections which is brilliant......glad to have them on board as it widens the geographical appeal for all concerned. All these bands will receive a copy of the DVD free as I needed them to act quickly with their decision and they have agreed that they will enter the spirit of promotion as fully as the rest of us.

*Money! So far a third of you have paid to reserve your 5 copies and I know, having spoken to the rest that "it's on the way"...... . **Digby** and **Bed** have split so there are potentially some more spare copies. I'd like to take this opportunity to wish them well and thank them for their support.*

(Always using any opportunity to provide other updates and news which was part of the spirit of what I mentioned earlier I added in ...).

Late news from Russ Carlton (www.hyper-vale.com) is that the Marque/The Mill is opening up again in September. On Friday 29th there is a "meet and greet" at the place on Aqueduct St, Preston, at 7pm and all bands are encouraged to come along. They are looking to host unsigned bands on a Saturday when a touring band is not booked. The Wannadies, I understand- have a gig lined up there and Shed Seven, Electric Soft Parade and Hell is for Heroes too. Good news and I'm going- see you there?

Finally, plenty is going on this weekend in Chorley on the Flat Iron market (opposite the shopping centre and old bus station). Phil Baker (who did the sound for the festival) is hosting the event so come down an support it (12noon to 7..ish!). Out of town bands via Independent Sound (Dave Horrocks) are **The Smear, The Flares, Only 1 Mammal, Cassidy & Renton** *(a good indie band from London who I met at FJ Nichols, Blackburn on Thursday) – all of them will appreciate meeting fellow band members and it is an excellent way of looking for gig swaps.*

It will be worth it in the end and I will continue to make the whole project work for us ALL.

The menu bands were*:

Anodized (Carlisle) *Eat Yourself* "Ben Smeaton and fellow metal cohorts.... worth the purchase price on its own, faster than the rest with an essential ear catching chorus.....high production quality allows every word and guitar to feature effortlessly....a heavy tag with intelligence and ...musicianship almost taken for granted....."

Bushbabies (Preston) *Hard Getting Old.* A popular light Indie band I watched a few times and their singer who was doing sound at the Marque Club at the time.

Failure by Design (Aughton, Liverpool) *Anarchy is Frowned Upon.* I cannot remember whether I saw this band live, as part of a Wigan Music Collective gig or was given their CD by a member of the band at one.

Missed-Her-Bliss (Great Harwood, Blackburn) *The Rate of Nots.* "They are easily the loudest band I have heard at the North Bar. Sod this review just see this band live and be blown away by sheer ROCK!"

Atomic Hound Dog (Wigan) *Too Much Time.* Same situation as with Failure By Design, above.

Wowzer (Chorley) *Dirty Old Man.* "Every band has their idols and the collective vote goes to Pulp if we had the mandate on behalf of this tight little outfit...with an eye for the visually appealing*...in the mid '80s this would have been a massive Indie hit so here's hoping what goes round comes round as Wowzer deserve it on this outing". * refer to the only live gig I saw them play (Adelphi, Preston) when one of the band wore a dress -he was last seen serving at Appoco Music shop, Bolton St, Chorley.

There is a long list of people I thanked in the end credits and Clarke Design did a double sided colour cover which featured stills of most of the performers. The cover price was "pay no more than £15....for those who truly value live music!" Perhaps it is a fitting to end this chapter with the sound bites on the back cover to provide an independent tribute:

"....it had a great buzz about it. You can almost feel the passion and taste the ambition in the air. It seems the Preston scene finally has its own Hard Days Night".

(Kris Reid, Roadhouse, Manchester).

"A Big plus in getting lesser known bands in to new venues"

(P.O.D. Witchwood, Ashton and www.arcsounds.com)

"An excellent idea to promote new talent within the music industry. All the artists are energetic performers with a wide range of style and directions"

(Dave Horrocks, Independent Sound UK).

"All the bands seemed very professional and this could easily have a few future stars on it. The particular highlights were Let's Not Lose mars to the Commies and Idiom Lifeline who could go a long way, I was impressed with the sound quality...very well put together and I wish we had been on it!"

(James from Kid Conspiracy).

It's Not Cricket! II

On that Sunday (2nd February), I booked Strettles, on Fylde Road, Preston for the event. It was less ambitious than the first one and I did it in association with David Kay. The footage David filmed did not see the light of day, as he did not bring a sound technician. The visuals were good, but the lack of a quality sound recording meant there was no way of producing a usable product of Pretendgirlfriend's performance or any of the bands that day. To make amends he promised to do me a "proper" recording of Pretendgirlfriend in the future – which I held him to. One person I met for the first time at this gig was Rob Clarke – landlord of The Mitre Tavern, Preston. He took a copy of the first "It's Not Cricket!" DVD and invited me to discuss promoting his venue the following week...out of adversity and all that...and another indication of the more I put myself about the more I got in return etc.

DVD front cover.

07 Chorley Community Centre, M.A.C.Y & local bands

Sometimes I don't know when to keep my mouth shut and I end up saying something I later regret. This is a chapter to evidence this point and bear witness to what became my mantra that drove everything that followed.

"Give us something to do - town is boring say youngsters"

This is the title of an article by Malcolm Wyatt that appeared in the Chorley Guardian on 4th September 2002. It summarises the feelings expressed by half a dozen lads from the Pall Mall area who were upset about being asked to move on when congregating around town. One of them, a pupil from Southlands High School, talks about having nowhere to go or anything to do and how the Police keep "moaning" about them, even though they are not causing "problems." A representative from the Police and a councillor are quoted with their version and spin on these observations blah blah blah...

This is a matter of weeks after the final of The Battle of the Bands (BOTBs) competition at the Chorley Community Centre (CCC) and a few months into what I had been involved with musically. I had just set up A3H Promotion Ltd (Chapter 10) and was looking for an opportunity to flex my journalist muscle buoyed up on my contributions that Roy had published in *Pogo'til I Die*. I wanted to draw people's attention to the music nights at the CCC and how this could address the issues raised by the paper. I wrote a two page "open letter to the editor" of the Chorley Guardian to "...take issue with everyone in Chorley both young and old and to ask all your readers to do something about it". The key points in my rant were:

a). I had grown up in Euxton and, as a teenager, felt there was little on offer for a "youngster" in that small village back then – hence I had to go to youth clubs in Leyland. But, now, as a parent and father of two daughters (who would be teenagers in 4-6 years) it seemed little had changed as there was nowhere for them to go in Withnell or Brinscal at that time either – how little had changed in twenty years!

I wanted to be able to put them on a reliable bus service, confident in the knowledge that there would be somewhere for them to go that provided a safe environment while they entertained themselves for a few hours at the weekends.

b). Parents/grand parents had created the generation gaps but we/they could bridge this by getting involved in what was going on in their communities. *"....we are detached and the family unit is now very different to 20/30//40 years ago. Then the opinions/wisdom of age was available as a guide to the young. What can you offer now? You youngster take time to listen and have some respect for those who may have lived through poverty, fought in wars and even instigated the sexual revolution you take for granted (they)...have more to offer than you give them credit for or will ever learn from a glossy magazine or Technicolor web site. You elders be prepared to listen to the youngsters for they are often far more intelligent than you think and ....more concerned for their future - in a world you created for them – than you would imagine possible".*

c). *"The Media, news papers, TV, Local radio – what have you done to close the gap and advertise/feature what the youth really want? How many of your reporters/readers are in the age group you refer to (13-16)... let them have a stake- they are your future readers/viewers/listeners what opportunities exist for them now?"*

d). Finally, *"... as evidence of what is sadly lacking support and is a solution in front of your eyes, I draw your attention to the CCC. A music project has been set up and is currently running there. Notably voluntary input from people who give a damn – namely Russ Carlton, Ben Greenaway and Phil Baker who (with the help of a small grant from Chorley Council).... staged a BOTBs and attracted regular groups of kids in the 11-16 age group over seven weeks culminating in the final on 17th August...."*

On the 18th September the Chorley Guardian printed a shorter version as "make use of the facilities is John's rallying call... a community campaigner... says this is not politics but value for money. We expect that from supermarkets or holiday tour operators but not when it comes to what's going on, on our own door steps....."

I sent a copy of the video I recorded during the BOTBs to Lindsay Hoyle (Chorley's Labour MP) "... to show what this (CCC) ramshackle state of a place can offer... It did open on Fridays but due to lack of support is focusing on Saturdays until demand rises....it is there now with music and live bands, and aiming to be a non alcohol zero tolerance drug environment. And with support and finance in can be so much more".

I had not asked for the tag of "community campaigner" but shortly after the article was printed, I got a call from Colin Evans of the Board of the CCC trustees. We met at the CCC and by way of a news letter he edited from May/June 2002 (which I refer to now) he summarised the history of the building. *It started as a Baptist Chapel and Sunday school in 1900. The chapel was on what is now the car park until it got burned down in the early '50s and was landscaped by the then Chorley Urban District Council. The land was owned by*

Inskip -one of the oldest hirers who subsequently sold it to Chorley Council. In the '60s the local Rotary Clubs, Round Table and Lions got together to provide a venue for charities, groups who were starting up and others who could not afford commercial rents. Run by a trust and registered by the Charity Commission, the centre provided basic needs for the founding hirers. Due to economic decline and the lack of maintenance the centre nearly closed in the '90s. Due to the "unstinting effort" by the then Chairman, Peter Durrigan, improvements were made against a back drop of vandalism. Colin told me that the centre was leased at a peppercorn rent from the Council but there was a need to raise revenue against increasing costs. He asked for my thoughts on the future of the centre and what I could offer to help achieve this. I liked Colin and what he and the Trustees wanted and agreed to be co-opted onto the committee and I began my involvement with the machinations of running the live music nights. Chris Mellor was Cultural Development Manager for Chorley Borough Council and at that time the CCC was the focus of music and cultural projects that the Council wanted to provide for the community. The CCC was regarded as a cultural centre for young people to practice music skills, giving them the opportunity to meet and, along with other hirers, to form a powerful lobby to obtain Lottery funding for their individual interests. With an increase in usage there was a feeling that the CCC would have a knock on benefit from the improvements to the stage, lighting, public address, decoration, another furnishings for the benefit of all. To his credit Chris got the funding for the BOTBs competition and took an active interest in the CCC and we would often bump into each other at most of what I went on to do in Chorley.

The home grown bands that evolved from the Punk Revival gigs at the Labour Club (on Friday Street) had relocated to the CCC and the buzz about the place was electrically sweaty. By the end of the year Saturday nights at the CCC between 7.30 and 11pm was the place to be for the kids who liked the various genres of guitar based music. The success of the Saturday "Hype nights" that Ben, Russ and Phil organised had led to the formation of the Chorley Community Music Consortium. I was asked to join this too and, in due course, became its Chairman for a while. Over the following twelve months I was given the opportunity to take on a lot of other roles- most were linked to Chorley which had become the centre of a small music phenomenon. The reputation of Saturday night gigs at the CCC started to attract bands from Manchester and Liverpool and other venues in Chorley picked up on live music and quickly established their own nights (e.g. Harry's Bar on St George's Street). On line message boards like Prestone helped keep everyone informed of what was happening and if a band pulled out or needed help with equipment – someone was found who could play or help. I have many brilliant memories of that community spirit/buzz and the working week was geared toward what was happening in Chorley on Saturdays. I videoed as many of the CCC gigs I could get to. The place was packed with bouncing crowds giving encouragement to musicians to have a go at playing live. For many it was often their first time on a stage and we were swamped with requests from newly formed bands to play at the CCC. It was a fantastic atmosphere and for a while the confidence it inspired felt like the possibilities were endless.

The trustees wanted to ensure that things were run without incidents and the police liked the fact that the youth of Chorley had somewhere to go. But there were occasions when fighting broke out by the bus station between "Goths/Emos/Metal Heads and the "Townies" or CHAVS. I'd hear of some kids walking home being set upon because of the way they dressed – which reminded me of the Troggs/Bonehead rivalry and the opposing factions during the Punk Wars. Vandalism inside the CCC was a problem too and Ben organised security guards to work on the doors and inside the Centre. Bags were checked for alcohol or anything else that was being smuggled in and patrols back stage were to discourage any "in appropriate" behaviours. Offenders caught were professionally ejected and barred.

Meanwhile, Russ and Ben expanded the Hype nights to Preston and a flyer I have for 4th April 2003 advertises **Faultline, Enima** and **The Remote INCA School** to appear at "Storm (opp Bus Station) 6.30 till 9.30pm £3 members/£4 others". Ben offered me the opportunity to be part of the Hype Night "franchise" and suggested I arrange for an introduction to Ronnie Brown at The North Bar. This lead to what turned out to be a financially disastrous run of gigs there for me that I was left funding in the run up to the *"It's Not Cricket!"* festival in the June. I had committed to the nights out of a misguided sense of loyalty to the Hype ideal and the belief that if it could happen in Chorley and Preston I could make it happen in Blackburn.....but not... as it turned out, on a Monday night! Sometimes I wonder what stupid pills I was taking at that time!

Despite what I have said elsewhere against the practice of pay to play promotion, we did introduce an Incentive Scheme at the CCC in response to those bands who did make an effort to bring a crowd in. It was a mild way of preparing them for gigs out of town by getting them use to the reality of pay to play. We sold this as an incentive rather than a stick and advertised it as an opportunity:

You will find attached .jpg files of flyers with regards to your gig, there is one for each band. Please print, photocopy and distribute this flyers amongst your fans and all parties who might be interested in attending this gig. Tell them to hand in the flyer on the door as they pay their entrance fee (£3) when they arrive at the venue.

At the end of the night we will tally up the number of flyers we have received for each band playing. Whichever band we have the most flyers for will receive payment according to the following table.

Less than 20 flyers: No pay.

Between 20 and 30 flyers: £1 per flyer.

More than 30 flyers: £30

So each week one band will get the chance to earn between £20 and £30 providing they bring at least 20 people and they bring more than any other band playing.

Hype at Chorley Community Centre is a non-profit making event; all profits made are channelled back into the centre to improve facilities and equipment and to fund future events. We would love to be in a position to pay all bands that provide the entertainment for this event but due to recent expensive repairs and maintenance work this is just not practical at the current time. We believe this incentive scheme is .... a great way for us to help each other out.

We are aware that out of town bands may be at a disadvantage with this scheme, but it will still help to improve the crowd numbers for your gig, and who knows, if you play often, build up a following and get a database of fans you could be the ones claiming the rewards in a short time. If you for any reason should cancel your gig on this date it is your responsibility to tell the fans who you have passed flyers on to.

Code of Conduct

All bands are expected to agree and sign a code of conduct stating that they will respect the venue, other bands, customers and all equipment within. See attached Document for details.

Membership

We are encouraging all CCC band members and customers to become official Members of Chorley Community Music Consortium (CCMC) the group who run the 'Hype' gigs. This will have a number of advantages with creating a work-ing musical community surrounding the gigs....By January 1st 2004 member-ship will become compulsory and non-members will need to be 'signed in' to gigs, perhaps at a higher admission price. Membership is totally free and to register all you need to provide is your name, contact details (email preferred) and a date of birth. There will be plenty of opportunities to register at the gigs, or you can email back now with your details.

Meanwhile, back in Chorley I met Michelle Graham from South Lancashire Arts Partnership at one of the CCMC meetings. She encouraged me to form a splinter section and to apply for a Lottery Grant to address the needs of the under 18 year old kids specifically interested in music. This lead to the formation of Music & Arts for Chorley Youth (M.A.C.Y), for which I set up the bank account and took care of all the meetings and administration. I am proud of what we formed M.A.C.Y for as the words of its constitution and intentions are commendable:

Mission Statement.

"M.A.C.Y believes in the discovery, encouragement, and promotion of the longer term development in young people's talents for music and art".

Formation and aims.

A group of the younger volunteers who sit on the Chorley Community Music Consortium [CCMC] committee have decided to broaden the appeal of the work of the CCMC by setting the following aims:-

1. *To explore and apply for any grants and funding that is not available to the CCMC.*

2. *Should such funds become available, they are to be used to establish a legacy of music & art making opportunities in areas of social and economic need.*

3. *To improve the overall opportunities for musicians and artists across all styles and genres.*

4. *To champion the value of music and art and demonstrate that both have an invaluable part to play in advancing the education and social development of young people.*

5. *To establish opportunities through holding events and workshops that will prove how music and art are forces for regeneration in communities, fostering social inclusion and community cohesion.*

Organisation, structure and rules. *From the initial meeting on 3/6/04* this constitution has been agreed by the members and supported by the South Lancashire Arts Partnership [S.L.A.P] on the following basis*: -there followed 15 points on governing the day to day matters. We then set out our aims:

MACY has set itself up on the understanding it will be successful in obtaining grant funding in order to fulfil its initial aims for its formation. Therefore, assuming this to be the case the following are agreed as its initial objectives: -

Battle 4 the Bands *– the CCMC has empowered MACY to select, organise and arrange for prizes for this competition amongst unsigned bands and musicians who wish to enter. This started on 5th June 2004 and will end on the final on 31st July 2004.* From this a DVD was produced with songs and interviews with **Capulet, My Theory, Three Ways West** and (Winners) **Dead Jim.**

Music & Arts Festivals *– it is hoped that MACY receives sufficient funding to stage an open air event in Chorley with the help of other organisations [e.g.*

SLAP] with the first anticipated to be in September 2004. This will require the hire and /or purchase of appropriate equipment, payment of staff and associated costs in staging a festival of Music & Art. It would then be MACY's ongoing objective to hold such events at least twice a year.

Our grant application was successful and we got £5000 and we did set up and ran a BOTBs with the finalists being filmed at the CCC. We used Seal Films and the DVD featured **Hara Kiri, 3 Yards of Sausage** (one of whose Dad's appeared on it in interview with Michelle Graham), **Spaz The Apple Core, Elohym, Chris Cardwell, Matt Swift, Homemade Memory, Dead Jim, Aurota,** and Capulet. There was a bonus featuring **Magic Sam** (a magician), The Commies "Time Won't Tell" video, photos by Dave Gilmour of all the above, those who helped out on the day and some of the crowd. The back ground music is by Elcho and I got interviewed on camera by someone and spouted on about the event and future plans for MACY.

When the copies were ready we held another festival at the Football club at Windsor Park where I met Shaun Maxwell for the first time. A year later in October 2005 the money left from the grant had to be used up or returned to the lottery. We ran a competition to set up a website. The winners got cash and the remainder was used to buy a laptop and printer for the use of in publicising MACY and its future events etc.

In time, as I became too busy away from Chorley, I relinquish my role, bank account and equipment to Neil Aspinall who was doing a splendid job at the CCC with various youth projects and Chorley FM which stated broadcasting from the rooms there. It became a hub for kids to go and learn how to make music on computers as well as having the refurbished facilities in the CCC at their disposal. In that sense MACY fulfilled another of its longer term goals:

Workshops and regular events *– based on the success of the CCMC's Hype! Nights …it is MACY's objective to organise and run similar concerts that appeal to a wider genre of music e.g. Classical, Folk, Hip Hop, RAP, Drum & Bass and music derived from other ethnic minority groups on a rotational/regular basis. Artist, which can include painters, glassworkers, photographers, film makers, actors, dancers etc will be encouraged to hold exhibitions of their work/concerts alongside appropriate musical performances – hence culminating in the festivals as above. Furthermore, MACY seeks to link up with similar bodies to itself in other parts of the UK and abroad to undertake exchange events with local musicians and artists. It is also hoped that musicians and artists will hold workshops around the events MACY organises.*

None of this would have happened if the kids of Chorley had not wanted it or gone out their way to support it. They did this by picking up instruments, forming bands and attending the gigs. This is something every generation does and I will be eternally grateful to those who did and everyone who allowed me the opportunity to be part of it. This book is partly my way of thanking Chorley as well as documenting the people who were part of it. With this in mind I would like to record some names deserve a special mention here because of their involvement with this chapter.

Tom Farrington and Charlotte-Jane Seward. Tom, AKA "Son of Cheesley"- a student at that time who helped me set up MACY and was its first Chairman. Tom lived in Brinscal and was one of the CCC regulars who went on to book bands and help run the Saturday nights. He was the guitarist in **Drop in the Ocean** – a metal inspired band that I saw a few times and arranged to be videoed by Flea Pit films. Tom had to put up with a lot from bands and musicians as any promoter has to. But, at that very first level of the unsigned music scene there is no professionalism just plenty of tantrums amongst prima donna wannbees. Charlotte was a student too who helped set up MACY at the start and sometimes introduced bands at the CCC.

Michelle Graham – I never knew anyone else directly involved with the South Lancashire Arts Partnership and thought it was her own enterprise because everything seemed to revolve around her. She encouraged me and made a lot of good things happen for the youth and infrastructure available to them in and around Chorley. In particular she brought much needed focus and investment to what developed at the CCC. I never had a cross word with her, always approachable and willing to help when and where ever she could.

"Spike" and "Tink" – well know amongst those involved with the CCC who did their best to oversee Saturday nights. I saw firsthand what they had to put up with that others did not see. Spike had to arrange the sound on many occasions and the life of any sound tech is a thankless one. Tink looked after the "catering" area – which was where the old kitchen use to be and from where soft drinks, crisps and sweets were available.

Tony Brookes – long suffering sound engineer in the early days of the CCC before Spike.

Amanda – another student at the time who took the door receipts and helped me out doing the same at gigs I put on elsewhere. She was in touch with what the kids wanted and made a number of observations that helped with feedback to the various committee meetings I attended.

The door/security staff – I apologise for not remembering your names but you know who you are but amongst the credits to the MACY DVD are **"Emma, Dave, JJ, Shell, Chaz, "Punk" Alan, Lindsay, Andrea and Charlotte!"**

Finally, it is hard to pick out the best memories from all the performances I saw at the CCC but if pushed to then it would be: the BOTBs final in August 2002 for reasons stated elsewhere. **The Malibu Stacy** appearance was personally satisfying as it was my way of thanking Bruce McKenzie for the help he gave me. One of the more colourful performers were Baby Bitch a four piece that was fronted by Stephen Buckley and had one of my favourite tag lines *"sound of metal wearing a feather boa with slick riffs and dirty grooves.*

Last, but by no means least, I know that for many CCC regulars it was Saturday 20th December 2003 – Let's Not Lose Mars to the Commies last ever gig. Hannah and Holly came along and videoed the event from the balcony. This meant that what I wanted for my kids had become a reality and the principles of MACY were the legacy of one Community Campaigner – not bad achievement after all eh!

Left: The first gig flyer I saw which was given to me at Townsend Records advertising the BOTBs in Chorley - very significant. Below: Inside the CCC on a typical busy night.

08 Pretendgirlfriend

(Dedicated to every musician who felt they never reached their potential)

Are your expectations for this chapter prompted by any of the following?

a)   The suggestion of a clandestine relationship in my past?

b)   Your own interest in Pretendgirlfriend (the band) from Burnley and their history.

c)   To understand how and why this band became, and continues to be, so important to me.

I congratulate you on all of the above. No, I have not had an affair or any relationship outside my marriage – sorry to disappoint you, but I respect the thinking. Yes, this is a chapter dedicated to both of the later but it is not entirely one or the other as our stories are intertwined. I could add a fourth option of:

d) Interested in why local bands are not better known and who or what is the cause of this.

That last option is the deeper reason I wanted to write this chapter. In so doing I hope it will give the fans, relatives and others who know this band, what they want in terms of the background and the context of their story so far. It may help others involved - the bands, musicians, promoters, managers, fans etc- to understand either their own part in it – as contemporaries (past and present) or those of you considering or about to take your first steps into local music. What follows is a biography of a four-piece indie rock band that started as teenagers and is still going in their thirties. They have had highs and lows but I invite you to judge on what level you think they had successes and the causes of their failures to this point. Along the way, I wrestle with my own involvement - the positive and negative effect I had as their manager and will always have, I hope, as a fan. Therefore, their experiences and mine, should help everyone fascinated with what it is to be successful in this form of entertainment, art or business we like, love or loath, depending on our own perspectives to it.

A different kind of kitchen muisc

Can you recall occasions when you remember exactly where you where when you first heard a song that becomes a life time favourite. Consider a live concert you went to where a band's performance moved you so profoundly that the experience has stayed with you ever since. The following is what happened to me after taking the initial feeling, meeting the band and going on to managing them for a few years. The concert was a gig at The North Bar, Town Hall Street, Blackburn, on 4 July 2002 - a Thursday night at about 8.30pm- to be precise. The band concerned being Pretendgirlfriend. I was there to review their set and those of two other bands playing that night and maybe get some interviews. I hoped that, if the material was good enough, it would be printed the fanzine *Pogo'til I Die* or even the local papers. I wanted to enjoy the experience of watching three bands I had not seen before – the others being The Iinviisiibles and Goldblade.

The evening started with an introduction from, Ronnie Brown, to interview London base quirky Rock trio The Iinviisiibles in the upstairs front room. I was nearing the end of the interview, relaxing and chatting away, when Pretendgirlfriend struck up their guitars. Realising I needed to be elsewhere, I said my goodbyes and rushed downstairs. I knew instantly that they were a very different local band to **Rocket Dog** (from Darwen) who I had seen at the same venue the month before. They were older for a start and transfixed me by their tighter sound and no nonsense delivery. I had to jolt myself to hit the record button on my camcorder. As I stared down the lens, I knew I was having an extraordinary experience – a timeless *Eureka* moment.

These lads had grit and determination etched into every riff. *Over My Head*, in particular, stood out as an unrelenting tank of a tune. Three bars of three chords followed by the fourth bar two-chord riff - it bulldozes along at a moderate pace. Subject matter is the neighbourhood title tattles or *gossip radio* and how we should let it go over our heads! Wow, that had attitude, garden fence observations, and a realism that struck a note in me that still resonates today. Their set was over after a few more tunes of similar quality and I was stunned, motionless — my thoughts suspended during the brief moment of silence before the interval music came on. I kicked back to reality. I <u>had</u> to talk to them - I just had to! I was not thinking in terms of me the journalist but as an instant fan. I was a follower in whatever direction they were going which was a room at the back, which was the kitchen when the building was once Chequers restaurant. Its use now was for the bands to store equipment. I had to take a breath, collect my thoughts and process what I had just witnessed. I started to rehearse my words of introduction when -shit! I realised in a flash of panic – Ronnie had always been there to smooth the way with the others I had interviewed up to that point. I was going into this without an introduction. What if I ballsed it up...perhaps they would not be interested or sufficiently warmed up by Ronnie's words... and, if it got back to Ronnie that I was hassling his acts it meant....oh... double shit! However, before I could change my mind it was too late. I had knocked on the door, they opened it and, whatever I said must have come across all right. I stepped over their guitar cases, rucksacks and array of wires and was soon standing awkwardly amongst the cold steel benches and large redundant cooking ranges. I was "in", in the mix up of the moment and quickly into conversation with Simmy, Noel and Smit. Danny was elsewhere - probably at the bar.

What I remember most from this first meeting was the trio's down to earth ordinariness. The first band I met who were not on a record label, unfamiliar with giving interviews – but they were raw talent, East Lancashire locals and genuinely nice lads. I did not know anything about them, they did not know me and neither of us knew what use we could be to each other. I felt a need in me to help them in any way possible. I had a purpose to what I had started a few weeks before. Here was a band I liked both as people and for the Indie/Rock style of music they were playing. Simmy and Smit told me years later that a friend of theirs, Roy Bright (**Depon Eye** and **Exit State**), said to them that if anyone showed interest in them they should treat them "with respect". In our own ways, that was what we were doing on that balmy summer's night in 2002. We formed a bond that has grown stronger over time.

"First date impression with Pretendgirlfriend"

This is the title of my interview, which was a combination my scribbled notes and an edited version of a biography Simmy had put on the band's website at that time. My favourite part was when they ask if they could lie about their ages (19-26) which endeared me to them even more as we explored their hopes for the future *"We enjoy music but we play what we'd want to hear on our stereo...it's up to people to decide..."*(Simmy). He went on to explain their method of writing, which was that when he comes up with the bones of a song he is comfortable enough to let the others layer their skills on top. I ended the article with *"....I sense that there are no egos here."*

A few days later, I sent a copy to the band with a VHS (video) tape of their set and a couple of photos I had taken of them on stage. In the covering letter (dated 13th July), I wrote, *"I hope you get this in time for the gig on 17th. I printed off some copies that you may want to hand out or put on the tables and if anything gets used in the media – please send me a copy.... let me know of future gigs"*. My accounts show that the expenses for the p&p and materials was £8 for a sort of gift, but it did not seem to matter as I had acquired a new outlet or hobby and the costs were irrelevant. I had an eye on helping this band as well as testing whether my writing was any good. I had no idea what it would lead to but I did feel excited in a way I had not experienced before. I spent the next week on a high of sorts, boosted even more, when I read an email from Smit on 15 July:

"The stuff you sent has arrived I will be collecting it tomorrow from the post office. Our next gig is at the Albion in Clayton Le Moors on Wednesday 17th July. Short notice but only got the gig finalised today. There's another band called 76 Seconds sorry don't know anything about them. Cheers Smit".

This was all I needed – a few simple lines. It was a relief to know that they would soon have my package and Smit had made sure I had the details of their next gig – implying he/they wanted me to go to it. It was a small gesture but such things at that time for me, and I guess for anyone taking tentative steps into this type of unknown, was encouragement I seized upon. Layer by layer those scraps of help, introductions and word of mouth recommendations - builds you up as an individual as well as your profile as a budding journalist, come promoter and every other title I took on over the next five years!

I felt I now *knew* Pretendgirlfriend and they *had* expressed appreciation for what I had sent. All this added up to being the spark that spurred me on - it made me *want* to do more. This endorsement galvanised me into taking my bulky camcorder, pocket camera and awkward note pad to every gig thereafter. It became a behavioural template, I captured as much as I could and I went on to amass an extensive collection with every band I interviewed or wanted to get closer to. Initially, during the next couple of months, my working method was to duplicate a copy of the video footage, keep the original on the Hi8 camcorder tape and print extra copies of the photos to present as a sort of free mini promotional package. It was my way of saying thanks and, as I did not ask for any money, I am sure this helped overcome any suspicions of a hidden agenda. When they accepted what I was doing was genuine – for the love of the music, and my way to help them promote themselves – the result was in the winning of hearts and minds and forging a niche in this very small market. It started with Pretendgirlfriend and that first gig.

Before the end of the month I had a call from Noel, he said he would get a copy of their next recording to me, which I said I would like to review. I did not have a clue of what I could offer beyond being a fan of their music, to give feedback about their performances and songs. I was nobody as far as the music business was concerned so why would any band or musician want to get to know me. I had no record of accomplishment. Okay, I had written a few reviews – but, so what! To any casual observer I was playing at it. I had even justified it to myself as a hobby for God sake! The appreciation from this band and the other first few musicians I met became a tonic to sooth these doubts. I now know that had Pretendgirlfriend told me to "fuck off!" at our first meeting I probably would have and it could all have stopped there – in an instance, full stop, no encore, no decade later and this book etc.But, they did not and I owe them for that.

Claustrophobic Town

Sure enough, at the end of July I received a CD from the band. It is on a silver Memorex disc with "Pretendgirlfriend" written on it in black marker pen and the cover is hand written in blue biro with the track listing 1. *Down on Wednesday* (Oct 2001), 2. *Lemon & Lime* (Oct 2001), *Claustrophobic Town* (Oct 2001), 4. *Limbo* (Aug 2002), 5. *It's Not The End of The World* (Aug 2002), 6. *In Your Pocket* (Aug 2002) 7. *Over My Head* (Aug 2002). Below this is a note *"Hi, John we would be grateful if you could review our CD. Phone me on receipt, Cheers, Simmy"* - adding his mobile number. In those days, the post arrived early in the morning, i.e. before most people left for work 7.30/8am.Some details you never forget and that day I know that I was on my way over to Accrington on the newly opened M65. I slipped the disc into the cartridge, housed in the boot of my car – you could load about half a dozen – unlike the front loader I have today. Down the short stretch of the A674 to the Houghton Arms roundabout. At some point, I adjusted the stereo control panel to find the number of this recent addition. As soon as it started, I was struck by the quality of the recording. It was way beyond what I had expected. Professionally produced, it was not some hollow studio effort like those I had heard to date from other bands. No, this was at a standard I could put alongside any of the commercial CDs I had in the stacker at that time. The musicianship I took for granted but I had to remind myself that this was not a Beautiful South or the latest Manic Street Preachers offering. This was an unsigned band from further up the road to where I was going. You had to go back to The Milltown Brothers to find any artist from that part of the country who had made any impact on the charts and that was nearly ten years previously ("It's All Over Now Baby Blue" in July 1993 on A & M records, by the way). Pretendgirlfriend, from Burnley, just over that hill - I thought – a few miles away - on my bloody door step.... *and* , big deal......I actually *knew* them – I had met this band – they knew me and I was so incredibly proud. Yes, "proud" that what I was hearing was absolutely, undeniably and straight down the middle -GOOD.

Of the magnificent seven tracks - *Claustrophobic Town* was the song that hit me squarely in the chest as I cruised the rush hour that early autumn morning. I wanted to pull over and listen to it without the distractions of driving – to appreciate its perfection. Smit's distant riffing guitar intro comes closer, as Danny's snare and side tom steadily rise in volume - racing to the climax of a crescendo that hits the apex on Simmy's six note, six note four note four note lead repeat rammed home by Noel's driving bass. The song ranks with any of my all time favourites and the best of those times when I drift away to another place, as if the sounds have delivered me into an aural haven. The John Peel's *Teenage Kicks* epiphany when what your ears are sensing grabs you in a way that never lets you go. I know this is not unique all music fans know what that feels like - the raised hairs at the back of the neck, widening of the pupils and quickening heart beat. More famous songs that have done this to me are; *In The City* (The Jam), *This Charming Man* (The Smiths), *Dreams* (Cranberries), *Boy in the Bubble* (Paul Simon) and many more less known songs. In late 2002 it was *Claustrophobic Town* which became an addition to all these and it was **the** song that hooked me into Pretendgirlfriend. From then to now, I regard the band as one of the best of the unsigned scene I have ever had the privilege to know and I regard Martin Simm as being amongst the best songwriters I have ever met.

Volume 12

For those of you who do not know Pretendgirlfriend or for those who think you do – I have put the following band biog together with the help of Noel, Simmy and Smit; Danny and his whereabouts are unknown at the time of publishing.

At the start of 1999, Simmy and Smit had gone from jamming sessions at each other's houses to rehearsing at their friend's house. Her name was Manfa (Samantha Higgins) who was to be the band's singer as neither Simmy nor Smit felt they had a voice good enough to do the job. Eddie ("Ed") Stimpson, who was a work mate of Simmy's from Pendle Council, offered to play Bass. He was older, in his late thirties, and wanted to join, having listened to Simmy talk about his plans to form a band. Ed had two conditions for helping them out - he would stay until either they got a younger replacement or, two years had elapsed. After a few practices, Manfa moved onto backing vocals, as it was felt her voice was better suited to this role. Simmy took on lead vocals – having gained more confidence. Ed helped them find a drummer called Arnie (a "biker" from Leek in Staffordshire). Another friend, Matt Gains, got them gigs by asking around and was loosely referred to as their manager. Volume 12 soon had two original songs when they played their first live set at on open mic session at the Rhythm Station in Rawtenstall. Smit recalls a *surprising appreciation* from the crowd. This was Manfa's first and last public appearance with the band, and, Smit and Simmy felt that it was an amicable departure for all concerned *...there was no hard feelings*. Next was a gig at Arnie's hometown of Leek before he parted company too being replaced in July by the talented sixteen year old from Darwen - Daniel Spink who had spotted Ed's add in the local paper.

Unfinnished Business

After a summer of practicing, on 8th October, the band took on a new name "Unfinished Business" and played at the Kierby Hotel, Burnley. This was one week after the birth of Simmy's first child, Liam.

Pretendgirlfriend

Two months later, they had their first Manchester gig at The Star and Garter and changed their name to Pretendgirlfriend. The Pretendgirlfriend name originated form Paul Walby. Paul was a friend of Simmy and Smit. He was five foot four and they nick named him "Whopper". It was some years earlier when he thought up the name while they were kicking band names about one day when they had nothing better to do. Five years later, the pair recalled it and used it from then on. The Star & Garter gig was disappointing. Simmy recalls that *"...it were shite – proper run down place, where we took ten people with us and .... We had the cost of travel, charging our mates £3 entry to watch us play to them thirty miles from home"*. Undeterred, they soldiered on over the following twelve months with a series of local gigs, notably: Queens Arms (Darwen) The Carlton (Burnley), Cellar Bar (Blackburn), Starkies (Padiham) and the Punch Bowl (Earby). The attendance was good at first and then it tailed off as the novelty wore thin. Meanwhile, they got through a lot of rehearsing and socialising in their adopted HQ - Abacus Studios, in Hapton, where another band, **Spitfire**, also rehearsed and they did a few gigs with them. By April 2000, they felt ready to record their first EP at Abacus Studios entitled *Face of the Alien*. Produced by Ian Hartley, Pete and Shaun Tye, it is three tracks and a reasonable effort after all the rehearsing and gigs. The result is not unlike the Manics "New Art Riot" EP – which is how I described it in my first review – a snap shot of a band forming its sense of identity. Apart from the title track, it includes *19 St John's Road* and *Don't Care*. The main aim for the band was to have something to listen to outside the rehearsals - to get a better feel for the songs. In the summer of 2001, Ed, true to his word, left the band. Noel Duffy, who had been introduced by Spitfire, replaced him. Noel fitted into the band very quickly and made his debut at the Bands in the Park Festival in Burnley in July. His commitment to the band was cemented when he came back early from the Leeds Music Festival to play their next two gigs during the August Bank Holiday Blues Festival weekend at The Derby Arms in Colne.

With support from their growing fan base and, following a recommendation from Abacus Studios, they recorded a more confident follow up EP **Down on Wednesday** at Studio Studio, Whitworth with producer Pete Troughton in late 2001.Again, including the title track, were *Lemon and Lime* and *Claustrophobic Town*. This recording experience was markedly different from Abacus. Instead of the band doing all the work, all they felt they had to do with Troughton was play and invent.

2002 became the start of a major change in the band's fortune. The year started quietly after a few gigs at the North Bar including a support slot for **Fi-Lo Radio,** Simmy played a number of solo acoustic gigs around the area too and a support for **10 Stone Dead** at Kendal. Most importantly was securing the support slot to a sold out gig at The North Bar, with The Fall on 19th April. This lead to their return gig there a few months later, when I met them.

That is the end of the first part of the Biog. What follows is the continuation of their story from a suitcase of papers I amassed since and what all of us can remember. It is as accurate as we can make it but we are not claiming it to be the definitive version. Some of you will remember things differently. Hence, anything you do not agree with is perhaps due to our interpretation and a different angle of hindsight to yours. This is a story of the band and me on a joint quest, and, like any adventure, it does not always go smoothly or end as perfectly as we would like it too. It may not follow the path you want or bring to where you expected.

The first gig I promoted

The opportunity for me to help the band directly came when I asked them to be one of the four bands I wanted to play at the launch party of my business - A3H Promotion Ltd (see Chapter 10). This was at The Marque Club, Preston on November 6th. Some of those details are relevant to Pretendgirlfriend's story here as they demonstrate what options I had at that time and how the band fitted into what had escalated around me in the few months since I first met them. When Pretendgirlfriend played my gig, it was the second time I had seen them live. When they went on stage, due to being so busy on that night, I did not have time to watch their entire set. In time, I came to learn not to make my mind up about anyone based on the first sighting. Rather like listening to music, it can take a while to appreciate whether something is good or bad and if I truly like or dislike it and, more importantly, whether I wanted to be associated with it or not. Second sighting of Pretendgirlfriend was not a disappointment. Despite not being able to focus on all their set, watching the video of it a few days later was enough to confirm what I felt about them and made me want to be more involved with their future.

I hoped my way of going about things at the launch party did endear me to the four of them. I paid them the agreed cut of their ticket sales, a share in the door take *and* their van hire – an additional cost I had not paid to any of the other three bands that night. However, it was important to me to show my integrity as I remembered Simmy had been vocal about being ripped off by other promoters. It had stuck in my mind and was echoed by nearly every other band and musician thereafter. The "pay to play" side of the music business is a recurring issue throughout my time in the industry and still goes on to day. For now, let us leave it there and, for the record, it was as a matter of principle that I adopted a different way of doing gigs and I am certain this attracted me to Pretendgirlfriend.

Pretendgirlfriend on the airwaves of Chorley

The next opportunity to help them happened when they accepted my invitation to appear on the Chorley radio sessions. It was on the Saturday 30th November - Simmy, Smit and Noel came to do the interview with me. They arrived about 7.30pm, just enough time before their gig at Chorley Community Centre (CCC) the same night (which I had also arranged for them). Danny was suffering a cold so he stayed back at the venue. They handed me their four new recordings from their latest Studio Studio sessions grouped under the title track *It's Not The End of The World* others being *Limbo, In Your Pocket* and *Over My Head*. The other CDs they bought included The Clash, Guns'n Roses - *"...the first guitar band I got into in the late eighties"* (Simmy), Nirvanna - *"Who bridged the gap between Heavy Rock and the Indie guitar scene and made it cool to play guitars again..."* (Simmy), Sex Pistols and The Wildhearts.I have transcribed a section of the interview that summarises where they were at this point in their career:-

(Me) *What has been the worst gig you have played?*

(Simmy) *There's been a few...I'll tell you what it is with the local scene - it's hard work and I think we're at the point now when most bands call it a day to be honest with you. Certain pub gigs haven't gone down so well. We've playeds in our own town at the local pub...Starkey's and there were about six people there – some people get it and some people don't and they didn't.....*

(Smit) *Well, I think the problem is the people going into the local pubs are not generally going in for the music they are just going in for a drink. Proper music venues where people have come to hear bands play, we will go (down) a lot better there.*

143

Simmy goes on to recommend the Carlton in Burnley where they *–are use to having bands on every Friday night and they are a supportive crowd even if they are not that keen. Like we've done a few gigs down there and lads said "hey, that were brilliant but it's not really our sort of music". They tend to be into Pink Floyd and there seems to be a Pink Floyd tribute band base there.*

Immediately after their interview that night, Russ Carlton came in for his interview. Russ was a part time gig promoter currently in the middle of running the hugely successful Battle of the Bands competition at the Aquellenium nightclub in Preston. The club was packed with students and other under 25 year olds – which was helped by heavy sponsorship and advertising courtesy of the Lancashire Evening Post. Entry on Tuesday nights before 10pm was only £1 and it did not close until 2am. Simmy and Smit had talked about single figure audiences in small pubs around Burnley in a depressed and some-what fatalistic tone. This could have given listeners one impression of the band and may have accounted for poor attendances at their gigs. However, Russ juxtaposed this. He was enthusing about his club night and the 200 plus people who were coming to see his bands there every week. The conclusion is obvious - either play in Preston at one of these nights or do something else to get more people to watch you! Pretendgirlfriend needed to get in front of bigger audiences if they were to make any progress. I made a note to see what else I could do to make this happen.

2003: was the year I managed **Let's Not Lose Mars to the Commies** and developed my company way beyond my expectations. Part of my A3H activi-ties included help to Pretendgirlfriend - bringing them to the attention of anyone who I thought could help alongside any opportunities I could provide myself. The band was doing their best to promote themselves and their efforts with the local press paid off. Well, kind of...On 17th January Clive Lawrence did a three quarter page feature on Pretendgirlfriend in the Pulse section of the Burnley Telegraph titled "We're not playing second fiddle now!" With a sub heading "... a support band who want to make their own mark", it has a large picture of Simmy playing guitar and quotes him in another sub heading, after AMBITION in bold type saying:

We want to do gigs that will be more positive for (the) group and move us on.

The article starts "Ambitious East Lancashire guitar band Pretendgirlfriend has a point to prove when they play their first live gig of the year next Friday". While this is an eye-catching start, unfortunately, the "next Friday" at both the start and end of the article, was in fact the 24th and not the 31st January which was the actual date for their gig! The "next Friday" –was the 24th - the night of my gig for Sex Pistols bass guitarist, Glen Matlock at the same venue.

What was their loss may have been my gain. Despite all that, it was a good picture and excellent publicity for Pretendgirlfriend. In his article, Clive highlights Simmy's frustration by the fact that nothing has come from the support slots they have done and how, having shed their early likeness to Oasis, "....the lads are happy with their own mix of guitar rock" quoting Simmy saying:

"It's difficult to pin down our sound to one style or genre. But although it's mainstream, it has got bits of punk in there and it's definitely got an edge".

The entrance for the gig was £1, doors opened at 8pm with "special guests" that turned out to be **Last Living Enemy** (not **Friend of Foe** or **Dumpstar** that appeared in the press cutting). I went to this gig and wanted to see them for a full set, with no distractions, as well as to support what they were doing. My next-door neighbour and good friend, Mick Guy, who had seen them at the Marque Club gig, came too. We agreed that they played with a fiery passion you only get with bands putting on their own gigs in ways you do not when they are part of a bill someone else has asked them to join or paid to play! It says a lot about how Pretendgirlfriend were trying to make something happen for themselves, on their own terms and after four years of mediocre experiences leading to very little, just as the article had noted. I understood what hard work goes into organising a gig. I felt they had pulled together a good night's entertainment. It was a landmark event for them. I was overwhelmed with empathy and got incensed by some scallies sneaking in without paying. I grabbed the microphone from the PA desk saying something like "... Come on lads put a pound in the bucket for the bands - they are doing their bit so do yours by supporting them eh!" Beyond words of encouragement, I did not feel I could do much more to help other than singing their praises to anyone who I felt could help them

That night, I also interviewed them. It provides clues as to what was not happening for them and the reasons why they needed help. It shows a certain fatalism as well as optimism that make me both sigh and laugh aloud when I think of then and now:

(Me) What was your impression of the gig?

(Simmy) – It were all right - good turn – errh.... (some) were fairly into it, but, I dunno we've done better and worse – it were one of them I didn't enjoy it as much as I should – but we haven't gigged for two months so... that'll come...

(Me) What does it take to put a gig together and organise (one) these days – can you talk me through that?

(Smit) Simmy does most of the organising of the gigs. I do the website side of it and I've done the publicity for this gig – the leaflets, Simmy's done the papers and it takes a bit of own funding..

Simmy interrupts by saying it took him four years to track down Clive Lawrence and, despite giving them a write up and picture *"....that was bigger than their piece on Christine Aguilera...."* Clive got the date wrong. With a laugh and a friendly dig at me, Simmy adds that he probably did me a favour as I have explained earlier – but no hard feelings!

(Me) How would you describe the local music scene for gigging then?

(Simmy) Shit! (Pauses). Not that good really you've got to put it on your-selves – you can have £150 at the Carlton or break even at North Bar.....(with a chuckle)...I'd rather break even at North Bar...

(Me) What attracts you to the crowd here – why did you choose this (place) to play?

(Smit) It's a good venue .... People from Blackburn are supportive really, lots of big bands play here, and (it has) a lot of live music..., which is the main reason we come...

(Simmy)...there's nowhere to play in Burnley – for the record don't bother to play in Burnley! You might get (paid) at The Carlton but you've 5 or 6 people watching ya and one man and his whippet at the bar – it's not worth it!

(Me) What do you put it down to – why do people not come out and support local music?

(Simmy) It's a good question John and for once I'm speechless!

(Smit) I think a lot of people (have) hung on to the dance scene – even though it's dying off they're still really into it.

(Simmy) You've got to go to the cities and I've said it before, you know we did Manchester when we first started out and its all basically pay to play. You've got to bring 25 people to watch'ya. You've to pay £50 to play in first place – what's point in taking people who you ram it down their throats every night anyway ...I dunno you've just to go out there and play out of your own town...."

Noticing the new tracks they played - *Barred from the Kings* and *Me and Strange Women*, I ask what they think the crowd's reaction to them was.

(Noel) It were good - they liked it. That other song, which isn't "Strange Women", it starts of in G durrrrrr dur dur dur dur dur dur durrrr (and after a phonetic rendition, he states firmly).... That's a superb song – they liked it!

(Simmy) I think tonight "Barred from the Kings" is the best song in the set. But, what we do is put ourselves up for criticism – we's doin our own stuff. We don't arse about with covers, we get up there, we play it if they like it they like it, if they don't I'm not right arsed about it! If I impress five people out of a hundred then it's a job well done John –d'yu know what I mean!

(Me, nodding no doubt) We first met seven months ago – how would you describe the band's development since then?

(Smit) Well, we've got more from the Oasis sorta fever .... we've had quite a lot of comments about Oasis and being like them so what we've tried to do is change the style of music slightly so it's a bit more up beat getting away from the root chords and getting into the power chords and different riffs. We've worked a lot on harmonies between guitars....

(Simmy)... the others on the local scene they're either really heavy metal or jangle Indie Pop - I think we fall nicely in between the two. We are not getting the attention or profile we deserve. We are, in my eyes, the best-unsigned band in this country – no worries.

(Noel mutters) "That's reet..."

(Simmy becomes louder and there's real passion in his voice) ....we all agree man or else I wouldn't be doin it - I wouldn't be bending over backwards to be getting it goin and we're goin to 'ave it man – I'm tellin ya!

(Me) You were telling me a few weeks ago, that it's a make or break time for the band, really...?

(Simmy) It went through my mind tonight – like this might, be the last gig, I ever play with this band...but you know we've got a little bit of interest – you know 2 or 3 people. I mean some have slagged us off tonight... but I won't go into that.... It's as simple as this reet - if you like us you like us, if you don't – if you've got something horrible to say don't bother saying it just get up there yourself and write better songs than what we're doin at the moment – bring it on –d'yu know what I mean!

(Me) What do you think would help promote Pretendgirlfriend now?

(Simmy) It would take a big, big cash influx –from someone with a lot of money like...errh....I don't know who's got a lot of money...Richard Branson, Tony Wilson, Bill Oddie – anyone like that- who is prepared to fuckin back us d'yuknow what I mean coz I've no money I mean all my money goes on kid you know.

(Me) The CDs that you have cut - what response has that had from sending it round?

(Smit) Well, everyone one who has heard (the songs) has liked (them) so far... some have been into the band and some haven't - even people who haven't have really enjoyed (them).

(Simmy interjects and asks me what my question was but picks up on my early point about) "...what would help...?" (...and adds emphatically....) "...Air play. If we're heard on radio and the records are in the shops, themselves would be emptied – simple as that!"

(Me) What about local record stores, why are they not stocking your CDs then?

(Simmy) Well it's what we're looking at - that –we're going to have a word with Action Records (Preston), Astonishing Sounds in Burnley...on a sale or return sorta thing and I think come spring/summer time we're goin to do an album launch, maybe get back in studio do another three songs and if no one else is interested we'll put it out ourselves....

(Me) I was talking to Smit before and you've brought in some of the old songs and revamped them – what was the thinking behind that then?

(Smit) Well....like I said before...Simmy's worked hard on them and brought them into more of the style we're trying to put forward to ourselves now..

(Simmy)...we're trying very hard to lose this Oasis tag....probably coz of my voice more than how the band sounds...you don't write songs for anyone else – you write songs for what you wanna hear.... "Oh you sound a bit like this, you sound a bit like that...!" I put my CDs on wi 'rest of my CDs you know with The Clash, Pistols, Oasis, Wildhearts – good British bands and that's what it is. I'm not gonna change the style of this band for anyone to get signed – I'll do it myself if I have to.

(Me) The lyrical content has always struck me – everyday situations- like "19 St John's Road" is one and "Over My Head" – what is it that gets up your nose that makes you want to talk about that sort of thing?

(Simmy pause, slight chuckle...pause...) nothing gets up me nose really.... errh, I dunno – everyone asks, "How do you write a song?" I dunno...I just do not know – words just come to ya – at first they just might rhyme but afterwards when you listen to it, when it's been recorded, and you think –yeah – I can get a bit of that – that's coming for me who writes them – I dunno what I'm on about – I dunno it sound alreet doesn't it?

(Smit) What Simmy said to me before is – he works on a song, on a riff and works on lyrics, which rhyme, and ....each song tells a story of some sort .... And he's always said to me that that is never really thought of until it's been written and I've sung it a few times and there is a story there and it's not just a rhyming lyric....

(Simmy) I don't know about any other song writers....that's the way I do it... there's no political stance with this band....there's no errh....no....no....

(Noel) There's no Stella left! (He declares loudly as he re-enters the room having gone out to get another pint......empty glasses salute the air....).

(Simmy) Yyeah – there's no Stella left...! (Laugher all round)....errh.... perhaps that why we're not where we should be – everyone has to have a stance... why bother! Just play music... if you're enjoying it you don't have to stand for anything......I dunno there's a lot of self doubt sometimes – but we're a laid back bunch we don't bounce about the stage...if they like it - it's a little nod of approval

and I know that's a cracking tune and if they're not interested in playin it then I'll dump the song - I'm no dictator. I'm the main songwriter but everyone chips in everyone has an opinion....were I going off the point there John...?

(Me) No... are you looking at an album later this year then?

(Simmy) It's all top of me head stuff this but hopefully a ten track CD out by autumn -be it by a record company or be it on ours own back but we'll do it!

(Pause...Me) – What about reaction on the website – what's the interest been there?

(Smit) It's been running for a year and two months now and we've had two thousand (slowly thinking) and sixty-three hits....and the biggest span of hits has been the last week actually– since we got a bit of publicity in the paper and since we've been promoting this gig tonight – yeah we've had...errh.

(Simmy interrupting Smit, again)... 2BR ....Andrew Turner will play local bands – you've got to meet the criteria: 1. you've got to have to be doin a gig. 2. it's got to be broad castable material (and grabbing my Dictaphone as if to make his point as if this interview was live on radio).... Andrew Turner – send him a CD – he's a good lad!

(Me smiling no doubt and thinking I should never interview a band after a gig, when the adrenalin mixed with alcohol has started to kick in...) *What about gigs coming up – got anything planned?*

(Simmy) 21ˢᵗ February, Northwich – Winnington Wreck – we are doing a gig with ..... Deep On Eye – they're pretty good.

(Smit) It's the gig I sorted out through an email I got by a promoter....

(Simmy) ...but nothing after that ...we might get offered another one after tonight...

(Me) What about submitting something to radio one?

(Simmy) Done that.

(Simmy) Just waiting on a reply! But, again, I dunno - I don't think we fit the bill...we're too poppy...

(Noel) ... they get to hear our new songs and they'll be fucking hell let's play them..! We're best band around here! Them new songs are superb –the crowd like them - we're superb!

(Simmy) It's hard when you're starting off to win a crowd over, like I said before...

(Noel, even more excitedly) - We've got some really good fuckin songs and I don't know why we're gigging round (here)....

(Simmy)... Limbo's a good track...

........and a debate breaks out and I sense that the interview is over and, besides, that the tape is coming to an end I do not want to outstay my welcome.

On the first Sunday of 2013, Simmy called round to mine to play me two new songs he had written - *Whit Sunday Walking* and another one he had not titled. At my request, he played *Squeaky Clean* – which is one of their oldest songs that I'd not heard properly before. Anyway, while talking of the old days, I played the recording of the interview above and another one I describe later about what is cool when it comes to musicians and bands. He creased up with laughter and we agreed that it captured exactly what they were like and felt at the time. The transcripts have not been printed before –and it just goes to show the benefit, as John Robb once told me, to "record everything!" This tapes cuts through the uncertainty of what we remember.

With a little help from our friends

Amongst others who helped the band, back then, was Phil Baker. Phil was (and still is) a local PA supplier and one of the most genuine blokes I met "back in the day". He is a brilliant sound technician who I hired on many occasions. A true professional on every level and always up beat. Phil liked Pretendgirlfriend and he took up my suggestion to let them support his Pink Floyd tribute band called **Pulse** (Echoes of Floyd). Phil played lead guitar and sang in this band and they had their own gig at Chorley Little Theatre at the start of March. I went to this and the stand out Pretendgirlfriend song in their set was *On the Sofa*. I noted in my diary.... "Excellent night. Discussed my thoughts on P/Gs future and how I can help e.g. intro to other out of town bands like **Cornerstone, Maybees, and David R Black** etc".

I kept in touch with all the bands I met and, by way of returning the favour; I would hope they would offer me a support slot for The Commies. Low and behold, that is just what happened with Pretendgirlfriend who offered them a support at the next gig they were putting on at the Inn on the Warf, Burnley in May. Other bands on that night, were, **Cornerstone** (co-incidentally) and **Tessem** (good friends of Pretendgirlfriend who I had met and got on the radio too). I accepted on behalf of The Commies but, as it turned out on the night, it was a miss match of styles. All the bands played credible sets and I took some superb publicity photos of The Commies but they told me afterwards that they had little in common with Pretendgirlfriend. They were right – The Commies were much younger and seeking an entirely different audience. I thanked Pretendgirlfriend for the gig and said I would return the favour by inviting them onto the "It's Not Cricket!" festival. At this event, Pretendgirlfriend selected *Limbo* as their recording and their interview was with all four of them sitting outside on the tables adjacent to the venue. Incidentally, if you get to see this DVD and watch the footage of *Limbo*,

150

you can glimpse Simmy's eldest son, Liam, toddling about and trying to get to the stage. Furthermore, in the festival programme I wrote a feature on Pretendgirlfriend:

"I will not attempt to hide my admiration for these lads from Burnley. Simmy is a song writer of immense talent and Danny, Smit and Noel provide the backbone he rests on in their working class brand of Indie Rock. Their CD is a white print with logo and web site in brick red brown and orange.7 tracks that give their diversity from the fist-punching stadium Rock of "Claustrophobic Town" to subtler slower forms in "Lemon & Lime" and Simmy's growing confidence in his (acoustic) work "In Your Pocket"...they have continually looked to gig and work on new material which is due out in the Autumn on an LPs worth, if all goes to plan. It is fitting that they take their place today as one of the areas only Indie Run's groups worth watching".

The contract I drew up for all the performers on the DVD for "It's Not Cricket!" is signed on Pretendgirlfriend's behalf by Simmy and dated 4th August. On the occasion I visited Pretendgirlfriend – at Simmy's home in Padiham, their reaction was good and I emphasised that they could use the footage as part of their own promotional packs – in addition to the CDs they sent out. No one else was offering this and it was A3H's unique selling point for the bands involved. Thereafter, I was heavily involved with promoting the DVD and The Commies for the rest of 2003.

In the Pretendgirlfriend story it is appropriate, I feel, at this point, to blow my own trumpet on the matter of the DVD. As far as I know, I was the only one offering the DVD package at that time. By comparison, when it comes to other companies help to musicians, this was by way of pay to play or an invite on CD compilation for a fee and promises of distributing it to the bigger concerns in the business. However, for £50, from me, they got an interview, the one song they elected to play live and have professionally filmed, edited and packaged with five copies each – a bargain by any standard. They could cut their footage and present it any way they wanted.

By contrast, an example of the Music Industry CD option came to Pretendgirlfriend from Chromium Records based in Wallasey, Merseyside. The contract is signed in advance by Rebecca Whitfield (Project Manager 24/06/03) and ,despite a bad start - "Dear Potential Girlfriend" (!), it expresses interest "...to place *It's Not The End of The World* on a new music compilation album entitled *Liquid Dreams*". It pushes for a quick response by urging "...that you accept or reject this offer no later than 2nd July 2003". It was similar to the promises that Matchbox Recordings had made to the band prior to our first meeting. For £80, Chromium Records would release the compilation on a CD along with 19 other bands adding "....the big deal is we approach major record companies, publishers and radio stations on your behalf to get you some kind of deal. We have a scheduled appointment with EMI in the summer to present them with this new music. We are hoping to put on a full-scale concert of all artists on this album, which will be in front of media types and industry scouts. We may even offer to sign your band to our label in the autumn when we will be looking for new artists.....the CD is due for release in August/September 2003". All promotional activity would cease in October 2003.The band went ahead in the end but perhaps due to a big response, Chromium Records put out an additional CD that year entitled "Industry standard" which featured the song. Co-incidentally, amongst the other 19 bands were **Black Lines,** who I did actually set up a gig for at The Adelphi, Accrington a few years later, but that had nothing to do with Chromium Records and more to the bands contacting me directly. As for the other 17 bands, I had never heard of at that time or since. There is a postscript to all of this in a letter from Rebecca Whitfield (now "Head of A&R") at Chromium Records, who sent the band a copy of a letter addressed to "Dear In The City "dated 12th April 2004. In it, she says (typo errors have been left in too)...

"I am proud to introduce to you a band called "Pretend Girlfriend". We first stumbled across this ultra talented band when they sent us their demo ten months ago. We then placed then on a new music compilation album called "*Industry Standard*". Having seen this band live myself, I can verify that they will blow the minds of industry professionals at In The City this year. We ask that you give them a strong consideration for performing this year as they have the talent o make it all the way. We cannot recommend them highly enough...."

We did not get an offer to play In the City that year so I will let you make your own mind up about this type of record company "deal" and offers of "help".

Meanwhile, Phil Baker was organising the Council backed three day music festival over the Bank Holiday weekend, in Chorley. He offered Pretendgirlfriend the headline slot for Monday 25th August. The event was on the Flat Iron market/car park in the town centre, featuring local bands of all styles. Phil had rigged up a stage on the deck of a long haulage side loader. This weekend coincided with the hugely popular annual music festival at Leeds and others in Manchester and Liverpool - it was a Bank Holiday weekend after all. Consequently, in Chorley, the attendance for its own "festival" was very poor. In fact, the crowd had dwindled to less than thirty, by the time they went on. The weather was cold and rain threatened all day. With all the elements were against them, they took to the stage sometime around early evening. I did note a very enthusiastic lad at the front singing every word of their set and I think Kirsten (Simmy's partner at the time) was holding Liam and Simmy's parents might have been there too. My diary entry read "...about 20 people watched – pathetic turnout!"

That day Pretendgirlfriend and I meet a band from London called **Renton** who hung around after their gig to watch them. Renton was a three piece from London who we all got on with. This lead to me arranging a few support gigs for Renton and a tentative promise from them that they would get Pretendgirlfriend a gig swap down south – possibly in London itself! There is a perception that any chance to gig in the capital needed to be an objective for aspiring musicians. I did not know if this was true at that time, but later, with the evidence of many who did take that path, I know it to be so, as most ended up with little to show from it other than inconvenience and cost. Meanwhile, given the poor turnout for the Chorley Festival and I posted a CD of their songs and covering letter to Dave Horrocks. He was always asking me to pass on his name to other bands or introduce them to him. I wanted to know what he thought of Pretendgirlfriend and if he could get them a support to bigger bands that were doing well. This contact may have been responsible for two gigs at The Queens in Chorley on 30th October (supporting **Helico**) and an acoustic set for Simmy on 2nd November. The year ended with an interview I had set up for them on a Chorley radio broadcast before a gig at The View (Frodsham, Cheshire).

2004 At the beginning of December 2003 The Commies decided to split up. We all agreed to fulfil the gigs booked up to their final one at the CCC just before Christmas. During this interim, I must have been in communication with Pretendgirlfriend - probably Simmy or Smit, as they seemed to be whom I spoke to most out of the four. I remember a bit of a cat and mouse situation at this time, a case of, who would or would not make the first move. I was considering what my next steps would be - especially management options as I had really enjoyed being the manager for The Commies. My diary entry at the end of 2003 reads-

"At some point before... (My family holiday in Italy)... I came to Burnley to hear what PG had to say about asking me to manage them. The fact that Danny wasn't there meant I would not verbally agree to anything on the spot.... they were all bought into what I wanted to be to them. I said I did not want to manage them the way I had done The Commies as I had lost the plot trying to case them into an A&R role for A3H. What I remember most was

Simmy saying "....we want to play the Apollo (Manchester) in front of 2000 people" How refreshing to (what most other bands would say which was). "Get signed by X records...or....be famous or get better gigs".

While on holiday, I had time to reflect on what I had done right and wrong in my role as a manager for The Commies and I did not want to rush into anything new with any other band. I was in an open frame of mind while mulling over what had happened and another series of "what ifs" was churned around. By this time, I had also become involved in the running of the events at Chorley Community Centre and I wanted to continue my strong ties to the town. Chorley had been good to me and this was my way of putting something back into the community (literally), by volunteering to attend various meetings. From this, I got involved in the longer term plans for the music in Chorley and the facilities available to the kids. I had also become a Director on the board of Chorley FM and put together another schedule of band interviews for the RSL broadcasting in the December - presenting two of the shows myself. Furthermore, I was spending a lot of time travelling, interviewing and reviewing gigs, making new connexions and developing others. I was still writing for *Pogo 'til I Die*, and kept all of the local media informed on what I felt would be news for their readers. This had the knock on effect of blossoming A3H's profile and my own personal reputation and knowledge was growing.

One result from 2003 and managing The Commies was working with David Kay (Red Brick Productions) who called me one day after watching a copy of the "Its' Not Cricket!" DVD. David and I got on very well and he did a promotional video for The Commies as well as filming their last gig at The Roadhouse, Manchester. He and I were tentatively considering a partnership between our two businesses promoting talent through his film company and my contacts with local musicians. The Commies footage gave us an idea. We could help each other while sharing our passion for local music. David had good connections. He had shot videos for The Proclaimers, The Levellers, and was currently working with Pete Doherty (ex Libertines) and his new band The Babyshambles. I was receiving a lot of mail from bands all over England due to the internet and A3H's listing in the Unsigned Guide. More people recognised me when I went out to gigs and I wanted to be at the centre of everything that was going on within a 25-mile radius of Chorley. If I felt, I could help anyone and very rarely charged for my services. I understood a lot more about how the music business worked and I had a lot to offer a band and certainly had more experience and contacts than when Pretendgirlfriend and I first met. Finally, while on that holiday, I read "Black Vinyl, White Powder" – the book written by Simon Napier Bell. He discovered Marc Bolan, and

managed bands as diverse as The Yardbirds and Wham. My dairy notes "…
it made me want the manager tag and the sense of being part of their experience". The key word being - *their*. I did a pros and cons of what being a manager
meant.

"To be or not to be"

The Commies showed me that I did not have all the answers and I did not
want to create any sense of false hope. I needed to make it clear what I could
do and what I was not capable or willing to do…. *if* there was to be a next time.
Nevertheless, I did feel that I understood Pretendgirlfriend as people in ways
I had not with The Commies – who I did not know at all before they asked
me to be their manager. Pretendgirlfriend, in contrast, I had known since the
start and I had a strong relationship with them. I knew I had more in common
with them. They were older: Simmy was a father, Smit was married, and I
thought it would not be long before he started to have kids. I had a paternal
instinct for The Commies, hence, I never drank while touring with them, and
the generation gap was a wide one when it came to conversations on subjects
other than music. Not that it was ever uncomfortable. The Commies were a
terrific bunch of lads but, by comparison, to Pretendgirlfriend, they were all
still teenagers and I was forty so you can guess what I am trying to say here.
Pretendgirlfriend's musical influences were more in tune with my own. The
talks we had had at gigs and by phone had common observations and themes
– we were on a similar wavelength. Their fan base was different – older or
at least closer to my age than The Commies'. Pretendgirlfriend came from a
background I could relate to as all four of them were working full time rather
than being students or recent ex-students. Furthermore, apart from Danny,
the other three were not living at home and I was warming to the opinion
that it all mattered in ways that were reasons to do it rather than for not doing
it. In making my mind up, I *could* see myself as part of their world. If I could
choose whom I wanted to manage next then Pretendgirlfriend was definitely
on the short list.

What could I offer any band as a manager? I was not starting at the beginning as I had done with The Commies. I could hit the ground running and
get them to a point where someone else could step in and take over. I could
see that more clearly within the boundaries I was working to at the start of
2004 than I had at the end of 2002. I sensed the direction I needed to steer
towards and, with a bit of luck, how I would help anyone get what he or she
wanted. All it needed was their agreement to let me give it a go and see what
happened. However, what did a band like Pretendgirlfriend want from a

manager? They said that not being signed would not hold them back and that they would, and had, put out good quality recordings themselves with no one else's help. That was the D.I.Y. punk ethic and technology was enabling bands to be more independent in getting their product to the market place – i.e. the World Wide Web. I could get a band, like Pretendgirlfriend, more gigs - especially further away from their hometown. It all added up to a plan to increase the fan base and, rather like The Darkness had done recently, and Led Zeppelin before them, to use the power of numbers to sell out gigs so that the music business came looking for the band rather than the other way round. Nevertheless, would boil down to mailing others understand that and would they want it? Were they prepared to trust in me and did they want to work as hard as I was prepared to do?

In the margin of a diary note on Wednesday 14th January 2004 I had put under the word "MANAGEMENT" the following list of " what turns me on" - "Impact, Lyrics, Style/does it swing, Image, Imagination and FUN!" and I had added "PG" to a small list of names for A3H in an A&R capacity. On that Friday, I drove up to Carlisle to watch **In Car Stereo** play The Brickyard and meet David Kay who introduced to Andy McCormick (who ran the venue). Others came to meet me there like Ben Smeaton and "Dave" from local band **Chapel Ten** as well as the members of **Cornerstone.** I was considering my options with David Kay and the idea of working together on an "It's Not Cricket II!" The musicians wanted to work with me. They loved the first *"INC"*DVD as it featured **Anodize** from Carlisle as well as **Cornerstone** (from Workington). I was flattered by all the attention. However, given the distance from Cumbria to Chorley, I knew that I had to stay within Lancashire if I was going to be effective. I did keep in touch with these bands for a while and Cornerstone featured in my band lists for gigs for some time after. However, the trip had demonstrated that I had plenty of ways to go next but the pull to be a band manager was the strongest. It was a case of: was I certain that Pretendgirlfriend would be the best for me?

The day after was busy too. I'd helped with the preparation for the CCC gig night line up of **Slick 50, Sudden Death** (who got replaced by **Geoffrey Bungle**, I think) **Resin** and **The Semi Smalls. Duckhunt** were on at Stockport Student Union and I had an interview with Dave Sharp (ex Lead guitarist for The Alarm) as he was playing The Roadhouse, Manchester. I entertained the idea of getting to Stockport to catch up with **Duckhunt** and then travel into town afterwards. At some point during the day, I set up a meeting for the following night with Pretendgirlfriend at Abacus Studios. However, I must have been drawn into the CCC gig as I ended up talking to Jake Maxwell

(Shaun Maxwell's son – see Chapter 9) and invited him to Manchester with me. Jake was great company and he gave me the update on what was happening at the CCC and his thoughts on what was being done well or badly by the management there. After the Roadhouse, I gave Bruce McKenzie a lift home. Bruce had set up the interview with Dave Sharp and asked Jake and me in for a drink. While we chatted, he wanted to know what I had planned. It was always good therapy talking to Bruce as I got things clearer when listening to what his opinions were. He told me that I was one of the few people he knew who were "doing it for real". He reminded me of what Dave (Sharp) had said during the interview – how music had been corporatized and there was a demand for Rock'n roll which was being stifled by people who did not understand the true spirit of Rock'n roll. He praised me for what I had done since I had become involved and gave me a huge boost by saying I had plenty to offer. He said I was someone who got things done by getting out at the grass roots level - whereas others just thought and talked about it but never actually did anything, I did! I don't recall discussing Pretendgirlfriend specifically – had I done so, I might have been there for breakfast as we left the venue after midnight and it must have been close on 3am when we arrived back in Chorley. Driving home, I reflected on one of my favourite Alarm lyrics that refer to people who have plenty to live for and nothing to lose. Why not – I *did* want to manage Pretendgirlfriend.

Definition of success

The meeting at Abacus Studios went well. I had sat in my car outside the unit for a while giving a last minute pep talk to myself and making notes on what I wanted to say, ask and hoped for as a successful outcome. Given my day job as a business manager, I was going through what I knew - preparation, planning and "visualising the outcome" – old habits die-hard! However, inside, upstairs and in the rehearsal room, it turned out to be a lot less formal. I sat on the floor below the drum riser and all four of them sat in a row facing me, smoking and drinking cans of lager. Over the next hour or so, we talked candidly about what we all wanted. I noted that their "definition of success" was:

- *To play the Apollo, Manchester in front of 2000 people singing their songs back to them.*
- *Make a living! £350-£400pw each.*
- *Radio airplay*
- *Recognised by fan base – i.e. one that was reliable/loyal be able to sell loads of records to.*
- *Moreover, make good venues want us to play for them.*

In turn, they wanted me to be their manager. They admitted to being naive in the belief that they could manage themselves. They were not getting anywhere with A&R representatives and felt they needed a "sponsor" for their talents (my word not theirs). I suggested this was the function of a manager – a belief in the band and their abilities- an essential attribute–they agreed. Getting gigs had been hard for them and they had only managed ten in total for the whole of 2003 and I had a helping hand with a few of those. We also agreed that they needed to be doing four gigs a month and ideally one a week by the end of the year. I committed to this being my first objective for them. I talked about image and stagecraft. I offered to video their gigs and analyse them together afterwards. We needed regular meetings to discuss what was working well and what was not. There would be a structure towards improvement in the quality and quantity of the gigs. I threw in the idea of gig swapping with other bands outside East Lancashire as well as with those closer to home that were playing a similar style of music. The theory was to build up a fan base amongst similar bands – even if it meant winning over other bands' fans! Names we banded about were **The Cherries, The Flares, Renton, Cassidy, Only One Mammal, Scary Billy Bob, If All Else Fails, The Bushbabies** and **Atomic Hound Dog** – essentially anything that was not punk or metal. They gave me details of Chromium Records and mentioned the band **Riverside Happy** and Hebden Bridge as a place to gig which is where Smit worked. We concluded the meeting by agreeing that they wanted me to manage them using the resources of A3H to do this and promote them. It was a "shake of the hands" deal between us five to "do our best to make it work". We felt that there was no need for contacts - we either trusted each other or we did not and it was the former from day one to this.

Our first tour

The following day, I set to work by contacting Dave Horrocks. With his help, I set up "The Demo" tour in a matter of days. The lads were flabbergasted by the speed ,number and geographical spread of venues. The tour started at The Shed in Leicester on 22nd January and (initially)12 gigs later it finished at the Peterborough Biker Festival over the bank holiday at the end of May. In fact, as the tour progressed, more dates were added and eventually ended up into the start of June as 25 gigs in total. That number, for six months, is about the same as the total number of gigs they had done over the last two years! Venues along the way included The Limelight Club (Crewe, twice), Night & Day (twice) and Star & Garter (both in Manchester), Slaughter House & Bar Fly (Liverpool), as far north as Carlisle (supporting Nick Harper with **Helico**

–courtesy of David Kay- at the Brickyard), and the Dudley Arms (Rhyl, Wales) as well as Casablanca's (Southport). The closest gig to home was The Queens in Chorley. All I had to do was update the publicity and photocopy more material. Under A3H, the promotional packs I sent to venues included flyers, CDs and posters that read:

"Pretendgirlfriend are a 4 piece working class indie rock band from Burnley. Out to demo a powerful collection of songs about everyday life that appeal to anyone who values faith in the human spirit and a desire for truth and honesty. There's no hype as we know it is you who will decide if they pluck your conscience and stir your desire for no frills rock n roll..."

It goes on to ask the reader to log onto the band's website to "let us know" their "verdict". I also asked that if they have a flyer to bring this to the gig for a discount on the normal entry price and any CDs were to be copied and handed around their friends. It sounds a bit desperate in hindsight but I had seen how flyers and CDs were <u>not</u> used as a marketing items. I wanted them to be picked up not thrown away or used as beer mats.

That first gig in Leicester was a solo acoustic set by Simmy as Danny was unavailable – I think he was doing an evening college course on Thursdays. I drove and Noel and Smit came down in my car with Simmy and his equipment. It was a freezing cold night and the venue was deserted. Apart from us and the other bands on the bill - **The Riptons, Unchosen** and **A is for Ape** with a couple of their mates between them - there was no one local. It was empty which was sad as the venue, in terms of space, size, lay out etc was, ideal for bands – just no audience. I spotted an Attik flyer and noticed Adequate 7 were playing at that venue on the same night. I had been to The Attik was close by and I had been there with The Commies. I took it as an opportunity to keep in touch with my contact there, update him on The Commies and drop off copies of Pretendgirlfriend's material to see if he could help. I headed over and The Attik was a hot buzz of 40 to 50 kids going wild to the bands. In contrast, when I got back to the Shed it was stark, barren and very cold! Nevertheless, Simmy did his set perfectly and we headed off as soon as we could. The other bands did not impresses in sound check and we could not see any point delaying our 2-3 hours drive back. Despite the disappointment, it was the first of many adventures I had with the band. Every gig we did at a distance from home had something memorable about it. This one was notable for the fact that the Police pulled me over just as I got on the M6. Apparently, my headlight was faulty! They insisted I take a breath test, which scared the shit out of me as I had had a pint of Guinness and could not afford a blot on my driving licence. The others just pissed themselves laughing and, having calmed down after the negative result, I saw the funny side too. We were behaving like naughty school kids who avoided detention on a technicality. We sang songs and intermittently repeated the officer's reprimand "...make sure you get your light fixed", all the way back to Padiham.

I tended to do all the driving to gigs and I used the time to get to know the band better. Their banter was hilarious and everything I thought it would be. Despite all the pressures and preoccupations for a manager, organisational logistics and a sense of doom in preparing for things that could go wrong, the day of a gig was a special day. It was exciting on all levels and whether it was with The Commies or Pretendgirlfriend, it was equally unique every time. With Pretendgirlfriend there did not seem to be any generation gap, which made the crack all the more fantastic, especially when we got "home" from gigs, usually at Simmy's. These ended up as a riot of laughter, booze, occasional "substance abuse" and good-natured piss taking – I loved it.

After supporting **Renton** at The Cellar bar at the end of January, the next gig was the Night and Day Cafe, Oldham Street, Manchester on 11th February. I had organised this gig through Jay Turner who I had met the year before. Jay struck me as a genuine music lover and we got on well during the few times we met. The Night and Day Café was one of *the* country's prestigious gigs for any band to play. It regularly featured in the music industry magazines on most people's lists of favourite venues to work with and many bands like to play there too. This, I am sure, had a lot to do with people like Jay being involved. It had a bohemian feel and its location was ideal - the Uber cool Northern Quarter of the city, which dripped with credibility amongst the students and music/social elite. However, in places it was a bit dusty, tired looking and in need of a good scrub - but that was its charm. The stage was to the right hand side at the far end as you took a dogleg entry through the narrow wood framed doorway at the front. The bar was to the left and you walked pass the side of the stage to the get to the toilets down stairs. When I did speak to Jay, he was usually perched on a stool at the bar. I remember he told me that he gauged if a band or any performer/act would be successful by measuring the length of the queue of fans waiting outside to get in to see them not just the number of people who were in the venue for the gig - I have never forgotten that.

The running order that night was one that was stuck to as Jay always ran his gigs well – still does no doubt. 9pm **Bunny**, 9.45pm **Four Kings**, 10.30pm Pretendgirlfriend and 11.15pm **Spiral Rocks**. I remember **Four Kings** impressed me enough to ask for their contact details and we stayed in touch for a while. The attendance was good and we got invited back to play again in May. Members of **Tessem** came to watch, as did my neighbour

Mick and his cousin Rick. Stu Taylor took up my offer to meet me there for a drink and he up dated me on his promotional use of compilation CDs for his bands. The set for Pretendgirlfriend went well – no problems on stage and the sound mix was good. At the bar afterwards, Smit introduced me to a former work colleague of his, Steve Fenton. Steve had gone self-employed and set up his business, Calder Recordings, in a studio on a small industrial estate in Hebden Bridge. He was complimentary on the band's performance, singling out *Separate Bedrooms*, and he said he wanted to know if the band would be interested in letting him record it. I think we all agreed on the spot as any free help and recording time was welcomed – a bonus so early on in the tour!

In between this night and 13th March when they did the recording session with Steve, my diary is a blitz of events. It is crammed with notes on event details, gig flyers stapled in and my scribbled notes on what I was planning. I wanted to be everywhere all at the same time. During the early months in 2002, the more places I went, the more people I talked to and the more I offered to get involved with - the more I got in return. It ran like a formula. I was continuing this way of working, as, every now and then; it paid dividends, which were not always apparent at the time. Much of what happened was a consequence of co-incidents, if that makes sense.

That Sunday (2nd February), the band played the "It's Not Cricket II!" event. I had wanted a dynamic film of them performing their latest songs. I did not get one but David Kay did promise to make up for this. Rob Clarke (Landlord at the Mitre Tavern, Preston) came to the event, which made up for the setbacks; as I talked and I went on to help promote bands there for a while.

Meanwhile, the weeks ahead were equally busy. 999 and the **Hyperjax** at The Royal Oak Hotel: Poulton-Le-Fylde: **The Shotgun Fairies** (Rob Clarke's band) with support from **Super Nova** at the The Mitre Tavern: **Kid Conspiracy** at Nottingham Junction supporting Skindred: **Crouch Mog, One Degree, Southpaw** and **the Hawthorns** at The Roadhouse, Manchester, **This Product**, and **The Passion** at The Mitre Tavern with the **Stolen Ponies** probably at the same venue over this weekend too: The Meteors and **The Hyperjax** at the Star & Garter (Manchester), **Kid Conspiracy** at the Witchwood (Ashton) and **Anti Placid, God Botherer, Abiosis** and **22 Drop Out** at the CCC all on 6th, leaving the 7th with notes referring to a "Saturday afternoon gig at The Cellar Bar, Blackburn, **Capulet** and **If All Else Fails**" written and then ruled out, "Pretendgirlfriend, **Leaf** and **This Product** in the 6th? !" It looks a mess but made sense to me back then -just one week of many over those months. It did not feel like I had taken on too much as I needed to know what was going on and I was selective in using everything that worked in Pretendgirlfriend's favour. However, slap bang in the middle of all this was the consequence of my offer of help to another band some months previously, which pulled my attention away from Pretendgirlfriend.

In Car Stereo

Going back to when I met In Car Stereo at The Brick Yard at the start of the year, just before agreeing to manage Pretendgirlfriend, their performance that night had been so impressive that I said I would sort gigs in my area if they came down. It was a genuine offer and there was mention of a tour in February, which I indicated I would help with. This was a promise called upon by front man Jordan Yates. I had agreed to honour my commitment with a few dates which included an invite to the "It's Not Cricket II" event. I did not anticipate how it squeezed my schedule arranging the Pretendgirlfriend gigs and everything else that was happening. However, a promise is a promise and there was an ulterior motive that could work in Pretendgirlfriend's favour. Firstly, I had organised some of these gigs at venues that I had not dealt with before (Barley Mow, Warrington and Mitre Tavern, Preston) and I could see if they were suitable for Pretendgirlfriend. Secondly, to keep their costs down, I hired a small PA and mixing desk off Phil Baker. I wanted to try one out to see if buying a PA for Pretendgirlfriend was a feasible investment. The gig was my way of a trial run - a way of testing the logistics versus costs. It gave me the experience of transporting and setting it up, messing about with mixing the sound, dismantling it, lugging it back and storing it. My plan was to put on our own gigs at places that did not have a permanent PA – like the North Bar. Other venues were trying to host live music to compete with those who were doing it successfully. If we could do gigs as a self-contained act, we would get more gigs and be able to keep more of the money. The going rate for a full PA hire, with sound technician for one gig could be £100-£150 plus. Later, we could consider getting a van, loading up our own equipment and going on a tour. I had seen some bands do this, which impressed me and it made sense if you wanted to build a fan base. I could understand how this might appeal to A&R people who could "see" where a band was playing and as an indication that their commitment to be successful.

When it came to PAs, back then, size was everything. The bigger the rig "tops" and "subs" (bottom cabinets), the bigger gigs you could put on and the better the sound mix. A vocal only PA utilised the "tops" and meant that the band had to be careful with the volume levels on their guitar amps in order to get the right audio balance. The drummer and vocalists had to fend for themselves as there were no monitors (other speakers which feed the sound back to them on stage).This meant a lot of faffing about in sound check which is done when no one else is around. When the audience comes in, they fill up the space, altering the acoustics, which can cock up the sound completely. It is a nightmare to adjust while performing which is why you get shrieks and piercing whistles at the start of some gigs you may have been to. The only place I found that a vocal only rig worked well was in the very small pubs like the Mitre Tavern or tiny clubs like The Cuba Café in Manchester. Cost, storage, transport etc – naaahh, I ditched the idea – one of my better decisions as a PA always seemed to be available or hire costs could be shared or we could borrowed one off another band.

Meanwhile, Pretendgirlfriend's gig at The Queens in Chorley had to be rescued by support band **If All Else Fails** as Simmy's voice packed in after the third song (hence the date does not appear on the band's official gig guide). IAEF went on again, after their set as support band that night, and did a set of cover versions to make up for the gap and I owed them one for that (See Chapter 11). I had my debut gig at The Mitre Tavern at the end of February and **In Car Stereo** headlined. The flyers/posters artwork came via Steve Hodgson who had moved on to playing drums in support band **Capulet**. It is an eye-catching pencil drawing of a Manga warrior, in profile holding a dagger. The sub headings I added: under Capulet read "(from Chorley.... out of the ashes of **Let's Not Lose Mars to The Commies** and **Rebekah** the finest phoenix to arise on the local scene"). Under the other support band, **Titus Gein** I put ("On tour with their Glasgow stable mates who play as tight as F_ _ k. You will not see a more cutting edge instrumental power crushing trio south of the border"). All three bands played blistering sets and the event did seal my association and friendship with Rob, which enabled me to put Pretendgirlfriend on there a few months later.

Simmy's voice recovered sufficiently for them to do a gig at the Retro Bar, Sackville Street, Manchester at the end of February, with **Leaf** and gig organiser, Gus Fairbairn's band, **This Product**. I had met Gus and interviewed during my first visit to Bury Met back in 2002.The gig was my first sighting of **Leaf** who impressed me instantly (see Chapter 11) and it was the first time I met Roy Bright, who Simmy introduced me to and with whom I got on instantly. Pretendgirlfriend played a competent set – nothing out of the ordinary and they got paid £30 – nice one Gus! I like the Retro Bar. It has a tiny long cellar under the main pub. It was The Swinging Sporran in the 1980s, where I watched Senseless Things play when Pete Buttle was managing them. In a way, I had become a music promoter like him and wondered if I would go on to set up a record company too! Meanwhile, the intensity of the gigs and wanting to be everywhere at the same time, meant I really could have done with a Tardis. Not that it ever interfered with my commitment as Pretendgirlfriend's manager – I always looked out for what could benefit them. It is indicative of how, in trying to be everything to everyone who I felt I could help, I had to spread myself out and maybe at times I did it too thinly to be as effective as I could have been for the band. On reflection, I may have got this balance wrong and wonder whether, if I had been concentrated on one band 100% of the time, would it have made a difference?

"Songs, Ideas & Philosophies 2004"

This is the title of a diary Simmy started around the time of the first Night and Day Cafe gig. It is a school exercise book containing the lyrics to two songs, so far unrecorded or played live - called *Compromise* and *Miniature Me* (both dated Feb 2004). The diary provides a revealing insight into Simmy 'observations and opinions. He writes:

"Pretendgirlfriend are the only truly original rock band around. They look good in casual style clothing, no need to dress up with fucking gaffer tape around denim jeans...its not a fuckin Halloween party, these are fuckin good songs that mean something, and if I look angry when I'm singing that's because I am......I've had more arguments and fights with myself than anyone else......Northern Soul, Northern Grit, Northern spirit, call it what you want. We are a band for the people."

The recording session at Steve Fenton's studio was over the weekend of 13th March and, while there is no comment on this in Simmy's diary, it went well. Unfortunately, we did not use the *Separate Bedrooms* track in its own right as an official single but we did put it on CDs we burned off and gave out at gigs. There was a rough recording of *Barred from the Kings,* used as a demo only. On the 11th, the band went over to Liverpool to promote their gig at the Slaughter House on 24th. The advance visit was an idea I had, in that the lads could go to new venues a few weeks before they played the gig to check the logistics, such as directions on how to get there, where to park etc. They could see how gig nights were organised, gain a feel for the place and get to know the staff. It was a chance to hand out flyers, make sure posters were up and find out who to contact in the media plug the gig etc.We did this together for a gig over in Sheffield at The Casbah. Impressed by our proactively, this venue let us in for free to watch Marky Ramone who was playing there the same night. Thereafter, the only other tour dates for that month were the Star and Garter, Manchester, (18th) and Chorley Community Centre (20th).

Simmy's next diary entry, Thursday 1st April 2004 is:

– *The Casbah-Sheffield. April fool's day in the steel city...and somebody is taking the piss. Whoever designed RAC route planner is having a real laugh on us. We finally arrived at the venue at 8.30pm to find a proper backstage area, complete with rider. Fuckin hell! One of 1ˢᵗ gigs with a free bar and yours truly is fucking driving. This must be April fools, okay. Gig went well though. Set list: Streets of My Town, Apologies, Live in Hope, Down On Wednesday, It's Not The End of The World, Limbo, Separate Bedrooms, Barred From The Kings. Gave a few CDs out, chatted to a local band about race riots. Set off back at 11pm. Got back home at 1.10am. WIDE AWAKE. Grit Rock is born! "It's a fine line between Rock Star and Professional".*

I did not go to this gig but was at the next one – Sunday 4th April the Mitre Tavern (the building was changed to a Vets practice). Simmy's diary records:

*"Our third (full band) gig. Smit does the honour of driving which means I have from 6pm to 10.30pm to have a few beers. First impression of the Mitre Tavern is something from Sky One's toughest pubs in Britain. However, friendly venue owner Rob (a lot younger than I pictured) welcomes us. Rob has provided us with our greatest compliment yet "A band from Burnley who sound like a band from Burnley" – Top! We go on last - after **The Runs** from Burnley and **One Man Stand** from Stockport (who played Safe European Home). 10.30, 6 pints later – a storming set in front of a huge four+ audience, mission accomplished. Another pint and I would have been shit. Two local lads think we are ace and look the part. Things are looking up."Separate Bedrooms" mix is finished. Not keen at first but growing to like (it) very much"*

In time, I went on to use Simmy's words, or similar, to introduce the band when they came on stage. "A band of the people for the people" and we coined their musical style as "Grit Rock" on our publicity –especially during the **Live In Hope** CD/DVD launch and tour. The credit goes to Simmy for the inspiration to how we were trying to make the band stand out by defining its style as no longer Indie/punk/rock etc but as something new that captured the fundamentals of who they were, where they were from and what they were about. In the same way that the music press labels reflected other styles like EMO, House, Acid, Hip Hop etc we came up with the phrase "Grit Rock" to make it easier to triumph <u>our</u> own label that we would be comfortable wearing.

Finding an audience amongst the crowds.

At that time, it was hard for Pretendgirlfriend to find their place on the live circuit. The gigs during that year were usually a miss match. As an Indie guitar band in the 1980's sense of the word, they would end up on bills with teenagers doing their take on Punk or the Americanised Skate/punk version that was prevalent due to the influence of bands like No FX, Blink 182 and older stalwarts, Green Day. I had seen it all first hand with The Commies and with my involvement at the CCC; Punk, Metal and every other style but Indie seemed to be dominating the unsigned scene in the North West. **Supernova/ Underdogs** and (at a push) **If All Else Fails** were the nearest comparisons to Pretendgirlfriend in terms of their contemporaries but there were no local venues catering for their style at that time. They got at good gig at The Brickyard, Carlisle on the 13th with **Helico** (who were based around Chorley), supporting Nick Harper, which David Kay promoted. But, in Lancashire, I had to try my best to widen my search which is what I was doing and what was making my diary so busy. Casting my net as wide as I could or spreading myself too thin – please feel free to debate! It was a fact – there was no audience in the places I knew then, before Fraser started at The Mad Ferret in Preston or Paul Fox at The Attic in Accrington and no one had heard of the Arctic Monkeys at that time either. The band was equally frustrated. Simmy writes:

Pretendgirlfriend are about turning people on to proper Rock'n Roll songs. Songs with lyrics and tunes. No dress code needed. What's all this "taking bags to gigs" when they go out these days! (i.e. rucksacks)... I can't do with this skater types...ska punk, they are a fuckin disgrace and an insult to the proper Ska bands that went before them...I hate this geek look thing. You know: 1) Beanies and Butt Head style laughs in between songs. 2) 15 and 16 year olds with scruffy beards-unshaven, unwashed to be individuals – bollox to individuals, they are all like that.3) ....and I have seen this from a band from Preston...putting on an American accent when introducing songs...why pretend to be from fucking America......but I am sure they hate my music as much as I hate theirs. (Despite this he ends on an optimistic note) *We are 100% committed and confident of becoming a top band that people will come out to see...we are genuine and ...the majority of our audience...don't regularly go out to local gigs. They are people who go to the pub and work full time...this is why we need to get air play...I suppose if we are gonna be a townie band then so be it, although I want everyone to like us".*

To emphasise how wide the chasm was between Pretendgirlfriend's music and sense of fashion, to what was popular, en vogue with the majority of the youth audiences, Simmy's next entry sums it up perfectly:

*Dudley Arms, Rhyl 17th April 2004. "God bless Kruger!"...we met the other bands on the bill. "Capulet"...nice lads...but... (**In Car Stereo** and **Cameron**)... are the basis of Pretendgirlfriend's hate agenda...Butt head style humour and wanting to be American. You just knew that these boys are going to be as heavy as fuck and are going to dislike us as much as I'm going to dislike them. The venue is* *like a box type room with a stage. Brilliant jukebox... set list: Streets of My Town, Apologies, Limbo, Live In Hope, Down On Wednesday, It's Not the End of The World and Barred From The Kings...but a mixed response from the.... "You're good but not really my cup of tea", crowd...then it's always the folk who look most frightening who turn out to be the friendliest. Thank God for Kruger, a bald, heavily tattooed glass collector/bouncer. He excitedly asks me for a CD and heaps praise on us for a good ten minutes before single handily carrying Noel's bass stack out for us.....not that bad after all.*

Promotional tools and marketing

I sent out many press packs throughout this first tour. They contained a personalised letter (if I had a contact name): a CD of their songs, copies of press cuttings and a list of tour dates or flyers. If I had a contact number, I followed up the mailing with a call. For the Rhyl gig, I even sent a pack to Mike Peters (The Alarm) who I thought might be interested as the PO Box for his contact address was in Prestatyn. I was hoping he would remember me from the interview I did for *Pogo'til I Die* with him when The Dead Men Walking tour came to Darwen in 2003. For the record, he did not show up but I know he was ill at that time. It is an indication of how I used every contact I could. Apart from this, I sent a press pack to everyone in my contact address book who I thought would be interested and could help the band, but it was a hard slog. The money did not worry me as much as the lack of immediate response, which amazed and disappointed me. Why couldn't others hear what I heard Aaaahhhs! Frustrating then and even more so now! We needed a break and no one seemed interested. I consoled myself with the few things that were going right and those who did like what they heard. The introduction to the Dudley Arms, which came from Gus Fairbairn – meant that the net working with bands *was* paying off! Landlord, Peter Johnston and Lorraine did like the band and tried to do their bit. They got a piece in the local paper, The Journal, on 14th April:

"The Dudley Arms will be presenting....on April 17th ...Pretendgirlfriend (who) adhere to a very simple credo indeed: produce and play the kind of music that they themselves like to listen to and do it with no compromise of their ideals or selling short of their integrity. It's not done them any harm so far, an after supporting The Fall...they've inked a management deal that has got them playing gigs at a rapidly increasing rate..."

You could not beat good publicity but I wanted to demonstrate we had more to offer to the venues and other promoters who put us on - that we would do our part and be original. Probably my most individual idea for publicity came about for our return gig at The Night and Day Café, Manchester on May 4th. The Wildhearts had a gig at Academy, Manchester on April 23rd. A Friday night, and, Noel, Smit, Simmy and I had tickets for it; Danny was skint so he stayed at home. My idea was to burn off 100 CDs and package them with an invite to the Night and Day gig. We would hand these out as we talked to fans at The Wildhearts' gig and ask them to come to watch Pretendgirlfriend. The plan being that Pretendgirlfriend was influenced by The Wildhearts so Wildhearts' fans may like what they heard on the Pretendgirlfriend CD and come to their gig eleven days later. Even if only a quarter came we felt that this would be a success as they would be there as a result of hearing the CD and not some hype a journalist wrote. This would increase our fan base and we could repeat the stunt when other similar bands were on tour close to places where we had gigs coming up -good, in theory.

We met up at The Night and Day Café and laid flyers out on the table. I met **Leaf's** manager Dave Collins as one of his bands was playing there. It was a Fierce Panda (record label) promotion night and I went next door to The Dry Bar as I had seen **The Maybees?** Name on a poster for the same evening. They were from Liverpool and I had met them the year before and showed them round Preston. I thought they might be able to help with gigs over on Merseyside. When I made enquires about them I spoke to Vuz Kapur "they hadn't arrived yet" he told me and offered to pass on a message. This was my first meeting with Vuz and, in conversation with him that night, he told me he was the Manchester arm of Liverpool based Glaswerk Media. Glaswerk are a prolific and well run out fit, putting on loads of gigs, reviewing bands, recordings and had lots of useful information in their website. I mentioned I knew Matt Ong from Glaswerk (I did an interview with Puressence and Echo Boy at Preston University back in 2002 for him), and Vuz took a keen interest in what I was doing and suggested registering Pretendgirlfriend with his "V Man Events". A few days later, I did this and at the foot of the form I emailed to him is Vuz's rallying call "Eat, Breath and shit: music" – he was a great one for "Spin". I gave him a copy of the Pretendgirlfriend CD, told him what we were going that night and he seemed impressed. Thereafter, we had a mutual respect for each other and did find that, quite often, we were useful to each other. I know that there are many opinions about Vuz from what musicians, managers and other promoters have told me but, from my own experience, I know that he ran his events as professionally as I could expect. Meeting and keeping in with Vuz, was all part of the networking process I needed to do if I was to get tangible results for Pretendgirlfriend in the future.

The Wildhearts gig was brilliant and we handed out all the 100 CDs. I came back to Simmy's to celebrate and stopped over. I woke up round 11am and read Simmy's diary. I then wrote eight and a half pages covering the above and my own philosophy for the band. Amongst the ramblings is this gem when I describe Pretendgirlfriend as a *"...body. The bones are Smit – plain, simple, always solid, a frame work, a structure - the website- the midway between the rest. Danny and Noel, the back bone, the power house the muscles, the rhythm of life. Simmy, the head, the mouth piece, the gob! But, the heart of this band is the music - the lyrics and tunes – it lives and breathes. Me? I add the skin and try to point its direction... We are five; we are a "gang" – a fighting unit that doesn't move alone. We move as one, think as one, believe as one, achieve as one! I am proud to know and be part of the finest band in the world.... "finest" is Art. It's an opinion – just like a Constable or a Turner or a Lennon or a McCartney...its not what we say or what we think we can do it's what we know we are and what we actually do that's of the people for the people. I give you Grit Rock. I give you Pretendgirlfriend!"*

25th April: Simmy's diary entries note: "Air plays on 2BR *It's Not the End of The World* and: "Pretendgirlfriend No 6 on Rock Box Radio" (internet). On the 27th there was a "write up in the Burnley Express". I do not have a copy of this, but it all added up to an increase in focus from both the media and the lads' awareness of it.

29th April – email from Simmy at 12.54 (while on his lunch). Mentions how he's found *The Ordinary Boys* while searching the internet *"...currently being played on radio One...sound a bit like us...I think we should look to the bands that are breaking and try and arrange some support slots.* He copies in the review and I make a note to check them out and start thinking about how you get to know who is breaking and get the inside track, support slots etc....? Fuck knows! Is what I concluded and thought of easier options instead.

Going back to the idea of increasing our fan base, I had a lightning thought – where better to start than in Burnley and specifically Turf Moor, home of Burnley FC. If we could appeal to the terraces and they could relate to us then we had a captive audience. The club had a loyal support fan base for everything Burnley related – could the football loyalty stretch to music and Pretendgirlfriend? If we could get gigs at venues in the towns where the football team were playing an away fixture – round lunch time- we could advertise that fact to pubs who would welcome away fans. We present this to Burnley FC supporters in the hope that they would adopt Pretendgirlfriend as a sort of mascot band. I would have to work on the how but in short all they needed to know is that if they go to X venue at a time when they were planning on pre match drinks then they would be hearing songs about their hometown and surrounding villages from "their" local band. The venue would get more punt-ers in and pay the band for the gig and who knows there might be an evening gig too –more exposure, more fans and more money etc......But, there again... thinking this through.....it all depended on the result of the football match. It could make it a good, bad or ugly situation! Okay, dump the evening gig and stick with the lunchtime slot. It would be limited to Burnley FC supporters only – but it would be a guaranteed attendance, money and a good reason to watch Burnley FC if nothing else! An example of how my mind would kick around ideas and then I would look for the most practical out come. I settled for getting a Pretendgirlfriend track played at half time and see what response this got. I worked on this in the background.

30th April -after the Landlord failed to appear at The Wagon and Horses in Adlington, I cancelled the gig I had set up for Pretendgirlfriend with **The Hyperjax**. Next was a slot on the annual four-day music Festival at The Cellar Bar, Blackburn. I did a deal with "Timsy" (AKA Jonathan Timms), who was supplying the PA, sound engineering and organising the scheduled. I sold him the idea of putting on some out of town bands amongst the run of the mill locals. He took to this and I booked slots on the Saturday night for **The Dangerfields** who were on a short tour and **Renton**, in return for Pretendgirlfriend playing on Sunday 2nd May. To add to the mail out and general publicity for Pretendgirlfriend, I asked my friend, Dave Gilmour, to do some photographs when they played this gig. Dave is a talented photographer. I met him through my eldest daughter who was at school with his daughter. He was looking for opportunities to try his new equipment by photograph-ing bands I knew. Brilliant co-incidence as I needed better publicity shots for the press packs! All went according to plan, and the gig was notable as it was the first time we met die-hard fans Ashleigh Garratt and his girlfriend Sandra. "Ash", as he insisted we call him, signed up to our mailing list (which was another one of my innovations and something we took to every gig). He and Sandra made Simmy's night by coming up afterwards and expressing their enthusiasm for the set. They went to every gig they could whenever they played locally back then and ever since. Dave did a great job with the photos too and they were ready just in time for the next series of gigs.

Amongst these was the return to the Night and Day Café. We were hopeful of a new fan base after the Wildhearts promotional stunt. The gig advertised us with **Wires, Orinoco Shores** and **Crosbi**. The attendance did not swell with an influx of new fans – perhaps one or two, but the photos I took are amongst the best I had done to date – small consolation and I was deflated! Maybe the next gigs in Southport, Crewe and Leicester and the prestigious Carling Barfly, Liverpool would be awash with those hungry for Grit Rock. But... sadly, no! These were, largely, dismal attendances and, despite a Fly Magazine listing with **Crimson Rise** for the Barfly, Liverpool – it ranked in Simmy's list of career low points as they played to the sound engineer! Bang went another of my ideas – to secure a sponsorship deal with the drinks company who manufacture Carling lager. I had the thought of selling the band to them: "who went down a storm at recent gig at their esteemed venue in Liverpool – the city where modern pop music was born...blah blah blah". The punch line and deal breaker rested on Simmy's lyric in homage to their brand of lager in the line "I'm not swopping Carling for Lemon and Lime" (*Lemon and Lime*). We had a few dates with London based band **The Perishers**, which Dave Horrocks had set up, but I could not go to these and some was cancelled. Surely, our luck would turn.... And it did by way of the only direct response I remember getting to my next mail shot.

This came in a letter from Gary Ward who invited Pretendgirlfriend onto the Darwen Music Festival on Sunday May 30th. Headlining that year were The Buzzcocks and Pretendgirlfriend appeared in a listing and article by Gail Atkinson for the Lancashire Evening Telegraph two days before. Gary put my write up in the festival magazine with one of Dave's photos, it read:

"The UK's first grit rock* band. Four working class lads from Burnley who sound like a band from Burnley ought to sound. Borrowing The Wildhearts guitars, they fill the void left by the Stereophonics and Oasis with songs that capture Lancashire's soul with all the confidence of The Clash".

This was great exposure along with the flyers we distributed using this with an added "*" inserted below emphasising:

"Grit rock is today's saviour for those who want songs with integrity from a band who are of the people for the people. The agenda is simple: to sing about what is real in the lives of ordinary folk taking inspiration from the streets of their home town." (www.a3hpromotion.co.uk)"

They played The Mill Stone at 3pm after **Easy Street** and before **Strange Days**. I took the family and stood the kids on beer crates at the back in front of the mixing desk. It was a good gig, plenty of festival revellers and it lifted our spirits.

Finding our spiritual home in Accrington.

In mid June, we all went to see **Ten Stone Dead** supporting Tom Hingley and The Lovers at King Street Working Men's Club, Accrington. Afterwards we had a meeting at Simmy's to discuss our plans for the rest of the year. Holidays were coming up for everyone and we had done a lot so far and deserved to ease up, relax and take stock before deciding what to do next. Steve Fenton had sent me an email at the start of the month in response to mine thanking him for his work. I had asked if he had had any feedback on the *Separate Bedrooms*. He had loaded a sample of the tune on his studio's website, in addition, I ask for his advice on what the band should do next. His email highlight:

Most people who've asked about the track wanted to know where the band were from and whether it would be available as a single or part of an album ...They're very good and it would seem a logical step for them to...release an album, backed up with press and tour....I believe the "SB" track has huge potential as it's topical and relevant to most people, plus the hooks great too.

He ends by saying that:

PG should consider having some of their tracks "produced/studio polished".... recent albums by Keane and Snow Patrol...were very "studio polished"...once done approaching a suitable label would be the next step.

We discussed this but we did not go back to him or take the "studio polished" advice. Our feeling was a mixture of being satisfied with the raw, live edge quality to what they had done at Studio Studio and the costs of those sessions balanced against what it would cost to get the "polish" added. It was more time and more money but we were sceptic cal about over produced songs! Steve had hinted that he had to concentrate on paid work so was not offering to do it free himself and we could not blame him for that. We did not know anyone else who had gone to the extra expense of doing this either and I had no contacts or the money to fund this – especially as it was unknown territory. We concluded that we had to weigh Steve's advice against the possibility that we could get interest based on what we had done and to see where that lead. The songs were good enough as they were and should sell themselves, adding anything else (i.e. "polish") to them had no guarantees. Instead, we did a mass mailing over the summer months selecting two/three tracks to burn onto CDs that we each felt, individually, best represented Pretendgirlfriend with an packaged as professionally as possible. The band decided to take turns in this DIY exercise, posting the press pack to as many record companies and following up as many leads as we could. I was to continue to look for other places to play and make contacts with local bands where possible. We met regularly to review progress.

Back in Accrington, local entrepreneur, Paul Fox, arranged the June gig. He set up www.thesongmachine.co.uk and Pretendgirlfriend appeared at their next event, over the weekend of 17th and 18th July at the same venue. The line up was a "who's who" of local talent. Both days started at 2pm and went on until 11pm. The afternoons were mainly acoustic sets from some of the bands doing a full band gig later on the same night. Simmy did a solo set at 2.30pm on the Saturday and the full band played at 5pm. Also on that day were **One Day Heroes, Johnny No Stars, Tessem, Last Man Standing, Fashionable Wino's, Natasha Jones, Spanglefish, The Scribes, Stalker** and The Burn. Apart from Tessem and The Burn, I did not know any of the others, at that time.

The Burn was the most successful band to come out of Blackburn since The Stiffs during the post punk years – see index. They did not impress me (had I missed the memo or something?), and I had not been aware of their presence, which, looking back now is incredible given that they had achieved what most local bands wanted to and were still based in Blackburn. That Saturday in Accrington, they played a short stripped down acoustic set and their Indie take on folksy/blues, again, failed to leave its mark on me. I did recognise the drummer, Lee, who had served me, drinks at The Cellar Bar where I think the band rehearsed. In my mind I didn't asked the obvious question like how does a supposedly "successful" local band explain stopping around Blackburn and doing gigs at the local working men's club? Should I have made more of this opportunity? Had I gone out of my way to talk to The Burn I may have been able to get an insight on the dos and don'ts of how to be signed and secure quality support gig slots? I did not and this may have been a missed opportunity.

Meanwhile, fuck me! David Kay turned up with a film crew in tow! He shot an interview with Pretendgirlfriend and the whole of their full band performance. I was in shock as it was one of those conversations I had with him a few days before, at short notice, and a case of David saying he would try to do it but had to wait and see who was available on the day to help. Hence, I was not counting on it, had not motioned it to the band and that is why it was a surprise when he did actually show up. However, again, the quality lacked a useable sound recording but we did use it for self-analysis on stagecraft and image. It did register with everyone else there as no one else was having a film crew to record them! Mr Fox was okay about the filming and he introduced his wife, Julie. For the record, the running order for the following day featured: **The Grim Beavers, Bret Classical** (acoustic), **Last Man Standing, Macky, Nod and Scouse** (acoustic) , **The Scribes** (acoustic),**Ten Stone Dead, Karma, Gone Beggin**, Tom Hingley (acoustic), **India Mill, Citizen Band, Strange Days** and The Mill Town Brothers!

The Mill Town Brothers - Bloody Hell! "Impressive, even if, like Tom Hingley, a bit passed the sell by date", is how I recall it, cynically, and why I did not bother to turn up for the gig. I was doing a lot for local music in my area and good luck to anyone else doing theirs in their neighbourhood. However, it did not strike me as anything earth shatteringly different. There was nothing exciting about what "thesongmachine" was doing, nothing fresh, raw and prolific. It was a case of the Indie tag over all the acts and Pretendgirlfriend were the most original thing on that weekend as far as I could make out –shit I was cocky git! I had a kind of "so what!" attitude about the gig that this rival business was organising....and I let that cloud the gig and other possibilities I could have explored at that time. Furthermore, we did not know at the time, but this was the start of an association between the band, Paul Fox and the Attic nightclub that would see Pretendgirlfriend perform their greatest gigs. But, in July 2004, I had our sights set on bigger and more original ideas when it came to promotion... Burnley FC!

Correspondence and phone calls with the club had lead to the playing of *It's Not the End of The World* during half time at their home games and there was a suggestion of a music festival at the ground. However, *500 miles* by The Proclaimers became the preferred choice and the stadium rock gig did not materialise. In fact the nearest we did get to playing at Turf Moor was a private gig for a wedding reception held in the club bar about a year later. A grand and original idea had not worked out; I put it behind me and moved on.

Unfortunately, there was nothing tangible to show from all the mailing and phone calls. We had many debates on why. Was everyone else on holiday too? Was our press pack up to standard? We did not have inside contact names: maybe there is a corporate "hold" on signing new talent: Indie is dead etc...? The band consoled themselves with a few gigs. They played an afternoon slot at Marsden Park Festival, Clayton Le Moors on the 10th September followed by another at the Rosendale Biker's show on the 19th. The mood was generally flat and we all needed a break to set new horizons.

Over these months, I made loads of trips to Manchester and anywhere else, I thought I could create opportunities for Pretendgirlfriend. I haunted the Roadhouse, Dry Bar, Night and Day Café and went to whatever Vuz was putting on at Jabez Clegg (off Oxford Rd in studentville). In addition, apart from dipping in and out of what was going on in Preston and Blackburn, I decided to see what Bolton had to offer. On 25th August, I went to the Albert Halls, in Bolton town centre. David Kay was filming the bands that night, paid for by the Council. **Leaf** were on as well as **Catcher, The Newds, Billy Club** and, I got my first sighting of, **The Minions of Jeffrey** who, to quote the over used expression, totally blew me away with their firebrand take on ska punk. Talking to the Shepherd twins from **Leaf,** they were dismissive of their hometown when I asked them out about putting on gigs. At that time there was very little going on in the town. They said that there were only a few places for bands to play. The Alma was a very small pub in the centre of town that allowed gigs, as did The Dog & Partridge. The later was even smaller than the Alma–so small, in fact that the "stage" was the floor space left when the pool table got moved to make way to create a playing area on gig nights. I went to see for myself and watched a gig at The Alma around this time when **Leaf** played there. I offered them a gig at the CCC in return for their candid help. David Kay also confirmed what they had told me and I concluded Bolton had nothing for Pretendgirlfriend or A3H either – sorry Bolton

The recording process – wizards and magic...

September was quiet so that the band could get back into Studio Studio to record the new tunes. Done over a weekend toward the end of that month Pete Troughton's easy going nature captured some of the band's best output which went on to appear on 2005's *Live In Hope* CD.

I had no input into the making of the music with either Pretendgirlfriend or The Commies. I would give my opinion when asked but knew my limitations. I am not a songwriter or a musician so I stick to what I know. However, having heard Pretendgirlfriend's new batch of songs live, I did feel that they were musically distinctive and laced with lyrical vitriol. I understood the views being expressed having got to know the band during the time they were written. Whatever they did in rehearsal to get the songs to the standard they were satisfied with the unique chemistry that exists between the band members. The only person(s) who should influence or interfere in the product of a recording is the engineer and/or the producer – Pete was both of these to Pretendgirlfriend. I understood this from how the last Commies recordings were on a level far superior to anything they had done before due to the technical work that went on at Prism studio. A band can go into a recording session with songs that they feel need to be reproduced the way they want or hear them in their heads but the studio wizards work their magic in ways that make the end product sound totally different. I was reminded of this reading Peter Hook's autobiography "Unknown Pleasures". In it, he expresses his admiration, for the work of Martin Hannett (producer) with Joy Division. Hannett created works of art for this band in their two LPs and singles that have stood the test of time, pioneering the early stages of digital recording techniques and moulding a sound that was very different to what the band wanted or performed live. This is what Steve Fenton was on about – the "polish" – which worked wonders for Joy Division and no doubt many bands before and since. This is what a record company paid for and we were not in that league – well, not yet!

Contacts, concerts and more co-incidences

Around September, another opportunity came from Chris Cardwell, who put me onto a Battle of the Band (BOTB) competition held in Skelmersadale – close to where his parents lived. Chris had sung in **Boddah**, who had split up by this time and he was looking for help in promoting his solo work. We met up at The Dungeon Club, in a small shopping precinct on a large housing estate. "Captive audience" I thought, parking outside this modern venue. The entrance was at street level and a sunken area housed a bar running along the right hand sidewall. The stage was at the opposite, left hand side, with seating and a small dance floor in between. I liked it instantly – well spaced out, not too big not too small – cosy in fact- with an in house PA, lighting and everything you needed. Chris introduced me to the promoter, George Long, who was about my age, maybe a bit older. I think he was new to doing these events and we talked loosely of me being able to offer gigs at the CCC for bands he wanted to direct my way and vice versa after the BOTB ended. I secured the 17th October for Pretendgirlfriend to play in one of the heats. The gig was okay, about fifty or so in the audience and we were part of a four-band line up. We got through to the final at the end of November which local band **Smudge** won if memory serves. The lads were not fussed as we had only done it for the exposure. The prize was "£500 to spend on sound and lighting equipment" – which, I read as a tie in with a local PA firm who would supply it for any gigs you put on. Our apathy shows how unimportant all this was to us by that stage. However, it did lead to an offer from the landlord of a nearby pub called The Viking, which they played as part of the tour. On a final note, it was on one of the two nights in "Skem" that we heard "I Predict A Riot"(Kaiser Chiefs) on the radio as we drove there – or should I say got lost on its many roundabouts –worse than Warrington for the sodding things! "What have the Kaiser Chiefs got that we haven't" we debated with loud resentment, as we got frustrated at running late. Even now, it is a fact that I will argue with anyone, that Simmy's lyrics are ten times superior to anything that band have written.

In the summer, Steve Fenton had floated the idea of putting on a joint gig in Manchester. His pitch to me was to showcase some bands he had recorded who he felt had potential- including Pretendgirlfriend. He wanted my help promoting, organising and running the night as well as sharing the costs-splitting the financial side 50/50.The idea was to get anyone we knew in the industry to the gig as well as giving the bands what they all wanted – a gig with similar genre/sounding bands at a prime Manchester venue. He mentioned Jilly's Rockworld and we met the owner at the club on Oxford Rd (since closed) at the end of September and agreed terms for the next date available, which was

Wednesday 27th October. The club did not hire out to private gigs at the weekends – it did not need to as it was usually packed- hence, like most Manchester venues, we had to make do with a mid week slot. We called the club night "Revels" – like the sweets – *bound to be something you will like* was the tag line if anyone asked us about it. We advertised it as a *Calder Recordings & A3H Promotion presents*. The line up was **Blue Hobo, The Mushrooms, Operator Six** and Pretendgirlfriend who were to be the headline band. We both felt that this would be excellent and well deserved recognition for Pretendgirlfriend. Doors open at 8pm and we had the club until 2am.Charging £4 a ticket (£3 in advance). Steve did a brilliant job on posters, flyers and met me, with a mate of his and my mate Mick in Manchester a week before for a PR stunt to street walk, hand out flyers and talk to as many people as we could. It made the listings in all the usual media ads and the night went very well. About 120 came through the doors, which, for a first time gig, were very respectable numbers. A coach brought fans and the other bands that were from Yorkshire. Financially, we just about broke even – a result in itself too as the aim was more about exposure for the bands and winning over new fans than us making a profit. One or two "guests" did show but they were mostly mates or associates Steve and I knew. The bands enjoyed it too– Steve organised a buffet and drinks back stage and the feel of the whole night was very warm and had a buzz we knew was worth repeating – which we did but with a different line up in the New Year.

On a high whilst organising it, I think Simmy came up with the idea of putting on our own showcase gig. This was our way of flushing out local bands to identify with, as well as making some money for a tour/recording costs in 2005. We sold the idea to the media asked for bands to apply to us directly. This lead to a meeting at a pub in Hapton to discuss the event and agree terms, running order etc.It was a genuine and credible profile for the band and we booked the 27th November at The Kierby Hotel in Burnley town centre. We met **Ad Nauseum, Re:verb** (sic), **Asimov** and **Counteract** and reached an agreement on the spot to put the whole thing together amongst ourselves. I contacted the media playing on the successful tour we had done and how Indie was having a resurgence on the back of the 10th Anniversary of Oasis debut LP and the commercial success of a new wave of bands like The Future Heads, Maximo Park , The Ordinary Boys and (yeah alright) the (chuffing) Kaiser Chiefs. One feature, in the Leader Times Newspaper on the 19th November, was a black and white photo I'd taken at their last Night and Day café gig with the head line "More than Pretenders!" All the details were correct too: "Tickets, costing £4 are available from the Electron shop, Burnley and you are advised to get one to avoid disappointment of not getting in on the night". Splendid free coverage and the night was a triumph on all fronts netting the band an £80 profit – albeit most of this went on booze soon afterwards to celebrate!

Spitfire got wind of what we had been up to and offered Pretendgirlfriend the support slot for a gig they had organised at Bacup Leisure centre at the start of December, paying them a £40 fee to appear! In return I offered them a slot on the A3H end of year gig at The Cellar Bar in December, with Pretendgirlfriend, **The Phlegm Fatales** (Rob Clarke's new band), and **Dead Jim** and **Three Ways West.**

These gigs boosted our confidence and to top it all off Smit had an email on 1ˢᵗ December from Got Rocks 4x4 Film Company based in Utah, USA. They were looking for songs to accompany their DVD recording of Super Crawl III, which was the extreme sport of off road "crawling rigs" which look like supercharged beach buggies going over obstacles in the desert. They wanted to use *It's Not The End of The World, Live In Hope and Streets of My Town* and Smit replied "yes" subject to:

1) You use part of each song and not the full track. 2) We get a Pretendgirlfriend credit mention and the title of the track for each song you use. 3) Pretendgirlfriend is entitled to a proof copy before release. They chose *It's Not the End of The World,* got the track listed while being played on the video footage and the band name and website was printed on the back of the DVD case. Well done Smit!

Simmy went through spurts of research on the internet. He would send me contact names, addresses and websites to have in readiness for our next release, or for me to get started on making contacts. I either did so, on receipt, or logged them for a planned approach when I had time to do more of my own research. Drownedinsound.com, ukbands.net, pogomotion.co.uk, Poptones Records and thechartshow.tv –all of which I got onto straight away as I had heard of these. We even got hold of a PO Box for The Wildhearts and sent a press pack to them too. I already encouraged Simmy to register with the BBC's Radio 2 Search for a Songwriter competition in June. We would try anything we could – there seemed to be plenty to go at and it was a case of sorting the wheat from the chaff - like an email Simmy sent me on my Birthday "John just been looking through some emails from Chromium Records..." He attached a list of radio stations, record companies, management and publishing companies that they had sent copies of the "Industry Standard" compilation CD to. It was a year old and phone numbers only – no names or any direct dial or mobile numbers. I filed it.

However, few days later I got an email from Phil Scarisbrick who was working for INFX Productions, it started off "Hi John, we are currently looking to record a showcase CD which will be heard by our industry contacts (Warner Music, Beggars Banquet, Atlantic Records, Mean Fiddler) to name but a few...". Oh Dear! Another Chromium Records deal I thought. The cost was £50 and all travel costs, accommodation and expenses would <u>not</u> be covered "...but we will make every effort to assist with these matters..." – just as well as the studio was in High Wycombe and the recording of two songs would be over 2/3 days. Only "four or five bands ...who we consider are good enough to reflect the project in a positive light..." would get full use of the studio and assistance of in house producer Warren Bassett who had worked with The Fall, Bob Marley, Manfred Mann, ELP and, most recently, produced the Bloc Party album. Phil adds that the most "exciting part" is that if the CD is a success there would be a live event and mentions Camden Barfly – i.e. a London date. The recording would be Feb/March, around the time all this we would have our DVD/CD available, a tour penned in and a London date could really help. Result!

I knew Phil as he was in **The Message/ Super Nova/ The Under Dogs**. When I called him, he explained that it was part of his studies at college down there. We could be helping each other and knowing Phil made me warm to the whole project. I pondered this for a few days, chatted to the band and then sent an emailed out to Pretendgirlfriend and some other bands I was helping who I felt Phil might be interested in **The Hyperjax, Three Ways West, Leaf, Sterling Rose (Daniel Rossall), 13amp, Kid Conspiracy** and **Dead Jim**. I wrote that, while I would be sending in a CD of Pretendgirlfriend's material and offered to include any of theirs, I wanted to make my position clear. "...I don't know this outfit and have had experience of such "pay to record" arrangements....could be a load of shite, there again it may not be....see you all on Friday at The Sir Charles Napier (Blackburn) for **Kid Conspiracy**" (another gig I organised).

Surfing on this wave of good things happening, we started to plan our next release. This would be the new Studio Studio tracks with the possibility of any new songs that may be written in between, as Simmy's output was gathering pace. *Working Holiday* and a re-working of *19 St John's Road* were on the agenda along with a price tag of £6/7 for what we referred to as a "mini album". This showed pride in what we were doing and, if done professionally, merited the price tag. Simmy thoughts on the following year included talk of possible gigs abroad – well sort of –Jersey if that counts. He had a family friend who lived on the island who had a mate who ran a club there. It put bands on from the mainland in return for covering expenses. He went on to list record companies to target. Selecting five labels that suited the band and Noel had been sending CDs on this basis already. Under "gigs and stage craft" he felt that *"although this has improved we are still not there yet...we should rehearse twice a week...look at a tour...and get a support to a band like Malibu Stacey (Bruce McKenzie's latest protégé) maybe revisit the idea of going out with a covers band like The Jamm"*(see index). It was about this time that we started to kick about the idea of a promo pack with a DVD of the band playing live as well as a CD of tunes. This took some six months from that point to becoming a reality, but at this stage, we pencilled April in for a release date. "....proper packaging and everything". I agreed with everything and gave my vision of a double cased DVD/CD along with agreeing with the need to work on the stagecraft –especially the need to engage the audiences more than they had done. Danny talked about workshops the band could go on to get help on this aspect. We had a meeting of minds on what we wanted and agreed that we had come a long way since January.

Severing ties and cutting to the chase

I had a renewed vigour. I wanted to manage Pretendgirlfriend full time in 2005 and I focused on reducing my commitments that were pulling on my time. These centred around Chorley - the CCC and the CCMC in particular. New people wanted to get involved and the same was true at Chorley FM. Chorley needed people who could dedicate the time it demanded - I needed to let go and it felt the right time to do so. I handed in my resignation from the Committees in October.

When the band asked me what makes me believe in them my answer was (and still is) *"you – you all have the talent, the songs and you deserve to succeed!"* To cement my belief I had to commit fully too. During that autumn, I was accepting work from venues to supply bands and organise fee paying gigs when asked by other bands like – **Kid Conspiracy** –at them CCC (sponsored by a local Fish and chip shop), Sir Charles Napier (Blackburn) and The Mitre Tavern. I had to cut this role down and funnel A3H activity towards Pretendgirlfriend's benefit exclusively.

Our final publicity of 2004 was a half page feature by Caroline Innes in the Lancashire Evening Telegraph on 31st December. It had a coloured picture of Smit in profile and Simmy staring directly at the camera. The headline "Pretenders to The Indie Throne" had a smaller coloured photo of the band I had taken at the Revels gig. The article talked about their successes in 2004 and ambitions for 2005.Simmy says: *"Live In Hope is about us and other people aspiring for their goals and that has been what the last year has been about".* Smit concurs, *"2004 was a good year for us, we played some fantastic gigs at (Jilly's) Rockworld in Manchester and at the Kierby Hotel in Burnley where 200... came along".* Simmy adds, *"...there is a gap out there that has been left by the likes of Oasis and the Stereophonics....we want to bring back real lyric-based songs that you just don't seem to get any more".* The article states that The Burn has joined the audience at various gigs... (?)......Maybe they had or was that wishful thinking? The final paragraph advertised the return gig at The Cellar Bar (Blackburn) gig on 29th January and the first gig in Manchester at The Late Rooms on February 6th. Brilliant, probably the best newsprint the band had up to that point. We used it in our promo packs full of full of promise. I was about to say Eastern Promise – for those of you who remember the Fry's Chocolate Cream TV advert. Smit's comment in the article mentioned how 41 per cent of hits on their website came from Saudi Arabia *"They seem to open the site, look at us staring back at them and decide it isn't quite what they wanted. I don't think we will be getting many fans from the Middle East!"*

2005: We hit the ground at full pelt. I had secured a gig at the Late Room after meeting Richard Lynch during my many visits to Manchester. The venue on Peter Street was below the Life Café – both venues have changed names now, but back then, they were the places to play on that side of the city centre. My first visit there was with The Commies back in March 2003, with **Zombina and the Skeletons** supporting **Fi-Lo Radio**, who Richard was heavily involved with at that time. I think one of the lads from **Leaf** mentioned what Richard was doing there, under Charabanc Promotions. Their flyer stated "Club Biscuit" Friday nights with DJ "Dil", drinks promotions and dancing to Indie Music from 11pm "Til late". Crucially, it was tied in with HMV Records. The glossy double-sided coloured card (i.e. expensive) listed a month's worth of gigs with 3-4 bands under the headline: "The HMV showcase featuring up and coming bands from around the UK". **Leaf** had a gig there on October 22nd. I did not go as I think there was the possibility of Pretendgirlfriend doing a gig with **Counteract** at The Station in Helmshore, which in the end, did not happen and the band rehearsed instead. However, my mate Karl Stanley and I had tickets to see Carbon Silicon (Ex Clash guitarist Mick Jones's new band), at The North Bar the same night. Before the gig, I rushed Karl over to Hapton to meet Pretendgirlfriend while I mentioned the Late Rooms and explained what Richard was doing. Furthermore, the deal included having your CDs on sale in the HMV shop in town – wow! "... We had to have some of that!"

I told David Kay about it too and pushed him to come good on his promises to do a proper video for Pretendgirlfriend of their performance and hire

181

a decent sound engineer! The plan was to use the footage as part of the new twin DVD/CD release in the Spring. David and I were still in the last chance saloon on the dual business idea and delivering a professional job was what I wanted if we were to make a go of it or not. I hedged my bets though - a student, James Riley, had sought me out and offered his services under his "Flea Pit Films" project. More the merrier and he lived in Hyndburn – which I took to be a good sign. We needed to get a many fans in as possible and capture the atmosphere the best way we could. Having two film companies there had to pay off and was bound to impress anyone from the industry who came to the gig.

Mid February, I got an email from David Bash who selected bands for International Pop Overthrow (IPO). David organised and ran the IPO festivals, primarily in several USA cities. For the past three years, he had also brought the festival to Liverpool during the bank holiday weekend at the end of May. His email explained that Mark from had referred Pretendgirlfriend to him **Re: verb.** Having listened to some of their songs on the website he wrote " I would love to have Pretend Girlfriend play" I accepted and confirmed their availability and was asked to send press packs to an address on Magnolia Boulevard, Sherman Oaks, California. It gave me a bit of a kick when I did that at the local post office. Later that month, when confirming some more of the contract details, I felt I should do what Mark had done for Pretendgirlfriend and recommend several bands for David to consider. These included **Leaf, Ad Nauseum, Minions of Jeffrey, Hyperjax, If All Else Fails, Kid Conspiracy, Sterling Rose** and I copied the email into them. Things went quiet; David had IPO Nashville and Chicago before Liverpool. Meanwhile, I kept gigs to a minimum to allow the lads to rehearse, socialise and get as many friends, family etc committed to coming to the Late Rooms gig in February. I arranged two warm up gigs: The Dudley Arms (Rhyl) and The Viking (Skelmersadale) before the end of Jan. I did not want them to play locally as they had just done that and I hoped any new fans from further afield would take a trip into Manchester – on a Sunday.

I researched the other bands on the bill for the Late Rooms and summarised this in an email to allow the band to check them out and arrange for equipment. Sharing equipment was normal practice but I tasked them to cast a critical eye on anyone we gigged with in advance. I did not want them to be upstaged by anyone, knowing, as much as we could, should guarantee this would not happen. I hoped this activity would sharpen their minds on every gig from now on. The line up for The Late Rooms, was **The Window Right**, then Pretendgirlfriend, **White Haze** and (on last) **Rob McCullough**. Going on second was ideal as it meant the fans for all the other bands would be inside the venue and at £4, a ticket you should want to get your money's worth and see all the bands. Playing any later, as we had often experienced, especially last, meant that you invariably played to your own fans as the other bands and their fans had packed up and were long gone.

Reality and some success at last

During a lunch break, I delivered a batch of CDs for Richard to his office in Sparkle Street, Manchester. He was busy but I was there long enough to see his desk space full of piles of CDs, letters, posters, leaflets and bits of merchandise. The sight was a throw back to that wakeup call backstage at The Bar Fly, Liverpool in 2003. While taking in the intensity of it all, I asked myself, what does it take to make someone realise that your band is better than anyone else is? Walking back to work, I mulled over my deflated feelings. Going in I was on a high confident in the great artwork we had put into the promotional packs, I left wishing we had the full DVD package now as maybe that would give us the edge to stand out from the crowd. However, on 21st February, I walked into the HMV store in Manchester and located a rack of CDs about three quarters inside the large ground floor. It contained the Pretendgirlfriend CDs. I stared at them proudly on the display in the country's leading music retailer shop, in one of the world's most respected music cities! Slowly, I drew in a deep breath of satisfaction and selected one, paid the £2.99 and kept the receipt with the HMV bar code and reference number on it. This was tangible success finally and worth repeating!

The Late Room gig went very well. We had plenty of people down for it and the film David shot of their performance is probably the best footage of Pretendgirlfriend that exits to date. A three-camera shoot and a sound mix from the venue's mixing desk is the best I could have expected, finally!

Live In Hope CD/DVD

I-Profile provided the cover picture as the last work for me as A3H's web site engineers. It is a coloured painting of a pair of man's hands; his dirty fingernails clasp a faded coal dust grey cloth cap. It is a humble, working class image, implying honest toil and pride. The band's coloured logo is in the top left corner and "Live In Hope" in white type set is in the bottom right corner. On the reverse cover is a black and white photo of a woman's hands – chunky ringed fingers pinching a half smoked cigarette, to convey anxiety. The inlay is a black and white picture of a man's torso wearing a loose fitting black shirt, elbows rest on his thighs and his fingers are loosely entwined and below the track listing in the centre is:

"Borrowing the Wildhearts' guitars, they fill the void left by Steoephonics & Oasis with songs that capture Lancashire's soul with all the integrity of The Clash".

We used high-grade gloss paper for the cover and it unfolds with the words to the three songs repeated across both sides. The CD has on body printing with the band's logo in colour at the top and bottom, centre is the tracks *Live In Hope*, *Streets of My Town* and *Apologies* with the email address on the right. The DVD is in beige with the band's coloured logo to the left at the top and to the right on the bottom. Also at the bottom is "Live the Late Room Manchester". The back inside cover is a black and white photo of a man's shaved head. It is a shot from the back, and his left ear lobe has three earrings and "Pretendgirlfriend" stretches across his lower skull from the top of one ear to the other. Above it on the rest of his skull is:

"We are the finest indie guitar band of our generation. We are about substance rather than style. Caring more about why people have to choose between stealing and dealing instead of what hair gel to use".

This is in tattooed styled italics and on his collar is *"Concept and many words of encouragement A3H Promotion Ltd"*. The DVD menu opens up with *Separate Bedrooms* playing. The three options are inset inside a strip of 35mm film. First, is "Flea Pit Film" and as you click on it the *It's Not The End of The World* is the background music to the credits. I do a two-minute introduction and name check the other bands and as many people as I could remember who had come down to support the gig. James' footage is a mix of live, freeze frame and fading in and out, which I liked. Second is David Kay's "Industry" version, which has my voice over again with his logo introducing the band as a one-liner. David's edit is two songs shorter i.e., *Lemon and Lime* and *Down and Wednesday* – the slower ones. It is equally exciting, without any effects and the little jump imperfections I accepted as they give the live feel of cameras jostled by fans. The final option is a picture gallery with Dave Gilmour's photos from The Cuba Cafe gig in March (the first gig I did for Vuz). *Claustrophobic Town* plays as the photos fade in and out and ends with a wall of logos credits the final one shatters to the sound of breaking glass. All the artwork, printing, DVD formatting and the gallery section was the work of my mate Pikemanmick and it must have been a labour of love as he put a note with the proof disc through my letterbox, adding "P.S. I was up till 1.30am!"

This was the most complicated package I have ever commissioned and I am immensely proud of it. At last, I had obtained what I had wanted from day one – a good quality film of Pretendgirlfriend playing live – a flawless performance both they and I could be happy with. It did take a few months to put the finished product together, and we had a lot of meetings and discussions over its content. We argued over whether to use James' footage at all, was the double/two disc worth the expense and would anyone be bothered to watch it etc etc.But what we did not disagree on was the fact that we had got something we had not seen any other band produce at our level. We believed that the DVD, in a double case, with the CD, was unique, for that time. We felt it was guaranteed to win over the curiosity of whoever got it. We put 25 copies together – five of which was for our own use to show people and the rest were for marketing. It united us in the belief that it would impress everyone, as long as anyone could take the time to watch it!

The master plan Part I

We took four copies each and targeted who we thought could offer that much needed break. I chose radio stations in Manchester and varied my approach to suit what I felt they were looking for. Radio was one area we had not tapped in to and we had relied on the plentiful coverage in the local newspapers. Manchester's press and magazines were reliable for listing the gigs promoters had paid for. But radio, I knew from my Chorley radio experiences, reached a different audience. It was free, more independent and its listeners tuned in to hear new and local music. "Want your demo's played on radio or fancy a live set?" -was the title of an email Smit forwarded to me in February from Matt Kendall. He was asking for material to be sent to "Hayley and Naomi" at Fuse FM at University of Manchester. I sent one of our existing press packs to them with a hand written letter. I drew their attention to the Cuba Café gig and mention their next Late Room gig with **Ad Nauseum** in May. The following month I was in correspondence with "Zara" from All FM along similar lines. These small stations were fine but how did I get to the bigger ones like the BBC. I had to work on this but accepted anything else that came along.

Meanwhile, Steve Fenton and I had arranged another Revels gig at Jilly's Rockworld for 23rd March and I used this to introduce myself to the radio stations and sell the A3H/Calder Recording concept of our businesses helping bands helping each other. I also plugged the Pretendgirlfriend gigs in Manchester and their "extensive" tour - as far north as Barrow-In-Furness and as far southwest as Wales, culminating with two appearances at The International Pop Overthrow Festival in Liverpool in May. I tried every angle I could. I considered TV but I did not know anyone at Granada or the BBC and no one I knew had any contacts. The best I could do was waiting for the

Live In Hope CD/DVD to be ready and send that in – by which time I hoped I had the name of someone who would be interested.

A slight interruption from Laura Edwards

When all was going well on many fronts, the band got a kick in the balls. Sending out press packs and encouraging traffic to the website material, down loads etc, invited criticism as well as praise. It did not occur to me at the time, but most of what the media had written was, more or less, what we had told them or what was on the website. There had not been many, if any, serious music critiques of live performances or recorded material. Our fans liked it and those we worked with but, looking through all our files now, I cannot find any in depth and independent analysis of Pretendgirlfriend's work. This is something I have tried to address in this book and why I feel it is necessary to show the warts' all. Hence, one review of their songs from Laura Edwards was scathing. She was not known to any of us and I do not remember when or where the review appeared exactly but it must have been sometime in the early part of 2005. I do know it incensed Noel in particular. He went so far as to print up a batch of CD covers with "Who the f*** is Laura Edwards" in the title. Here is what she wrote;

Limbo – *a Green Day-lite power chord led pop-punk racket with snotty vocals and a meandering bass line. The backing is reminiscent of a million other nu-school punk upstarts.....hardly unique...* It's Not The End of The World – *ironically the gravel-voiced singer sneers at one point "no need to mimic/No need to mine" – while Pretend Girlfriend might not be lip-sync friendly, their music is heavily borrowed from other bands...*In Your Pocket – *the band morphing into some kind of Oasis tribute act. A banal meat and two veg rock backing highlights the lead singer's desire to be Liam Gallagher, his tendency to distort words almost comical...a poor man's She's Electric".......The nasal vocals and frankly crap lyrics are so typical of the no-brain rock of the mid-90's you imagine Pretend Girlfriend to wear fisherman hats, think Shed Seven's break up was a tragic loss and go on stage with a bottle of beer, a fag and an anorak on...*19 St John's Road - *...it is impossible to hear that sneer without thinking of the two-bit Gallagher wannabe, who here also sounds out of tune and monotonous.... The accompaniment...relatively unremarkable.* (In summary) – *Pretend Girlfriend are unconvincing...their songs are uniform and basically non-descript and...simply not good enough to indicate a big future for the band. Any chance to impress is also marred by their frankly terrible lead singer who needs to be told to front a band you need to develop your own style and, more importantly, be able to hold a tune. Pretend Girlfriend may be listenable to in a pub on a Saturday night, but that's all they will ever be.*

To continue and put the master plan back on track...part II

I put the most positive spin I could on what she wrote. I acknowledged that she was entitled to her opinion. I put the damage into context – was she someone with an axe to grind? Was it limited to whomever her website/blog attracted? She was not a name any of us recognised. My counter attacked picked out the "good" things she said – her opening line was *Pretend Girlfriend's four track EP is a professional sounding affair with tight musical backing and good sound quality*. The dent in the band's pride was bashed out after a drinking session and they moved on. I did what I felt a manager should do by not dwelling on it either. We had to take criticism professionally and what we all knew was that the material she had reviewed was old and the band's sound had dropped the Oasis tag. Simmy's song writing had progressed and he *had* found his own style. Danny had provided backing vocals that drew out harmonies, which were not present in their earlier songs. A few years in any band's development made earlier recordings seem like they were performed by a different set of musicians. Compare debut LPs of say: The Jam's In The City to Sound Affects or The Cure's Three Imaginary Boys to Faith or Echo and The Bunnymen's Crocodiles to Heaven Up Here etc etc.Finally,the review did serve to demonstrate that we had to look to the future and push the new material more. We could not change the past and it was right to leave the material on the website to show the development. This did come at a risk but the band was prepared for that and they didn't want to duck any punches. I had to respect this and hope it paid off.

It is not what you lose rather what you have not gained...yet!

Another frustration I realised at that time was the 21-day gig rule. Vuz had pointed this out when I booked the Cuba Café gig. It meant that you could not play any other Manchester gigs/venues 21 days either side of the gig you did for him. This was sensible, as he wanted as many of your fans to his gigs by reducing the number of gigs you played for anyone else in the city. It was not a problem when we were scratching around for gigs. However, as we planned a major push in Manchester, we did not want to refuse any gigs that came our way. We only booked the one with Vuz for now and used the Late Rooms gig in May as the launch date for the *Live In Hope* release. In fairness to Vuz, other venues and promoters applied the 21-day rule at that time. The Charabanc Promotions contract, which ran into five pages, had the same condition in clause 5 of the 22 in the Terms and Conditions pages. It emphasised the "pay to play" issue that I, and most bands I dealt with, hated. You had to pre sell a minimum of 25 tickets at £4 each but after the first 25 sold you received £3 on every ticket thereafter i.e. "...if you sold 50 tickets you got £75". Richard was up front about this and he was always vocal about running his business on these terms. I respected him for that and it was in plain English, not hidden in legal jargon and small print. Furthermore, it was a testament of his both his recognition of potential talent and risk assessment. The gig offer, and the expenses of the package he promoted, had to be to people he felt had demonstrated a sufficient standard and degree of common sense. This quality control cannot be said of others operating at that time who put you on with little thought to genre matching and geographical foresight. The money you paid was weighted against the costs involved to make the whole showcase work. I understood the need to have the £100 in cash to hand over before we could load in. I could see the value of this in the facilities of the venue- a clean, modern, efficiently managed and cool subterranean nightclub. Then you had the advertising in the 5000 coloured flyers the street teams distributed around town. National and Regional media band listings including The NME, The Fly, City Life and all their websites. The band profiles released to over 100 record labels and publishers. In return, it was our responsibility, not his, to get A&R interested so that they attended the gig. This was the crucial fact that few bands appreciated. Playing Manchester, or any city, was one thing, but the trick was to get people who mattered to show up and offer you the deal you wanted!

The IPO Liverpool festival was a stab at whatever we could get from that City along the same lines. In between, The Queens in Barrow gave us good exposure ahead of our debut gig in Cumbria. The Live music section of the Evening Mail on the Thursday before the gig had a half page write up and colour picture of "The Real Thing: Paul "Smit" Smith of Pretendgirlfriend in action" under the main heading "Queens welcomes the great Pretenders". We took **Ad Nauseum** with us and had support form locals **Synko, Silvertones** and **The Usual Suspects**. The last two bands featured my wife's best friend's son, Matthew Whatley, who I had watched grow up and who had become an accomplished guitarist. **Synko** was Carol Hodge's other band to **Sadie Hawkins Dance**. Carol and I had kept in touch after the interviews I had done for SHD for *Pogo'til I Die*. They were under Stuart Taylor Promotions – both Stuart and Carol had good connection to Manchester. Carol had set the Barrow gig up as a return favour for me putting on **Synko** with Pretendgirlfriend, **Baby Bitch** and **Supernova** at the CCC on 26th February.

We got a boost to our advanced publicity for Liverpool from an email Smit replied to in March. Mark Lee had made an enquiry Liverpool Reporter.com - an internet radio station. He had been in the audience when

Pretendgirlfriend played at Casablanca's in Southport. He said, "...the gig wasn't too well attended but the band played a great set regardless! The station was looking to give new North West bands exposure and wanted to feature the band's music. It broadcasted 24 hours a day with band information and a link to their website. It was in the process of moving to include video clips too. There was no fee but also no payment for tracks being played as Mark wrote "...it's simply about playing new music". The station worked with local contacts and the main venues in Southport. He offered to pass on CDs and pointed out that "...they can't pay for bands sadly (gigs being organised by proper rockers so they're skint)". I concluded that no matter how small the attendances are at any show you should always play the best gig you can for you never know who is watching and where it may lead. Furthermore, when it came to expressing gratitude to those willing to help Pretendgirlfriend, I also sent a letter to Caroline Innes thanking for her feature at the end of last year "... which generated a lot of interest for our shows". I pointed out how important the support of a regional paper is by adding "...your work, along with that of John Anson and Clive Lawrence is invaluable and deserves to be acknowledged".

Meanwhile, to earn some money for the trip to High Wycombe, the band played The Duck & Boot, Burnley on 20th March and the Cellar Bar, Blackburn on 26th March. There were gigs at The Top Spot in Hindley, Nr Wigan with **Audio Rush** and **The Layne** on 9th April and The Dudley Arms in Rhyl, the following weekend all of which paid too. This left a gap of nearly three weeks to plug our return to the Late Rooms on the 6th May – we had to focus all our collective efforts for this gig to be the most successful one of their careers to date.

The final pieces

I put a mail out in April to everyone in my A-Z Filofax pages. It must have been over 200 strong by then, bands, promoters, venue owners, all the media people I knew and anyone I had been associated with. I even suggested we invite Laura Edwards as we got over her comments quickly and what a win that would be to make her re-evaluate the band's new material and a live performance! I told other bands that came to the gig that I would name check them from the stage during my introduction. We had coaches laid on for pick-ups in Burnley and Blackburn. I wanted everyone's help to break the 200 we had for The Kierby Hotel concert. So much was resting on this I made a weekend of it in case anyone did show up who was interested in signing the band. I was confident we had maxed out the preparation.

At a band meeting at Simmy's at the end of April, we prepared our story for interviews. We agreed on some standard questions and answers:

"How would you describe your music in 5 words?" –Answer "Indie, alternative, melodic, guitar driven".

"Why call the band Pretendgirlfriend?" Answer, "Wouldn't you want to get slotted behind Chrissie Hynde (Pretenders) while showing your arse to Primal Scream!"

"Why should people take time to listen to Pretendgirlfriend?" Answer, "Because we know why people have to choose whether to steal or deal rather than agonise over which hair gel to use"

"What question do you want interviewers to ask you?" Answer - "Are you here to make the dinosaurs extinct?" Answer "Yes! Any stadium filling act has had their day and it's time to fill the void in the towns they can no longer relate to with our terrace anthems – we'd like you to have the privilege of hearing what we've learned!"

We set out a summary of who was going to contact whom over the next month. Simmy took Island Records, Poptones (Alan McGee) EMI and Fierce Panda. Danny – BMG, Complete Music Ltd, Hit And Run, MCA Music, Polygram, Sony, Warner Chapel and One Little Indian (Jamie Graham). Smit – Big Life Muisc, Chrysalis Music Group, Dick Leahy Music Ltd, EMI Music Publishing Ltd, Island/Polygram Music, Momentum Music and Rondor Music. Noel – Pye records, Warner Bros and Angus Blair at Chrysalis. I was to do the usual round of local press as well as, Alan Wells (Delta Sonic) and promoters; Pogomotion and Drowned In Sound

Helen and I had booked into the Midland Hotel just a short walk up from the Late Room. It was our wedding anniversary and I wanted to celebrate both in style. I had invited a lot of family friends who we had not seem for some time. They were equally interested to see what I had been doing in the music world. For some of them it was their first experience of the Unsigned Scene and they were as excited as I was to have them there to share it. I wanted to have the gig recorded and had been approached by Chris Hughes. He was charging a small fee running a mobile digital recording studio called Studio-Nyne. Really nice person who had all his gear packed in a small suitcase. He recorded both **Ad Nauseum** (on second) and Pretendgirlfriend who were headlining. I had agreed to help promote **Ad Nauseum** under A3H since they asked me for help shortly after the Kierby Hotel gig for a small monthly fee. The recordings I got for Pretendgirlfriend and **Ad Nauseum** are very good quality. The other bands on that night were **The Chase** and **The Aftercast**. This gig was the culmination of the plan along with the hope that we would sell out the Late Rooms, get offered a deal and be rewarded for our unique CD/DVD promotional tool and professional marketing campaign.

The night of the gig was unlike any other I had been part of. Helen and I had had a few drinks at the hotel before tottering the short distance along the glitzy row of other cubs and pubs on Peter Street. The weather was warm and I had a great feeling of something very special about to happen. I had a huge smile on my face as we descended the long wooden steps to the kiosk at the bottom. I could tell from the welcome I got from the staff on the door and the noise inside, that the place was busy. Walking inside I felt I was on air, the music was all the latest Indie tunes, I was nodding and saying "Hi" to familiar faces and I could see Pretendgirlfriend's fans had arrived and I was so in love with the anticipation of the evening ahead. I found most of my friends in the cubicles on the left side and, having got Helen and myself a drink, I took it in turns to sit and chat with them. I checked in with the bands and all was well despite the draught beers not working which upset a few of the heavier drinkers, as there were only expensive bottles available. I took this as a sign why the place was not full - that more fans had gone to fill up at other watering holes to save money and would return later on. Then **Ad Nauseum** came on stage and delivered a cracking performance – fired up on nerves and keen to impress the appreciative audience. By this time there were about 60/70 people in and two bands yet to play. The key now was not to lose anyone and hope that there would be a steady increase in numbers coming in.

By the time, Pretendgirlfriend took to the stage the numbers had increased. I did my introduction name checking **Elcho, Aurota** and **Sterling Rose** – as members of all three bands were in the audience. Kerry McGregor and Alex Martindale were there and I plugged her *Burn Out* fanzine. I kept the speech short and said thanks to the fans who had made it down to see "...a band of the people for the people – PRETENDGIRLFRIEND!" My last frenzied words were Kermit the frog like, as the band started to strike up behind me. On fire, I energetically leapt from the stage to join those at the front for *Barred from the Kings*. The lads were tight. Noel was doing backing vocals too – such was his confidence. Segue into *Streets of My Town* and at the end of the first Chorus Simmy shouts "Happy anniversary Helen". The next, *Out In The Cold* "...about a homeless person who got a bed for the night as one of my mates took her home". Slowing the tempo down Simmy starts *Down On Wednesday* to the strumming of Smit's guitar before the tidal wave of noise crashes in on the third verse. *19 St John's Road* in homage to ".... Shaun Tye, Abacus Studios" – nice one Simmy and thumbs up from him! *Live In Hope* follows before a short thank you to everyone and another "...happy wedding anniversary John"

191

then straight into *It's Not the End of the World* to end the set. It was over. All the planning and promotion had come to this point. Nothing more we could do now. What a ride and now we had to wait and see!

We *did* sell the required number of tickets and everyone there *did* have a brilliant night. However, it was not the massive turn out that I hoped for. As gigs go, it was successful but I knew that it was only "Okay". There was about £10 for sales over 25 – i.e. about 35 people who paid on our head count to get in officially, that is. It was not what I had hoped for – I could not deny that fact - the turnout *was* disappointing. There were no crowds waiting outside, queuing to get in and no one of any industry influence came to watch as far as I could make out. My mobile did not ring with offers of "talks" and my email box was empty. I came to realise that the band and I had given it our best shot but, as the weeks went by, we had nothing to show for it. I was at a loss to think of anything we did or did not do and consoled myself with the thought that maybe Liverpool would be different!

The great debate on what it takes to be cool

Before Liverpool, they had a gig at Nirvana's in Wigan with **Anderson Shelter** on 19th May. I could not go but the feedback was positive. By co-incidence, **Anderson Shelter** were to appear at the Cellar Bar, Blackburn, a few days later, along with **If All Else Fails** and pencilled in were Pretendgirlfriend and **The Usuals**. As it turned out, only the first two bands played but Pretendgirlfriend and I went down to watch with a few mates. Simmy invited me to stop over at his place. I had my Dictaphone with me and I recorded part of the drinking session that followed up to 3am when the tape cuts off. I have transcribed a large portion of what I can decipher as it highlights some interesting attitudes and thoughts amongst those present in the aftermath of Manchester- being Simmy, Smit, Noel, Christian Thwaites and Ray "Fergie" Ferguson (Simmy's mate and Pretendgirlfriend's self-appointed 5th member).

Topic of conversation at the start is Noel's account of a CD (containing 14 songs), by Audio Rush from Westhoughton/Wigan. A3H had received one of their press packs and the standard of it stood out. I had asked him and the other three to review the CD, photos, and covering letter and press clippings. The press mentioned airplay on Canadian radio and I was attempting to get the lads to appreciate what it is like for those in the Music Industry to make decisions on what they received through the post. I knew what it was like to get mail from bands and others hoping for representation, a review or just a gig or two. I would get 3-4 packs a week as A3H attracted mail from all over the UK. We had spent a considerable amount of time and money putting the

192

Live In Hope package together, as well as doing several of our own mail outs. I was wrestling with why nothing had come of it so far. This led me to the idea of turning the table on the band to see what they thought of another band's promotional pack. That way we may discover what works and what does not or, at least understand, what we may need to do differently to make an impression. I had developed a criterion to assess mail. I only allowed five minutes for each of them to do this – i.e. listen to the CD, read the material before delivering their verdict. I wanted to make it as real as I could, so I put an added time pressure in to give their opinion. It was to be a two minute summary of what they thought of the music, its style, the lyrical content, professionalism, what track stood out and why and, finally, a decision on whether they would sign them or not. For the record Noel would not sign them but said if they were playing a local gig, he would "...nip down and watch them".

At that time I, always carried my Dictaphone as experience had taught me I could meet someone to interview. However, that night, I had brought it to play to the lads so they could hear each other's comments. I dumped the idea as it was not going to be one of those meetings and most of us were pissed up and talking shit. However, I thought this would be an opportunity to capture more feedback on what opinions we have of another band after watching them play live. Building on my managerial objective of trying to get Pretendgirlfriend to be analytical on what made something a success or failure; I let the tape run as Fergie sparks off the banter claiming emphatically to Simmy:

"I don't think your band looks fuckin cool!"

It sets fire to a debate on what it is to look cool as a band and as a member of one. Fergie says that Smit looks cool whereas Simmy and Noel do not. Then Simmy and Noel interrogate Fergie on what it is that Smit has and the other two do not. After a good natured series of exchanges that threaten to breach Fergie's contention that they cannot take criticism, and, as the pair become increasingly louder in their counter claims that they can, we conclude that Smit is cool because:

-   He dresses in clothes that have a (rock) look – loose fitting and dark.
-   He has a bit of charisma and style.
-   When he walks on stage, he looks like he is in a band and plays cool.
-   Whereas, Noel (in tracky bottoms) looks like he has turned up for a five a side game of football.
-   Simmy is almost cool but not like Smit is.

Fergie adds that Smit has confidence - an ingredient for coolness. Simmy fires back by saying that Smit is not the most confident man "no offence

Smit!" Smit acknowledges that this is true. Fergie comes back with the fact that when Smit walks on a stage you know that he is in band. I interjected and remind the band of the first video I did of them way back in The North Bar the day I met them, by saying, in a way that tries to appease everyone, about the being cool issue:

".....Smit was at the right hand side of the stage and he stood out. However, when they are performing, Simmy and Danny (to a degree), look really into the music and Noel and Smit look detached. Bill Wyman looked detached in the Rolling Stones but he had a certain charisma just doing it. Moreover, it is that confidence that once Noel and Smit join in vocally - it then becomes a band. When they played the Late Room and Noel, bless his cotton socks, was having a go he was more confident. I've always said to him; don't put your head down, look at the back of his head (meaning Simmy's) if you don't know where to look....and when you saw Simmy at the Dudley Arms – you were on fire there".

The talk moves onto what we are all wearing and I state that Fergie, who is dressed in black, looks menacing – but "up for it "cool. Whereas Noel, who is in a red top, looks pail and washed out – it does not suite him. Noel, defuses the observation by saying that he is in the red and is cool because he does not care if he is over drawn! We drape black on to Noel – a coast or shirt to hand and immediately congratulate him on the transformation. Fergie says:

"You look darker and serious, and, as a guitar player – that's all you want!"

While admiring Noel's new look Simmy contends that he looks like a burglar that we have just found trying to break in and we have asked him to sit down and have a beer. The conversation moves onto a repeat of earlier opinions on what it is to walk out on stage and look like a band. I maintained, as I have done from day one, that image and stage presence is important and should to be taken seriously. Someone mentions the NME and how the pictures of the bands has every member of them wearing thin ties and how that is the look of a successful band at the present (Franz Ferdinand, Kaiser Chiefs for example). Simmy grabs attention by saying:

"...what I've always said about Pretendgirlfriend is that we are coming from somewhere different...for the common man....to come and watch us and look and think....what you get with us is straight out of the pub onto fuckin stage.... some might think we are fuckin roadies...and all of a sudden were plugged in and on.... I think though...but I don't think I fuckin know, and this is gonna sound big headed, but of all these fuckin local bands we have got the tunes far, far above anyone else...so I don't give a fuck what I look like ...when I'm selling half a million records I won't give a fuck what I look like you know what I mean...!"

Thwaites joins in after Smit leaves for home saying how Green Day signed to a small label and toured extensively. This is his way of explaining that, by starting small, you can build on something. Simmy counters by asking how many bands that did that and did not make it. Thwaites ignores this and goes back to the analogy by referring to Pye Records (who **Spitfire** signed to) and, as if a red cloth had been waved to a bull, both Noel and Simmy wade in by stating the fact that (Noel) feels how they could sign to Pye records tomorrow but that it won't mean anything. Simmy says how signing to Pye records made **Spitfire** think and act as if they were better than they are. He says that when he does speak to Wayne or Lee (the brothers in the band) and he ask them:-

"...do you fancy a Burnley gig and (mockingly mimicking their voices in their reply) ...yes as long as it's in a good fuckin venue – we're not doing nothing less than the Mechanics...they already think that they are there (raising his hand up high and then, lowering his hand)...but they're there... ". To drive home his point he uses a football analogy that **Spitfire** are *"... like a fuckin Scunthorpe United trying to be Premier league!"*

More booze splashes about a series of opinions on subjects on the video player or TV and, in between, Simmy's strums an acoustic guitar. The tunes include, *Graffiti* (several times), *I Don't Like Mondays, Green and Alcohol*, a song about the Titanic, *You Can't Always Get What You Want, World Turns Upside Down*. I am urging Simmy to play a song he played to me one time some weeks ago called "I Hate My So Called Mates" – without success. Topics range from what it is to be working class (Simmy's dad's attitude to what is wrong with the youth of today): debating Cold Play's success, what they stand for: Porno movies: ring tones: kids of today are spoilt: German bombing of Manchester and the loss of life in WWII. At ten to three in the morning, Fergie has crashed out on the sofa; Thwaites and Noel are still going strong. Then Simmy starts to strum the tune to *Blockbuster* by The Sweet he gives us a rendition of the alternative Mac Lads lyric "The Fat Bastard". Subjects turn to Coca cola, America and how they do everything right and I add how they do everything big "big country, big motorways, big cars – big heads!" More songs follow: *500 Miles*, a Wonderstuff song, *Barred from The Kings*. Then, as Simmy strums the intro to *"Ziggy Stardust"*, I start the song with an ad-lib:

"Now, Fergie fell asleep on the settee

Noel is sick 'n bored while we watch the telly"

Cigarettes and Alcohol, a song by Outkast, *Graffiti* (again!), *Build Me Up Buttercup, Up the Junction, This is how it feels, Hello*, then to the tune of *Alternative Ulster* is the Mac Lads Sweaty Betty alternative. It goes on: *Friggin'n the Rigging: Bodies* a debate about Sid Vicious: Pete Doherty/Libertines: the Camden clique and The Coral. In a final comment, Thwaites is making a case for Pete Doherty and TV documentaries claiming him to be the next John Lennon. The last words on the matter are mine "wouldn't go that far –they use to say that about Liam Gallagher!"

These sessions made us all feel alive and equally alert to defend Pretendgirlfriend against any detractors - no matter how close our mates were!

International relations and opportunities

My association with International bands started from the point when Pretendgirlfriend played the IPO festival, Liverpool and ended a year later with me working with David Bash to offer overseas bands an opportunity to play in Accrington. We did not know what to expect from our first festival but appearing at The Cavern Club was an exciting prospect for a starter! The festival was very well organised and spread over several venues in and around that Club on Matthew Street. All the gigs had free entry running from the Thursday night starting around 6pm and early afternoon on the Sat, Sun, Monday playing none-stop, almost, to the early hours of the following days. Hence, it tended to be busy with people moving from one venue to another. It sounded like a proverbial wall to wall of bands all the time. My initial enthusiasm dampened slightly when I got David's email in March pushing for bands to apply for their songs to be included on the official IPO CD. The previous year's was a 3CD set with 69 tracks *"...and it received rave reviews in several quarters"* ...humm.... sufficiently vague I thought! This year's offer was a 1000 pressing, *"Which will be given out to those who attend the IPO Los Angeles festival to be held from 22nd July- 7th August. Not Lame recordings will also press additional copies, which will be placed in stores in the Los Angeles area as well as made available on internet sites such as Amazon.com. Not Lame is still receiving consistent orders for all seven IPO CDs, which is testimony to their success......if you're interested in having a track...,please send CD-R of your track plus $300 submission fee..."*.......At this point I felt something swell up in the back of my throat! We did not take him up on this offer and adopted a sceptical approach to the gigs. The other venues were Flanagan's, Lennon's and Mood Indigo. Our slots were both on Monday 20th - 6.15pm at Flanagan's – fifth on an eight bill line up and 9.45pm (second from last) at the Cavern Club (front/main stage) – excellent, no problems with that.

We arrived at mid afternoon and loaded our instruments into Flanagan's – an Irish bar at the bottom end and round the corner from Matthew Street. There were plenty of people milling about and, as the day went on, watching some of the other bands, I discovered that a large proportion of any audience was composed of other musicians. The musical standard was high amongst the

196

bands and occasional soloist but very little grabbed my attention. I was happy with this, as I knew that Pretendgirlfriend would wipe the floor with them all and they did at both of the shows they put on. Looking back at the festival programme, the only ones that stand out now are **Harrison, The Black Jackals** and **No Standards**. However, what did impress me was how well the festival was organised. Fifty plus performers over five days on an eight-bill rota across four venues – and the Cavern had two stages so in effect that's five stages in total. Each had a sound engineer and David would move from one stage to the other introducing the acts. Not that he did this for every one -it would have been impossible - so the bands just got up and played a 25-minute set, then got off and on went the next. It ran like clockwork, David had done his research well and none of the performers I saw over ran or acted like prima donnas – which helps when you have a packed schedule to stick too. The IPO gave us was two good gigs and exposure to all the other bands who watched them. Nevertheless, there was no contact from anyone in the music media or write up/reviews of Pretendgirlfriend's gigs – so it was a "lame" duck in that respect.

Stock taking after nearly a year and a half

We had done plenty of gigs - mostly away from the local venues and we had ninety-nine per cent positive publicity. We had a quality DVD and CD package with a brace of cracking songs delivered in a professionally tight live set. We had respect amongst our peer group; we had received several offers to produce our material from varied and independent sources in the UK and as far away as the USA. We had hit the record labels, promotion companies and anyone who we felt should be interested in us. We did not have any enemies as far as we knew and the music industry appeared to be returning to our style of music. However, we had not had any firm offers of management or credible record label interest. We did not know why and we did plenty of self analysis-seeking ways to improve every aspect of style, image and presentation when performing live as well as on the internet. We had a loyal fan base and we were attracting new fans with every gig. Summer was approaching and I had to think about what to do next. I was mulling over the idea of gig swaps with similar styled bands. The idea being, that we would put on a local gig for an out of town band who we liked. We would guarantee them travel money, beers and a packed gig. In return, we would expect the other bands to be able to do the same for us in their hometowns. This was a form of networking. Gone is the risk of travelling 50-100 miles to play to one man and his whippet like the Shed, Leicester scenario. We could hire the North Bar but preferred something closer to Padiham/Burnley – then luck played its hand in our favour.

How we found our crowd in The Attic

What was to become the highlight of Pretendgirlfriend's live performances and take them to the point of realising the dream to "make it" – started with guitar lessons for my youngest daughter, Holly who was ten and half at that time. When Holly wanted to take up the guitar, I encouraged her while secretly hoping she would go on to excel at it. She was disappointed with the rigidity of formal lessons at Blackburn School of Music. I asked Simmy if he could show her a few chords and teach her some tunes. This lead to him suggesting he came with me to buy her first electric guitar. We arranged to meet one Saturday in Accrington sometime in May when he had his second son, Oliver, for the day. He knew a good music instrument shop in the town and after the deal was done we decided to find somewhere for a brew.

Around this time, I had heard of a new venue opening up in Accrington via a chance meeting with Lee (from The Burn) while out drinking in Blackburn. He handed me a flyer that advertised: The Attic. 48 Warner Street, Accrington with a mobile contact number for someone called "Sam". The week started 11th May with an open mic nights leading to the Saturday 14th May (12pm-2am) line up of *Karma*: *powerful and visceral with nods to the like of Hendrix, Cream, Free and The Family. Karma fuse blues, funk and psychdelia into their own unique style*: **Sam Salon** *normally playing as a solo act, tonight Sam will be playing as a trio doing everything a 3 piece can do from jazzy blues to blues rock and beyond, currently plying his trade in London and with big labels sniffing around this is a great chance to see him up close and personal*: **Rebecca** (no, not the Commies inspired trio from Chorley) *Soaring vocals and searing anthemic songs Rebecca are signed to Fat Northerner records and have just won one of London's biggest battle of the bands and have sold out of their current CD in Japan where HMV Tokyo are massive fans*. The flyer ends with + *DJ*. I stapled it into my diary but did not go to any of the nights for some reason and assumed that more would follow if it became an established venue. Hence, when Simmy mentioned getting a drink, I suggested we check this place out. Warner street is a short walk from the main street in Accrington and we climbed the three flights of stairs to the top of the building, which nestles above a Victorian Arcade below. Slightly out of breath, as we had carried Oliver's push chair all the way up we got a greeting from the man behind the bar confirming that coffee was available and kids could come in during the day.

After settling down at a table, we surveyed the place. Back then, The Attic had the stage at the far end directly opposite the entrance. It was a boxed in on two sides with a wall that came up to your waist. To the left of the stage were the doors to the toilets and the right side lead to the fire exit and kitchen, which doubled as a dumping ground for equipment. The bar on the right of the entrance had wood panelling with mirrors and one of those hot drinks machines that you have in branded coffee shops. At the other side of this was a small gap before the sound engineer's area housing a mixing desk and room for 2/3 people to stand. A foot high step allowed the only entry point to this enclosed corner adjacent to the right of the entrance door. On the left hand side of the room was a selection of heavy wooden chairs and tables with a raised seating area in the centre backing on to the wall that over looked the street. Two large windows provided the only natural light. The PA speakers were at the front of each side of the stage and the floor area was free of obstructions. I could picture where a crowd of 100 or so people would stand with a clear view of the stage. A perfect small venue is how we summed it up to each other. Then Simmy leant over to me. For those who do not know Simmy, he has a way of saying what he feels is a gem of wisdom by cuffing his left hand wrist to his mouth. This, I learnt over time, meant he was about to say something revealing – a sort of "...for your ears only..."and on this occasion, as he did so, he said - "John, I think Pretendgirlfriend have found their home here – what d'yu think mate?" I took a deep breath, did a slow 180 degree visual sweep and looked back at him with a nodding smile..."...yeah, I think you're right mate!"

We were the only people in at the time; I went over to make enquiries about getting a gig. The bar man, "Sam "was, as I later found out, a member of **The Citizen Band** and he noticed my enthusiasm for the place. He knew of Pretendgirlfriend when I mentioned their name and my association with them. After that relaxed discussion with Sam, we left our calling card and he did the rest.

Pretendgirlfriend's debut gig at The Attic was on 10th June, with support from **The Palms** (who we had stuck up a link with after a seeing them at a gig in Manchester).The success of the Attic over the years was down to owner Paul Fox and his vision. He had a passion for music as well as being an entrepreneur. I shared the former and lacked the later. Everyone got a warm welcome from "Foxy". He has a beaming smile that draws you in and makes you feel immediately at ease. He said that Pretendgirlfriend were exactly the type of band he wanted to play his venue. Indie guitar styled and local – what a refreshing change, I thought. He had ambitions to attract new breaking bands and needed similar genre supports that were reliable and able to bring in 20/30 of their own fans. He did not present this as a "pay to play". Foxy was subtler in that he felt that any self respecting local band, serious about being taken as a contender for getting on in the music business, would demand these numbers of themselves and not have a problem with them. If they did, then it was better for all concerned that they forget it and not waste each other's time. This was fair as it was up front and made sense on a "challenge yourself if you don't agree with the logic" kind of a thing – I liked his style.

Pretendgirlfriend played the Attic four times before the end of the year and had eight gigs there in 2006. I cannot say I remember much about their debut but it was attended by a reasonable crowd – Foxy had no complaints and my diary noted "Brilliant – we've found our venue and our crowd" -Simmy was right!

Very soon after this gig, Foxy called me over to his office at the Attic for a meeting. He wanted help promoting the venue and asked me to supply bands for Friday and Saturday nights. He offered the venue for hire if I wanted to put on my own nights there. This kicked off a successful two-year relationship between A3H Promotion Ltd and the venue. I learned a lot, personally, from Foxy. For Pretendgirlfriend, it meant I could ensure they got the right gigs there. The Attic became their home. It was ideal for the gig swap initiative, our own show case nights and support slots with those further up the food chain to commercial success. All was perfect for once.

The rest of the year settled down to a series of selected gigs – including a Charity gig at Burnley Mechanics in June. On the back of their set at Arts in the Park in Blackburn (over a weekend in mid July), Kerry McGregor did a full-page interview which was published in her September issue of *Burn Out* (number 6). The band had a good slot in bright sunshine. Kerry took some photos during their set and inserted two with the interview. Simmy and Smit are wearing shades and in the sound bites she captured you can detect a new optimism:

"...every gig seems to get better...people said it sounded good out front" (Simmy)

"We have about 25 songs – about 8 of which we do....our strongest...we are a live band...and the last time we played Wigan we went down really well" (Paul).

He mentioned this because they had a gig at Nirvana's with **Ad Nauseum**.

"We made a few contacts in Wigan and they're coming down again tonight... they've been on the website leaving messages, said they'd never had our CD out of the stereo" (Simmy)

They pay a flattering tribute to my input too:

"To be honest we were only playing with it up to John becoming our manager. We did more gigs in the first two months with John than in the year before, so you DO need a manager. It's a fifth voice as well. Good thing about John is he won't

talk about something he doesn't know about. He's not in it for the money; he's in it because he is a genuine fan. We're probably not doing as much as we should but we're doing what we can. I've two children, Smit's gonna be a dad soon, everyone works full-time....I know that it sounds cliché but we've never chased the sound of the time or dressed a certain way. We've always been honest. This year's been our best so far, still waiting to hear from a couple of labels as well that have asked for our stuff. A couple of majors, but I'd better not mention any names" (Simmy – with economical truth!).

I struck a deal with Kerry to help promote Pretendgirlfriend's "In the City" gig at the Retro Bar in October. In return for her help/interview etc, I gave her copies of Pretendgirlfriend's live CDs (from the Late Room gig in May). I had burned these off myself with Retro bar gig flyers for her to give away free with the first 100 copies of the fanzine. On the inside page of the issues under "FREE CD" she added my editorial:

"Pretendgirlfriend are pleased to provide free CDs to help support Burnout fanzine. The band hope you enjoy their performance, recorded live with no tarting up in a studio or fancy remixes- what you hear is exactly what came across during their dynamic performance. The band wants their music to stand or fall on its own merits. So as a live EP, people know exactly what to expect when they go to one of their gigs. The band would appreciate your feedback. Any criticism, as long as it's constructive, can be directed to them at www.pretendgirlfriend.com or via a3hpromotion@aol.com, Finally, anyone who wants to become a true fan can register at the above and help support their In The City gig at the Retro bar, Sackville Street, Manchester on 2nd October – doors open at 2pm – several bands and cost to be advised in next issue".

Kerry adds underneath "Thank you to John and Pretendgirlfriend for CDs, interview and the support they've shown me". The band got their picture on the cover too **above** The Undertones – get it in there my son! Another job well done!

Next Foxy offered them the support slot to Tom Hingley's debut appearance at the Attic on 29th July. I was on holiday but the band said that the gig was a success and Tom had said that "he really liked us" as Smit relayed to me later.

Telling you about the young ideas

We were all floating on a new sense of achievements. Things seemed to be happening and The Attic was fast becoming the place to play if you were an Indie band. We were also very busy sending out the press packs for the In the City gig. It was a lesson we had learned that there is no point playing city centre gigs if no one who mattered showed up. In the City was the few days each year when Manchester was stuffed with Music Industry people. Thanks to the efforts of Tony Wilson and his team, Manchester had its very own show case event – which was a series of lectures, exhibitions and concerts. It was our first time and well known that bands had been signed off the back of being noticed playing gigs during this event in the past.

I had a subtle way of approaching the "targets" we had selected for the mail outs. From the pages of music industry magazines, I cut and pasted sound bites. So, for example in one letter/email I wrote:

"...if you're good enough A & R will find you..." (Dougie Bruce A&R at Sony Records).

"It's important to give a great show; people are going to gigs again and want to be entertained" (Angus Blair, Chrysalis Group).

"...don't play London unless they're from London....just send a CD and contact information" (Gerard Philips A&R Independente Records).

"...ultimately what counts is the music and a band that believes in themselves"

(Dave Campbell, The Cluny, Newcastle).

I added:

"All your words have been absorbed...and I would like to know you. You probably won't have heard of me or the band I manage called Pretendgirlfriend from Burnley, Lancashire." I mention their website and go on to say "... I have developed their talent to the best I can and recorded this on a DVD for the people who I feel may be able to help". I end by saying that I would like to send the DVD/promotional press pack to them but wanted their response indicating how I should address the label to ensure it reaches them personally.

The best response I got was from Phil Catchpole - A&R Manager at Chrysalis Music Ltd. I had quoted him as saying:

"Don't pander to A&R people. Just get on with what you are doing and if the act is great and the time is right, you will be discovered".

I started the email to him "Not that I want to pander but...I'd hate you to get crushed in the rush to sign this band" – I thought you would appreciate my personal invitee to see them at the In The City Showcase, the retro bar etc... ". I got an email back "hey john thanks for the mail...please send a demo to the address below (The Chrysalis Building, Bramley Road, London).

I sent the pack and we lived in hope!

Not everything was plain sailing. We had become use to disappointments and knock backs and these continued to balance all the positive things. For example, on the eve of Colne Music festival over the August bank Holiday weekend , Simmy got this from Holly Davies at www.drownedinsound.com www.repeatfanzine.co.uk & www.shoorfromthehip.co.uk :

"I looked at your site and read some of the reviews and I'm not sure you'd really be my thing – the comparisons to Feeder and Aerosmith, who I don't like, and general use of the words "Classic Rock" indicated that your sound might not be one I'd go for. Did you think those reviews were accurate? If so, is their some sort of X-Factor, which makes you, transcend the genre? Only I never listen to anything, which I think of as classic rock at home, and I switch the radio off when such tunes come on. So do feel free to try to persuade me – but going from those reviews you would be in grave risk of an uncomplimentary review from me! So, it's your call really....Sorry I can't be more unreservedly enthusiastic – but I am being honest, and I would be up for giving it a try if the above warning leaves you undeterred.... Holly(i)y xxxx"

The email is 5pm on 25th August– close to her bedtime I was thinking. Later there was an email exchange between her and Simmy, which resulted with her response of:

"Cool. I'm fine with reviewing live stuff. Send the CD to (an address in Cambridge)..Holly xxxx."

I have nothing to show where this leads – another dead end. I had a few other setbacks. A gig at the Liquid Lounge in Blackpool for July/August did not come off – neither did one with **Occasional Rauscudos** at the Royal in Poulton, as one of our lads was not available. On my personal profile side, there were positive but distracting matters. I had M.A.C.Y and Chorley FM meetings as I was still giving input to them and I wanted to be available to DJ as a way of promoting the band. I had paid gigs to book for the Attic and the Cellar bar had asked me to put bands on for them too. The band bookings boosted revenue and there was queue of bands wanting me to manage and promote them as well.

Banking on a change

It was summer. I had family responsibilities and all the parental logistics that go with it while fitting everything else in between. To add to what was on my mind in the mid to late 2005, I was not happy in my day job and I had not been for most of the year. I was disillusioned with the role of a Business Manager. The title "Manager" was in name only and it was little better than being a sales representative. With every customer came the pressure to sell – flogging overdrafts, loans, payment protection and introductions to consultants who would sell other financial service products. This is what I had escaped from doing three years previously. There was little time to manage a customer in the traditional sense of what I had been doing on the personal side back in Barrow in the mid 1980s. The role I pictured for a business manager was someone taking time to understand a business: what the owners planned and to develop a long-term relationship that delivered what they expected i.e. give sound advice rather than persuade them to buy expensive products that seemed to be swelling the Bank's profits rather than those of their customers'. It was time to make a change. I put in for a move when we all had to re-apply for our jobs. I had been good at my job and was offered the Wigan office, keeping the same grade but given even higher targets. No, I wanted out. Fortunately, my new boss was one of the very few old school staff left who had his integrity in tack. I told him I did not want to take the job and he simply asked me what I felt I would be happiest doing. He recognised my need to move and was genuine in his desire to see that I settled into what I wanted to do next. I said I needed three things from any alternative: to work closer to home, have a seven-hour day and not have to sell anymore. I would consider a sideways move or even a downgrade, as I knew that by getting out of Business Banking meant I was stepping off the career ladder. The runs on it had proved to be a slippery and I was tired of playing the game.

I still wanted to stay in the Bank – no way could my music support me and there was no offers of redundancy this time round. He came up trumps with a move into Group Operations as a document checker based in Clayton Green, Chorley – flexible hours and, with no customer contact, there was absolutely no selling. Excellent, I applied and got the job. Meanwhile, a property deal Helen and I had been involved with in Spain was going belly up and we had to resolve that next. The autumn proved to be significant, as it turned out, for all the above – and especially my focus on Pretendgirlfriend.

Tony Wilson – the moment he got Pretendgirlfriend's package

October was a major turning point on many levels. Manchester, In The City, was the next horizon we had to conquer. By now our pre gig, publicity was at its best and we knew we had done as much as we could on mail outs, the internet etc and all that was left was to see what happened at our slot on the Retro Bar. I went to Manchester the day before as Bruce McKenzie had invited me to a showcase gig he had organised during the day at an underground club called South on King Street. I took Shaun Maxwell with me and made a point of visiting as many other venues as I could while we were in town to hand out more flyers and talk to people, in particular, those wearing convention passes. These cost hundreds of pounds and got you into all the gigs and conferences. It was a safe bet that those who had one *were* involved in music industry - the trick was to find out *what* was their line of business. Ideally, you wanted them to be A&R on the lookout for fresh talent to sign. I never met anyone like that. Rather it was people plugging their own city's venues or talent. They had their own compilation CDs to hand out with superior looking leaflets to mine – glossy coloured and eye catching – unlike our plain black and white photo copies. It was hopeless – saturated with everyone doing the same thing. I did not know anyone significant to hand our stuff to either. No one had been in contact to meet me off the back of the mail outs. I tormented myself by asking if I had I done all that I could do. Come the Sunday I did much the same - street walking before their set handing out flyers telling people what time they were due on stage. Then luck played a hand. I found out, while in conversation with some Geordie delegates that the majority of the people who mattered would be hanging around The Midland Hotel. Sure enough in the centre of the Hotel's reception were big tables full of flyers, CDs and other free bees left by bands and other hopeful promoters. I decided to spend as much time there as possible, taking it in shifts with the band.

I did not recognised anyone in the roped off area that overlooks the reception. It seemed the place where you needed to be to smooze with the elite. I kicked myself for not doing more homework, studying the faces in all the trade magazines. I ran a vision: an invite across the barrier by someone from a major label who had expressed interest in the CD/DVD I was handing out. Later, they would appear at the gig and we would shake hands on a deal. A dream I tortured myself with. Damn it, I should have invested in a convention ticket/pass, brought a pocket full of cash and wormed my way into conversations offering to buy drinks and anything else that would get me an edge. I was feeling utterly frustrated by being on what seemed to be the fringes of a game. I did not understand the rules that everyone else appeared to be seasoned professionals at playing it. I was out of my league and I was at my lowest ebb. I was about to head back to the Retro Bar with Smit, when I spied a car pulling up outside and out stepped Tony Wilson.

Tony (Mr Manchester and music legend) Wilson! I knew this was it - no time for holding back. I gave a "heads up" nod to Smit in the direction of the glass doors and darted for the right hand one meeting him just as he was about to go through. My heart was pounding; my head was a jumble of opening lines and my brain screamed, "... don't fuck it up!" In the whirl of it all, I said something like:

"Mr Wilson, I just wanted to shake your hand and say how thankful I am to you for all you have done to promote local music in the North West of England." I thrust my hand out confidently.

He stopped and nodded a "thank you "as he shook my hand. Remembering I had once sent him half a ten-pound note, during The Commies days, I said, as I struggled with my jacket to find my wallet:

"I don't expect you remember but I once sent you half a £10 note promising to give you the other half if you went to watch a band I was managing at the time..." (His expression turned to a puzzled frown and his colleague smirked ...." and now you want to ask for it back eh Tony...!"

"No, in fact (thinking quickly I changed tact and pulled out the CD/DVD of *Live In Hope*)...I wanted to hand this to you and assure you that no bribe is necessary to want to see this band...."

Then the most amazing thing happened that would stay with me forever. He looked down at the case; I watched his eyes widen slightly – which I took as a hint of being impressed. Then the fantastic moment went by in slow motion as he accepted the copy and stared into my eyes, saying slowly and very deliberately:

"I'll take this and listen to it later..." He smiled reassuringly, took the CD/DVD and patted it into his left suit pocket. He was through the door and gone into the throng of people waiting inside.

"Wow John, Tony Wilson......" Smit said as he joined me on the steps outside.

I starred up at the sky, took a deep gulp of the fresh evening air. I was standing on the steps where many famous and powerful people from all over the world had stood. I gave myself a moment to take it all in and savour how I felt. I had done something brilliant. I was happily dazed by the encounter. I replayed it over in my mind, breathing in calmly, I had to process the sequence, rewinding repeatedly as Smit and I stared at each other - stunned. Slowly a smug feeling of contentment and pride at what we had done poured into my soul and I blushed with the widest grin ever! Wow! I had met, shook hands and delivered the best material that Pretendgirlfriend had to the one man we all knew could make our dreams come true. If Tony Wilson liked what he saw and heard then there were no doubts anymore. He still had the connections and influence, even then while in failing health, he could pluck anyone from obscurity and into the big time. Forget Simon Cowell, Tony was still the king when it came to the genuine article and his seal of approval had integrity stamped all over it. Yes, indeed we had saw, come and conquered Manchester finally. What could any of us have done that was more impressive than that! The man that mattered most in our world who got the package said he would "listen to it" – at last, we had our break!

We had to rush back to the gig and I think I floated there. Smit and I slapped each other's backs all the way back to Sackville Street and the lads were all a gasp when we retold the story. The gig –ahhh- it did not seem to matter as much now. We got a result no matter what happened next!

And.....yes you guessed it...nothing happened. The call from Tony or his PA I played in my mind was :" Mr Winstanley, Mr Wilson was most impressed with the Pretendgirlfriend CD/DVD and he wants to know when you would be able to meet him with a view to signing a contact letting him take over the management of the band for a six figure sum?" No, that call never came. No one else called either. No one important came to the gig that we recognised. We harboured a hope that maybe he would send out a scout to see us play a local gig before making the offer. The next one was at the Cellar Bar, Blackburn on Saturday 22nd October with **Dead Honchos**. The gig came and went and still no call, no email or letter as the weeks went by. Bollocks!

The beginning of the end...or the end of the beginning?

I remember Simmy being annoyed that I had not cancelled that Cellar Bar gig in favour of them supporting Little Man Tate at The Attic the same night. Foxy had arranged the gig and it was only after I had confirmed Pretendgirlfriend at the cellar Bar (which paid a fee) that he asked me to supply the support slot (free). I gave this to **Star 27** as a thank you to Russ Carlton for all his encouragement back in the beginning. **Star 27** featured him and others in the group I had know from way back – including ex members of **Wowzer**. However, Simmy later reflected on my decision and agreed it was the right one. We had never pulled out of any gig and were not about to. We had advertised the gig on the flyers taken to Manchester so there was always a possibility that someone from Tony Wilson's team may turn up to watch them in Blackburn. They played a cracking set and, as it turned out, we all got over to the Attic to see the Little Man Tate set and met the band afterwards. This band was breaking through at that time and was where we wanted to be. I asked them what advice they had in "making it". They said to keep going, playing as many gigs as possible and never stop believing. So, nothing new then! I could have been pushier and played up to them with the intention of getting introductions, contacts and anything that would get Pretendgirlfriend and me onto the inside track. But, I didn't. It was not my style and maybe that was a flaw.

The end of the year was approaching and I had to think about 2006 and what I wanted to do next. I thought about setting up my own record company. How difficult would it be to produce my own label and sign my own bands – what was stopping me? Why wait to be signed why not set up your own label, produce and sell your own CDs. This is what Pretendgirlfriend had been doing for years but did not have the "label" name behind them. We could make one up and tell everyone we were a signed band. That would generate publicity and get one of the ticks off the career wish list. What would it cost? It cannot be that much more than what I had spent on setting up A3H, registering the name and having it printed on everything I had done since. The DVD/CD could be relabelled along with the band's entire back catalogue. Simple! When I put it to the band in the past, they came up with the name Unfinished Business but we had not pushed the name or what it meant. Was now the time to do so? I put this on hold as Foxy asked me to organise a gig for Tom Hingley and his band **Too Much Texas** in Chorley at the former Labour Club.

Relatives of Foxy's had taken on the Labour Club on Friday Street (Chorley) and wanted help promoting it. **Too Much Texas** was the band Tom was in before he joined The Inspiral Carpets. He had put the band back together for a few gigs and had asked Foxy for help. It was a lifetime ago since I had been to the club and it had closed for a while. I did not know this band but felt there would be any demand to see them because of Tom's connection and name. The whole thing was a challenge but the opportunity to work with Tom was attractive. It was a favour to Foxy, who had helped me and who knew where it might lead. It was a lot to take on in one go and I had that to process amongst everything else. The 12th November was penned in alongside a gig for Pretendgirlfriend with **Shorn** at the Attic on 19th November.

The two went hand in hand. I needed Chorley based bands to support **Too Much Texas** and asked Shaun Maxwell. He agreed to help by putting **Shorn** on the bill and recommended **The Shoks** who had a huge local following, as their drummer was local boxer Mick Jennings. To add variety I invited **Colorpool** to play too. I asked Timsy to supply the PA, more out of gratitude for his work to me at The Cellar Bar, than a snub to Phil Baker, who I wished I had asked as Timsy turned up late and nearly ruined the gig. Jake Maxwell saved the day by setting it up working the mixing desk as well as performing with **Shorn**. Tom was easy to work with and he was delighted by the turn out, which was massive. We all made money on that gig and Tom did a solo acoustic set at the end of the night. I cannot remember if it was planned but he did one despite the fact that most people had left. I stayed in touch with Tom for a while and I think he gave me some contacts. Again, I could have made more of this but did not and nothing came of it for Pretendgirlfriend.

It got very chaotic very quickly. I was everywhere at once again with my diary a blitz of gigs, phone numbers, times and notes. Chaos, in a good sort of way for A3H as money was coming in from gigs and new bands were banging on its doors for representation. The weekly mailbag was well into double figures! Other venues wanted me to supply them with bands. Some of them I had not been to or heard of before and I had to make time to visit or check them out by asking others about them. I was also curious about their suitability for Pretendgirlfriend to play too. During all this, I had the thought of getting Pretendgirlfriend better support slots using the Attic. I surveyed who was "hot" and I sent out requests to play the Attic on one of the nights that Foxy had reserved for me. I was prepared to offer up to £100 for expenses etc out of A3H's money. As a result, Polytechnic got in touch and played on 2nd December (my birthday – a good omen I felt). I put **Leaf** and Pretendgirlfriend on as support. Foxy gave me some cash toward the costs of flyers and the gig was a success in that it was well attended and enjoyed by all. I did not make enough of the chance to get to know the members of Polytechnic and seek out any connections they had. I don't think they hit it off with the bands as they were off as soon as they played their set and had my cash. I was not into sucking up to bands and didn't feel that this was going to work out unless I compromised on this issue. I would let Pretendgirlfriend find the bands in future and do the networking instead.

That weekend Pretendgirlfriend were back at Studio Studio for a recording session. From this came *Shopping for Free* and *Green and Alcohol* – probably the pinnacle of tunes by the band buoyed up on an eventful year that delivered more than we were disappointed by. Lyrically, Simmy was at his observational best and the band was at its tightest. They were ready to make the next step up to being signed – especially when they played the Attic as taxi, fares for the faithful were less expensive than going to Blackburn and further afield. The place was buzzing and you sensed something was about to happen.

Internet and the webs we weaved

Around this time, I had asked Smit to take over running A3H's website and to boost my cyber space presence.Myspace.com – had established itself as *the* place to be where you could up load tunes, a profile, gigs and photos. It made the world a smaller place. The market became your PC; in the comfort of your own home you did not need to see a band live, you were spoilt for choice on a global scale. Both Pretendgirlfriend and A3H were on it. We unashamedly drove traffic to Pretendgirlfriend's page by playing all the tricks we could, going on other bands sites and making comments about why everyone should visit theirs. At that time, MySpace was an excellent platform to display your songs. The power of the internet made us obsess about getting "friends" and upping the number of plays of our songs. You did not have to rely on Royal

Mail anymore – you could send a hyperlink of your MySpace address or attach MP3 of your tunes to whomever you wanted. Soon my email box was filled with others doing the same to A3H. The industry changed very quickly and it was not long before the Arctic Monkey's broke. The story at that time as that their success paid credit to their internet presence, everyone was hoping that they would be next band to succeed this way.....and for a while we believed it too land ....the rest is history!

My home life had changed too. Helen and I finally bought a small place in Spain and I had relocated to work in Chorley, accepting a downgrade. I was closer to home and joined a local gym as I was becoming fat and had done no regular exercise since stopping judo in 2002. **Capulet** asked me to put on a gig for them at The Adelphi, Preston between Christmas and New Year, with support from their newly signed label mates on Motive Sound Records. I asked Jake Maxwell to do sound and supply the PA. It was a great gig and a brilliant way to end 2005.Both the music and personal side of my life was busy but what next for Pretendgirlfriend?

2006 I did not know what more could I do as the band manager. I had spent the last few weeks of 2005 gnawing at the idea of setting up a collective of bands that had either asked me to manage them or become closer involved with promoting them. It hatched the idea that became the Digger Movement (see Chapter 11). I set about writing out a contract agreement with the bands I wanted to join. I posted this out just before the Christmas break and waited for the response. I also chewed over the idea of the record label again. I had developed a friendship with Sean McGinty by this stage. He was the BBC Radio Lancashire local music presenter and saw the impact of his shows on promoting local bands. Sean was/is a great advocate of local music and we got on very well. Sean had helped Pretendgirlfriend by playing their songs on his show and provided one of my favourite opinions of them *"a meeting of Oasis in the street with moderate violence"*. I felt my appeal to him, and perhaps a lot of others, was in my capacity as A3H and not just as the manager of Pretendgirlfriend. This realisation changed my direction. I had to face facts and I knew that I had never been entirely devoted to a single band at any point.

On reflection, I can trace all the way through this chapter, how I was continually preoccupied with matters outside Pretendgirlfriend. To be fair to the lads I think they knew I had done as much as I could for them and their priorities had changed too. Consequently, I embraced the Digger Movement, planned to put out a CD of these bands, and focused on that. This is the point when I knew I had come to the end of being the manager for only one band.

I did not know that at that time but I had tried everything I could over the last two years and I did not know what more I could do. My belief in the band had not changed and never has to this day. As I saw it, I had to make a choice: what was the benefit of continuing to manage the band if someone else could take over and do a better job or was there something I could do that I had not done already.

Towards the end of 2005, Simmy told me he was content with playing locally rather than for me to set up another tour. I was very busy organising and promoting the Attic and Cellar Bar gigs and relieved by this comment. When I floated the idea of The Digger Movement, Simmy said he would rather join it than have me pushing Pretendgirlfriend as I had done. There was no big discussion with the rest of the band as there had been at the start we just accepted that I was no longer their manager but would continue to let them know of anything I could pass to them. We had returned to the way things were before. It was as simple as that and this is where I could close the chapter. However, there were one or two highlights that I think deserve a mention.

Vibes from the Attic

Green & Alcohol was track 7 (lucky seven) on the "Vibes from the Attic" CD (see Chapter 10) which I released to coincide with their appearance at the IPO festival in Liverpool at the end of May. I paid for an advertisement for them and **The Making** (who had also joined The Digger Movement) and were playing IPO too. Pretendgirlfriend played Lennon's and The Cavern (back room) and I gave away loads of CDs while plugging their appearances. The band did do their part of the gig swap idea playing Pure in Sunderland after an invite from local band **The Pits**. They played the Attic with Sheffield band **No Av on the TV** and North East based **Junkser,** but never got the return gig. By the end of the year, Pretendgirlfriend put three tracks on The Digger Movement CD. These were: *Shut the Door Behind You (Demo), Shopping for Free* and *Out in the Cold* and I took pockets full of copies to In the City, Manchester at the end of October. Foxy asked them to support Northside, Tom Hingley and ex Oasis Bass player, Bonehead at the Attic. But, perhaps the biggest and most satisfying thing I set up for Pretendgirlfriend before I got out of the music business, was their support slot to Ginger from The Wildhearts at Riffs night club in Blackpool on 20th Jan 2007. Thereafter you can read Pretendgirlfriend's continuing story at www.pretendgirlfriend.com.

Epilogue

I transferring my interest from Manager to the fan and friend I was from the very start. It took the pressure off all of us. Since then I have had many chats with the lads about what happened or didn't and at no point have any of them had a critical word to say about what I did for them or did not do as their manager. They are generous in their appreciation and "blame" has never entered the vocabulary between us. However, this chapter is a study of failure as much as it is of success. I know what I wrote between the lines and I do blame myself now for not making more of opportunities I had. The benefit of hindsight is one theme of this book and that is a good thing as it gives me closure and helps me make sense of it all. I hope it helps to put into context everything the people involved inside and outside of the band need to read. It may raise more questions than I have tried to answer and perhaps the best fact left from all of this is that it is not the end. The band is still playing and who knows what might happen next. The future is unwritten.

Song by Song – a personal discography critique

It is important to me to express my opinion about the songs Pretendgirlfriend have written. Most of what follows is about recorded material you can hear that for yourself by visiting the www.pretendgrilfriend.com. I hope that you will be able to appreciate that they have taken the time to record their best output, spending money on what they could afford. It is a credit to all the band members that they have not put a foot wrong. I know that there are moments of influences that can be sighted in the their songs; of something borrowed in vocal or guitar styles but the end result is always a quality that stands above the majority of their peers in the unsigned geography of East Lancashire. They were in competition with some notable peers too – **New Breed of Monkey** and **Spitfire** on the indie side as well as **Exit State** and **The Freespirits** on the metal/rock edges.

I spent a lot of time with the band on tour, at meetings, rehearsals and just chilling. I know something about their private lives that perhaps gives me a better insight to the songs than most to talk in terms of themes that run through the work to date. This is my opinion on the meaning of the songs. No one has confirmed if my interpretation is correct or not and the conclusions I have reached are my own. I do know that the lyrics of Pretendgirlfriend have been central to my attraction to them and worth studying more closely.

Trust and fidelity

Simmy is the main songwriter in fact, as far as I know; all the songs recorded to date are his compositions. It is a reflection of his personal life and he has had several relationships in the years I have known him. He confesses to his own lack of self-confidence in his own abilities:

I look in a mirror and what do I see I see?

I don't see a success staring at me

I just see a liar who lies through his teeth just like me (It's not The End of the World)

He is also painfully aware of this in relationships too:

Do anything she tells you to

Speak only when you're spoken to

Agree with everything she says

Coz you know she's always right.

Lose your self-esteem make it easier (Miss High and Mighty)

In Your Pocket is a song in which he is mockingly respectful of a friend who invites himself into his home, does not bring his own beer and takes up all the room on his couch. Yet his ability to be so selfish, boasting about his latest winning horse while falling out with his host has a cautionary tale for those who are taken in by his charm:

Mind your girl coz he might steal her

And keep your cigarettes close by

Turn your back keys in your pocket

Lock the door to keep him out.

However, Simmy is not the same as this person, he admits he has made commitments and when these have failed, he tries to explain why. The Martin Simm I know has never let his band or me down. Maybe he has had to make choices in his life when it came to his song writing and the band that set him at odds with his partners, family and friends. Like Shaun Maxwell, decisions had to be taken and if these do not sit comfortably with what you believe in then where do you go? What do you decide to do? Whom do you upset and whom do you pacify?

I know that in the pursuit of what I was doing musically I had to make choices that I am not proud of in retrospect - I spent time away from my children and Helen when I could have been with them. The money I invested could have been spent on what they wanted. I did what I wanted for reasons of my own and in my own way denied them something. This was never done in a fit of selfishness or on any level of greed, it is just what I did when I did it and for the reasons that are entirely justifiable to me. I hope that you can identify with Simmy and his predicament, as I do, when we all have to face our own cross roads. How we live with the path, we take and the consequences of where they lead us to make us who we are. For Simmy, in his songs, it is trust and other interpersonal issues that do not sit easy with him. He wrestles with what he had to do or has done in an effort to understand, exorcise and confess. He exposes his weknesses and answers his own question in:

I never learn I'll never earn respect
What damage she will turn up next?
I never trust I know I must
Give up my vice tonight.
I am the one who has done wrong....

No compromise I'll never change...
I'll say I'll change but never do
I'll carry on the way I do (Green & Alcohol).

There are times when he puts the blame on others without mincing his words:

I don't think I ask for much,
Just a girl I can trust (live In Hope).

Perhaps it is not necessary to have the analysis that delves into the personal reasons and circumstances for him writing these lines. He may not want to mention names and get graphical. He is trying to express both shock and guilt at the same time at his own failures and in the actions of others. Some songs direct blame towards friendships. He feels discretion, or lack of it, brings out another sullied trait in people and their surroundings.

Privacy

The confinements of life in a small town, with its nosey neighbours and the restrictions to personal freedom they impose by their behaviour. *Claustrophobic Town* is all this in the song title and the litmus line is *...And the gossips know just where I've been.* One of his earliest tunes touches on the depression this can cause while he reflects on his circumstances at work:

Down again on Wednesday and its feeding time for me
In a cage for all the world to see, in a show that I can't handle
Coz I know that it's not me; I think they picked a part for me.
CHORUS
And I don't know why I'm here- Listening to all of their problems
I've got problems of my own -and I fall asleep for the third time. (Down on Wednesday)

Simmy grew up in Padiham and has spent all his life there. His family are from a working class background in the East Lancashire sense of the meaning. The demands on his life by others are a burden and his frustrations surface repeatedly throughout his songs as if the strain has left a stain on him. This makes his journey from the crossroads a circular and vicious one. From the songs up to 2003;

An honest man trying to please everyone (It's Not The End of the World).

My time is no longer my time (Over my Head).

And I'm sick of all the compromising; why not put the blame on me (Limbo).

When I had started to manage the band, I was able to see how fate went for him first hand. How, despite his attempts to improve his life and circumstances, relationships coupled with the eventual lack of commercial success for the band, meant that he exposed the failures in others and himself – a case of a return to issues of trust and commitment. On the *Live in Hope* EP, he puts it all into a one-song confessional that is *Apologies*:

Taking the blame for the words of a friend

Disguise my thoughts send me round the bend

Chorus

I'll say I'm sorry, there's no need to be on my knees

I'll say I'm sorry, there's no need for apologies.

Sometimes the desperation of his lot is so bad that he can see no way out other than a miracle. This brings me to the glaring question as to why, with so much unrest, uncertainty and conflict, Simmy has not chosen to take a stab at why bigger forces in our lives have let him down. He seems to shoulder the blame, is singularly responsible or sees the gossips and turncoat friends as the targets and not the world at large. He does not single out politicians or religion like most songwriters. He is not a class victim like other writers such as Paul Weller who sees himself as some warrior for the Socialist cause – where the good of all is second to the triumphs of any one individual. Simmy does not make any statements on, interestingly, either Politics or Religion, as they are both absent in all his songs. The words pray, faith, God, worship etc are not in his vocabulary –why?

In the end, that miracle he feels we all need is the lottery. A pledge we take that appears to be the answer to all our problems, which Simmy triumphs in The Streets of My (Claustrophobic?) Town. Since its launch, The National Lottery is more popular with the people who can least afford to gamble – the low paid and usually the desperate. Simmy leads us to conclude that in his world people worship the Lottery every week when they pray for a financial windfall to solve their problems:

We live in hope that we will win the lottery or anything (Live In Hope) or

Win the lottery and move away (Claustrophobic Town).

Drugs and Alcohol

Drink and substance abuse feature in passing or very specifically. They are what cause the down falls and are blamed for both Simmy's failures and others. *Green and Alcohol* is the whole theme in one song. Green refers to "dope "or marijuana – being the colour most associated with the leaf of the plant it is extracted from. In the first song he ever wrote - *Lemon and Lime*- the drug is a source of comfort while passing time and casually referred to as a relaxant *meeting my dealer and staying up late.* In time, he becomes more aware of its use by others. The sinister stranger who *Smokes so much green he needs to be alone* (Shut the Door) as well as in the down fall of others – notably in women he has known – such as the Girl in Shut the Door (*..Until she can't afford another line*) or Shopping for Free (*...now that she's a dealer I don't care*). In On the Sofa, he is apologetic for smoking all his fiend's "gear": *They couldn't shut me up, And that's a poor excuse I know for the stupid stuff I took.*

The damage he leaves in his wake is noted but he it is equalled by the respect of its cause:

Salute the green and alcohol

Alcohol is a regular cause of problems and runs along the same lines. Again, in *Lemon and Lime* innocently he gives testament to what he feels are his props that he is reluctant to give up. He mentions drugs (above) and the thrust of the song's chorus is that he is *not swapping Carling for lemon and lime.* He has made his choice, and as he often declares, he is sticking by it. Simmy confesses the nature of the volatile relationship he has with drinking:

One drinks too many and ten's not enough (Apologies),

Have a drink to smash it up (Limbo),

Sold my soul on the sofa of a friend while I drank all his beer (On the Sofa)

I was thinking of the past looking through an empty glass (Live In hope).

He also sees it as a cause in the downfall of others who usually end up homeless like the girl (another girl, again) in Out in the Cold who sells The Big Issue *to "Finance her alcohol".*

I know from my personal involvement with the band that drugs and drink play a part in and around what they do together. Maybe both are partly to blame for the band's failure to focus on the task in hand when it was most crucial to do so. Equally, I could blame myself too, for I over stepped the line and I did get too involved with them on too many occasions when I should have asked them to restrain. I doubt that they would have paid attention, as, by the time I became their manager, both were endemic and part of what the band were about. This is not a rock and roll thing, this was reality for the kids they once were – drugs and alcohol were as much a part of their lives and

216

psyche as music, football or fish and chips! I could add violence into this too but will cover it as another theme below.

Violence

There are references to smashing things up (It's not The End of The World) and flying off the handle (Claustrophobic Town) and the subtle ...*ashtray in my hand is gonna prove a useful tool* (Barred from the Kings). It all adds up to the ever present threat of physical abuse. Simmy addresses this in Street of my Town. It is another confessional observation of how the environment we grow up in shapes the person we become. The fatalistic opening lines are as Everyman's;

What have I got – stick to dealing
What have I got - stick to stealing
I'm walking down the streets of my town.

This leads to not having any friends other than "street villains" and even they are knocking down his door. Eventually he is in too deep, paranoia, inevitable beatings and alienation from anyone who knew him. Not a pleasant place to be is the message to any would be dealer or thief. As a parent, he is sending a lesson to his own sons and others he loves who may be tempted not to make that choice. So is this Simmy the moralist?

Fall from grace/decline of the innocent and band analogies

The women in his songs usually meet with disastrous endings. *Separate Bedrooms* tells the tale of a woman who leaves her partner to seek fame and fortune in London as a topless model. She falls on hard times and turns into a prostitute seeking the charity of anyone who will offer her a floor to sleep on. This is the literal interpretation but it could be a rebuff to any temptations. Whether this is the old adage of the grass being greener or not all that sparkles is gold analogy could apply too. *She hates the smell of London* is the harmonised refrains to the song and very different reality to the streets she imagined. It works as a story song and a warning to himself that the band and his own song writing should be good enough to be discovered up north. This hometown belief is commendable but in practice rarely works.

There is another interpretation of *Separate Bedrooms*, which I wrote and put on my website. I subtitled it as *an allegory of racial tension in Burnley* and pointed out that as the band were based in and around the same town; it could be a reflection on the emptiness and decline in racial harmony as witnessed recently in the area. The extreme right British National Party (B.N.P) had gained a seat in nearby Oldham. The song's choice of the words *segregation* and *eastern music* is an indication of a deeper relevance than a couple squabbling when set against the real back drop of racism that was rife at the time. Simmy is pointing out that we either live together, embrace diversity or we call it a day and fall apart. I pushed the comparisons by saying that her indecisiveness, confusion and bad choices leads to her entrapment. The voters of Burnley shared a similar frustration having seen a rise in the Asian population and a fall in property prices. Capitalising on this parallel some politicians seduced them into believing that the break down in their moral values is the fault of the moderates push for a multicultural society. Our female in the song, like Burnley, is left to regret putting hope in short sighted solutions. One conclusion is that, in any relationship, it is better to face up to your problems and to work them out together rather than to look back and regret thinking and acting apart. Furthermore, life's divisions and tension have to be settled within a community and not by a distant Government – otherwise its help is like the empty charity she is left with in London.

In the early naughties, London seemed to us as to where you had to be if you wanted to make it in the music business. I know from sending countless CDs, press releases and DVDs to agents, record companies and A&R reps that their UK offices were mostly in the capital. Bands were lured to doing mid week gigs at prestigious venues like in Camden and others places in the belief that they would be discovered. In essence, this was symptomatic of the pay to play culture that, in fairness to London, is not restricted to that City alone.

On this theme Simmy provides his own reality check using the homeless girl in Out in the Cold...*No money for taxis look like I'm sleeping rough in this shelter*. Ironically, she does not accept that she is a tramp as she says *that people mistake me for someone who is homeless*. Again, Simmy could be allowing us the interpretation that her predicament is a reason why bands do not succeed. Often I witnessed that members in a band are too close to what they are doing that they do not face up to the fact that they are what they fear most - which is not being good enough. This girl is both physically and mentally lost:.... *miles and miles away from home, and I look like a tramp with no place to go*. Indeed, if the song is about the music business then it is either a diversion or a nod to someone actually giving him some evidence of the band's failures or the pit falls they were heading for. The girl is not self critical and with no one to tell the truth she/they continue to be disillusioned *people abuse me I sell Big Issues to finance my alcohol.*

Paul Smith AKA "Smit"

Smit went to the same school as Simmy but was in the year below. None of Simmy's junior school mates went there but there was one, "Ormy" (Paul

218

Omerod) who lived at 19 St John's Road (see later*) who was a friend of Simmy's and Smit's that introduced them to each other. In 1989, Smit was playing guitar in a folk group at St John's The Baptist Church, Padiham. One day Simmy asked him to play a tune and Simmy instantly liked the guitar – the simple tunes impressed him. By the fourth year, they "connected" as they shared their interest in similar bands – namely Gun's and Roses and The Wildhearts, which they discussed while hanging about after football games. Smit had been playing guitar since he was eight but it was all new to Simmy when Smit encouraged him to try his hand. For Christmas 1992, Simmy monopolized Smit's present -a guitar and amp and soon enrolled with the same guitar teacher as Smit. Simmy's constant practicing made him proficient very quickly surpassing Smit's abilities.

They spent time in each other's houses jamming along to a lot of folk music. At 15/16, Smit would join up with Simmy and his mates for heavy drinking sessions – often in Accington on Friday nights – the College grounds near the Fire Station were a favourite haunt. Someone would bring a stereo and it would be boisterous but it was always good natured, no fighting just a common interest in having a good time listening to their latest best tunes *there was a mix of different eighties music until some skin head later ruined it.* Smit's first attempt at being in a band was with Nicky Rushton who was into heavy metal and they rehearsed in a church hall – no *lyrics just a lot of shouting and scream-ing, playing on boxes in a shopping trolley.* Simmy had a natural talent for guitar and the pair soon moved on the idea of forming a band. This was the early 1990's and despite their best efforts this didn't amount to much other than *a few broken windows of church halls playing metal.* Simmy and Smit drifted apart as they pursued separate interests only to meet up again in the late 90s via a mutual friend. At Ormy's house in Padiham, Nr Burnley, armed with guitars, drugs and alcohol they started jamming again talking about getting a band together.

Smit wrote a note to me saying that he remembered my introduction to them as *a journalist for a local fanzine* asking to interview the band. He added that *we were excited to have someone showing genuine interest in the band and felt like rock stars to be interviewed, accompanied by (Bez style 5th band member Fergie) and lubricated with alcohol the interview felt like it should have took place at the back on the MEN.*

Smit told me that his best memories over the years was when *we were play-ing to people we did not know like at the Cellar Bar, Blackburn and then later at the Attic, Accrington.* But his worst memory was when he became comatose drinking Dominican Republic rum in an attempt to be Rock'n roll in front of hosts **Spitfire** during their after show party. His favourite song was *Squeaky Clean* especially when they played it at the Kierby in front of loads of their mates. *Limbo* is an old favourite too but feels that *Shopping for Free* is the one he looks forward to most as it gets the biggest reaction. The highlight gigs to date were those at the Attic in 2005/6 and gigs with **Underdogs** (from Preston). Family life for Smit was always pulling on his ability to commit as deeply as he wanted to. Indeed Curtis "Stigers", one of Simmy's friends and guitar pupils deputized for Smit on several occasions towards the end of their initial ten-year run. Final word from Smit was *it's a shame as I like regular gigging.*

Daniel Spinks – born and bred in Darwen. At fourteen, he started playing in a covers band for two years with some lads from Accrington. Then one day, by chance, two lads at school were looking for a drummer. Meanwhile, Danny's mum worked with someone who was a part time jazz drummer, called Ian Bell to whom Danny went to have lessons (at a place called Vox Jam in Nelson). By the time he left college at 18 having completed an Access to Music course at Blackburn College, he knew more than his teacher did. Danny wanted to play in a band that played original songs. One day Darwen Citizen ran an advertisement for Volume 12 who needed a drummer for up and coming gigs – quoting Ed's number. Soon after calling it, he was jamming with Ed and Smit at the Unit in Hapton. Danny said that he was *so happy that they had their own tunes and lyrics and I clicked immediately as it was something I wanted to do.* He said that the songs they had were Rumour, Honesty, Changed Man and Yesterday's Old News. At that stage, they had done a couple of gigs and an open mic session. He cannot remember the venue for his first gig with Volume 12 but it was the Kierby gig under their new name of Unfinished Business which he describes as ...*fantastic. We went on second to last around midnight. There were loads of people, dancing, I had loads to drink, and I knew this is where I wanted to be before I started my first term at college in October 1999.*Danny's commitment to what he had discovered, as his future was a positive focus when his father died. Danny was seventeen and he had a gig three days later at Starkies but he played it telling me determinedly *I was not gonna sit at home...*

Their friendship grew quickly as Simmy, Ed and Danny all had birthdays within three days of each other. Socializing was as a group that included girlfriends and sleep overs with Sunday dinners thrown in by Kirsten. When I asked him what was his best memory he said that the gig at Queen's Park, mid 2001- it was his first time on a large stage and a full PA specifically recalling the acoustics bouncing off the surrounding trees in the distance. This was equal to a series of Attic gigs during their peak period. He compared this to the disappointing Mitre Tavern gig, Preston when the band played to two Irish lads who were gypsy fighters with nowhere else to spend the night. He also regrets the times he missed rehearsals *due to the piss heads that I was living with at that time.* His favourite tunes are Claustrophobic Town and Over My head *due to their simplicity and how they relate to living in a small town.* It's Not the End of The World is the one tune he looks forward to playing as *it's a cracking song – a bollocks of a tune too.* In the last conversation I had with Danny he said he felt others in the band *seemed to be settling down* and told me that he wanted to "make it" before he was twenty five.

My own views on Danny are on two levels. As a drummer/vocalist, he is one of the best I have seen on the unsigned scene. Rock solid and he contributes essential backing vocals. I have seen him single handily recover some lacklustre gigs when the rest of the band have been ropy on intros or failed to pay attention to what they were playing. He would shout and drive them like an irate goalkeeper forced to make a save due to those in front of him no doing their jobs. I would like to have been as good as Danny if I had kept up my drumming and a reason why he is so good is that you do not notice him. He fits into the songs seamlessly as it should be and some are built around his beats – namely It's Not the End of The World. By 2008 uncertain where Pretendgirlfriend were heading, Danny started playing in his side project band Haiku. He wrote songs with them and the songs I heard him sing at the last few gigs with Pretendgirlfriend were commendable and promising signs for a developing writing talent.

Danny was instantly likeable and we often shared the journey's to gig together on our own, as I usually transported his kit to and from gigs. He was generous with his friendship with me and shared many personal opinions and stories that gave me an insight into the teenager who matured into the young man. I know I am a better person for knowing him as some of his experiences took me by surprise and made me feel he had done more living by the age of twenty-one than I had done by the time I reached forty one! Initially though he was usually the quiet one until he got to know you and then, he would soon be telling you dirty jokes or stories and was always on the lookout for women to bed. He had, unfortunately, his demons off stage. The last time in his company was during a lift I gave him to pick up some equipment prior to a gig at Bohemia (the new name for the Attic, Accrington before it changed back to it again). He confessed to going on binges that lasted days and he could not remember but was over a thousand pounds lighter at the end of them. My last contact was a telephone conversation in September 2008 during which he told me about Haiku "...it's going alright" and he had just written a song called The Richest Man in the World. He said that the binges were behind and I have since lost touch with him after he left the area. All the band are concerned for him and hope he will be back in touch soon. Danny there are four pints from us waiting for you at the bar, wherever you are mate!

Noel Duffy

Noel's musical journey stared when he was 12 years old. He and his best mate, Brian Ford watched Oasis on Top of The Pops and argued the merits of the band and their songs which were receiving a lot of air play. While Brian hated them, Noel was *turned on* so much so that he wanted to learn of to play guitar. Noel's father was a jobbing Disc Jockey and they both liked Queen, so he when Noel asked for a guitar he bought a Bass and a copy of Total Guitar book. He began to teach himself following the melodies from the tabs developing a lead style. He became good enough to help on bass for **Spitfire** during rehearsals while they were looking for a replacement. Noel knew Wayne Ford (one of the two founder brothers of **Spitfire**) and had previously formed Astoria with Wayne (R/G), Christian Thwaites (Bass), Russell Hosker (songwriter guitar-ist and since deceased), Craig Etherington (drums) - Noel played lead guitar and the band did couple of gigs locally. Noel said that in his mid teens he *was heavily into drinking too – going out five nights a week getting pissed. I was so young I didn't have a clue when we started out as Astoria and did a gig at The Brookes Club (behind the bus station)* – a gig that Danny remembered seeing by co-incidence. *We had three Marshall Stacks and played Magical Mystery Tour.*

However, he first saw Pretendgirlfriend when they supported **Spitfire** at a gig at the Carlton, Burnley in 2001. *I was not impressed with the band, I felt they were a ripping off Oasis and dismissed them.* Noel wanted to play lead guitar in a band that met his standards in terms of integrity. He was looking for bands in the music papers that were playing the current "indie" style. Noel did not have long-term plans with **Spitfire** and it took Simmy to persuade him to join Pretendgirlfriend over a quite pint at The Railway in Hapton. Noel recalls that despite his earlier reservations - *Pretendgirlfriend were my kind of people, easy to befriend.*

My personal view of Noel is a series of flashbacks. The detached one at our first meeting and during early performances I never felt he was very comfort-able on stage. He tried to take my advice and "big up" his presence by adding backing vocals or shouts when perfect pitch didn't matter – like the chant-ing on 19 St John's Road. On one drinking session at Simmy's we ended up wrestling on the floor and I think my superior Judo holds earned respect between us. I respected him for his often cuttingly insightful observations and criticisms that pierced many debates. He would be the Devil's Advocate and say what I initially took as negative comments. However, he could back them up and I never chose to ignore his opinion, as he was usually right. He acted as a quality control so that if any songs were presented lacked the "buzz" in the rehearsals then they were dropped and did not make it to a live gig. This was a collective maturity that most bands I knew did not have. Such bands would usually develop a song to the point of trying it live and then judge the audience reaction. However, as Simmy and Noel reminded me in a discussion in October 2012, Pretendgirlfriend would drop songs if they did not "punch through and made you feel it". This self-imposed demarcation applied to many songs that Smit wrote and some of Simmy's lesser know tunes or versions of songs (like the original Ballard version of *Over My Head*). They both concluded, in retrospect that, "other people said that we wouldn't play a shit song" and that in itself is a credit to them.

Noel has a warm smile and generosity. He would always put any differences to one side if we had disagreed on something at a previous meeting. He did not hold a grudge and I never heard him say a bad word against anyone who did not deserve it. To me he is the band's conscience – you do not always agree with him but you want to know what he is thinking and hear what he has to say. I also suspect that he harbours a deep sense of disappointment. Not just at the band's lack of success but with life in general. Perhaps he has experienced all that life has to offer at a young age and found it wanting. In October 2013, however, this may have changed as he married long-term partner, Deborah.

Martin Simm

I admire Simmy for many reasons. Yes, undeniably he is a gifted songwriter and a guitarist who has stayed true to his beliefs and set standards in both that have benefitted Pretendgirlfriend in more ways than are obvious. My friendship with him is based on mutual respect. All through the early days, then as the manager and to the present we have never had a cross word and this has a lot to do with his ability to read a situation and see a disagreement a mile off. During my management, he would act as mediator between what I wanted to see the band do and what he thought the band were capable of doing. He would not seek a confrontation, preferring to say *"wait a minute lads let's look at it from a different view...maybe John has a point about XYZ, maybe we should consider this and not dismiss it out of hand...I can see where he's coming from, that's not to say I agree but let's give it a chance...".* **Simmy the diplomat. That is a skill that he may not have been born with but by 2004 he had it in buckets. Let's just take it as a "given" – call it part of his DNA and agree that it has made him and the band survive where others have imploded through bickering or chasing a false sense of their own worth.**

He is the anchor in much the same way as Smit is – maybe as the older two in the quartet but each has shared enough of each other's admiration for lager and the other's company to know how each is thinking. I admire this quality irrespective of how it is gained. I am equally curious to know why so many of his relationships outside the band have not lasted as long.

While I ponder this, I return to those formative years and the influence of bands like Oasis, Sterophonics and the Sex Pistols, which show me a very precise clue to Simmy's own need to tune into singers who are not natural vocalists. This is because, as I later found out; Simmy is/was painfully shy as a boy and into his teens. He had little confidence as a kid and as he formed the band, he doubted for a long time that he was a singer. Therefore, if Noel, Kelly and John could do it then it was worth a punt for Simmy to try too. I reassured him when he confessed this to me by quoting Mr Rotten to him: "....a trained voice is a tamed voice..." I added Ian Curtis, Morrissey and Tom Waites who have made it as vocalists because they are/were not natural singers.

His lyrics touch the common chord in people in a similar way to these people too. Cashing in Giros' going to Cash Generators, being barred from the Kings and the use of Green and Alcohol are things that people identify with. Everyday things that connect and audience with a songwriter and the performance is the confirmation – the seal of approval – the glue that seals the two. Fans like Ash and Sandra are evidence of this. They are two of the band's more ardent followers who turn up to most, if not all, the local gigs. Certainly every time they played the Attic, they would come in and be standing at the front. Ash fisting the air while spilling his drink and Sandra flicking her hair as she sang the words back to the stage. ".... they are just brilliant at what they do and what they are...." or something along these lines is how they answered me once when I asked them why they like the band. But they did single out the lyrics and Sandra made the point of telling me once that Simmy's lyrics were as good as any she ever heard and then she broke off into singing "Unguarded Moment" by The Church as if to make her point that it was equal to what Simmy wrote that made you feel he was in touch with what touched her inside.

In his exercise book Simmy wrote some notes for a radio interview announcing the end to Pretendgirlfriend and some of his comments cut to the core of what his vision of the band is all about – passed and present:

– I think the band always spoke to the common man. We never tried to dress it up – the songs are basic Rock 'n Roll songs with simple lyrics telling stories of everyday life, memorable tunes and an air fisting chorus.

Why does it come to an end?

Ultimately, the songs dry up. I am great at writing new riffs but with age, the lyrics don't seem to flow like they use to. It's over two years since I wrote a song and, without new songs a band starts to die. Songs are the blood that keeps a band breathing. Personally, I feel every song I wrote was as special as the last and after it stops ebbing that the end is near.

Highlights:

- *Going to Blackpool by the sea to support my musical hero Ginger.*
- *Supporting and meeting Bonehead from Oasis.*
- *Supporting and meeting Dermo & Northside from 90's.The Fall. Inspiral Carpets, Seahorses*
- *Cavern club, Liverpool in 2005*
- *Seeing our following almost double overnight after finding out home at the Attic and having our songs sung back to us. Having people genuinely care about the band.*
- *Just good nights out on the beer and playing to new crowds and meeting new mates.*

Low points

- *Losing my voice at The Queens in Chorley.*
- *Having to wait after performances to get our gear.*
- *Barfly (Liverpool) – playing to the sound engineer.*
- *My advice to anyone is get a driver.*

What worked against us –?

- *Luck – we didn't have any the way some bands do* – he mentions Oasis and the story of how Alan McGee saw them unintentionally when he missed his train one night and wondered into King Tuts. *But what is the likelihood of him doing the same in Accrington!*
- *Pay to play venues*

I do not delve any deeper into analysing Simmy – the person as I think that is private and best left for him. I do know that what Simmy puts down in his songs is genuine. I cannot detect any instance in a line from any of his tunes that is not real. He does not do what other songwriters may do to please others. He does not write love songs or overtly politicised opinions. He sticks to what he knows and does not pander to anyone else's tastes or fashionable trends. In this respect, he is the same as Shaun Maxwell. They both have that integrity that does not waiver throughout their writing and they are equally matched in the quality control standards. If it is not good, it will not be played or get recorded. That takes guts and a single mindedness, which I admire. It makes me respect their integrity in doing so.

Who knows what the future holds for Pretendgirlfriend – Simmy does. However, he does not do it alone. Pretendgirlfriend is a band, equal in parts to each member in it. The band does not survive without Simmy and his songs - songs forged into shape by the others in the band –so one is dependent on the other.

Other members

Curt Foulds. After a series of guitar jamming sessions with Simmy, Curt (AKA"Stigers") was asked to join the band to help cover for Smit when he had family commitments. This was after 2007 and he did a good job as a 5th member.

Bynod – ex **Spitfire** joined in 2012 to fill in Danny's prolonged absence.

My final word is to suggest that I have left sufficient evidence and clues to what has kept them less well know than I feel they should be. A loosely guarded secret is how I like to think of Pretendgirlfriend now. A secret I want to share with you in the hope that the band will get the recognition they deserve – as indeed many of the bands, musicians in this book should is the future is unwritten. I have a sense that you, the reader, have the pen in your hand now.

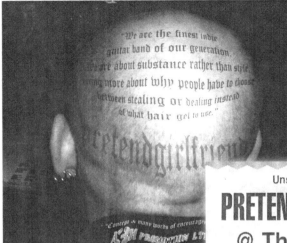

"We are the finest indie guitar band of our generation. We are about substance rather than style. ...ing more about why people have to choose between stealing or dealing instead of what hair gel to use."

pretendgirlfriend

"Concept & many words of encourage...

PRETEND GIRLFRIEND

@ The Marquee,
Home of Live Music

Wednesday 6th November 2002
Open till 2am Price £4.00

The Mill
...educt Street, Preston PR1 7JN

O.A.R. !IF IT AIN'T LIVE IT AIN'T 'ERE!
Dress Code: No Sportswear
Tel: 01772 883617   00023

pretendgirlfriend

LIVE IN HOPE

⊙ **Polytechnic**
⊙ **Pretendgirlfriend**
⊙ **Leaf**

The Attic Warner Street
Accrington BB5 1HN

2nd Dec 2005

Free Entry

Starts before 9:00pm

Legendary Wildhearts frontman
GINGER

Saturday 20th Jan
at
Riffs
Blackpool

with support from

pretendgirlfriend

Promo

Tracks
1. Shopping for free 3:35
2. Out in the cold 2:54
3. Green and Alcohol 2:46

for booking email a3hpromotion@aol.com
or Tel John Winstanley on 07812 577 987

www. pretendgirlfriend.com

copyright unfinished business records 2006

A3H PROMOTION LTD.

Pretendgirlfriend

One of the few English bands around today that sound English. They are 4 working class lads from Burnley who ride the Rock'n Punk cycle at full throttle all over the North West and into a venue near you. Their guitars pack a fist full of songs about everyday life that touch the hearts of all who crave integrity and honesty in their music. This band delivers with the emotions and edge we all live on in tunes that you'll be singing for weeks later or until you see them again. A band to watch in 2004.   [A3H Promotion Ltd.]

26th March - Chorley Community Centre [Reget High]
15th March - Slaughter House, Liverpool [with Strike Out & Vegas Daughters]
1st April - Corbas, Sheffield
12th April - Brickyard, Carlisle [with Belts u supporting Nick Harper]
17th April - Dudley Arms, Chirk with In Car Stereo, Capulet & Chatreun
18th April - Slaughter House, Liverpool [with Luzon & Spatts]
19th April - Oyster, Chorley
20th April - Waggon & Horses Adlington with Hypodex
2nd May - Cellar Bar, Blackburn "The Long Weekend Festival"
5th May - Night & Day, Manchester with Cornectio Sleeps
7th May - Casablanca's, Southport
6th May - Corvos, Limelight Club
8th May - The Vault, Leicester
14th May - Just Fly, Liverpool with Filter 6z & Crimson Rose
18th May - Slaughter House, Liverpool [with The Parishers]
20th May - Queens, Chorley [with The Perishers]
21st May - Waggon & Horses, Adlington [with The Freakers]
28th - 31st June - Peterborough Boston Festival
2nd June - Corbas, Sheffield

For more information see www.pretendgirlfriend.com

Pretendgirlfriend

A3H PROMOTION LTD.

Proudly presents

Kid Conspiracy
At
Mitre Tavern, Preston 19th Nov
[plus Phlegm Fatales & Synko]
&
Chorley Community Centre 20th Nov
[+ White Rod, ADI, 3 Yards of Sausage]
&
Sir Charles Napier, Blackburn 10th Dec.
[with Capulet & Free Falling Camels]

And
[In association with P Lighting]

Pretendgirlfriend
At
The Keirby Hotel, Burnley
27th November
[+ special guests:
Ad Nauseam, Asimov, Re:Verb and
Counteract. £4 on the door]
&
The Cellar Bar, Blackburn
22nd December & January 28th
[+ special guests]
&
The Late Room, Manchester
6th February 2005

In Association with
www.calder-recordings.co.uk
We are looking for band demos for our

---

pretendgirlfriend

LIVE at the Keirby Hotel 27th November

special guests
Re: verb
Ad nauseam
Asimov
Counteract

£3 with flyer / £4 on door

sponsored by
A3H PROMOTION LTD.

Calder Recordings & A3H Promotion Presents

REVELS
"the finest unsigned bands in the world..."

pretendgirlfriend
Operator 5
the Mushrooms
Blue Hobo

PLUS SPECIAL GUESTS

WEDNESDAY OCTOBER 27th 2004
Doors open 8.00pm till 2.00am
£4.00 door / £3.00 with this flyer
Jillys Rockworld
65 Oxford St
Manchester
Tel: 0161 236 9971
dave@jillys.co.uk

www.calder-recordings.co.uk   www.a3hpromotion.co.uk

Danny
Drums

Noel
Bass Guitar

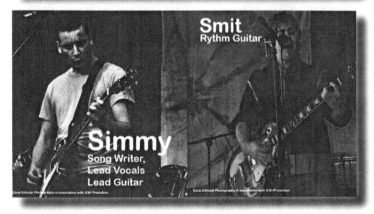

Smit
Rythm Guitar

Simmy
Song Writer,
Lead Vocals
Lead Guitar

My first sighting of Pretendgirlfriend North Bar, Town Hall Street, Blackburn, on 4 July 2002 - a Thursday night at about 8.30pm- to be precise!

Curt Foulds – in The Subliminals a covers band that Simmy was in for a while when Pretendgirlfriend took a rest after their Attic gig 5th December 2009.

Backstage at Pure, Sunderland September 2005- Noel, Smit Danny and Simmy.

Me, Noel and Simmy on Noel's wedding 2013

Pretendgirlfriend 2013 Simmy, Smit, Noel and Brynod.

09 The Penniless Playboy (Shaun Maxwell)

(This chapter is dedicated to the memory of Mr Norman Martin)

People never cease to disappoint me. Mostly I feel under whelmed by their lack of originality or being brave enough to be different. But I suppose that has always been the case. The recycling of dirge and fashion speeds up every time. A new fad, maybe flavour of the moment or seconds of fame instead of the Wharolian 15 minutes is appropriate today – and less so tomorrow. Everyone creates their own truth but some are more honest than others and these are usually the lepers and outcasts. No body wants their bubble burst but I wonder who's blown it in the first place and I mean that in more ways than one. Some one once said "music's not that important you can eat it"– that's because most of it is shit!

Shaun Maxwell wrote this in a series of letters and notes he gave me when I first started to take him seriously as a musician and then later as one of my closest friends. I am attracted to his unique and often cutting observations of human nature and the way we exist together in spite of our excesses, short comings and squalor. Shaun's songs are like canvases that capture his outpourings as art or bile. Some are simple and child like; others peddle poetic themes, stories of love, the sadness of its loss or the loneliness of depression and the consequences when regrets are allowed to fester. His musical styles vary from the playful chronicles on the decline of English football (complete with terrace hand clapping) to an increase in minor keys for darker dirges about sinister individuals and social flaws. Character assassinations abound, focused on the hideous who venture out in public or reflections on the famous or infamous celebrities of our past. Song structures and lyrics ebb and flow along his fret board with the power of a single pluck or the crescendo of chords. His fingers conjure up images with equal feelings of the delicate, delightful or disturbed when warped on the wah-wah pedal or stranded on the sustain. Experiences are weaved in as voyeur or victim – tinged with caustic or coy humour. To step into his world is to discover an appreciation of our own lives set in comparison to it. His "musical journey" is one of contrasts which demand that we ask what has led us to be where we are in our lives compared to his and the reasons we are, who we are, depend on our own personality and unique travels. You may not like him or his music or ever want to be able to understand what he has seen or suffered, absorbed, abhorred, dignified or dismantled. However, for others this could be the arrival at a station of shared truths where someone else has expressed your feelings as perfectly and as simply as he does. Even his song's titles have the capacity to condense and juxtapose such as *"Leafless in Eden"* or *"Beautiful Song for the Ripper"*.

On a one to one with Shaun I glimpse a mirror of myself that stirs emotions of admiration, confusion, envy, and frustration. I wanted his story to be a chapter of its own - it deserves to be as, externally, it is a contradiction to my own life but internally, very similar. Where I can I have used his own words or those of others who know him and included and excluded details he has asked me to. It is not a comprehensive biography but it should explain why someone once gave him the back handed compliment *"you're the only person I know who is proud of their own defects".*

Shaun lives an easy few miles from my home. We both have an awareness of our "over fifty" age bracket which stimulated a mutual willingness to put our stories in print before we expire! His chapter is the first one I wrote six months after the last gig I put on as my "retirement" from the music business in September 2007. The pages rushed by with key moments of his life entwined around the many reincarnations of the bands he has fronted. Intermittently, as now, I continued to make an effort to catch one of Shaun's gigs or we would venture out together to watch others play. In many conversations with him it became apparent to me that while I was "growing up" and, to the moment when we first met in August 2005, I did not understand the difference between living to make music rather than making music to live. His life in a word is "authentic" as this is what he and his music represents. The size and variety of his output over forty years is staggering and his best work is always what he does next. His back catalogue is evidence of this being either in tune or just ahead of its time but always fresh He is an artistic musician who, like all genius's, does what he does because something inside him drives him to do it. His lyrics captivate my attention and draw me into his perspective by the way they are painted into the musical styles he uses to express them:

When I write the songs I always imagine them with choirs, orchestras or brass sections. So, the bass riffs are the brass section – my guitar is an orchestra by using tuneful discords or drone notes – only playing first form/ordinary chords or traditional bar chords to punctuate certain points. You can hear a ghost riff subconsciously due to the way I strum and catch certain strings systematically. When all the music comes together, drums, bass, guitar, vox it makes a solid statement. I often leave out the obvious so the listener can fill in their own parts – to feel a part of the songs. I try to avoid Rock'n Roll leads and I use either soul or folk type riffs.

Shaun (Ali Bongo) Maxwell was born in October 1959 at Chorley

Hospital. His father was an Irish Roman Catholic (from Lifford, Eire), who supplemented his main job as a brick layer, with other *standbys* or foreigners. One winter he was working in a plastic factory.... *All he had to do was push a button but one day he went to the pub and forgot about it. When he got back it got clogged up and he got the sack. Mind you his dad (mi granddad) was a character to. In World War II he took part in the second wave (re-enforcements) during the D-Day landings in Normandy. His troop was given bicycles to speed up the advance but, being an alcoholic and not able to ride one, he swapped it for three bottles of wine with the first Frenchman he met. He had to run behind his comrades for the rest of the advance.*

His mother was born in Chorley and raised into a Methodist family which had been settled in Chorley for a long time before she got married. Shaun is a middle child flanked by three year older sister Julie and thirteen year younger brother Paul. Shaun understood his place in the world from an early age *...treated as one step up from the black immigrants and way down on the social scale.....the only solace I had growing up was my mum and her parents...and mi panda! My mum or dad - probably dad- kept trying to chuck it away' cos it was so mucky but I retrieved it from the bin each time - eventually they gave up n stuck it in the washer were it disintegrated. I knew I had to be physically tough and clever to survive.*

In the year of Shaun's birth all was well in the Maxwell household. Even the UK number ones for that year had the positive signs too as *Here Comes Summer* (Jerry Heller). Other songs of that same year do give pointers to some of Shaun's own character traits and attitude from the ironic timing of *A Fool Such As I* (Elvis Presley) *Dream Lover* and *It Doesn't Matter Anymore* (Buddy Holly), to the final hit of that year -*What Do You Want To Make Those Eye's At Me For* (Emile Ford and The Checkmates). For the first few years he lived with his grandparents on Yarrow Road *a private rented house not like our council house in Northgate Drive were we moved to in the early 60'sand. My first memory were playin in the back garden wi' me granddad – I was really close to me grandparents especially me granddad as he took me all over the place. But oddly enough though whenever I have nightmares or bad dreams they were always set there. The house had no bath or hot water only one tap in the kitchen and an outside bog which use to freeze in winter - it had lead piping. It where the first place our Jake* (Shaun's son) *lived as a child – not right for an asthmatic kid! Yet it were POSH for a council estate as every one had jobs and cars – not like it is now though....* This close knit family didn't move far to Northgate Drive and then to St James Street when Shaun was seventeen. At the later Shaun was impressed by his mother's determination to live in more modern surroundings.

233

She saw to it that central heating got installed and proper carpets were fitted – both were a luxury to the stone flooring or the peculiar smelling linoleum he was use to. Soon after she bought their first colour television ....*under water things were amazing...... the colours of water fascinated me.*

His formal education started just before his sixth birthday at St Joseph's Catholic Primary (off Harpers lane) without being able to read or write. There he met long term friends – Colin Farnworth and John Martin as well as sadistic teachers. One woman had a fondness for the *Scholls* (a wooden sandal with a leather strap) that was often beaten onto the palms of small outstretched hands. For more serious offences the strikes were doubled to six and a cane or strap was an optional instrument of corporal punishment too. On refection though, he *fancied* one of the female teachers dishing out the punishment, adding with wicked swiftness *...even at that age I was a perv!*

Mischievous rather than wilful, trouble hung on his shoulders and one of many instances involved the school bell. This was rung in much the same way as in schools today (assembly, lessons, and breaks etc) a key piece of kit not to be tampered with! However, Shaun's mechanical curiosity got the better of him one day. While *mucking about with the "donger"* he unscrewed the chain that fixed it to the inside of the brass shell. He was disturbed and in a panic he threw it into the cloakroom – only to land at the feet of a teacher keen to sound the next event of the day. As if in a scene from a popular TV show of the day "Whacko", the comic moment unfolded with inevitable palm swelling....*they would probably have me down as having ADAH – that's the trendy thing instead of being just a bad'un.*

Educational discipline extended with equal vigour to the clergy which Shaun encountered on another occasion while walking behind John Martin. John was going too slow and eager to move quicker Shaun accidentally caught John's shoe and tripped him in front of the incumbent Reverend Father. As if delivering the 11th commandment the enraged Father grasped a generous clump Shaun's hair bellowing "...YOU CAN NEVER WALK TOO SLOWLY IN THE EYES OF GOD!!!" Maybe God himself was angered by the way his children were suffering or how else could you explain the bolt of lightning that stuck the carpet in front of the school's alter. The hole it burnt made a lasting impression on Shaun happening as it did between his ninth and tenth Birthday.

Hymns had their affect on Shaun and carols were his favourite as they reminded him of Christmas and *getting presents.* It wasn't so much the tunes but the imagery he preferred when it came to *All Things Bright and Beautiful* and other Church standards. Shaun's voice broke at the unusually early age of

234

ten. *Suddenly it went like a donkey – I never got it back and I use to have a good one!* Determined to keep singing he was attracted to and developed an affiliation for Lou Reed's vocal style.

Despite his best efforts at cheating in the mock Eleven Plus exam he was split up from Colin for the real one, which he failed and went to St Augustine. Colin passed and went to Preston Catholic College. St Augustine was a boy's only school on the site of what is Holy Cross School, today (off Burgh Lane). His first two years were *horrible* – going as far as to describe that time as *evil* – bullying and violence prevailed and he survived the hardship by his wits. The teachers were just as bad it seems - one was regarded as a religious zealot reaching for the cane as much as the Bible to inflict the learning of the Catechisms. Here he met other long term friends Nicky Smart & George Tweedy.

Since his time at St Joseph's he had volunteered to be an altar boy so he could exploit the opportunity to play football. He was tall for his age and this, combined with his natural ball skills, made him popular enough to play with the older lads in older teams that met on St Joseph's field. *I never got any shit off anyone coz I was respected for me skills.* Matches were against the Shakespeare side that came from the other half of the estate separated by the old railway line. It was about this time he learnt about religious discrimination for the first time. Shaun wanted to go to camp with his friends who were in the Boys Brigade but he was barred on the grounds that he was a Catholic!

In his teens, Shaun's passion for football continued and he grabbed every opportunity to have a kick about. He became a regular on the sides that would huddle around the local parks or recs. During his second year at St Augustine's Shaun played in lots of six aside tournaments which often attracted talent scouts from Wigan, Stockport and Blackburn football clubs. Wigan Athletic were willing to offer him a playing contract, but Shaun only found out about this years later when is dad explained that he wanted him to continue to be an athlete! Shaun had developed a talent at race walking and between 13-16 he held records at National English Schools and 3As championship level. *He was very proud of me and very protective even if misguided he never took what I wanted into consideration* - hence Shaun went into the Police Cadets later on so he could train professionally before sponsorships were available – *it's the way you did things back them at amateur level.*

Shaun had swapped his steam engine for a set of Premier drums. He practiced *...to the tunes of old T Rex* and The Glitter band at times when his father was not around *so as not to annoy him.* However, one day some burly blokes turned up and said his father had told them that they could take them which they did. Later, his father explained that he *was getting on his nerves!*

235

Shaun's friends by his early teens became the source of bonds that endured. Colin Farnworth has been a *massive influence* – showing Shaun how to read and write. *Colin explained how words worked* rather than regurgitating the parrot like State methods of the day. They played in bands together up to the early 1980's and then in 2012 when The Sinister Chuckles reformed. Colin's mother was a staunch catholic and what we refer to today as a pushy parent. On the other hand his dad was very laid back and someone who Colin admired *for his lack of ambition*. If his mum thought he was going out with the wrong sort she would hail him back like a taxi. Obediently and apologetically Colin would concur to her claim that he had forgotten to drink his tea. *Later Colin use to try and come round of an evening undetected!* He self learned acoustic guitar and, crucially, it was Colin who gave Shaun a book of basic chords which took his education in a totally different direction.

Growing up in Chorley was a mixture of adventure and survival. He and Colin spent hours sat under the bridge over M61 down by Botany Bay. They were *hiding from a hiding* so to speak from their parents – Shaun from his father's beatings after the pubs closed and Colin for minor misdemeanours. *Colin took two months to assemble a model aeroplane that only had 20 parts to it.* When his mum asked "why's it taking so long and what's that smell!" no one had the heart to explain the reason for the prolonged odour was due to his experimentation with solvents. Gangs offered comfort and stability. *All estates had gangs. The Bagganley Estate gang were up by Spar at the back of the Post Office on Eaves Lane – they were Bikers – grebo types. Ours were the Thornhill Mob back in 1971 we were Skin Heads. I were the youngest member and we had a half cast member called Gassy so we use to get into "rumbles" with other Chorley gangs. Acceptance into the gang didn't involve any initiation ceremony you were in if you lived on the estate. Most of us played football together....* Being in a skin head gang did not, at first, exclude black people – to Shaun it appeared that Richard Allen's book "Skinhead" (one of the first "adult" books he read) changed people's attitude. Being southern orientated it had a narrow perspective which was a world away from the north that did not resonate with reality in Shaun's world ......*Gassy were half caste anyway!* Shaun's sister was a skin head... *wi that feathered cut at the front and she'd play Tamla Mowtown while she got dressed in Ben Sherman checked shirts, cream trousers, red socks and monkey boots.*

Chorley had some notable families *like the Morgan's, Donaldson's, James' and McFadden's. The Williams' though were one of the original and few black families to settle in Chorley. They were Jamaicans and used to own the Odd Spot and had their own band called "State Penitentiary".* Playing soft Soul Shaun thought they were good when he heard them practicing as he passed by their house in Corporation St. John Martin recalls how he *...used to deliver milk to their house on a Saturday morning and I loved looking through the window at all their gear set up in the front room. It was the first time I saw an electric guitar for real.* The Odd Spot was off Knowsley Brow- and when the bands were playing there Shaun use to go and mind the Crombies while people danced to Soul and Ska. Age didn't seem to matter as the oldest were fourteen or fifteen and he was eleven or twelve *...its seemed as though people didn't bother how old you were back then.* Comfort and conformity could be confusing to the impressionable. Rites of passages and the experiences of vices lead to familiarity and extremes *-I didn't start smoking until I were 17 – I liked it as it made me dizzy – it were a PUNK thing to do- all mi friends smoked and I couldn't coz I was an athlete.* (Gambling)- *never use to up to few years ago – only 50p accumulators not a habit!* But Alcohol and drugs were very different– *The first time I ever touched alcohol was at the first gig with Pleaze sharing a bottle of Woodpecker cider with Colin.*

Fighting & the Scooter Years.

Shaun begrudgingly admits that he was looked up to – not just because he was taller than his peers but he was mildly *crazy* and known as Mad Max (...well!). Younger or weaker members of the gang would seek his advice about who to take out first in a fight against home supporters at away games or on local park kick abouts or rival scooter club meetings. The stories of Mods and Rockers fighting, drinking and drug taking were experienced firsthand by Shaun. *It was nothing to be ashamed of as long as no one got severely hurt or caused damage beyond what was considered acceptable.* Alongside all of this culture was fashion, the iconic Vespers and Lambrettas and, most important of all, the music. *We had crap second hand scooters which use to break down regularly and fights broke out along the way.* Separate to this, and while a Punk was happening, Shaun knew the lads from the Scooter clubs but could safely go to the Punk shows at Wigan Casino as these gigs were on before the Soul all nighters. He also went to gigs at the Electric Circus in Manchester. He saw many of the bands of the day from the well know (e.g. The Buzzcocks) to the less famous now (i.e. The Cortinas from Bristol). Shaun remembers this place as *a great venue but it were a right dump and kids chucked stones at the windows.* At one gig he stood on Wayne County's toes and on another night back at the Casino when he watched the Stranglers he got his picture taken for Blackpool fanzine "Viva La Resistance".

Wigan Casino put on Northern Soul nights which attracted scooter clubs turned on by the dancing and songs that became a cult genre of its own. The Casino also offered somewhere to stay instead of walking home. The "all nighters" were exactly that -you'd go in on one night at 8pm and come out just after 8am the following morning. He'd often *fall asleep after the Punk gigs, pissed and someone would always lend you a few quid 'til next week so you could get home next mornin – it was a scene that encouraged a kind of brotherhood.* He also met The Lurkers in Preston; two of them were salesman – *ordinary people - that's what punk is all about!* Colin liked them even though Shaun hadn't heard of them but *they were dressed normally and not in the accepted Punk style.* Shaun at this time was labouring on building sites (cash in hand), grave digging for Kenyon's or at the slaughter house (in Limbrick) during the day and absorbing everything that happened at night. John Martin remembers that they all went to *Wigan when the Sex Pistols were due to play as the S.P.O.T.S. (Sex Pistols on Tour). The Pistols didn't play and were replaced by Slaughter & the Dogs whose lead singer Wayne Barratt used to wear a Dracula cape. At the end of the gig he lobbed it in the crowd and we got it. We walked home from Wigan to Chorley that night telling ghost stories about Johnny Red Clogs, some miner who got trapped in Bickershaw colliery and lost both feet – but his bloody clogs used to haunt people!*

Discography

Shaun's interest in music started when he was *about eight or nine - I were always singing – you weren't bombarded night and day with music as you are now. I'd listen to the radio and occasionally a variety show on TV. The break in between the gaps gave you your own space so you could formulate your ideas –you liked what you liked without a constant background.* "The Yellow Rose of Texas" by Mitch Miller *were me first memory of a song and I also remember hearing Mario Lanza on the radio while balanced on the sink drainer which me mum sat me on very Sunday while preparing dinner. No one played music apart from Dad – it were no "musical household".* Me sister bought records and was into *Tamla Mowtown, the two volumes of greatest hits were me first consistent block of music and some Reggae.*

Underground Mongs – started and ended its six months life span in Shaun's box bedroom in Northgate Drive circa 1973. Not knowing what they wanted to create they were spurred on by the desire to do something that was "musical" in nature. They didn't know anyone but they'd listen to Marc Boland together. The sum of its parts was: George Tweedy – who played a white padded, backless stool with a stainless steel bottom. Dowels from his mother's clothes line acted as sticks. Phil Price - who had a Wharfdale organ ...

a horrible shite plastic brown thing like an accordion... Billy Dyke gave him his Beatles two string plastic guitar that had pictures on it – a collector's item today which got smashed up during an improvised performance of a Who standard. From this ensemble came Shaun's first "record" – which was self made from the inside "disc" from Led Zeppelin's III LP as it had a hole in the centre that fitted the spike on a record turn table. Coloured in and made to play it was dubbed "*Scritch Scratch*"..... *on account of the same noise it made.* Other notable sessions from this start was *Flush* a piece of performance art recorded on the trusty Phillips cassette player. This was the sound of a toilet chain being pulled and a voice uttering "flush" – childish humour that survives today.

Pleaze- formed in 1973/4 around the core members of Shaun, John "*boring*" Martin and Colin "*Mr Raggedy*" Farnworth. They would practice once or twice a week in John's bedroom – at his parents - Healey Cottage off Eaves Lane at the bottom of Froom Street (*behind the old Thomas Witter's carpet factory at the foot of the Nab*). John had a fondness for Status Quo and Black Sabbath riffs but Mott the Hoople was his "fave" band of the time.... *I was also into T Rex and Ziggy era Bowie (mainly Mick Ronson's guitar sound) more than Sabbath or Quo. I'd add "incompetent" to the "boring" tag* (which Shaun gave him) *as well. I actually bought the electric guitar (Avon Les Paul copy) before I could play a single note. I'd been to Colin's house one day to discover that he had a jumbo acoustic guitar <u>and</u> he could play it! He'd never said a word and I was mightily impressed. This spurred me on. My parents forked out the £35 for the second hand guitar on the proviso that I had to learn to play it. I always remember being so chuffed when I managed to hold down a bar chord although my Dad preferred it when I played ⊠Scarborough Fair' on one string!*

Colin Farnworth –had a liking for Folk music. His style was to play acoustic guitar with elaborate recurring melodic leads over which Shaun could make up songs. His dress sense was *squaro retro –a Nottingham Forrest FC shirt and flared trousers and brogues, his hair cut was the clone of Coronation Street's, Ken Barlow and, in homage to his Dad's squareness, old before he were young.*

Meanwhile, Shaun's skilful contribution was to beat a plastic bucket but with the technical enhancement of a cloth *so it did not sound too plasticy!* He sang as he was *the most outgoing* and decided he would do so fuelled by a desire to perform. *Loads of recordings were done* on 2 track and were of a three chord *bashed out* nature. Subject matter was culled from the humour of Lou Reed/ Velvet Underground in tracks such as *Do the Electric Plug* and *Yeah* which was like *Sister Ray* in style. Other tracks included *Saved by Rock and Roll* and a cover of *Walk on the Wild Side* though this was seldom with the right words or chords. John recalls:

239

We used to spend hours in that bedroom. I suppose we were even developing a style back then mainly due to the fact that we weren't competent enough to do proper covers. We used to do B sides of The Move and stuff we could pass off as our own. The 2 track consisted of a reel to reel tape recorder and a cassette recorder. We would play guitar and sing into the reel to reel then play it back and overdub whilst recording on the cassette. By the time we'd finished the original tune was barely recognisable under the squealing feedback! I remember Shaun got an alto saxophone around this time and we did an impromptu jam that became 'Sax in the Cupboard'. The sax was so loud that Shaun played it from within a 'walk-in' wardrobe; the key for me to start the riff was when he loudly announced from behind the cupboard door "screaming Max and his alto sax". There was a lot of laughter on those recordings. We once worked through the Complete Beatles song-book with percussion provided by clanking 2 metal ashtrays together (Youngers Tartan and Lions Mild if I remember correctly). Incidentally, the riff to 'Saved by Rock n Roll' (or Rock 'n' Roll Saviour as we renamed it) was pretty close to Anarchy In The UK or most Ramones tunes even though it predated these by a few years.

The trio were confident enough to gain their first few gigs at St Mary's youth club and Chorley youth club (off Lyons Lane) with the brashness of 13/14 year old youths "Hey we are in a band can we play". They knew the drummer Jimmy *straight and boring* Dawber who worked at St Mary's on Devonshire road and he offered to fill in on drums for them. John Martin recalls that i*n those days all the church/social clubs had a resident organist and drummer who would accompany whichever travelling vocalist was in town. He was, as Shaun says "straight and boring" but he was a great timekeeper....and he had his own kit! At the back of the stage, before the gig, we found a big wooden sign which said 'Sanctus'. It was obviously something from a religious celebra-tion or event. However it was impressive enough to use as a backdrop so, for one gig only, we performed as Sanctus. Definitely remember playing Sweet Jane and Walk On the Wild Side as well as a couple of originals.*

That first gig was a non event but everyone remembers the second one as being dramatic in more ways than one. A coffin was assembled: an old kitchen work top for the base; cardboard and cereal packets painted brown were used for the sides and lid. Shaun wore a fire orange and gold cloak made by Angela Murphy...*someone we knew form round the corner.* A Dracula collar, platform boots and shredded black pants completed this costume. The build up to this performance was a rock and roll baptism too. Colin and Shaun had acquired a bottle of Woodpecker Cider and drunk it between themselves as the time drifted by before the stage début finally arrived. The poll bearers stifled laughs of teen embarrassment as they shuffled their load to the side of the stage. Shaun was lying inside the coffin, his head gyrating to the disco tracks and muffled hubbub of the crowd. He clasped the microphone across his chest. This was his moment - the beginning of fame and fortune had come at last and sensing the need for the dramatic he announced, *"Oh No! It's the wild thing!"* – Cue Colin, John and Jimmy blasting out their version of *Wild Thing* by Troggs. Meanwhile, Shaun was stuck and the microphone did not work. The audience's attention was focused on the rectangular box in bemused curiosity. Ominously, the clanging riffs of the likely lads searing away at the intro brought the moment of truth closer. Unfamiliar with the on off button Shaun had started to use expletives as his efforts to escape became more frantic. Any sense of solemnity and reserve soon dispersed as, one side of the coffin split and Shaun rolled out shouting *I can't fucking get out!* Undaunted and equally unaccustomed to the workings of a Public Address system, Shaun utterances of *"Its shite this mic is not working"* could be heard by all who could be shocked no more. They had witnessed Shaun's arrival onto the world stage. He had made a start in his own uncompromising style, albeit in a small town in Lancashire that no one knew or was bothered about.

Their run of age restricted gigs at the local youth clubs was enough for Shaun to know he wanted more and where talent failed lying worked to secure others elsewhere. They were playing on the politeness of their elders who placated their bleeding ears with the comfort of knowing they were keeping kids off the streets at night. Shaun sensed a challenge and a direction which he did not appreciate until some three years later during the summer of Punk. Shaun reflects philosophically on those early gigs: *we didn't want to be musicians we just wanted to perform –to show off and entertain people. We looked at everything from a ridiculous point of view –using humour to overcome fear so we took the piss out of each other. This was in direct defiance of something I read in one of John's music papers. Ian Hunter from Mott the Hoople had said that you can't play in a band unless you've got £10,000. I thought this was unreal but it always hung over me so I told myself I can show you –you don't need that!"*

Pleaze's last gig was at the youth centre (where the Boxing club is now off Lyons Lane) remembered as a custard pie flinging event. A case of shaving foam on paper plate affair which upset everyone not taking part and *"....that was the end of that!"*

London & Punk Rock

Mid 1976 Shaun was in London where he experienced two ends of the political spectrum. Conformity, to his father's attempt to sort out his son's wayward ways. The short sharp shock treatment of compulsory National Service was no longer available. Second choice was coercing Shaun into joining the Police Force to train as a cadet. Shaun did what he could to settle in but he soon discovered he had more in common with people outside the barracks –"Civvies" –as they were referred to- *"ordinary people"* to Shaun The only exception were the few Geordie cadets that he could get on with who shared a similar sense of humour and austere back ground. By way of contrast, non conformity stabbed him in the stomach like an agitated pensioner.

London at the time was the epicentre of what we know now as "Punk Rock". By definition, any band daring to play this new style set themselves apart from their peers. This capital was where it was happening, at ground zero - but Shaun he took it all in his stride. He had The Velvet Underground's LPs since 1973 but bought second hand copies from a record shop called Verve. He could equate them to Punk especially their *undergroundness – bleak but embellished with middle class views while mucking about with drugs and prostitutes.* He was attracted to Punk Rock's musical form as it was *fast and energetic.* On reflection Shaun recalls 1976/77 as a period when he *liked* the Dammed's *New Rose, hated* Rock music and sensed a need for something new. His favoured Lou Reed was *becoming samey,* Roxy Music *were weird,* Bowie was *simply crap* and TV's "The Old Grey Whistle Test" streamed the obscure Bob Harris' *hippy left overs.* When he heard *Anarchy in the UK* he considered it Rock'n Roll – *"...a faster version of the New York Dolls with Steptoe on vocals".* He was *fascinated* with the Pistols but *preferred* the Dammed who he felt were *better.* He kept a scrap book of the bands he liked and his focus was on singles - the instant hit rather than albums. He got about travelling at night on his own. He once bumped into the archetypal Bromley Set - remembering the Cat Woman as *stunning but titchy.* There were very few Punks about but when he caught sight of one the impact was immediate as they ...*really stood out even if not all of them were dressed as Punks some even had long hair and string vests!* He didn't see any live bands because on the one occasion he got to find out about a gig it got cancelled due to fighting. Also the college curfew meant he couldn't risk not getting back in time either. He hunted for clothes in second hand shops on the Kings Road, dressing in a woman's short box jacket, Paisley shirt which he wrote over and stuck safety pins to. He didn't find the "Sex" clothes boutique and even if he had he *would not have paid £15 for their T shirt!*

Back up North Tony Wilson put the Sex Pistols on the Granada TV show he presented and a handful of the seventies youth were embracing the tidal wave of change that would continue to rattle contemporary music decades later. Shaun was one of them and on his return home he was on a mission to start the first Punk band in Chorley – maybe the first in the North of England for all he knew – he named the band Hangman!

Hangman–1977 (Chorley's very first Punk band). Bass- George Tweedy or *PLJ* ironically nick named after the lime fruit juice that was popular with slimmers of the time - *he seemed to attract all the fat chicks.* Guitar -Colin Farnworth – *Peter the Perv as he actually got off with girls* by this time. The drummer was, Andy Gilgun, the *cutie one or "Dan" for dandruff (which still sticks with him today).* Vocals – *Johnny Thud*....a stage name that did not last long for Shaun. There may have been another member as John Martin recalls someone called Eric who lived in a flat on Park Road. This was, in the main, a covers band, practicing regularly at the youth centre. Hangman's early gigs included a notable one at the Rivington Festival. It was organised by the local hippies who got to know about the band through mutual friends such as Mick Bamber (who later played guitar in Sinister Chuckles). He worked with Shaun during a two day community scheme painting a mural of Lou Reed's *Transformer* LP cover. Another, Mick Henderson (dubbed "Marco Polio" as he was a sufferer of the crippling disease) had access to a van. Transport was very hard to come by back then. No one of Shaun's age could drive and very few people from council estates had cars - even those owned by the middle classes were usually perks of their jobs. The incidents surrounding that year's festival were so violent that it put an end to future events there for some time. At the centre of the mayhem was the infamous Hell's Angels who descended on this otherwise tranquil village nestling on Lancashire's side of the Pennines not far from Chorley.

The Hell's Angels are organised biker gangs represented in most countries today. In the 1950s and '60's, teenagers flocked to their ranks, influenced by Marlon Brandon's character in the film *The Wild One*. Back then it was a male dominated order clad in black leathers riding powerful Norton and Triumph motorcycles. Their appeal then, and now, is to all ages who share a passion for speed and the freedom of the open road. However, in the 1970's, their fearful reputation for danger was sealed in tails of horrific initiation ceremonies and triple X rated deeds, spread in whispers in many secondary school corridors. In short no one messed with the Angels. The Angels animosity towards Punks to Shaun seemed to be due to a culture shock. The Angels dominance as the bad boys on the street was being challenged. Punk was the flag a new breed of 70's rebels flocked to. The media had made Punk and its exponent's front page news. The "look" was aggressive: multi-coloured spiked hair, facial studs and safety pins pierced lips and cheeks. Trashed out clothes and heavy makeup for both sexes gave a new meaning to being seen as an individual in an "anything goes" acceptance before it became high street fashion. It was collectively primitive - Mohican like- on a war path dancing to a new rhythm that was frightening, phlegmatic and exciting! Greasy head banging warriors were on a collision course with the colourful, pogoing upstarts in the small village of Rivington. Anyone in touch with either persuasion realised you had to take your side as your life depended on it.

Colin thought the Angels were *cool* – up to the point when one of them slashed opened his shirt with a Bowie knife and threw him on a camp fire. When it came to the Angels' attention that Hangman was a Punk band the two opposing ideologies were set for a battle. Shaun received a message that he would be shot if Hangman performed. This was not an idle threat. In the aftermath of the festival, there were word of mouth accounts of rape, countless fights and the random slaughter of live stock. What mattered to Shaun was that all his experience up to that point had lead him to a sense of self worth, but, should he play or should he go - what would he do?

The freedom of expression which Punk unleashed bestowed a spirit that inspired a whole generation. In time, some of Punk's off spring such as Bob Geldoff, Midge Ure and Bono, for example, would go on to change international opinions on world poverty, and human rights violations by bending the ears of our world leaders. But in 1977 faced with a life or death situation you had to truly believe in what you stood for. Dressing in the Punk style risked bodily damage in the same way wearing the wrong colours at a football match got your head kicked in. Hooliganism was at its height and football "fans" organised punch ups with rival gangs on the terraces or pre agreed spaces outside the grounds. Bank Holiday weekends witnessed clashes amongst tribes of Mods, Rockers, Teddy Boys and now the Punks in running riots on the beaches and streets of English seaside towns, amongst the buckets, spades and kiss me quick hats.

Meanwhile, adding to the musical chaos that the Rivington Festival was descending into, a shot gun had been fired. It blew a hole into the stage roof during the **Accelerators** set....*they were from Liverpool and were big hard scousers*...recalls Shaun. But what had he decided to do? Should he tell the others......Humm? Well, *Mr Raggedy (Colin) - was spooked enough as it was and Dan had "fucked off" long before their allotted slot*, in the end ....*we bravely ran away over the moors avoiding the roads. ... though one thing was funny when I told an organiser were not going on 'n explained the situation he just said 'don't give off bad vibes Maaan' I just turned round n said 'Me give off bad vibes you fucking wanker go tell them that..."* and as I walked off I just turned

244

and said "you useless cunt". We all returned the next day, except for George, so I played bass. During their set Shaun defiantly spat mouthfuls of beef burgers over the hippies at the front. But more than this, it was a moment that divides those who think about doing something and those who actually got off their arses and did it. That day, and in *that* moment Shaun Maxwell stood shoulder to shoulder with everyone who saw what the essence of Punk was all about. He believed in himself and all that Punk embraced. This performance was one of the first memories Shaun and I discussed during the start of our friendship and I remember recounting an abridge reference to it when I introduced **Shorn** (see later) at their Chorley Labour club gig supporting Tom Hingley in 2005.

Another notable event in Hangman's life was a gig in Preston for Newman College students. The attendance at The Duck Inn was high being a Freshers Rag Ball and they were supporting a hippy band called **Hungry Freaks.** *It was the first time that the music came together coherently albeit it a monotone melody delivered over a one string bass rhythm.* It seemed to work well up to the point when some Nazi Teddy Boys turned up through an open door. They were older than the members of Hangman and just at the point when they thought their lives were over in another Rivington incident, *a huge Rasta bloke and his mates stepped in with "You getting any shit Maaaannn?"* The Teds thought twice and headed home but the reprieve was short lived as the Rastas turned on them announcing *"...coz we wanna do youuuu!"* Somehow Shaun talked them out of it by telling jokes and odd ball stories with the ease of a bomb diffuser. Shaun's ability to communicate with those marginalised by their non conformity is a characteristic that permeates many of his songs. This was still the "early" days and his embrace of the ideals of Punk meant that any challenge was met head on no matter how insignificant by today's standards. Hence, when the land lady of another Preston gig threatened to shut the bar if he didn't stop swearing at faulty equipment, he proclaimed as loud and as clearly as he could, *"Fuck off! You old twat!"*

There is a cassette recording of Hangman *somewhere* at Chorley Youth Club or Tatton Community Centre depending on Shaun's or John Martin's recollection. John says *a version of "Suck" was definitely one of the songs from this session and possibly "I Wanna Smash a Hippie". I remember watching them at a gig in the basement of Chorley College on High St and a real hippie slapping Shaun across the face because of that song. Shaun just burst out laughing in the guy's face.* However, the band split soon afterwards due to a dispute over a double booking – on one hand a prestigious gig at Rafters in Manchester on the other an earlier promise to play ,what one faction in the group viewed as a more inferior venue, that the sands of time have long since buried. Such is the fate of many bands – often the subject of an argument is just a spark or the catalyst to other deeper rooted issues. There was little money in playing Punk then and I know that, financially, it hasn't changed over the decades since. To emphasise this and the historical irony of the golden age of the genre Shaun pointed out that one day Colin's bogey (push cart) crashed at the bottom of the hill on Seymour Street and they were given more money to use it to help move a fridge back up the road for someone than the gig they were due to play! The demise of Hangman gave birth to Shaun's next band – Sinister Chuckles.

<u>Sinister Chuckles</u> (**Parts 1-3 end of 1977 to early 1978**). This band had a couple of line up changes but the main players were Colin – R/Guitar and who named the band as a reference to obscene phone calls. Shaun "Conrad Hinowski" on Bass *"...box is buzzing and me ropes gone slack!"* who use to put stickers on the frets to see what notes to play which meant he always had to stand under a light to see them. John Martin – L/Guitar. John told me that he was *rehearsing with a band, whose name escapes me, upstairs at the Imperial Inn (Union Street, Chorley). They wanted to do Stones and Deep Purple covers and I kept turning up with my own tunes which were "a bit too fast". At one rehearsal I looked over my shoulder to see Shaun and Colin peeping round the door. They didn't speak but the next day Shaun told me that Hangman had split and would I like to form a band with him and Col – brilliant!* Chris Ball – Drums – John said that they had a couple of other drummers before Chris. *One was Dave Compton who was actually a 'Neb' (Hells Angel /Greaser). He was great but I think he packed in due to peer pressure from the rest of the Nebs. Then we had Topper (can't think of his full name) who had played in a college band called* **Cyrus Teed** *who did standard rock covers (All Right Now etc). Another great drummer but he didn't last because he didn't really like punk and he was on a different wavelength to us. Chris couldn't play for toffee but he looked great, blond spiky hair a cross between Billy Idol and Paul Cook.*

They practiced at John's where Colin and Shaun took turns at sampling John's father's home brew – hence there was no direction or emphasis to anything. But there was plenty of opportunity to develop attitude and their self deprecating humour which has stayed with them to this day. Shaun didn't want to stop annoying people so they became famous for playing crap. Going against the grain John and Colin's playing leaned towards Rock riffs as it felt like Punk was a passing trend. Shaun surmised that it was a time of pigeon holing styles and he feels that he would like to describe as "pop". *Pop is a dirty word for people who aren't talented enough to do their own and make it their own.* John's opinion was that they were a *proper Garage Band because that's where we practiced. In true punk ethos of 'do it yourself', we didn't even have a microphone so Shaun bellowed down the earpiece of my headphones to amplify his vocals. My dad has since told me that the farmer nearby complained about the noise saying that his cow's had stopped producing milk!*

In terms of fame and fortune – they did get a visit from Pete Wylie who went onto form Wah! (....and its many manifestations) alongside the Liverpool scene that blossomed in the early 1980's. John says *this was whilst we were practising upstairs at the Leigh Arms. It was Martin (Skull) Rigby who brought him along. Skull had actually seen the Pistols on the Anarchy Tour in Manchester and had the first copy of the single that I saw. It was on EMI and in a plain black sleeve. I later got the same version from a cheap box on Preston market for 40p. We met Pete Wylie again at The Clash gig at King Georges Hall in Blackburn.* But who cares for name droppers' ehh!

Shaun was writing songs on his bass (e.g. *TV Generation*) and the gigs included pubs in Wigan that often exploded into fights. Night clubs like The Moonraker in Preston a strict age limit but they often ended in brawls such as at their support slot to Heavy Metal band **QUAD.** Shaun blames the fighting on some local football fans. He jumped off stage with a broken drum stick in hand ready to flatten them but tripped over a stool and got trampled himself. However, the most memorable gig for John was: *at a Christmas disco in Chorley Town Hall, Dec 1977 we supported boring old local farts,* **Legend** *(Leg End as we called them). Also on the bill was punk DJ Radio Doom who was touring the UK at the time. The place was packed (at least 600). We were playing a great, powerful set as we'd got pretty tight by then. Some Nebs started shouting for 'Smoke on the Water' and began throwing plastic beer glasses onto the stage. Shaun goaded the audience and screamed "why don't you try chuckin' proper 'uns?". Next thing there were bottles and glasses raining down. Ever defiant we started playing one of our songs 'No Surrender'. Martin Rigby's younger brother was onstage pogoing directly in front of me (he was in a 3 piece band called* **Stupid Six** *who's set, I seem to recall, just consisted of a 15 minute deranged version of Iggy's "Lust For Life") when, out of the corner of my eye I caught the glimpse of a bottle spinning through the air. Everything seemed to be in slow motion as the bottle hit him square in the face splattering blood all over me. It was an ugly event but good for our reputation. Radio Doom sang our praises to everyone later and condemned the cowards who'd done the bottling.*

This is an example of when the passing of time distorts memories of events, their sequence and facts vary amongst our protagonists. Shaun remembers a crowd of only *300 locals* and thought it was Hangman who played this gig and were on first. His version has him greeting the audience with sneers and, as he grabbed the microphone from the stand, he smacked his face full on chipping a tooth and bursting his lip. As the song came to an end his agony filled the lyrics with screams of "Aaaahhhs and fuuucccks". Luckily, as he double up in pain someone threw an ashtray that missed him but split the head of *"...some poor sod pogoing on the stage"*. Punk seemed to attract this kind of subtlety but, alert to the violence now erupting; he was upright and caught the next missile - *a beer glass*. As the ambulance arrived the place was well on the way to being trashed and the media headlines of the event went down as "Punks cause riot". The end came quickly for part I. A gig at Trinity Youth Club in Gillibrand Walks got cancelled as Chris got locked up for burglary. Beats the usual lame excuse of my auntie has just died!

Part 2 - John joined the band and recalls - *"I actually played a few gigs with this line up before 'leaving'. George and Jimmy came to watch us play the Joiners Arms gig (now Last Orders) on Market St.* Shaun said that it was a support slot with Hippy Rock band called **Loki** as he puts it *"....rhymes with crappy".* He band was: *Colin (bass), John (guitar) Shaun (drums) and Mick Roberts (vocals. I don't know how we ended up with Mick. He was a great lad and a good laugh but couldn't sing. He just had no timing at all. It was straight after this gig that the line up changed with George and Jimmy coming in. Col went back to guitar and Shaun on vocals. From a musical point of view this was the best line up so far as George and Jimmy were very competent, gigging musicians although they did seem to be yonks older than us. I remember playing a 2 night 'residency' at The Viking in Warrington when Col was away on holiday. I bust my bottom e string mid song and whilst re-stringing George started playing a rolling, funky bass riff to cover for me. Next thing, off the cuff, Shaun broke into the words from a popu-lar TV advert of the time "Lilt, with da totally tropical taste" happy days! We also did a great gig a Jalgos Caribbean club in Preston where I got in a fight with some prick who kept grabbing my guitar strings from the front of the stage. This gig was recorded by George so, if you do ever make contact, I would love a copy.*

Another memorable gig was at Trucks in Wigan where the stage was the tail-board of a lorry. We played a blinder on a Saturday night and Shaun intro-duced a cover version of Quark Strangeness and Charm that we did as "this is by Hawkwind......that's when a Kestrel farts". I also remember this gig because some idiot kept coming round the back of the stage and chucking water at the band (mainly me). My girlfriend (now wife) Ali was sat at the rear of the stage and the next time the pillock appeared she booted him square in the meat & two veg. The fact that she was wearing thigh length pointed leather boots made it doubly effective. Needless to say that put an end to the showers. We went down so well at

Trucks that they asked to play mid week and we would get all the door money. It turned out to be a 1.00am slot on a Tuesday night/ Wednesday morning with about 12 people in! I didn't leave as such. I went away to Scarborough for a week with Ali. When I returned I bumped into Col and asked when the next band rehearsal was. He sheepishly told me that they had got a new guitarist because they thought I wasn't committed enough. I was really hurt but it's all forgotten now.

Part 3 saw Mick Bamber (who was in his 30's) replace John along with George White (bass) and Jimmy Catterall (Drums) collectively referred to by Shaun as *The Baldies*. Both George and Jimmy had asked to play in the band – they had lots of contacts and a background in Pub Rock and Blues. They practiced at a pig farm in Bickerstaff, Mick provided the transport there. The room they used flooded regularly and they had to stand on wooden pallets to avoid electrocuting themselves. Shaun almost didn't get to play his first gig in Warrington as he and Colin went for a walk and got lost via a couple of pubs meaning that the band ended up going on last with them totally pissed. At a Labour Club in Rainhill Shaun *"totally off me box"* (again) decided to sing "knives and folks" for lyrics to every song to see if anyone noticed. But George and Jimmy were very tight and fast versions of *Jonney B Goode* were crowd pleasers before their set was halted by Bingo. John told me that *Mark Torkington – or Tosh as we knew him... briefly managed the Chuckles but got cold feet after a gig upstairs at the Royal Oak where Shaun royally pissed off Leg End by trashing their mike stand. After the gig we went to a party at Tosh's house in Queens Road. One of us was attempting to open a bottle of beer on the corner of an old wooded table when some longhair declared "tables have feelings man!" We left immediately in fits of laughter.* Shaun described this band fondly as an *"interim"* before Dance Troop and they did a recording at Rochdale's Cargo Studios. All that remains is the memory of the producer's comments at how much alcohol the band consumed –always in the pub and they dowsed crates of Holstein Pills in between. Hence there was a tinge of irony to the songs such as *Green Man* and *Wolf* (complete with howls in the background) were named after the Alsatian puppy that grew in front of their eyes becoming the premises guard dog. Others; Who *Shot the Rabbit* and *Terminal Acrobat* may survive somewhere!

Part 4 (April 2012 to present). The trio of Shaun, Colin and John – who had remained in regular contact with each other - decided to rehearse as Sinister Chuckles once again some 35 years on. Shaun on vocals only, Colin took bass duties with John on guitar. Short of a drummer Shaun was going to telephone Mark "Spook" Speakman (Ex Shorn drummer-see later) but he bumped into him while shopping in Aldi at the time. Once Spook agreed to join the Chuckles, Shaun introduced the selection to the others as *"I've got our drummer in Aldi".* Spook fitted in smoothly to the practices in the cramped cellar under The Railway – whose Landlord's over the years had been god to both this band and The Taser Puppets (see later). Their debut gig was at The Railway too and after few others in the town I caught up with them at The Guzzling Goose, Ashton –U-Lyne (Manchester) on 30th June. Mick Guy, my next door neighbour, came with me and I described this band's history and the sense of occasion this gig represented for me. Sinister Chuckles represented the pinnacle of what was the originality of Punk Rock. Forged in garage land, nurtured on nonsense, fuelled by fun, cheeky as chips with alcohol attitudes, destined to burn brightly for a short time rather than fade away. They were all this at the time when it was exactly right to be so. I oozed enthusiasm by describing to Mick this lineage rather than it being simply a case of men being boys again. For the former late teens/early twenty year olds from Chorley in '77/8, it was a time when writing a song, any song, was a statement of what was around them or on their minds. It was not going to be the sophisticated lyrics or a musical mystery like Punk's sworn enemies (Pink Floyd and Prog Rock) but the raucous rage of a rebellious rabble. That was what I promised him and when their set of eleven bombshells had been dropped on the good folk of Ashton less than thirty minutes later he admitted it was a promise kept.

Shaun wore his lightly tinted Elvis Presley steel rimed sun glasses. He gyrated and gesticulated in Pub Punk pastiche. The set list: was: *Tony Thornborough's Sock, Suck, Wiggy Brown, Dorian Grey, TV Generation, Fed Up, I Wanna Be Batman, Marilyn Monroe, I Wanna Get Pissed, We Are Outrageous* and *Schitzo.* John on his right and Colin opposite were nonchalantly cool with no attempt to distract from Rock Star Maxwell, being motionless compared to Spook sweating over his snare, slamming his sticks with all the stamina he could muster to keep up with the onslaught. It was blisteringly beautiful – everything I had hoped for and nothing like the U Tube footage of searing static and indiscernible vocals. By being forthright in his delivery Shaun's words could be heard clearly – aided by the repetition and simplicity in songs of two minutes or less. *TV Generation, I wanna be Batman* and *I Wanna get Pissed* had angst and levity delivered with the classical three chords riffs - no effects, no nonsense and no encore!

My notes from another gig I went to read as follows:

7th Oct 2012 at The Railway, Chorley – "Bongo's Big Birthday Bash" with: 1st **Dusty Moonan** *(G/v 15 minutes of light social observational melodies). 2nd* **Luis**

Drayton (all in black cross dresser with Nazi tin hat, spouts 4 letters words to backing tapes -very aggressive, instantly annoying but mildly absorbing and intoxicatingly memorable).3rd Sinister Chuckles (Shaun worse the wear for drink, Luis did vocals on "I wanna get Pissed") Didn't see the rest as I left about 8.30pm but they were:4th **Cactus Knife** *– unimpressed by the U-tube footage of this bunch of student shoe gazers. 5th* **Kill Pretty** *– seen previously, worth the price of admission anywhere for no frills hard core Punk value.*

Co-incidentally, Shaun has helped write and direct Luis Drayton's "Rising Scum" LP and pulled the live band Glamour Pussy together for the launch at The Kings Arms (Salford) that supported **The Things**.

The Sinister Chuckles first releases, after 35 years was; the **Blitzkrieg Mop EP** (circa mid 2012). Shaun's attention to the art work for the cover, like many of his bands, is a cut and paste of any material close at hand. This child like simplicity, is, in itself what the D.I.Y graphics of Punk championed. This particular CD comprises: (front cover) a black & white photo of a woman dressed like Hilda Ogden (a former character in the TV soap *Coronation Street* who cleaned the Rovers Return), she is bent over a floor mop that has a swastika on its head. (Back cover) a photo of the band live on stage at The Railway, Chorley. *Recorded at Shabby Row studios, Shabby Road, Chorley, Lancs.* Song list: 1. Tony Thornborough's Sock (on the radio). 2. I Wanna Be Batman. 3 I Saw the Ghost of Marilyn Monroe. 4. Dorian Gray. There's plenty of affection for this band that continues to gig today – check them out!

<u>**Dance Troop**</u> (1978-1980). This band represents the closest Shaun has come to "commercial" success. Named by Shaun and put together at the time just before The New Romantic scene went over ground. Bands such as Spandau Ballet, Duran Duran, Heaven 17 and the Human League took a lead from Bowie's cross dressing and sanitised it to excess. Perfect make up for boys, bouffant hair and sculptured fringes, yards of frills draped over the cuffs and chests of regimental regalia. The music was defined by the synthesiser, thumping bass lines and piercing lead guitars competed with saxophones or electronic string instruments to define a short period of appeal that claimed charts success and many a dance floor. Shaun paid £20 for the "skunk" look with a long blonde fringe and wore a military jacket. His assembled band this time was - Colin, Ian "Watty" Watson (Drums) a scouser from Bootle. Through knowing Watty at secondary school, Shaun met Nathan "Nat" Birchall to play saxophone (and who is now *considered one of the best saxophonist on the Jazz circuit*). Also, Mark "Eric" Howarth – Bass (who *played it like the clown Pirot*).They got a Manager – Mark Torkington who Shaun now dismisses as *"phoney"*.

251

Rehearsals were above The Imperial pub which is opposite what was then the site of the town's bus station on Union Street. One day Mark was drinking down stairs and asked to watch what was going on. They had Sinister Chuckles' PA and generally better equipment. Mark agreed to arrange them gigs which would get them noticed. These venues included Pluto's (Wigan) and one during the College Rag week at Blackburn Tech. The gig at the last one emphasised how flamboyant some elements in the band were becoming. Colin, for example dangled a cigarette from his lips but got positioned between a piano and an amp and ended up being wedged and stranded at the back of the tiny stage. The rest of the band were in hysterics as the fag smoke burned his eyes causing him *to squint excessively like Popeye.* He didn't learn as he repeated the impression at the very next gig there. The series of gigs lead to the band's highlight gig at Chorley Town Hall attracting *400 odd.*

Drugs were endemic by now amongst the band's Scooter club fan base contingent –speed and "Barbs" washed down with Alcohol. There was another larger social group emerging – who soon attached themselves to Dance Troop.... *hard core of 30+ people with money to spend who met at The Imperial and were joined by clubbers from Wigan.* At this time Shaun met Kathleen "Kit" Jordan who was a groupie to begin with. There grew a tribe of hangers on and, encouraged by their entourage, the band bathed in the egos it massaged.

At the brink of getting signed and looking forward to a guarantee of stardom, Shaun took a step back. He had a moment of reflection and decided it wasn't for him. He felt he'd been shown a lesson in a lack of product over style. Best friends Martin and George refused to watch them *"...they thought it was fucking shite".* Money was being paid to the band but they didn't see any *only Tosh did and we are talking up to £200 a gig* which even by today's standard is generous for any unsigned band. Dance Troop did fill a need to get all the trappings and crap it attracted out of Shaun's system before his next reincarnation. They did record a demo and sent it to Chrysalis Records but the band split into two factions. The rival one called **Ice Cube** formed by Kung Fu exponent Nicky Smart and comprised: Mick Bamber, Colin Farnworth, Graham Watkinson and Eric(*useless*) Howarth but without a driving force it went round in circles and soon broke up.

Nervous Desire It was circa 1981 -the summer of the riots at the height of Thatcherism. Shaun, says *the only notable event in Chorley was someone throwing a brick through one of Woolworth's windows....no one joined in and the poor sod got arrested- one dick head with no mates – silly bugger had to pay for the cost -biggest window in Chorley – plate glass –" Disaffected youth" – just some time wasters excuse to go robbing.*

Shaun was reading more than he had done before, while reflecting on his decision to end Dance Troop. Although short lived, Shaun felt Nervous Desire was a *"proper"* band for the first time – reaching beyond the Youth Club scene and it also consisted of: Nathan Birchall (Bass & Sax) and Ian Watson (Drums). Their main focus was playing the small feral like clubs such as The Warehouse (Preston). This was a return to their Punk roots – much faster songs like *Heretic Chant* which they went on to record. They were influenced by the blossoming Liverpool bands such as Teardrop Explodes and Echo & the Bunnymen etc. More importantly their friend Martin (from the days of Hangman) was studying French at University there with Pete Wylie who knew the lead singers of these bands –Julian Cope , Ian McCullough and many others in those fledgling "Indie" Mersey beat days. Regular "trips" in all senses of the word around Liverpool put Shaun in the presence of these contemporaries and the infatuation with all its seductions. By this time Shaun and Kit were *going out together* and he was teaching her how to play Bass guitar. The band's highlight was second on a bill at Tatton Community centre *just to annoy Ice Cube* who they *blew away*. A tape of this claim may exist but is not made available at the time of writing.

Adesire. Morphing out of Nervous Desire as the name suggests, Adesire's line up changed constantly but, initially it was Shaun, Kit, Watty (drums) – who was in and out of the band all the time and Nick (*bull shite*) Beardsley and Graham Watkinson (Drums). Another band member of some note was Keith "Finger Nails" Smith - *because they were long and he wore a snake skin jacket – bit of a hippie type and a keyboard player who was very good too.* His mother was from the Seychelles and half French. This gave the impression that he was of Asian descent and often got called "Pakki". One occasion, while changing his contact lenses in a toilet – he'd dropped them on the floor. In came some Nazi thugs who called him Pakki in Shaun's presence. Shaun educated them with *"No he's not he's from the Seychelles" –there tended to be a lot of their sort hanging around the music scene at that time".*

Keith lived in Anderson Street and they recorded at his house using a drum machine on a 2 track TEAK deck which did them very well even if crude by today's standards. Shaun immersed himself into poetry & literature- *Rossetti and the Pre- Raphaelites. – Dante's Gabrielle – all chopped up.* He and Kit were in love. No one was doing simple love songs at that time but he did as well as smoking a lot of dope. His consumption was such that when signing on one day mid way through the year, the clerk had to point out that he'd put the year 1983 when it was 1984. The mind set was psychogenic and minimalist – *it got a lot of people's interest as it was very accessible* and, from the songs I have heard, slightly ahead of its time.

Contemporaries at the time ranged from U2 to Monochrome Set and Shaun went to meet the former at a University gig in Manchester with Martin & Pete Wylie – "liggin" with bands was part of the norm for musicians at that time following the drugs often let them into this underworld. Shaun wanted purity in his music...*we were Ok when recording but fragile live – poor equipment - but that seemed to be the attraction at a time when everything was too perfect, precise and sterile.* "Some Noware" came first followed by *My Sister Sleeps, Statutes* and *Vocation Paradise*, described by Shaun as *J Kerouac in mood.* Returning from the pub one night a radio was on and John Peel played the later song. Furthermore, after a support slot to The Membranes at The White Heart, Chorley where they *got loads watching* them, in the crowd, was someone from Radio Lancashire who suggested they enter a Battle of the Bands competition the station was organising. Adesire were runners up and their prize was eight hours recording time in a studio in Bacup where they cut *What Is Love,* and *Lucian Song* recorded with Lila (Kit's sister in law) *who was taking pain killers and slurred her words as if pissed.* Later *Beyond Calvary* followed with another song that was *produced by someone famous from the Liverpool scene at that time* in Rawtenstall. He was *not keen on us at first but once he warmed to the band after a few weekends he like us and was a really nice fella. Reg – who put on New Order at Tatton, put the track on a "best of "studio compilation tape.*

DASH RIP ROCK. Before the end of 1984, Shaun wanted to change the name and have a new start as Adesire's style was quickly dated. Things were moving fast - music had changed with the arrival of the simpler stripped down/back to basic guitar and drums of the "Indie" sound. The Smiths were at the forefront at one end and Frankie Goes to Hollywood bringing up the rear. The New Romantics were dead over night and a ground zero had arrived again as it had done almost midway through the previous decade. "Dash Rip Rock" was the international jet set playboy "star" character of the Klampetts TV show featured in an episode at the Mammoth Studios in the salubrious Beverley Hills. Meanwhile, back in the dull foot hills of the Pennies, it was Shaun (Vox), Kit (Bass), Watty (Drums) & Jim Ball (Guitar) that formed the Chorley equivalent. Jim was originally from Wigan but lived in Broad Gate (Preston). He knew Watty from his studies at the same College. Jim was a keep fit/body builder who cycled everywhere with his guitar strapped to his back. Even though Shaun didn't like students as a rule he got on with Jim and he encouraged a lot of his mates to come to their gigs. The Band manager was

Phil Roberts or *H.M (Heroin Man)* as he was better known to Shaun. Like most of managers Shaun encountered there were alleged financial irregularities or discrepancies as Shaun recalls.... *the band members got paid £10 each for a gig and we were charged £20 for the use of a van when the band were paid £200-£250 a gig. But, he had his "uses"....!* Initially, this was providing rehearsal space in his cellar when their usual place (at Parrots) was shut down.

Gigs were still localised within short van rides like Witton Park Festival (Blackburn) and The Warehouse (Preston – supporting The Babysitters). At King George's Hall (Blackburn) they supported Ten Pole Tudor. Afterwards, on his own (as Kit had gone home), Shaun went to the post gig party with the group. *I freaked out Eddie by walking along the balcony rail of some flats in Shadsworth, three stories up. Shared a taxi back – great guy.* They headlined the Rag week at Preston Poly (now UCLAN) for two years running. The second year gig was a *pissed up* set resorting to a drum machine. On the first song Shaun stepped on an over loaded homemade foot switch which exploded. Ever the improviser...*we just turned up the speed and did a punky Jive Bunnyesque medley of our songs.* Somewhere there is a Video "Dash – The Movie" recorded at Chorley Town hall too.

Shaun records their worst gigs too like when they got asked *by some middle aged guy* via a friend to play at his girlfriend's 21st Birthday at a club somewhere in Partington. It came about as he'd seen Kit and Shaun play as a duo at The Wheatsheaf (Leyland). He was so impressed with their cover of *Heroin* that he thought they had written it and miss took them for junkies as they played so long out of necessity to draw out their set of two songs which is all they had at that time! As a group though, they were used to playing in front of large audiences. Disappointingly, when they arrived, they discovered that they were doing *a private show for this guy to impress his mates and their girlfriends.* But, they did play as Shaun understood them all to be gangsters *proper ones!* Another was at the Top Hat Club (Blackburn) when no one turned up as it was too rough. They had to clean the stage floor from vomit and broken glass from a previous gig there and someone got stabbed the week after they played. Kit got *scared to death* by an encounter with a transsexual *"complete with stubble and tit scars, showing them to kit in the women's toilet. Deep man's voice – his boyfriend was a midget who was feeling him/her/it up in the passage leading to the gig room while some guy was wanking under his mac – looking like a clique flasher".*

At this time they came in to contact with Jerry Kenny –*a mad hippy* – who was in the band **Naffi Sandwich.** He lived on the old American WWII Burton Wood air base turned into a storage facility. He had bought old BBC

255

Recording equipment which was being unceremoniously dumped during the switch to digital. These had old valves and 8 track, songs got layered *a real sense of what it was that worked musically – Psychedelic Punk – British not the American version!* Friends Mark & Gill *who were Goths* lent the band their keyboard for recording *Almost Classical*. Also they knew the DJ at Clouds and through him got an introduced to Ronnie Brown (see Chapter 2) who was putting on bands at the same venue.

Lyrics and poetry

I want to introduce you to some of Shaun's songs from this time and I hope that the selected editing I have done reveals some of his talent as a lyricist and poet. I would like all his songs are made available someday as their number and variation is vast and an enigma for someone else to unravel!

TAPE- March 1985 – recorded with Watty just before he left (apart from *) *Recorded at an industrial unit on Moss Side/Fox Lane in Leyland* – 1. "Cat Fight" – *about women being vicious – we were meeting strange people at the time- heavy Bass.*

And to destiny a daughter
She leads them down dark alley ways
I've tasted love straight weird and awful
I need a girl who lives life strange.

2. "Honey & Blood" – *Dali after one of his pictures*

If your lovin's so good
Why is honey sweeter than blood?
On the canvas you paint illuminate
What I can't understand
Is why the..... falls from your hand
Press your eyes and just wait hallucinate!

3. "Here Lies India" – *Anti Hippy song – India being exploited as no one played concerts there -they just went there to take drugs and find their souls but gave nothing in return.*

In what strange time of what strange cause
Blow your sails to India's course.

4. "Beware The Stars" – *my favourite* on which Shaun plays lead.

Fly the messiah in the sky
Shoot away the strings that keep them high
Loves in to life, lives of luck out of control
What price a touch?
(Chorus) Beware, Beware of the stars

Beware, Beware of what you are.
Instant simple giants often cry
Burning their fingers and their eyes
Greed dictates the convenience plastic wild
Needle cuts the victim vinyl child.

5. "Almost Classical"* – never sung live but the first professionally recorded and structured song. It is his earliest recording I have heard in which I identified with the depth of Shaun's lyrics:

A silent maybe between white walls and corridors
Did I sense you blushing; your eyes touched the floor?
If I know what you know
Then you can be the sun
If I know what you know
It's almost classical.
Can't you see reflections?
Love and that kind of thing
Tragic men write songs about
But sadly rarely mean.
What a wonderful feeling I'm down
The princess she danced with a clown
As we sit here observing
Some Gothic lament
Framed by a window
That's all we'll pretend to be
Statutes excluded from time
....that you can be the one.

There is mention of another session at Rawtenstall "Rex's Studio" with tracks; *Disco Bomb. I Love Fire* and *The Man from Vietnam*. A split 7inch single "Garbage Head" appeared on Chorley Records – with a track from **The Fluffies**. They did recorded a second session at Jerry's adding more tracks – a lot darker without Watty who was replaced by Howard Facey who was younger and Shaun knew him as he was someone who he use to hang around with some of his mates who had to go to Youth Advisory Service. Out of this came "Monsters Are Blue":

Nightmares a district
I'll take you to it
Where people are shadows
And monsters are blue
Bottles are bubbling forensic blood pumping

Lighting becomes you and
Monsters are Blue
The girls from who knows where?
Taken into care.
"Here Lies India" – with a subtler use of keyboards. And "I love Fire"
You know I can't marry you
My mind is dissected into peace and disorder
You wanted a mystical man
Who changes colour like a soup can – can.

Then another session in November yielded: "(I want) A picture of Dorian Grey"

I want a picture of Dorian Grey
A public fixture and a private face
I want no-no-no stains on my soul
I'm tattooed in the Attic
On a canvas wall.

"Insects & Matadors" and "Ghost of Marilyn Monroe" – *more up tempo* but by this stage the drugs had taken hold of Shaun and he was on the edge of a nervous breakdown and his words reflected this:

"...never met a creature who was so run down
A tethered metaphysical dumping ground"

Kit was heavily pregnant when they entered a Battle of the Bands contest in Preston....*she had to sit down on stage and balance her Bass on her belly. We had all her stuff for hospital in the car boot – just in case*. In May 1986 Shaun's son Jake was born. He was baptised "Jacob James Maxwell" -Jim after his friend but Shaun only realised afterwards that Jacob is James in the same way as John is known as Jack *so Jim Jim it is*. To add to his responsibilities he and Kit were evicted shortly afterwards and they moved to Hope Street.

About this time Shaun went to watch Pop Will Eat Itself with George, Mark and Gill at Manchester. It was the other band – Wonderstuff- that they thought was better and when they met them afterwards they shared the same sense of humour. There was a gig arranged for them to play a support slot for The Wonderstuff at Horwich leisure centre but the PWEI got signed and went to America instead.

Shaun sent material from their second session at Jerry's to Miles Hunt (Wonderstuff) which *he liked* and a video made by Keith at college out of random footage of the band. Nothing came from it and further disappointment followed toward the end of this band's life with the imprisonment of their manager. About this time Shaun met Martin Hannett (Joy Division and

Factory Records) producer – at a house on Park Road near the dentists – where they were recording. Shaun played him *Disco Bomb* and Hannett said that he wanted to record it but he was also *"off his head"*. Shaun had only one condition that he laid down to Hannett – *"...don't fucking die you twat!"* .... and then shortly afterwards he did......who knows what might have happened if they had met some years previously.....and Shaun philosophically quips.... *must have been the excitement of hearing our track!* Ironically Shaun remembers watching Joy Division at The Warehouse (Preston) and how Ian Curtis *just starred and was dazed out of it too...*someone else who died soon after being in the same room as Shaun!

Froyd Egg. Mid 1980's was a period of social unrest. The miners' strike of 1984, and the deepening grip of recession had the effect of making the poor poorer while the rich got richer. Thatcher's government sold off of our national assets such British Telecom and other utilities. *Me and Howard disagreed a lot about politics, as me n kit was really left wing. Howard was the Tory and as I grew disillusioned with left politics .I became more of a social realist as there is nothing up with left wing ideas just left wing bureaucrats that are self serving. Seems trivial now but the lines were divided in the Thatcher years. Me and Kit were so skint I sold Jim my guitar amp and used his guitars. Kit used his DIY bass amp. Jim started going out with this really middle class feminist tree hugger type. She hated me because I were never pc. One day I went round to H.M.s house to practice but all the amps were gone. Jim had quit without even telling us.*

Without an acoustic guitar and bass Shaun and Kit could not play live. They retreated to home recordings on their Teak producing *Profumo Affair, James Bond in Drag* and a version of *Dorian Grey*. Other songs recorded at her mum's house were *Sacred Cow and Blood Sports*. However, Shaun stopped playing when Jake was born. There was another band about this time called Eric Spears (named after the Coronation Street song composer) which was female fronted from Chorley/ Coppull/ Whittle. They used some of Shaun's songs written in between Dance Troop and Dash Rip Rock e.g. *Clap Hands* and *Big Banana Song* But *all their own songs got the worst review ever* .....Shaun's songs didn't!

Occasionally Shaun put songs playing solo guitar this collection (i.e. *Beautiful Game* and *who's that under the blanket*) also included two songs which recently featured in Shaun's solo sets. One of these being at The Ducie Bridge at the top end of Corporation Street, Manchester –in July 2012 during the Olympic opening ceremony. I had driven Shaun there and he played *Dream Rider* and *Wicker Man* which I think he'd played at the first solo acoustic gig

I'd seen him do at the Guzzling Goose in Ashton earlier in the same year.

Very Hippy George was another variation during this period. This time it was Shaun (Vox), Ian Mather (guitar and deceased in 2011), and Keith Smith (synth) – used to practice and record at Keith's house. Very short lived but they did play one gig at Chorley Carnival with notable tracks being: *Do the Electric Plug*, *The Statues are Victorian* and *Partners in Clay*;

Partners in clay – wasting away
There's my impression here the wife
Flat broke are we just penniless to see
She looks over my shoulder all that time
There is no wild wind
Or that kind of thing
(Chorus) Just the seasons passing by
Here comes the summer time again
It's the summer time again.

The 1990's and the football years.

The nineties are part of what Shaun fondly refers to as his *footy period*. Watching Bolton Wanders took him all over the country. However, drinking and violence relegated supporting the team during the match in to second place. Football hooliganism of the seventies was still a menace during that decade leading up to the Millennium. Football stadiums are very different now to those in the 1990's. There was a noticeable step change that had gained momentum after the Bradford City fire and Hillsborough atrocity. Steadily, health and safety considerations forced grounds to provide seating for every-one rather than the standing terraces. This costs, coupled with and the domi-nation of Television and Satellite broadcasting interests , increased prices at the turnstiles and for season tickets - which pushed away a lot of the hard core supporters. This impacted on the hooligans too and in time they grew older and watched the matches in pubs or at home with supermarket crates of discounted alcohol instead.

The 1990's for Shaun meant the type of friendships and situations which often lead to serious bodily injury and even the prospect of jail on other occa-sions. In his early to mid thirties by now, Shaun, like most men, needed an out let to get away from the humdrum of being a father, provider and strug-gling musician. Football had the camaraderie of the gangs of his youth and those fond days of kick abouts. Now he had some twenty years of life's experi-ences and the benefits of knowing how to use and be abused by drink. Shaun has recounted many stories to me of what he and his friends got up during those away fixtures as Bolton struggled in the lower leagues. However, he has asked me not to write about them in detail as some ended in severe injuries to others. All he will say is that there was never an event that he went to in search of trouble, it just seemed to be something, scent like, that hung to him. In the same way a pack of wolves will see off a rival, the encounter ends the same as nature's way of settling the primitive instincts all men have in common. But, while most games were *fun and about bravado*, there were those that, looking back, he'd rather forget.

Out of this period, Shaun developed a very strong friendship with Brian Cliff. They'd take turns on getting arrested during their adventures and especially while going to away football matches. Today Shaun freely admits to being over *attracted to alcohol* but he says that Brian *was worse* and he creased up in laughter when he told me of two incidents to highlight the point. One day Brain's girlfriend, Christine, knocked at Shaun's door and the conversation went along the lines of:

"Hiya Shaun, sorry to disturb you but you're about the same measurements as Brain –same height, weight?"

(Pause) Shaun ponders and says "Ehh, (puzzled, he adds)… yeah I'd say so – why?"

"Its Brian, he's only gone and got himself so drunk he's been arrested found walking naked down the M6 back from Preston. God know what he's been doing and I don't want to know but the Police are keeping him locked up and won't release him until someone fetches him some clothes to wear!"

Brain, like Shaun, at times just had to get away from people and the furthest and most remote location the better. On one occasion he drove to such a place in the north of Scotland. He parked in the pitch black of night at spot miles from the nearest village, undisturbed where he could neither annoy or be annoyed by anyone. Alone and with plenty of alcohol he'd gone to sleep, naked (again) in the back of the van he'd driven up in. I pictured the image of what happened next as Shaun told me. He must have woken with a pinching urge to pee. Believing himself to be far from the sight of anyone on the planet he leapt out of the back door. Clasping his cock he let the urine splash out on the wild undergrowth outside. Eyes clenched in abandonment at the blissful release eventually his stream trickled to a dribble he opened his eyes and became conscious of the sounds around him. Not the brush of the highland's sweet breeze through the heather or the baaaa or moan of a stray sheep or cow. Instead, there was a muffled chattering of people whispering and giggling that was getting louder. Perplexed at this human intrusion his eyes lids opened and he turned cautiously to his left and then to his right. He took in the rows of vehicles neatly parked behind trestles and pasting tables filled with all manner of bric-a-brac and chintz. Equally bemused beside each make shift stall were more people serving a crowd of the same composition looking for a bargain or meandering by. In the early hours of dawn it seems the locals had set up for a modern day Car boot sale by the time the unshaven Neanderthal Brian from South of Hadrian's wall bounded out at them. Something those gentle folk would never have expect to find amongst boxes of scratched vinyl, rusting spanners and no longer best selling paper backs.

Dynamo Turettes. *"Half Man Half Biscuit esque!"* This comprised: Jason Hurley, a guitarist, who was as a fan of Dash and lived near Shaun's mum – *one of the music crowd.* Using backing tapes with Shaun on bass they played The Ship Inn on the dock road in Preston and the Adelphi, with their backs to the audience wearing football shirts NOBOV FUKOV printed on them - in mock tribute to the influx of foreign football players. They played football songs as they both liked Bolton Wanderers and got round to recording a 4 track over the course of a year *Stumpy Argentinean Cheat, The Decline of British Football in the 1970's, Gruel* – later to be used for describing Stupid Little Cars – as better than *Gruel* and *Blood Sports*. Shaun wrote all the songs including their final gem *Nose – What's that mountain on your face! Dolphins* were the last recording done on an 8 tracks in Whittle. Kit was upset at the mix as it made her sound like a Dalek. Shaun is not certain what year this was but remembers it as being during the time of the Halle Bop comet.

Shorn (1995-2006). My first contact with Shaun was and indirect one in November 2002. A CD was handed into the "Live and Let Live" radio station - a forerunner to Chorley FM (see Chapter 4). Titled *The Occasional Pieces* I was immediately taken by the first track *Dolphins* which I played on air soon afterwards. This is the only song Shaun has recorded, that I have heard so far, on which he does not sing lead vocals. Kit's voice sounds like how I'd imagine a mermaid would sound. High pitched with the gurgling of bubbles while the rhythms gallop along with the swishing fins of salty sea life occasionally bursting through the surf on the echoed choruses. I didn't know how significant the CD would prove to be in time.

OCCASIONAL PIECES (A cure for toothache)

The title appears on the back of the cover. The picture is subject to copyright and those of you who have a copy you'll appreciate the image and the message it conveys. For most of you who will not, it highlights how uniformity stifles imagination and the freedom of expression by depicting the drudgery of labour. Black and grey shading is used to play on our fears of something sinister lurking in the shadows. Given the period of the Artist's life it could be a comment on communism. At the top; Shaun has typed "A band of outlaws became the inspiration of England's oppressed peasantry". He expressed his views about communism to me... *as a younger man I felt drawn to the left but in later life I've shifted the other way*. The back cover is framed on three sides by motifs – a simple drawing of an animal head, chevrons on groups resembling a tree or a flock of birds. In the centre is a macabre carving of a disfigured face. One side of the face is being stroked by a primitive Quasimodo like character who is gripping a thick stick with a studded clump the top. In the bottom left is a monk staring at you with a perplexed gaze. The tracks are 1/ Dolphins 2/ Beautiful Game3/ Decline of English Football in the 1970's 4/ Gruel. 5/ Nuclear Brown. Also on the inside is handwritten *"the last one don't work. Vocals Shaun & Kit, Guitar Ray Shaun, Bass Maxi Jason Drums Spook"*. With a Chorley phone number beginning 410....I did call the telephone number but no one called me back.

The song lyrics which follow are explained by Shaun. However, the words and how they are set out is how they appear in Shaun's song book with the dates he has written in at the top. They do not match the one's on the recording exactly and, as is often the case, words get changed or altered as their playing gains a momentum.

SHORN EP I – The Shorn EP "A quest for wealth, fame and new continents"

The back cover picture is of Jake, Spook and Shaun taken while on stage at Chorley Football club for the MACY supported afternoon gig (See Chapter 7). Below the band are www.Shorntheband.rocks.IT and the following track listing: *Vanity Cases* (17.11.2004) - *The arrogance of age and youth – the generation gap of "I know better than you!" attitude of self righteousness with a good smattering of peer pressure.*

Waiting for the boy
Just to break his balls
Just to break his fall
For you dear no pretty things
Given away it's a price to pay to think

Melt (May 2000) *Having the guts to go it alone, facing up to tricky situations when your life's in ruins and your "head's" in bits – being optimistic despite these draw backs.*

These things shouldn't happen anymore [repeat]
It's time that you were leaving

And you stopped believing

These things shouldn't happen anymore.

Birthdays (Feb 2004) _the love and suffocation that family life can bring. Big Brother is watching you. Support if behaviour is acceptable to set rules. A song designed to bring both Jake and Alex_ (Shaun and Kit's daughter) _together and appreciate each other's talents._

All my birthdays

Are illusions

It's a slight of hand

Someone's watching

Always watching

Inside net curtain land

Claps Hands (Oct 1989) _Wrote at the end of the Thatcher years. Being active against Right wing fundamentalism both socially and economically. Seeing the effect of the disenfranchised in the country. Anger at elitism and favourites in a corrupt western empire. Fuck Milton, Friedman, Thatcher and Conservatism – this country's erosion._

I want to teach you – clap hands

Said the one armed man

To believe in God and the burning cross

I held belief in my hands

And I thought I'd choke

After all it was a.....

[Chorus] Clap hand teach me clap hand

You wanna teach me!

Some ten miles high

Some ten miles low

There's a girl in a box

And many down below

All the rusty signs they point to zero [repeat]

SHORN -EP II Play, Art, Myth and Ritual on B.D.I records. The front of the sleeve has Shakespeare's face with a safety pin on the forehead pasted onto the head of a butterfly. My copy is on blood red paper with the tracks are listed as they appear below _"Shabby Road Studios" recording by Davos Productions courtesy of B.D.I records 2005._ There is a comment "A ripe ear in the process of shattering" is at the bottom and to the left of the cover credit to Lee Rheinheimer!

Monkey Sue March 2005 – [lyric not used] - _A tongue in cheek look at the injury claim culture. Chimps being scalded at a Chimp Tea Party._

264

Reality TV playing up and not being honest. The Jackson show trial – imagine "Bubbles" ever suing him because everyone else has! Watch the like of Jade Goody [Big Brother] and thinking are they really the same kind of human as me. Darwinism Reversed.

.....Bubbles, bedtime for Bonzo II
Monkey mind if monkey loose
No monkey bikes or monkey boots

Grace [The Last Punk Song] Sept 2005_*Visiting Liverpool – seeing the junkies, tramps, crime and prostitutes. Putting on a plastic face for "European City of Culture" sweeping the unwanted away. Suicide of the unwanted falling from one of the graces. Sick of The Beatles, sick of the funny man, sick of football – what else has it got to offer.*

She comes in waves
I'm soaked in audio
She my friend and only audience
I'm your little taboo
Frosted packets of glue
I'm your little disgrace
I fall from, I fall from
I fall from, I fall from
GRACE
Oh! Sparse Billie – we're European now
A quick one two – I'll be your sacred cow

No Oxygen*_Panic attack – the breakdown of relationships. Thinking too much about things past.*

I seem so instrumental
Like a chord without potential
What does it feel like?
When I'm fine
Everything is alright

I first met Shaun on Saturday 6th August 2005 a hot and sunny afternoon at Victory Park – home to Chorley FC. It was an all day music festival, arranged by the Music & Arts for Chorley Youth (M.A.C.Y) in the members' social club. Shorn were the first band on and their set featured some of the above songs. According to a list in my diary the bands started at 1.30pm with 11 bands on a 45 minute rotation which meant they had 45 minutes to get on, line check, play and get off. According to the asterix on the list of the bands I only had input for **One Day Life, Synko, Auorta, My Life in the Making** and **Zero Scope.** The last two I cannot remember at all but the others I definitely had association with but I had nothing to do with Shorn's involvement on this gig. Given my future involvement with Shaun I would like to say that their performance was a diamond in the rough moment, but I cannot as it did not stand out as anything special. However, I do know it <u>did</u> prick my ears as it had an old school punk edge. I mean that in a "classic" punk sense and not the Emo/Skate/Green Day/Blink 182 version that was the type of style that the youth of the naughties was performing as "Punk". *Clap Hands* impressed me the most for that reason alone. Shaun sang and played bass. He looked menacing with his shaved head, olive green shirt, three quarter length combat trousers and well worn trainers. Maxi (the name I knew Shaun's son Jake by) performed competently on lead guitar and backing vocals. He wore a white shirt that had the sleeves ripped off, slackened black tie, black trousers and a two inch thick strand of hair hanging down to his chin. Spook had a greaser style black vest, shoulder length hair and he beat his kit energetically positioned in the centre of the other two. Visually the overall impression was one of an odd mismatch of styles and ages.

I didn't have any intension of speaking to them other than to say ".... thanks for going on first, hope you enjoyed it when/where are you playing next?" I found this type of low key touch worked as the bands felt someone was showing some interest in them and it could help me if anyone made enquiries about them to me afterwards. Jake was at the bar and apologetic about their lack of preparation and, as he started to introduce the other two, Shaun cut his son's humbling tones dead with "it was alright - better than anything else on today....!" There was a pause and he starred at me. The moment was frozen with a menacing silence; the confrontational eye contact was eventually punctuated with him adding "well what d'u think?" Simultaneously, a big grin transformed his face and a huge hand extended to shake mine. It put me at ease as well as on the spot. My reply was positive, as I recall, if a little apologetic. I had a fleeting pinch of guilt as I had not seen all the set and I prided myself on giving comprehensive and constructive feed back when asked. But, in the short time I'd been there I had been circulating with the crowd, paying little attention to the performance. This is what I did most of the time in those days as I was always too involved with what was going on to pay any singular attention to a full set from anyone beyond those I was obliged to listen to either through my management or for a written media piece. Furthermore, I had no detailed knowledge of Shorn. If Jake had mentioned anything it had not registered. He'd never pushed this band on me and did not play up his father's extensive career either.

This first encounter was memorable in most part to Shaun's directness and my spluttering about like I'd let a pocket full of change scatter across the floor. I must have said something he liked as he didn't hit me or walk away unimpressed.

Shortly afterwards I arranged them the support slot for **Say Jansfield** at The cellar bar, Blackburn. This was an A3H gig as I was putting bands on at the venue at that time. Financially, this gig was a three way split and I paid Shorn £30. Say Jansfield provided the back line so got £10 extra, £30 went to A3H and I did watch all of Shorn's set. It confirmed my initial opinion. I was not wildly excited and yet, equally, not disappointed as I sometimes was after a first time watching other bands. I know that they were different or distinctive, but given my previous three years experience of classic punk, I felt that their market, and what I could do/offer them, was limited. I did keep an interest in Shorn but not as closely as I did other bands for these reasons and, if you pushed me, I felt their sound was heavier than what I or A3H was generally known for at that time. But their CDs, gig flyers did find their way to me and I did provide further help.

Shaun had impressed me as a person and in October I asked him to come to Manchester with me. I drove and the main reason for going was in response to an invitation from by Bruce McKenzie (Townsend Records). He had put together a showcase acoustic gig at an underground venue called "South", on South King Street. The *In The City* festival was on at the same time, **Leaf** were doing a set at the Dry Bar on Oldham St and I had another invite to Cliff de Carteret's house party in his flat somewhere out of the centre. I chatted to Bruce, but Shaun stood at the back smoking and looked out of place amongst the corporate music "bizz" types that the festival attracted. I knew that the performers were too ordinary and unoriginal for Shaun's taste. We stayed long enough to catch **Jade Gallagher's** set that Bruce had been talking up. It was a long day/night and I it was the start of many enjoyable jaunts in Shaun's company.

Finally, the rest of Shorn's existence in my memory is vague and I have to refer to the CDs and odd diary notes I have found. I am sure Shorn CDs were done in batches of 10 or 20 a time. The order of songs or art work varied depending on what the latest recording or enhancement / order of preference was when being burnt. The gigs recorded are: Monday 22nd August – Harry's Bar Chorley, **The Shoks** plus Shorn Monday 3rd October, Harry's Bar- Shorn plus **Arty Zyph**. I did put Shorn on at The Attic in early 2006. – it was to be a support slot for Ex Slits singer Ari Up but she didn't play the gig in the end but Shorn did. There are other songs that, according to Shaun's song book, were written in this ten year period. However, this episode is one which Shaun has not told me much about. He says there is a lot of "personal stuff" which he would prefer to remain that way.

Stupid Little Cars (2005-2008). Extract from Shaun's blog:

The History of Stupid Little Cars [the true facts!]. Thurs Aug 30ᵗʰ 2007

[Current mood –Crazy], [Category – Music].

Handsome Shaun son of Wilberforce & Margarita Scuttlebuck was born in Chorley Bottoms [an actual place] in 1798. Tragedy was soon to strike! A travelling band of gypsies inadvertently stole the young Handsome Shaun mistaking the sprog for a gooseberry pie cooling on the window sill. Realising their mistake as gooseberry pies tend not to cry out when bitten, they abandoned him in the windswept foothills of the Pennines where he was adopted into the family of a rare breed of "Oswaldtwistle weresheep".

He spent a relatively happy and vicious youth savaging folk musicians who ... unbeknown to them.... had played "The Irish Rover" just one too many times and they were "no nay, never no more!" With his solid musical background behind him, he decided to leave the tranquillity of his dank dark cave and move to the small but famously in bred town of Adlington to seek his fame and fortune.

On reaching this close [too close some may say] tumbleweed town he befriended the local bog beast- known to the inhabitants as "Dancin Ste". He had a sometime career as a go-go dancer at the nearby Conservative Club but he was soon asked to leave due to the fact that disco leper appreciation had took a tumble and was now unfashionable. More to the point, this whirling dervish of a bog beast was a wee bit too peaty for their liking. The savage folk singer and the Dancin bogtrotter called themselves "Stupid Little" but something was missing like a school bell without a donger – it didn't seem right – in fact the name had no ring to it!

The final piece of the jigsaw is when they crossed paths with Terry Oh! Oh! Oh! Oh! Oh! A name that was later to inspire the opening to one of their best loved songs "Carousel". He was a drummer and recently exiled convict who had an amazing escape from Australia by taping himself to a migrating leatherback turtle! Terry had a job building round like barrow things for disenfranchised Aggy Hobbits who had been on the wrong end of the Chorley Orc purges led by master dodgy builder Londsey Hiyle MP. Terry, more out of pity than love of their music, decided to join the determined duo. So the gruesome twosome became the Dodgy Threesome, now known as the almost legendary funky punksters the one and only Stupid Little Carts!!! Somewhere on the road they stopped for tea and lost a T and became Stupid Little Cars – the purveyors of lounge punk to the Queen...and the tiddlywinks says flippantly "the rest is history".

Their repertoire of songs included:

Amazing Flying Saucers *– influenced by a really intelligent guy I worked*

268

with but then found out he were a UFO 'ologist [well down in my estimation]. Also they were going to stake out Chorley nab. We were going to dress up as aliens with ray guns etc and scare 'em.

Ain't no Ghost Running in tune with "Amazing Flying Saucers" is about going paranoid about a Ghost only to find out it's a wanker at the window – hence the line "fingerprint on my window pane – a ghost of a beast and a suspect stain". Also childhood paranoia and my phobia of cracks in curtains and a friend who thought T.V was a two way camera and I was talking to him.

Fossil – anti ageism juxtaposed people who don't know when to stop from cutting edge to cabaret. Also, tongues in cheek dig at unoriginal teen bands and "yoof" culture.

Superman's Gone –Anti hero – reliance on someone to save you and finding out your hero is all too human and usually a dick.

All New Pussy Cat Show Anti celebrity-my disgust at the cult of celebrity-where being famous at being famous is all that matters.

Flight of the Do Do – extermination, cultural and literal. Genocide, invasion – feeling isolated in your own country and a second class citizen. From positive discrimination, to the ethnic cleansing department. Not letting people be who they are and don't want to jump into the cultural melting pot just because the majority of politicians and do gooders say so. True culture is not a trend it's a collective soul.

Chico's Shabby Affair. We've all had them – the S.T.Ds. The stalkers, one night stands etc and lying about affairs and a shag to regret- holiday romances of sad old gits and waiters.

Dali Is A Dalek Anti Fascist – the so called freedom of art juxtaposed with the restrictions of dictatorship. Dali originally supporting General Franco – loving the thing that destroys you in the end.

Jellyfish – The crassness of a sea side town – the revenge of jellyfish for people and litter pollution. A "leave me alone or else" song! I'm deeper than you think and I'll surprise you in the end. I hate Blackpool it's everything I'm not- false fun, humourless I always feel a foreigner there. "I'm a cry sallid" comes from John Wyndham's sci-fi class book The Chrysalides about people who are a different evolutionary strain – a when the revolution comes type of song.

Broken Dolls

> There the man who would be king
> Head too big for his shoulders
> Gets a doll pulls off her arms
> Life couldn't get much colder

Child cruelty – sadism and the abuse of power. From sexual to military and politics- all are linked. Dig at pseudo Fraudism – when it's plain to see some people are Bastards and some victims are conditioned to act out certain roles.

It's also a prime example of dualism in my songs. It's also aimed at the music industry building up bands and destroying them – an N.M.E gutter press preoccupation – the elevation of bands with a couple of decent good songs to the Next Big Thing. A plaything for the journalist –who are playing God. Also the preoccupation of city bands who are usually more amateurish and less adapted than out of town bands. They become local heroes who sell more because of the population. Bands are often in the shadow of what came before. Oasis was a strange example that stretched across the Manchester/ Liverpool divide. In essence, a piss poor Beatles. They were "bigged up" solely because they worked their way into the scene and did something familiar – stealing riffs and in my opinion oxygen. The only song of note was "Wonder Wall". So, Broken Dolls carries on from Voodoo Dolls by Shorn – the plaything is ripped apart once the owner is bored of it.

Furthermore, "The Man Who Would Be King" is a Rudyard Kipling book made into a film starring Sean Connery and Michael Cain. It's about a couple of chancers who desert the army in Victorian India and con their way into a Shangri La type of place. Where one is treated like a God then found out to be mortal but believes himself to be a God and is killed. The other escapes but is tortured and mutilated to tell the tale.

The emperor's new clothes is the fairy tale about a foolish emperor who is conned by his tailor into believing he is wearing invisible clothes. Everyone says how good they look- not daring to say anything else until an innocent boy shouts out "He's no clothes on!" Then everyone laughs and the emperor feels foolish. The crowd laugh to cover their shame at being taken in. This is the band [Emperor]. The Tailor [the music industry], the crowd [the fans] and the young boy [me].

Finally, the action man – is when a band has lost its flavour of the month appeal –plastic and artificial people create artificial scenarios and some make a lot of money in the process. It's like killing the one you once loved. Taking great delight in publicly destroying it – a master and servant relationship.

Carousel – A parody on pop songs – hence "oooh oooh etc" showing that you don't have to write amazing lyrics to do a good song. Set in the confines of a "Logan's Run" back drop where people are disposed of in their twenties [on the carousel].

I went to watch SLC on as many times as I could and they were always worth the effort and the banter between Shaun and Steve was worth the price of admission regardless of every tune being some of my favourite of Shaun's output to date. SLC's last gig was at The Imperial, Chorley on a wet night in October 2008. I took my camcorder and interviewed the three down in the cellar underneath. An abridged version is as follows -Shaun, as usual, does most of the talking:

What have been the highlights for SLC then? – *Playing with Bez* – they all agree and add ...*and recording.*

The low points? Shaun defiantly declares *"Oldham" it were the first gig after Terry's shoulder injury- no one responded to our set or talked to us afterwards. So when we have a bad gig we refer to it as "doing and Oldham!"*

Favourite songs? (Shaun) *Power of Twister – or always the last one we write.* (Steve) – *Carousel at the start* (Terry) *Flying Saucers – the fast strumming – all different songs in different times.*

What do you think you have achieved? *We started in Chorley and ended in Chorley. We showed other bands that you don't have to do the same stuff – generic material. We're recognised by others, like Bez, as not sounding like anyone else to be pigeon holed.* (Steve) *having no boundaries.*

What will be your legacy then? *To be remembered by our type of music* (Steve)... *and having fun* (Terry) *All those pretentious bands posing instead of getting on...* (Shaun).

What's the next chapter then? *Change name, new singer – watch this space* (looking at Steve)...*between Steve's ears! Close the chapter and do something else.*

Final message to the fans? *Thanks for supporting us it's been fun* (Terry) – rest agree nod and hold up drinks to camera with a grin.

Another reincarnation of Shaun's ends....a pity as I really did like SLC from the first gig I saw them play in Preston. The trio were distinctively mature compared to most bands I was dealing with to that point. I bought into Shaun, Terry and Steve lock stock and two smoking roll ups! I never witnessed them play an "Oldham" thankfully – they were always fresh, un -cool and ....yeah the word Terry used "fun". Dancing Steve's antics a perfect foil for Shaun to bounce off or on whom he'd shout abuse and ridicule – always humorously which made their set's unpredictable. R.I.P. S.L.C.

Taser Puppets (2008 – to present). Shaun [Vox/Guitar], Terry [Vox Drums], Jason [Vox and Bass]. *Check them out on the Web*

Songs and their meanings.

In all that you have read I hope that I have managed to convey the authenticity I mentioned at the start. The critique of each is left to your own knowledge of both outside what Shaun has told me or written down specifically by him as his intention in what the songs mean. The interpretation you put on

271

it all is for your own context. Perhaps, like me, some you can identify with against our own circumstances and back ground. A word of caution though as "Authentic" is sized up with an elasticised tape measure as Shaun is a chameleon song writer. His music and lyrical themes are often changed or adapted from one band to another. He scribbled down a few pages of "Song Links" and to pick out a few may help those of you who have followed or been involved with Shaun's career.

An example he gives is statues –as mentioned in an Adesire song in the final lines from *Almost Classical*;-"Statutes excluded from time" This reappears in Very Hippy George as a full song the *Statues are Victorian* the message being that *the majority of statutes are linked to war, the monarchy – static and unchanging- a reminder of the paradox of Great Britain – freedom bought by violence and oppression.*

Staying with Very Hippy George is an example of the music adoption in the song *The Electric Plug*. Originally from Pleaze, the riff is taken and put into *Bananas, Custard Jam* which has the same number of syllables as Anthony H Wilson which is linked into *Dali is a Dalek* (again 6 syllables) referencing Ian Curtis in the line "There's more to life than dancing to the rhythm of a drum".

Shaun also told me that his songs are rarely written on one level as words are chopped and changed over the course of a few days. Depending on what mood he is in. He could have several full sets of lyrics for the same music. Sometimes he picks the best lines from different versions to infuse all the different aspects of his songs. Different versus could be moulded together. The memorable lines may sound like a specific chord or riff.

Words are meant to conjure up vivid scenarios, bigger, brighter and darker than real life. It's like if Tim Burton did a cartoon of My Little Pony. Sometimes I substitute words by a vocal sound to convey an important rhythm or that I'm fed up with the meaningful Leonard Cohen, Dylan esque moan – i.e. the state of pop music or to lighten it all up a bit. I always feel like a human tablet – sweet and sugar coated on the outside hiding the bitterness inside that will do you good in the long run and ultimately not do you in. I learned to write rhythmically through reading "Under Milk Wood" the only Dylan Thomas I could stand. To avoid the generic rhymes like fire – desire, love- above unless I want to make a point of crapness. I tend to parody with fondness more than acid sarcasm.

Finally in Jan 2014 Shaun referred me to the following on his Facebook page to explain his method of song writing now: *THE MAKING OF A NEW SONG: 'Scene 5', got all the guitar parts, new n more effective lyrics whirling round my head all the time as I stalk about my flat drinking countless cups of tea... being me, being someone else, seeing it from the inside. Imagine I'm you looking at me performing the song ...where to emphasize parts n where to drop out- putting my guitar down ,chain smoking ,picking it up again, losing my glasses n plectrum ..,getting annoyed ,getting excited ,trying to mix it in my head like a human recording studio... what I want it to sound like & what will it end up like? .. I'm stuck with it now is...just wait till later..."oh hello insomnia not seen you in a while"...Oh the joys of song writing. MANIC!*

Conclusions and a challenge - Shaun Maxwell - a beacon in the music wasteland- discuss!

Sharing Shaun's company, for me, is always a laugh. He can be demanding or judgemental when he feels he needs to be to get the best out of others. This may explain why there have been so many line up changes, being single minded at times, mapping out his own direction. Those who chose to follow do so on his terms but I have not met anyone who has had a bad word to say about him. Shaun's personality is as varied as his moods. Like all of us he is up one day and can be down the next but he is always Shaun – no pretence, no verbal flannel, a *"take me as I am kind of dude"*. In another century he'd have been a dandy amongst his peers and his impact on me in 2005, was profound. I began to question what I was doing and I made myself a promise to seek out the integrity of the people I came into contact with. All bands, promoters, managers, venue owners etc would be judged against a new benchmark, when it came down to giving my time to anyone who either did or did not deserve it, I used the adage I'd almost forgotten about i.e. *What does it stand for!*

I know others have heroes or icons they look up to, track their careers, #tag them as is the modern tend etc. But, I do not. I do regard Shaun as a reference point in my life that I can refer to and from. His observations on human nature and the day to day slog of living show me the true worth of the values I take for granted. Being in his company, following his rants on Facebook or analysing the deeper meanings to his lyrics, reminds me of what I have and what I have not.

I will end with a quote and a challenge from some of Shaun's lines in my favourite Stupid Little Cars song "Chico's Shabby Affair"

"You should be checking me out coz I just checked out
Evolution you've got no shoes on - you've got no style".

I would be grateful if you would correct all this information. Eric Spears was actually Eric Spear (I was in this band). The bad review made no reference to any of Shaun's songs so take that bit out. Dynamo Turettes was Dynamo Tourette. I played bass, Shaun guitar. We never played the New Ship Inn - that was Shaun and Kit as Sumo Presley supporting Eric Spear, and we didn't play with our backs to the audience. The shirts said Fukov and Tsodov. We never did a song called Nose ¬ What's that mountain on your face! Beautiful Game and Dolphins were recorded and produced by me and Ashley Chadwick operating as Crumplezone. The 410... Number would be mine then. I played bass on all the tracks of 'OCCASIONAL PIECES (A cure for toothache)', Shaun all the guitar. All drums were drum machine.

Cheers Jason Hurley (Facebook message 3rd March 2014)

Record sleeve for Dash Rip Rock side.

10 A3H Promotion Ltd & other friends

A3H Promotion Ltd is the name of the company I formed in September 2002. Through the company accounts I can trace the financial details of everything I did over the nine years of its existence. Its profits and losses represent the consequences of the highs and lows from my many musical experiences. It is sobering to look back now and understand the failings of the generosity, naivety and at time recklessness nature of my adventures. Initially I had a paternal instinct for the vision of the company I created. Similarly we, who are parents, often behave in ways that do not make sense financially when we pander to the whims of our kids or rescue them from their own indulgences. By the time I dissolved the company I felt that the ten thousand pounds of director's loan capital, which was left in the balance sheet, was representative of everything in this book, rather than the loss it was in reality. The wealth of experiences it supported is an investment in time and memories that are priceless.

What's in a name?

The company name began as a way of signing off the articles I wrote for Pogo'til I Die. Rather than use my own name – which no one knew, I wanted to appear as though I represented something bigger than myself. I guess that's because all my working life I had the weight of my employer's name behind me in my dealings with customers and that does instil a sense of representing corporate values, some of which, despite the Bank bashing over the years, I still believe in. Hence, I formulated a set of ideals around my "promotional" outpourings based on family values which the three H's represent- being Helen, Hannah and Holly. Someone told me that if I wanted to be the top of any listings I should put an "A" at the start and a number which meant - "this has been a 3 H promotion"- got shortened to "...an A3H promotion". I went "Ltd" as a practical exercise in understanding how a limited company worked. When I wanted to be Business Manager I knew nothing about running a business apart from doing Helen's sole trader accounts (as a Dental Hygienist). Partnership accounts, I had learned from studying Accountancy, was one or more sole traders carrying on in business with the aim of making a profit. A limited company, however, was a fresh challenge and I felt it would help me have credence with customers if I knew what sort of issues it entailed. I only used an Accountant to set it up in September 2002 which was straight forward – as was most of the paper work thereafter- which I dealt with myself. I was the sole director and only share owner and Helen was the Company

Secretary – which is the way it stayed. The rest is a matter of public record at Companies House which anyone can view. What lies behind the official paperwork is what follows.

My first commercial idea

I had modest ambitions when I started. Writing about bands, venues and what was going on, the wheres and whens etc was what I was use to reading in national magazines. My favourite being Uncut as it had a free CD, features on films as well as retrospectives from the mid seventies. I was drawn to its Punk and New Wave features and one issue introduced me to a series of bands through the *Sounds of the Mid West* CD compilation. Among the tracks I heard some artists for the first time like Hazeldene (*Tarmac*) Emmylou Harris (*Wrecking Ball*), Kate Campbell (*Crazy in Alabama*), Willard Grant Conspiracy (*Evening Mass*), Lambchop (*Saturday Option*) and The Walkabouts (*On the Beach*). I thought this was what music journalism should be – bringing the variations of style and lyrical content to a wider audience. *I* wanted to do that too - and it is what I feel I did achieve in the CDs and DVDs A3H funded or was partly involved with. I have chronicled the occasions that changed my life in the other chapters and I know that this book is a testament to all that the company stood for. It is the prime reason my wife put up with everything then and in the time it has taken to write it too! I owe it to every-one who I knew, worked with or never gave them the credit they deserved at the time. What follows are those points that I have either glossed over or not detailed that provide missing links to a comprehensive appreciation of the facts. Additionally, there is further evidence to anyone wanting to shift through all the hours of videos I have kept and I am sure there is the potential for a documentary somewhere amongst it all too. Finally, if someone wants to offer me the rights, I can think of a film script too...here's to dreaming!

"Where is began.......(ah ah ah!...) I can't seem to....." forget!

The first visit to CCC during one of the heats in the BOTBs completion was the catalyst to get me fired up and the platform to witness the explosion of youth culture that was happening around the town at that moment. The final was my own "Sex Pistols at the Free Trade Hall" moment, if you will, and the effect was equally dynamic for what happened next in my life and ever since. However, it quickly occurred to me that I had to find out about unsigned/local bands through word of mouth or at gigs and by diving in and being at the very heart of the underground which was, and still is, unknown to anyone not directly involved in it. This gave me a spurt of inspiration - the idea to produce a portfolio of local bands that would provide a reference point for everything that was happening in this subculture. I felt this would be plugging a gap for the out lets that were linked to it, such as record shops, clothing boutiques and venues. Apart from word of mouth and being handed a gig leaflet or, as in the case of the Commies, a CD in Townsend records, anything else was limited to information on the material i.e. there was no other physical reference point to hand. I wanted answers to questions such as: where were the band from, who was in it, what was their style of music, how long had they been together, where were they playing next and what were their hopes and ambitions etc? Unless the shop assistants happen to know and had the time to chat, then where could you turn to? Perhaps there was a website but that meant having a computer, which, before the prevalence of lap tops and mobile phone technology, meant going home, plugging in and switching on your huge PC, monitor and something called a modem and then wait to "dial up and log in" (internet before broadband was frustratingly very slow). When you did find anything on the internet it was usually hit and miss and dependent on anyone from a band with the time to set one up, otherwise you had to sift through threads of comments on message boards in teenage speak. I did not like to rely on technology and my research made me feel that others of my age groups would appreciate and expect something tangible with a certain standard of writing that was lacking in the market at street level.

What if there was a catalogue with the CDs that told you all you wanted to know. Brilliant- one of my light bulb moments! I visualised a binder with an A4 size summary that was positioned by the shop counter. I saw punters picking up my "A3H Music Directory", musing with interest as they flicked through the pages that told them all about local and unsigned bands in the area. I ran this by Gordon Gibson at Action Records one day. After a pause, a slow nod of the head he said (in his broad Scots accent) something like "Aye that could be useful..... (thoughtfully adding a cautionary)....*maybe*". I started on a mock up and typed out write ups on the first few bands I knew, selecting photographs and compiling gig listings. I sourced ring binders, plastic slips and paid for a logo design for A3H. The first one was done by Prontaprint in Chorley and had A3H superimposed on three classical columns. The total cost for a couple of reams of letter headed paper with a light blue background ghost image of the logo and a two reams of white paper with the log in a board pattern around the edge of the page, together with two boxes of business cards was just under £400 (the basic cost of formatting a book these days!). The stationery looked good and presented A3H/me as officially (...or superficially) "in business" and now I was ready to make some sales.

"Why pay for something that you can get for free in a fanzine!" was the knock back I got from those I approached to buy a place/listing in the directory. It was a fair challenge and I had to consider servicing the outlets efficiently. I would have to visit them on a regular basis to replace any CDs sold, update the paper work and collect money. Unless the bands paid to be listed and the shops agreed to stock the directory and sell CDs for free, it could not be financially viable after my own costs, travel and time were taken into account. I ditched it shortly after buying a copy of the Jambeezi 18 track compilation CD and getting further involved with PTID. I had to have a re think and Roy came up with the idea of putting on our own gigs.

My first gig and the launch of the company November 2002

Roy's plan was a gig for a Punk band and we swopped names of those who were touring in the winter. But when we made contact with their agents the costs were in the £300 plus region - too expensive for Roy, hence I ended up going solo and booking Glen Matlock. But, it was Roy who gave me the inspiration to make gigs happen through my own endeavours. That D.I Y. ethos, central to Punk Rock, filled me with the belief that I could do my own gig and the first one was the launch party for A3H. By the Autumn I had got to know David Allen who had opened The Marquee Club (which later became The Mill) on Aqueduct Street, Preston. He allowed promoters to have their own night during the week when there was nothing going on at the club. I asked about terms and in return for providing the venue, sound engineer, the ticket booth staff and security he wanted a 50/50 split on the profit from the cash door take as well as 100% of the bar sales. All I had to do was supply the bands, my own publicity and take 100% of the advance ticket sales. I did not know any different and accepted thinking each band would sell most of the tickets in advance. I calculated that at fifty tickets each at £4, taking £1 for their own expenses, I would get £150, and if I had three bands on, that would be £450. Printing leaflets, posters and tickets would be £50 leaving a £400 profit plus half of what came through the door at £2 per head (net) – which was more than adequate for me to use on future gigs and maybe start my own CD compilation for bands.

I had seen **Duckhunt** pack out the Abyss in Chorley and asked them to head line, this was before The Commies asked me to manage them. Pretendgirlfriend were my favourite band and had to be on and they had not played Preston before. The third band was **Boddah** because they reminded me of The Manic Street Preachers, who Helen and I were deeply into at the time. Simmy met me at the club to have a look at the place and brought one of the Ford brothers from **Spitfire.** Before I knew it Spitfire invited themselves on the bill and I agreed as

the more the merrier! The date was 6th November -the anniversary of The Sex
Pistols gig at St Martin's college – a good co-incidence. The party was a triumph
for the bands and my profile as it was the venue's largest turn out at that time for
any independently promoted gig. However, I made a paper loss of £372.30 after
paying the bands some £250 for heir advance tickets sales and share of the door
take, £40 for the DJ, publicity of over £300 (including A3H logo T shirts advertising the gig on the back) and some £75 on raffle prizes and party poppers. I did
learn from my over generous enthusiasm, in time, but that first gig and a lot of
what I did was never about the money.

It's Not Cricket II!!

I did not mention this in detail in Chapter 6 as it was a flop compared to the
first one. I held it at Strettles, again on 22nd February 2004 12.30 to 8pm for
£3 entry or £2 for under 18s or card carrying CCMC members. Phil Baker
provided the same standard set up but I put it all together in a rush and for
mixed reasons. I wanted to work with David Kay on the music video business
project and generate a cost effective facility for bands to use. It was at the start
of my time managing Pretendgirlfriend so I had an ulterior motive of producing a quality film of them live as the INC I footage was dated. I also had gigs
to source for **In Car Stereo** who I genuinely felt were worth investing in and
Titus Gein were equally impressive. The line up for the day included **Capulet**
who I wanted to help after The Commies and I asked **Chapel Ten** who I also
liked. **Jumpskin** was a solo G/V friend of **This Product** – who played whereas
the latter, were due to appear didn't make it on the day due to one of them
being ill I think. **The Runs** were invited as a favour for Dave Foulds who was
helping a lot of punk bands in and around Blackburn by setting up his Noize
Anoize Record label. **Dumb Down** were Mick Pike's side project to **Pike** and
the headliners where the fantastic **Hyperjax**.

I have little memory of the day and as it was a poor turnout and the filming was a disaster. I did have the good will of the bands for making the effort
and I did meet Rob Clarke but apart from that I had sod all else to comfort
me and another deficit to nurse. It put me off organising festivals where I was
responsible for all the logistics and costs. Hence, I moved into providing band
line ups for venues and making recommendations to others who put them
on. This got me into the Cellar Bar festivals over May Bank holiday and the
series of afternoon gigs I ran there for a while. Helping Rob promote The
Mitre Tavern was fun and being asked by Foxy (Attic) and Darren (Adelphi)
in Accrington was equally enjoyable.

I got to help bands from abroad like **Gringo Star** and **Wormwood Scrubs** and did feel privileged to help **The Purpose**. But, some of the moments on those and other gigs toward the end of my time did not go according to plan or were marred with idiots who did not know me or respect my integrity. Without naming the guilty their absence in my story will let you draw your own conclusions.

A3H Records

The reputation of A3H built to a level that I felt confident to produce *The Vibes from the Attic* CD. The compilation of 20 bands I had brought to the venue in the first year. It cost £500 for 500 copies that I gave away free at the Attic after launching it during the IPO Festival in 2006. A3H was paid for the bands I booked but making money this way never sat easily with me and the Vibes CD was my way of showing them that I was more than a booking agent. I also wanted to help Foxy with what he was trying to do for Accrington – putting it on the musical map when all that anyone else seemed to care about was Manchester or Liverpool. If I could help the Attic, the bands that played there and people who turned out to support them and live music in the town – then maybe we could create a phenomenon like that which made those cities world famous for her musicians and clubs. A big idea and for a brief flicker during the hay days for Pretendgirlfriend it felt possible.

The following is my final round up of some people I wanted to mention who I may have only made a passing reference too so far. The first is from someone else who wanted to thank Foxy by paying his own tribute as well as putting some of what I have said above into context as far as East Lancashire is concerned.

Brother Bastion and the "Ribble Valley Delta" from '96 onwards...

By Dave Thorpe (aka Brother Bastion)

As a fan of the blues I always liked the idea of referring to the music scene in and around East Lancashire as the Ribble Valley Delta; based on the fact that many of the old mill town's I have gigged locally over the last few years all have brooks, streams and rivers passing through them that all eventually join the River Ribble. They are as characteristic of the towns they flow through as the old mills and chimneys that once dominated their post-war skylines there. The thing about the music scene around East Lancs is that it has always existed and stood its ground against the more fashion-driven scenes around places like Manchester and Leeds. Much of the music you hear around Lancashire as a whole is honest and unpretentious, it doesn't fit in with trends nor does it pander to the desires of cash hungry A&R people who are just looking for the next most marketable

282

Product. As a consequence, the mainstream recording industry has mostly left East Lancs alone, save for the odd X-Factor runner up from Burnley or wherever.

My story begins once upon a time in one such mill town called Accrington, my home. Back in the nineties, there was an annual event that took place every July called "Sound". It was organised by my friend Dave Fullalove and Mid-Pennine Arts. Taking place over a full weekend it presented live bands at the town hall on Friday, followed in the latter years of its existence by a dance music night on the Saturday and concluding with the big open-air festival in Oak Hill Park on the Sunday. If you lived in Accrington or any of the surrounding towns and were aged fifteen or upwards then there is a good chance you went at least once. As well as the very best in live music from around the North-West, there were the local cider warriors sat on the grass at the front with their bottles of White Lightning, the usual impromptu dog-fight, and more party drugs than an illegal rave at the tail-end of the 80's. You basically sat with your friends getting smashed, watched your mates' band play then when it was all over everyone piled into town to carry on the party until the morning light.

*I'd been in a few fairly dodgy bands at this point and in 1996 I was in a punk power-trio that went by the name of **Fetish**, whose line-up also featured my good friends Andy Mac and Matt Griffin on guitar and drums respectively, with me on bass and vocals. I don't really think in hindsight that we were a punk band; we just enjoyed getting wasted on booze, speed and marijuana, driving to gigs in my C-reg Ford Capri and making an arse of ourselves for laughs. As bad as we may have been, our tomfoolery usually won people over and we ended up playing our final gig at the all day festival in Oak Hill Park in '97. We'd decided to call it a day as Matt was going travelling round Australia for a few months and we all thought the joke of being this band whose gimmick was simply to act like dicks was getting a bit tired. When the day came Matt and Andy were feeling a little nervous and so decided to bomb some speed to "take the edge off" as it were. Although I'd tried most things once or twice, I wasn't really into that and just liked a spliff and a beer before a gig. So, as you can probably imagine, there were one or two different wavelengths floating around the stage as we began our set. About midway through our second song, our friend Craig led a charge of mostly metallers and cider-punks down to the front barricade and things were looking good, we had a mosh pit which was something I had never seen at this event. After a couple more songs I decided to greet the 3000 strong crowd, only to be interrupted by Andy on the other mic who suddenly began ranting: "YEEEAAAHH YOU FUCKING LAME C**TS, WERE GONNA FUCKING FUCK WITH YOUR FUCKING SHHHITBAG FFFF...FUCKER..." This went on for a couple of minutes despite me signalling to the sound engineer to turn it down (he* just stood there laughing). There were children in the crowd, young children, and middle-class Daily Mail reading conservatives who'd just come to see what the fuss was about. Best of all though; Andy's Mum and Dad were in the crowd. Yes that's right; our guitarist's parents were getting a birds-eye view of their youngest son on what was possibly his most abusive, profanity-laden diatribe ever. After he stopped, we just went into the next song, got a couple of our mates up for a version of Dead Kennedys' "California Uber-Allies", before finally all pulling a collective moony at the crowd which was then taken a step further when Andy turned round and flashed his amphetamine-diminished frontals at the unsuspecting audience. It caused every band that followed us onstage to swear like naughty kids daring each other to do it, and also caused a full page of complaint letters in the local paper the following week. It was a stupid moment, but a proud one nonetheless. Yes we upset people, yes we offended people, but they were probably the kind of people who needed that.

Fetish reformed a couple of times around 2001-02 for one-off gigs at the Albion Ale House in Clayton-le-Moors, a real-ale pub that had gained a reputation for live music nights and lock-ins until the wee small hours. This was all much to the dismay of the serious real ale drinkers and the insipid, hidebound fellow in charge of the micro-brewery who owned the place, none of whom liked any of this crazy Rock 'n'Roll business one bit. They believed live music, in fact any music at all, should be banned in all pubs, along with women probably, leaving nothing but miserable, lonely, real-ale Nazis drowning their sorrows with mild from their personalised barrel-glasses and choking on their morbidly self-righteous opinions. The Albion's licensee John, however, had other ideas. As well as having bands queuing up to play at the place, he also had a resident band in the shape of **Maupa**, who practiced upstairs and went on to release two critically acclaimed albums which were sadly under-promoted. Their first album was on the same label that brought us Hard-Fi, and it was Hard-Fi whom all the money got spent on, or so I heard. Whilst **Maupa** delivered complex and intelligent song writing, Hard-Fi appealed to the up-for-it lad-mag generation with their predictable chord progressions, and it was easy to see where the label wanted to go with their two-band roster. **Maupa** were by far the better band, and deserved the success. As I often say though, East Lancs has delivered some of the greatest bands and artists that the world will never hear of, and that is perhaps a sad fact to some but if you are playing your music for the right reasons then surely that constitutes success, right? You know it's not about shifting millions of units, right?

Around the start of 2003, and as the bubble burst around the Albion, and the real-ale purists eventually got their way in an expectedly bitter fashion, a local businessman had begun to promote regular events at the newly revamped King

St. Club in Accrington. Once a run-down Working Men's Club run by a commit-
tee of dinosaurs, it was now trading as a pub, and wanted bands to fill its fantas-
tic, custom designed function room. Enter Paul Fox, the music-loving carwash
owner who constantly beamed with enthusiasm for putting on live music, Every
band around at that time probably played one of his nights; **Maupa, The Burn,**
Tompaulin *(not sure if they did actually),* **Pretendgirlfriend, Depon Eye,** *and*
myself doing one of my first solo spots amongst many others. These were great
nights, and filled in the gap left by the demise of the Albion, by providing regular
live music. The most memorable of these nights for me was when the headline
band, a bunch of Radiohead wannabes from over Manchester, were playing their
set and taking it all ever so seriously. My good mate Duncan had been asked to
DJ the night in between bands and had ended up being stuck in a small dressing
room to the side of the stage during the bands set. He suddenly kept appearing
behind the band every minute or so, sporting a different clown/comedy wig each
time he appeared and would just grin eerily for a few seconds before disappearing
back into the room to swap wigs. This got people's attention as the band themselves
were failing to attract any, and very soon half the room were in hysterics. All the
while, the band looked at each other with confounded expressions; uncertain of
the apparent crowd reaction they believed they were creating and totally unaware
of their mysterious sixth member.

In 2005, Paul opened the Attic, and in doing so breathed life back into
live music for a town that had almost turned its back on original performers,
save for the Hope and Anchor and the Adelphi, both of which have now gone
and been turned into houses, or shops. The Attic became a home from home of
sorts for me and many other local musos. I gigged there, DJ'd there, hung out
there. Its opening night was played by myself, playing for the first time under
the name **Brother Bastion,** *along with my good friends, the* **Citizen Band**
and allegedly had darts legend Eric Bristow in attendance although I remain
unconvinced to this day that it was him. Paul had built up a good list of contacts
and along with Julian Clayton; they brought some quality bands and artists to
the place in the early days. Performers like former Inspiral Carpets front man
Tom Hingley, Ex-Terrorvision singer Tony Wright's new band Laika Dog, and
The Wonderstuff's Miles Hunt were just some of the bigger names who passed
through. I remember the Miles Hunt gig; I was second on the bill and played
a fairly short set as time was running on and I had to DJ as well. At the end of
the night, there was myself, a couple of bar staff and Paul stood around, when in
walked three girls. Paul explained that the bar had closed and after some harm-
less banter they left. Then, just a minute or two later Miles Hunt came back out
of the upstairs room he'd been using with a lost expression across his face, and

told us that one of his Yamaha Guitars that he'd left at the top of the stairs was missing and we soon worked out it must have been stolen by these three girls who had just left. Paul went with one of the bar staff to see if they'd gone to another pub, and in the meantime Miles and his wife both began to complain about how stressed they were about it all, which was understandable, and kept cadging roll ups off me. After Miles had cadged his 3rd in the space of half an hour I said "Look mate, I don't know how much you got paid tonight but it was more than me, so how about you get some fags of your own?", and so the cheeky fop then pulled out twenty B&H and said "Yeah sure"! Miles left with one guitar down that night, I can't remember if he got it back. Surprisingly, he never came back to play the Attic again...

I remember thinking the day after that I never would have imagined as a fifteen year old watching the Wonderstuff at Preston Guild Hall, hat I would one day be ticking-off the lead singer for scrounging too many fags. I guess it's funny how things turn out sometimes.

The Attic carries on in some form to this day, although it is a younger generation who frequent it now. The terrain of the town centre has changed, and the Attic with it. It still puts on live music but you don't pick up that sense of appreciation much from the crowd anymore that was there at the start. My most memorable gigs at the Attic included Sheffield Ska band **Bison, Downdime** from Leeds, Australia's **Derrin Nauendorf** and **Stringybark MacDowell**, Manchester Hip-Hop trio **Broke 'n' English, Grand Cru**, the **Hoover Dams, Exit State** to name but a few. There was once a time when if you wanted to find me, I'd most likely be in there if not gigging somewhere else. Now however, you'll more likely find me at a good open mic night out in the sticks or some small arts café in the larger towns and cities near my hometown. Still doing it, always will and I owe what I do in part to the existence of the Attic. I mean Paul, the tight bugger, rarely paid me for a gig but at least he had faith in what I do and that goes a lot further than money. I may not have been paid for gigs there but at least I had somewhere to fine-tune my act, develop my playing and become a better performer. That is precisely why people like Paul opened up places like the Attic; to provide a platform for new bands and artists to showcase their ability as well as bringing in more established headline acts. Most importantly for me though, and this is by far the best thing that ever happened there: the Attic is where I met the Love of my life and mother of my two children, and so without the Attic, our paths may never have crossed and that is just beyond unimaginable now. So if I were to thank Paul Fox for anything then it would be for giving us the Attic. It was a definitive chapter in my book for sure and will never be forgotten.

Ally Fogg (Big Issue In The North)

In the summer of 2002, I went on holiday in the anticipation I would have replies piled on my door step from the dozen or so people I sent my first mail out to. But I only had one and that was from Ally. His words of encouragement meant a lot to me and I made the effort of taking him for a coffee on Oldham Street close to where his office was in Manchester. He got the CD of The Commies to Conrad Murray who in turn provided a brilliant review which we used in the publicity for the tour with Farse as the magazine got a strong following and had a high standard the music reviews. He moved on and we lost touch but I never forgot what he did.

Mail bag and final round up

The following will be familiar to anyone who has received communications from any band or musician who wanted help or support.

13 Amp

This trio from Warrington were just one example of the many I received over the years and I did help in a small way as best I could. I know that one of their drummers died tragically young during that time and they soldiered on to produce a credible LP called *Moth*.

Hya John. Enjoyed last night and thought it went off really well. I've attached a promo pick to use and here's some text from our biog. We'll be up for gigging from January if you here of anything...

"13amp - Bright, Intelligent Agit rock from one of the UK's most promising bands. Kick started in 2002, the northwest 3 piece offer much and deliver everything in their blistering set. Writing about everything from love to death; soul to solitude, no emotional stone is left unturned. Successes this year have included the brilliantly received debut EP "Do You Think You Invented Drug Abuse?" accompanied by the bands first foray into movie making! Their support last summer with Too Pure signings MClusky was a real turning point and cemented the bands focus and direction. The full package awaits a label willing to take them on, but whatever the outcome of this campaign; you'll be hearing a lot more from 13amp in the future." By email from Jogga 28/10/2002

Chris Cardwell

Form former member of Boddah who I met at the BOTBs, Chorley –at ground zero – we helped each other when we could as mentioned elsewhere.

Chris Cardwell has been performing in various bands for several years in the Lancashire area. After successful stints in Doublethink (Lancashire Music Collective Hall of Fame winners 2004) and Ronin, Chris decided to go it alone and swapped his Les Paul and Marshall amp for a more acoustic setup. Chris has played in places such as Ormskirk, Skelmersadale, Chorley, Southport, Manchester, Liverpool and Blackburn, playing covers stretching from the 60's to the present day mixed in with original songs. As well as working closely with A3H and Tom Webb Promotions, Chris has resident slots at the Viking Pub, Shannon's Bar and The Owl and Pussycat Pub in Skelmersadale.

Duckhunt

"Variations on a Theme". *We have always had great admiration for this band from Leyland who headlined our debut showcase in Nov'02, supported our Glen Matlock gig and would have been at "It's Not Cricket I!" but were breaking in a new singer. They have shrugged off the Ska Punk tag with all the maturity you'd expect from this hard gigging and multi talented 6 piece. Opener* Fire In A Glass *is pure Speed Rock with a touch of Emo growling from giant keyboard man, Jim. Duckhunt's strength is the tightness of Scott and Si's guitars working with total precision to Rob's drumming.* You're Free Think What We Tell You *is heavier and has a refreshing burst of keyboards that give their sound yet another distinctive edge.* Dass Regg *is the most impressive song we have heard this year. With a Reggae beat and a stunning lyric in " ...I cannot see through the whites in their eyes" -at last a band who have a bit of intelligent grit in their agenda rather the my girls left me, my life sucks which the Yanks seem to have infected the music of the last decade or so with. The CD ends with* Q Club Tragedy *a popular live song as it pulls on all of their diverse elements. Name checked by fellow gig mates* **Echo Freddy** *in issue 51 of* Big Cheese *it shouldn't be long before* **Duckhunt** *are picked up by a prestigious label who we hope are capable of bringing their brilliance to a wider audience.*

This was my review in the *It's Not Cricket I!* Festival programme and they <u>did</u> go on to better things. By hard work and relentless gigging they changed their name to **Failsafe** and signed to Deck Cheese Records. Along with The Commies they were one of the most in demand bands of their generation and deserved all the success they went on to experience.

The Hyperjax

Rockabilly trio from Preston, I always admired for sticking to their roots and never wavering to the force of more modern trends. Regrettably I was never able to provide decent gig for them but I stayed in contact with Sam Woods and had an email from him at the start of my research – ever the optimistic:

Yeah, John I'm still gigging whenever I can. Times are hard these days as so many places are shut down. We've done alright never the less 2 more albums and some Radio One play since I saw you last and some trips abroad.

Sam December 2010

Last shops still standing

I could not pass up on the opportunity to reference two of Chorley's iconic records shops:

Townsend Records. Ross Allen – had a shop on Market Street where Wisebuys is now. It sold electrical goods as well as records. Shaun Maxwell bought his first record there *"Chug- a-Lug" by Roger Miller – it had a picture sleeve and I was attracted to that on a 7" seemed to be value for money, mi sister bought "Monday Monday" (The Mamas & Papas) -"Little red Rooster" was in the charts and was what I meant to buy and it shows how much better her taste in music was than mine.* It was there that the Maxwell family purchased their first "modern" record player – one that played 33.1/3 and 45 rpm instead of their existing one that only catered for 78s.The shop name moved to Chapel Street where the Pound shop is now before moving back to Market Street as **Ross Records**.

In the time of Punk the name changed to the **Slipped Disc**. When he was looking to sell up he gave first refusal to his neighbour in Accrington, Steve Bamber (current owner) – who later changed the name to what it is now "Townsend Records".

When it was Slipped Disc, I could not afford records so I would go in and ask to hear singles like *"Clash City Rockers"* until one day when I had enough pocket money and bought my first single - *"Hey Lord Don't Ask me Questions"* (Graham Parker & The Rumour" 1978). This was a momentous occasion as I did it off my own back and much to the disapproval of my mum who thought it extravagant. She felt buying LP's was a better bargain especially those embarrassing "sounds like" collections Hot Hits and Top of The Pops which always had a scantily dress big boobed model on them in some gaudy fashion disaster – it was the 70's after all! Later other more notable acquisitions from there were "The Smiths" (first LP 1984) and "Graceland" (Paul Simon 1986). At that time the counter was a small hatch at the other end of the shop to where it is now, on your immediate left. In 2002 I was told about The Commies by the clean shave headed Adrian who reliably passed my name onto the band. Later I met Bruce McKenzie who also worked in the shop back then. Steve's son, Chris who I first met when he did bar work at The Attic, now works in the shop and has helped me with my purchases on many occasions. He currently manages Chorley band **Fire in the Empire** in his spare time and promoted the highly successful first gig in Chorley for **The Virginmarys** at The Swan with Two Necks. All of these people are what independent record shops are all about – sources of advice on music tailored to your needs or just outside your comfort zone for you to explore.

Malcolm's Musicland, Chapel Street. Owned by Malcolm Allan who is currently the chairman of the Chorley Traders Association but back in the glorious days of punk his shop was in an arcade and he had more hair. The old shop had two entrances – one was directly onto Chapel Street and the other side lead out to a clothes shop adjacent to Cleveland Street where all the Punk and Northern Soul records sat in narrow boxes on the counter. I wish I could say that the most memorable purchase there was from one of these but it was not. Sheepishly I have to admit to it being Cliff Richards 40 Golden Greats (on a double cassette) paid for with some Birthday money. I knew *that* would meet with my mum's approval. I have another confession too - Cliff was the first gig I went to. I was attending confirmation classes sometime in the mid '70s and the church vicar put on coach trip to Liverpool to see one of his Tear Fund concerts. Nutmeg was the support band and it was awful saved only briefly when Cliff sang *Devil Woman* if you can call that being saved-more like being buried alive. But that was no fault of Malcolm's and the best memory I have is when he allowed me to take down a poster advertising The Jam's first gig at King George's Hall, Blackburn, which still has pride of place in my collection.

Audience Magazine

I subscribed to this for a while and used it to promote who and what I could. I got to know one of its writers – Gareth Thomas – who put me in touch with Steranko. This band played the Attic, Accrington and were memorable for the antics of their singer who ran around the place like a mad man. At some point Gareth asked me for my opinion for a short article he wrote, *"...focusing on the changing grass roots live music scene"*. It was headed *"Promoting the year ahead – calls for better planning and diversity"* and had my mug shot photo included.

It is a fitting end to this chapter and a rallying call that still applies today;

"A promoter's lot is not a happy one, or particularly lucrative.

While 2005 was, by all accounts, a great year for live music, will the good times carry through to 2006?

John Winstanley of North West based A3H Promotions (sic) says he would like more people scouring the country for talent. "They should be getting to more out of the way places like Accrington, Blackburn and Chorley" he says. "Well done Arctic Monkeys for catching them with their pants down". He also says he would love to see an end of bands "paying to play".

Left: CD disc for "Vibes from the Attic".

PROMOTION LTD.

Proudly presents

Kid Conspiracy

At

Sir Charles Napier, Blackburn

10th December

with special guests-

Capulet & RIOT To US tbc

Free gig in the upstairs bar.

Stardive Music
Are proud to present

Capulet

THE INJUNS (Burnley tbc) Chalpel ten

JUMPSKIN & THIS PRODUCT

IT'S NOT CRICKET! 22nd February '04

Stratilos, Eylde Road, Preston.

IT'S NOT CRICKET!

pretend girlfriend

@
the attic
warner street
Accrington
Supporting
14/1/2006 Four Day Hombre
28/1/2006 the park race/ colourpool
25/3/2006 Wiseman

A3H Promotions Presents

-Duckhunt-

pretend girlfriend

BODDAH

SPITFIRE

Live @ The Marquee, Preston,
Next to The Mill practice rooms,
Wednesday 6th November 2002,
8pm onwards,
£4

Digger Movement Tour [Est. 1649]

One or more of the following will appear at gigs:-

Founded on our English forefather's principles will be on Tour in November

Supported by the generosity of

www.myspace.com/theadelphi
www.myspace.com/_the_attic
www.myspace.com/riffsblackpool

&

www.a3hpromotion.co.uk

Avalon Way
www.myspace.com/avalonway
Colorpool
www.myspace.com/colorpool
Eicho
www.myspace.com/eicho
The Free Spirits
www.myspace.com/thefreespirits
Leaf
www.myspace.com/leafofficial
The Making
www.myspace.com/themakingband
pretendgirlfriend
www.myspace.com/pretendgirlfriend

11 The Digger Movement

(In memory of Lance Rawlinson, Gerrard Winstanley and The Diggers of 1649)

Music, Politics and Religion

In 2005 I met two members of The Levellers. David Kay (Red Brick Productions) arranged the meeting in a small room above a pub near to the theatre they were playing in Buxton that evening. The Levellers were the most commercially successful band that I had interviewed up to that point. Having formed some twenty years previously it had been a long time since they had chart success with *One Way* and *This Garden*. David had filmed, edited and produced their *Waking the World DVD** – a recording of their concert in Preston Guildhall in 2003 and the band had asked him to do another one. David hoped my interview would be used as an extra feature on it. I had several questions prepared and, after a brief introduction by David, to Jeremy Cunningham (bass) and & Mark Chadwick (guitar & vocals) we settled down to business. It was straight forward, nothing controversial and over in twenty minutes. Unlike other interviews I had done there was no chemistry between us. They were hardened professionals and I suspected that they could smell my lack of credentials and, while they were both very polite and attentive, I left feeling that I had gained more from the encounter than they did.

The Levellers trade mark was a keen ear for lyrics that were in tune with the squatters, tree people and columns of travellers that had been contemporary movements in their own right. They were modern day hippies who retained their popularity amongst those who shared their ideals and were prepared to pack out their tours. Like the folk and punk followers, mums and dads were taking their off spring to these gigs. Kids weaned on the ideology and vibes of their parents or who had worked it out for themselves. The Levellers had cultivated their appeal by refusing to take part in the music industry's games. The pair told me empathically that they disliked having anything to do with that side of the business. I felt, on the other hand, that the industry was no longer interested in those who were politically radical. By the naughties it had either tamed the insurgents or boxed them off to the margins. The Levellers concerts had become "cool" events to go to for families of Middle England. I'd seen a similar trend at the Otley Folk Festivals and the all day punk shows which had become sanitised and predicable. However, the band's name has its origins to

Levellers who were a political movement dating back to the early to mid part of the seventeenth century and the English Civil War. This is the relevance to my story and their part in what happened next.

The history books on this period usually concur that the *Levellers* were popular because their views appealed to the common people of England. The headlines of what they wanted included getting rid of the monarchy and the House of Lords; allowing religious toleration and giving the vote to all free men who should be treated fairly under the law. In those times this could not succeed as the means to do so was still in the hands of the wealthy or that of The Protectorate i.e. Oliver Cromwell the leader of the New Model Army and his generals – a kind of police state that governed Britain for a decade or so after King Charles I was executed in January 1649. The endurance of the names *Levellers* and *New Model Army* was forged at a unique time for "people power" protest in England and, over time, that weight of integrity in these names made perfect sense to the 1980's post punk bands who adopted them. I had interviewed members of both bands and, by the end of 2005, I couldn't help feel that this was not merely a co-incidence.

My time as the manager of Pretendgirlfriend was coming to an end and I wanted to make my next role a non exclusive one. I reflected on my options to form my own group of musicians to achieve several objectives. I had realised by then that it was always easier to share the responsibilities of bigger activities I had been involved with. My *It's Not Cricket!* Music Festivals: radio work with Chorley FM and roles in and around Chorley Community Centre were evidence of this and good learning experiences. Independent to these, I had witnessed others involved in similar collaborative ideas – especially in Music Consortiums or Collectives linked to Wigan, Bolton and Preston. They were organised by a mixture of people with an interest in music, musicians or the periphery that surrounds both. For example, Peter Guy (Wigan Music Collective) was a passionate believer in what that collective was doing and I'd seen a good spirit and attendances levels at their gigs – both locally (Wigan and Ormskirk) and in Liverpool at The Cavern. The group of bands who played in Bolton as a tribute to a former wrestler from that town was memorable for the collective spirit and affection for a local legend. Rob Clarke (landlord of the Mitre Tavern) in Preston had put on nights at his place with a panel of journalists, producers and radio DJs that passed comments on the latest recordings by local musicians. Furthermore, Rob's band, **The Phlegm Fatales,** appeared on The Preston Music Collective's Class of 2005 DVD. This was put together over two live recordings made at the Cavern, Liverpool on 17th April and

26ᵗʰ June, that year. The bands featured also included **Star 27, Baby Bitch, The BSI, Sleepercell, Asylum, Psillobian, Burn Machina, Elcho, The Usuals, Stone Devils**, and **Tin Gods**. On the back of the DVD case is the declaration:*"Preston is the North West's newest city and home to some of the greatest emerging talent in the country. Aided by Preston Music Collective, bands have made it their goal to put their city on the map alongside Liverpool and Manchester in terms of the local music scene".*

It is a bold testament for everything that was happening in Preston at that time and a credit to all those bands and no doubt the people mentioned in its production - Andy and Vicky Lyth, Dave Clough, Jamie Barker, Prestone. co.uk and The Mill. Like minded people united for a single event. Similarly, my work in Chorley led me to put together the collective of teenage musicians called Music and Arts for Chorley Youth (M.A.C.Y). I felt I was now ready to take all this knowledge and form my own version of a more imaginative collective. But first I had to start with a banner or headline to hang it on.

Gerard Winstanley – the inspiration*

"Whoever puts their hand upon me to govern me is a usurper, a tyrant and I declare them my enemy"

This appears on the reverse of The Levellers DVD case referred to above*. I had read statements on the same theme while studying A level History, in particular the writings of Gerard Winstanley and The Digger Movement which he speared headed. I researched The "Diggers" (as they are usually known) who also made their mark during the end of the English Civil War. They described themselves as the *True Levellers* and Gerard Winstanley had put a leaflet together in few days before King Charles I was beheaded. I dug out my old notes and the seed of an idea started to germinate as I reread them. In that leaflet he wrote:

Worke together. Eat bread together...Whoever it is that labours in the earth, for any person or persons, that lifts up themselves as Lords and Rulers over others and that doth not look upon themselves equal to others in the Creation, the hand of the Lord shall be upon that labourer.

I saw the struggle of labourers under the domination of their masters as similar to the situation in the music industry. The yolk of the pay to play practice used by a lot of venues meant that promoters were no better than booking agents for their employers. They demanded money from the quota of tickets sales expected from the performers before they were allowed to play. Diverting their energy at a time when they should be rehearing and developing their talent.

"...before they are suffered to plant the wasteland for their livelihood, they must pay rent to their brethren for it. Well this is a burden and the creation groans under".

This spoke to me directly as I saw the workers as the musicians who, like the diggers, were being exploited. But what of history and what happened to the Diggers?

While the Civil War ravaged England, the land owners had taken the opportunity to encroach on common land by draining fens and fencing off areas that were formally available to anyone who wanted to graze their live stock on and take anything planted therein. The day the people of England killed its King and, at the point when the monarchy was about to be replaced with The Protectorate, the country was a hot bed of radical thought, ripe for anyone to put their own ideas into action. The war had shown what could be achieved when people stood together against a common enemy and seemingly insurmountable odds. Gerard Winstanley seized his moment and, with others who shared his opinions, wrote his manifesto *The True Levellers Standard* (April 1649) in preparation for establishing a commune at St George's Hill, Walton, close to Cobham in Surrey. Winstanley used the Bible to support what he wanted others to believe in. Those who went to join him started to dig the land on that hill. They made shelters, planted vegetables, kept live stock and worked together, living as a group on the common land. As word got about people were inspired to form similar settlements at Barnet (Hampshire), Bosworth (Leicestershire), Cox Hill (Kent), Iver (Buckinghamshire) ,Wellingborough (Northamptonshire) as well as others in Gloucestershire and Nottinghamshire. It was all done with hand printed pamphlets and the determination of a few people who had the same focus. Quite good for a time when there was no internet, TV, radio or national press like we have today. When 2005 drew to a close, this collective action appealed to me as a model for what I wanted.

I played my copy of *Levi Stubbs' Tears* by Billy Bragg. One of the two B side tracks is *World Turned Upside Down*. It is a cover version of a Leon Rosselson song about the Diggers that Bragg played on his tour in the mid eighties. When he introduced the song at the gig I saw him play (King Georges' Hall, Blackburn) he explained that the messages it conveyed to him was relevant to what had happened to the Miners and the struggles of those communities under the Thatcher government at that time. Twenty years later, it gave me a platform to base my next direction on.

Gerard Winstanley argued that the land was a "common treasury" for all to share in. No one had the right to buy and sell land to make a private gain or financial profit from so doing. God, he felt, had given the land, rivers, seas and everything that walked on or swam in it for us all to share. If everyone pulled his/her weight and, according to what they were physically cable of doing when it came to the ploughing, seeding and harvesting of food and the construction and maintenance of homes to live in, then they had an equal right to share in what was available. Unlike the *Levellers*, who sought to use force to do this, Gerard and the Diggers were pacifists and preferred to use the words of God, common sense and non violent means. But, as in all good stories, there were villains in the shape of the local land lord, clergy and other gentry of the day who objected to this open display of freedom. They feared that those who were working the land on their behalf would join this Digger Movement. The tenant farmers and lower classes were their sources of income through the rents they had to pay or the work they were obliged to do. In effect they were slaves to those above them on the social scale and their spiritual well being could be manipulated by the Church: their servitude helped others sustain their wealth. What did that remind me of......!

The masters could not let the workers realise the freedom Gerard was offering i.e. to be in control and no longer beholden to anyone but their own class. This vision of an ideal social and economic new order could not be tolerated and the army was called in. The General who came to assess the situation had sympathy for those on the hill as some of the Diggers were ex New Model Army soldiers who had fought against the tyranny of the King. His report on the Diggers concluded that they should be left alone as he saw them for what they claimed to be i.e. a non violent group of people trying to survive. When the Army left, thugs were hired by those who stood to lose out and the Diggers' cottages were torn down and their crops were destroyed. With no food or shelter the Digger communes broke up and Gerard Winstanley and The Digger Movement became a foot note in English history.

The Legacy regenerated

I like to think that Gerard Winstanley and I are related in others ways than sharing the same surname. He was a failed cloth merchant who switched from being a capitalist to founding a not for profit commune. I worked for a Bank, a symbol of capitalism and I wanted to help artists and be unfettered by the rat race. He was from Wigan and my father's side of the family originated from that town which is now part of Greater Manchester. There is a small village called Winstanley near to Wigan and annual celebrations of The Diggers have been held recently in Wigan town centre at the start of September (see www. Facebook. com/wigandiggersfestival). I interpret his writings and actions as the first form of Modern Socialism or Communism. He was a pioneer, a man of his time who took the opportunity to put his ideas into practice. An ordinary man, who did an extraordinary thing by standing up for the better good of others, perhaps I could use this and the principles of The Digger Movement to form a collection of musicians and bands to help each other. This all came together just before Christmas and I set to work drawing up an agreement that I posted to those I wanted to join me. Everyone on my mailing list I had known for a while or were people who I felt would understand what I wanted for them. I put my ideas down in the "agreement". I called it The Digger Movement, registered a MySpace listing of the same name and waited for the New Year fizzing with energy and a new sense of purpose.

History repeating itself

Meanwhile, my day job demanded more of my attention and the timing could not have been worse. In the autumn of 2005 I had transferred from the Business Banking part of the organisation to the Operations side. My manager at that time was a family man too and he understood why I wanted to work closer to home. Holly and Hannah had started secondary school by then and I anticipated them needing more of my time. I'd spent most of my career working 25 or more miles away from home and I'd had enough of selling so pure admin suited me fine. The work was back office administration and there was no face to face contact with customers. This is what I wanted and I even took a down grade to transfer from Manchester to work at an office in Clayton Green, Nr Chorley. There was no reduction in pay and, with less stress, I settled in quickly. But, in the March of 2006, after months of rumours, the bank announced the unit was being closed and everyone was offered redundancy. Here we go again I thought! This time, unlike in 2002, I had established my music business. Tangible revenue being: income from A3H's booking arrangements with the Cellar Bar (Blackburn) and the Attic (Accrington) to supply 3-4 bands for Friday and Saturday nights – and more over the bank Holiday weekends; other venues were interested in my services too; **Leaf** and some other bands had asked me to help "manage them" and this had spurred me into forming the Digger Movement that could provide a regular income on top of the odd A3H gigs that had turned a marginal profit (**Capulet**, Tom Hingley and Polytechnic). I was better placed if I took redundancy this time round than in 2002. However, Helen and I had just taken on a larger mortgage to buy a property in Spain and the last thing we needed was for me to not have the certainty of my salary. Decisions decisions......four years on I knew I was not about to stop what I was doing but equally I was not going to take the music full time either. The uncertainty and negligible profits made me adamant of that. I realised by that stage that I would never be able to make the music side work on a financial par to my day job which made my choice much easier than in 2002. I didn't take redundancy and accepted an offer to transfer to another processing centre back in Manchester city centre.

This, and winding down my involvement with Pretendgirlfriend, meant I had to take my focus off The Digger Movement which delayed getting it established as quickly as I hoped. I needed to keep my income streams flowing but this was increasingly more demanding on my time. Other promoters were coming onto the scene too, such as *Corrupted* Metal nights at the Cellar Bar and Julian Clayton's Indie orientated *At it at the Attic* club nights– both were very well attended. I felt I had to stand out from this competition and be seen as a promoter rather than a booking agent which is what I was becoming to some as I was too busy to do anymore than that until the Digger Movement was fully formed.

I hit on the idea of producing a CD of people I had booked into the Attic since I started there. This resulted in *The Vibes from the Attic* CD compilation of twenty bands. I wanted it in time for the International Pop Overthrow Festival in Liverpool at the end of May as well as a way of thanking Paul Fox for giving me the opportunity and work at his venue. It was also a dry run for the official Digger CD but funded entirely by me/A3H so if I made any cock ups it was my own money being used and I would have no one else to account to. It did feature Digger bands who had joined at that time* along with some others who signed up later. I was adamant that The Digger Movement would be a self funded organisation that could succeed in the long term. More importantly, the A3H year end accounts were still showing a deficit funded by my increasing Director's loan. The financial stability of A3H Promotion Ltd depended on being independent to band management and had to become a platform for me to peruse other opportunities like, for example, finally writing my book and to take on future projects – that did not have to be necessarily connected to music. Our savings had been sunk into the second/holiday home on Spain and, at the start of the summer; I told myself that I had twelve months to make it all work.

The vision and the challenge

It took more time to establish The Digger Movement than I anticipated. Apart from my own distractions, I had to win over the hearts and minds of others and I spent a considerable amount of energy and money visiting those who expressed interest. Eventually, it started to take shape and The Digger Movement was crystallised by the summer. The founding members were:

Green Quarter, Avalon Way, The Making, Leaf, Colorpool and Elcho later on Exit State, New Breed of Monkey and **Pretendgirlfriend** joined too (and all appeared on the *Vibes from the Attic* CD*). Each paid their subscription and I agreed to use this to fund the production of 1000 copies of a CD that feature 2/3 of their songs. With this I would promote them and arrange a tour before the end of the year. Other bands that didn't join officially (by paying a subscription) did support our ideas and these included, **Auorta, Sterling Rose**, and **The Dead Honchos**.

Meanwhile, we would all attend each others' gigs. The unique selling point to the Digger Movement was my idea that each band would support the other to such a level that the Music Industry would work for us. I calculated that the average band had 3-4 members in it who had several friends each and family they could depend on to watch them play. If all the bands and these dependable family and friends went to any one of the other's gig, multiply that number by an increasing membership, it would swell the numbers to a level that would support booking larger and more prestigious venues to play up and down the country. Expected minimum attendance for any band/musician of the pay to play gigs was 20 to 30, so I knew that exceeding this was a definition of success for any Digger member. But, not by doubling or trebling the attendance - it would have to be at least ten times the expectancy. "The queue of people not able to get in to see you are what got you noticed not just your fans inside...." – or words to that effect- of Jay Taylor (ex Night & Day Cafe, Manchester promoter) came to mind. The Digger Movement had to dominate any gig and have an impact in the way that a flash mob works today. I always felt that musicians who actively supported each other were few and far between. Most of them always struggled to consistently bring people to the gigs they played away from their home towns. Here was an opportunity to boost those attendances by having a common reason to support each other as next time round the bands playing would receive help from the others. A simple ideal but it was based on a 350 year old principle!

The CD and first Tour (see pictures below)

I enlisted Dave Gilmour who did a brilliant job in providing photographs for the CD. Dave asked one of his relations (Alex Shorthouse) to be the model. He had him dress in what passed for a modern day Digger look. On the front cover he is on his right knee, plunging a spade into a collection of music magazine. The picture is in black and white except for the red A3H logo tattooed on his right forearm and 1649 is painted across the knuckles of his left hand which grips the spade handle. At the cutting edge of the spade is a bright light that pierces through a space to the right of the type set "The Digger Movement". The concept was direct - dig down amongst the media hype and you'll find that "common treasury" in the Digger Movement. Mick Guy helped put all the technical specifications together again. One of us came up with the concept for the back cover. We used a colour picture of the Alex in which he is stood up, his right arm is relaxed at his side but he has his outstretch left arm and hand leant against a wall. His stare is fixed at what is on the wall. In the back ground is a pale yellow washed thatched house, the sun is shining and the top two third of the photo is framed with rich green trees. In front of the house is a stone wall and a few delicate red flowers are in bloom. We cut out the wall Alex is looking at and inserted a lightly faded white scroll with The Digger Movement at the top and the My Space address at the bottom of the unfolded sections. In between the tunes are listed in a roll of honour which illuminates Alex's face as follows:

The Freespirits.
1. Free Your Spirits. 2. Shame my Soul. 3 Rock'n' Roll Royalty.
Avalon Way .
4. The Other side of me. 5 Had Enough. 6. Moment of Inertia.
Elcho.
7. For What its Worth. 8 Always.
The Making.
9. Times like These. 10. Tell Me Everything. 11. I Feel Love.
Pretendgirlfriend.
12. Shut The Door Behind You (Demo). 13. Shopping for Free. 14 Out In The Cold.
Colorpool.
15 Dark Harvest. 16. Get Out. 17. Yield Monkey.
Leaf.
18. I'm Not Emo I Just Forgot My Belt. 19. Demons. 20. Daytona.
To drive home the "vision" above Alex's head, in a halo effect is:
The Digger Movement will be on tour in November 2006
and this CD is a sampler from the bands who will be playing.
The Disc has a colour print of the Alex holding the spade across his shoulders to his right is:
The Diggers were a small group of people who protested against the greed of the landed gentry in 1649. They were lead by Gerard Winstanley and we are using his principles of self help and peaceful protest to create a platform for bands/musicians to stand united against the "pay to play" and instant TV smash and grab fame culture that has infected the music industry.

Opposite this is *The Digger Movement 1649-2006*, the usual disclaimers and contact details. Finally, I went to Digital Reproductions (in Bradford) again to source the manufacturing of the CD and packaging.

Meanwhile, I set up a 20 gig tour. The dates ran from November leading up to Christmas featuring 30 bands or soloists that were either Digger members or interested in joining the Movement. Geographically it started in the north, Lancaster to be precise (Yorkshire House), stretching out to Cumbria, (The Castle, Barrow In Furness), and west to the Fylde Coast (Riffs, Blackpool), over to the east in Yorkshire (Huddersfield University and Bar 120), across to Merseyside (Liverpool, The Cavern), Greater Manchester city centre (The Late Rooms) and as far south as Lincoln (The Bivouac Club). Other Lancashire events were dotted about in Preston (The Venue), Accrington (the Attic and the Adelphi), Hapton (Winchester Club), Chatburn (Pendle Hotel) and Chorley (ID Bar). It was the biggest tour I had ever taken part in. Posters and flyers were designed, printed and distributed. I put press packs together for the mail outs to the local media and radio stations. The costs were funded with as much Digger subscriptions that were available at the time. I supervised several of the gig nights and the musicians, other promoters and venues involved organised the logistics for at the rest. Everyone gave me positive feedback that all was in place and several bands were committed to gorilla/flash mob activities on the streets in Manchester during the *In The City* week as a further spurt to boost the Movement's profile. All the bands were satisfied with the CDs. Eyes lit up when I handed out copies to them and my net work of helpers who were equally positive about the quality of the product which added to all the pre gig publicity. I felt I had found my niche - being at the centre, inspiring and nudging all this activity along. All that was required was for the tour to be a huge success attracting a flood of others to join us.

Money, reality and trust (2007)

At the end of the year I sent out a mail shot to some forty bands/soloists highlighting the success of the Movement's achievements in 2006. I used the covering letter to stress:

1. That is was a: *Musical version of what evolved from the original Digger Movement* (brief historical references etc) *and existed as an independent entity, separate from A3H, as a platform for bands to promote each other as much as themselves.*

2. *To use the economies of scale to pool resources towards common objectives.*

3. *Whatever the Digger Movement does and becomes in the future will be because the members chose and agreed it.*

The New Year did bring in new members and the following joined over the next six months: **3 Gone Mad, Exit State, The Neon Trees, Dan Rossall, Small Amp, Sprungloaded, Stupid Little Cars, This Product** and **New Breed of Monkey**. Income started to roll in and at £10.50 per month or £100 single payment (discount deal) for a year's membership. This all helped cover the £150/250 per month expenses I was incurring. Based on the 2006 work load I estimated the percentage of costs relating to the Movement directly was an increasing percentage of my running costs. The biggest being my mobile phone contract at £75/120pm, followed by travel expenses at £35/£50pm and printing/ stationery/ postages etc £40/70pm – hence I needed 15-25 bands to break even. I had a reality check when I set out these facts in a two and half page email to the Digger bands on 6th January 2007. I was responding to a discussion I had had with Ritchie (**Colorpool**) at that time. There were some technical problems with the original MySpace for the Digger Movement and I used the opportunity to explain how I was going to sort this out with a summary of what we had done and planned to do. However, while being honest to everyone, I noticed that the list of negatives was longer than the positives.

On the down side I had not been happy about some members failing to provide what Mick and I needed within the timescales we had agreed with them in advance. This included the master copy of their tracks for the CD's to be manufactured and available ahead of the *In The City* week in the October. The planned series of gorilla events running up to and during that week was a flop. We did not have the CDs until the ITC week and the initial enthusiasm of people did not materialise into anything other than a handful of us wandering around handing out what we could carry. I contemplated buying a 5 day delegate pass but the cost and sufficient budget to do the smoozing (i.e. hotels, drinks and "entertainment") ran into a £1000+ and I could not justify that. I knew I didn't know enough people who mattered and smoozing was not what I did or what I was about. I'd have liked more dates and bands on the tour but that was down to some of the musicians involved not being available and being let down by other promoters, some local bands and there was a general lack of media enthusiasm to what we were striving for – they just didn't get it! Naively I thought we would have been better at supporting each other's gigs but the distance to some of them meant that unless I had provided coaches we were at the mercy of the local promotion away from home. I had trusted others to do what they promised and I/we got let down. Some bands only got one gig and others struggled to get double figures from their own fans attending the local gigs which surprised us all. I will always be grateful to the Blackburn/Darwen based 4 piece band **Morning Call** (MCUK) for bailing us out at the 1st December Attic gig. They pulled in over 35 people and were not even a Digger band but their ticket sales helped cover the fee for the **Former Bullies** (from Euxton) who headlines that night.

However, the positives spurred me on. We did produce a brilliant CD and we did put a tour together using the income from all sources to just about cover the costs. I took the words of encouragement and interest from new members to start 2007 renewed.

"Words and writing were all nothing and most die, for action is the life of all, and if thou does not act, thou does nothing" (G Winstanley).

I was busier than I had ever been. I had been asked by USA band **Gringo Star** to set up some dates on their UK tour for the end of January/beginning of February and The Purpose (in March). Meanwhile, I was booking bands into The Adelphi, Cellar Bar, The Attic and scouting out other venues who had made enquiries for me/A3H to work for them. In between I booked in or attended other promoters' gigs involving Digger members and those interested in joining. Finally, I got round to pulling everyone together for the first Digger Movement event of the year at The Sanctuary Bar, Burnley on March 7th. In attendance were existing members and all who had expressed an interest in joining. About 30 people came – mainly one or two members representing each band and I held a raffle with the proceeds paying for acoustic sets by **Brother Bastion** and the **Nashville City All-Stars**. From this I set up a Digger Movement members' night at the Attic a month later and reserved a date for a similar event every month thereafter.

The first one was very well attended but not without incidents. On the night, all current members performed their songs either live or by submitting a CD that was played over the PA. Directly after which, I took the microphone into the audience to ask their opinions. It was the first gig for **Sprungloaded** and joining them live was **Daniel Rossall, Small Amp, The Freespirits** and **Exit State**. I brought the **Wheeljacks** over from Blackpool as "special guests". There was a nominal £1 door charge for anyone who was not in the Digger bands - this was used to cover the cost of bottles of spirits I raffled off at the end. I had help on the door but, while I was occupied elsewhere, there was an altercation involving fans who had come down at the invitation of **3 Men Gone Mad**. The Attic had a dress code policy and track suit bottoms, trainers and the sports shirts were not allowed. I thought everyone knew this but some people had been refused entry for wearing such clothing. Woody from the band was unable to attend but he soon rang my mobile. I had not seen who was involved and got the details second hand. Hence I was unable to give an opinion and there was nothing more I could do other than suggest to Woody to tell those involved to: go home, get changed and then return. Woody expressed his disappointment that this was contrary to Punk ethics of people being defined by what they wore etc. I respected his opinion and we accepted that what had happened could not be altered but we'd be better prepared for the next occasion. It was a sour moment for both of us in what was otherwise a brilliant night and everyone said it was something that the Movement should repeat.

Radio One and the International Weekends

BBC Radio One came to Preston to stage their Big Weekend event in May and I was asked by Sean McGinty if I would be interested in being a speaker/expert on local music. It was a favour for him as he was stretched by being involved in other logistics for BBC Radio Lancashire. I used the occasion to print up and distribute double sided A3 flyers. It featured The Digger Movement's International All Dayer I had organised at the Attic (27th May), A3H's involvement with local venues (quoting their names and www. addresses),the May half term music orientated workshops happening in Chorley (May 29th to June 1st) and an advert for The Attic *Antic Comedy Club* (26th May). On the day of the Radio One event in the afternoon, an area in front of the Harris Museum had been set up with a stage, seating for an audience and I shared the platform with several BBC people. After a round of brief introductions, the compare took questions from the crowd. One of the speakers was the then late night Radio One Welsh DJ, Huw Stephens who sat next to me. He talked a lot of sense on the work the station was doing for developing/ unsigned talent through the "introducing" programme. At the end of the session he asked me if I could show him round Preston. What a complement I thought and I used it as a golden opportunity to talk about The Movement. Huw was easy to get along with, unpretentious, considerate and passionate about the role of a DJ. I think he was impressed with what I said and my knowledge of bands from Wales. We met up that evening and I walked him round Preston visiting Mad Ferret on the way to 53 Degrees as he wanted to catch **Yr Impossible's** gig. I took every opportunity to answer his questions; introducing him to everyone I met and told him as much as I could about what was happening beyond the boundaries of Preston. I pressed copies of the *Digger* and *Vibes* CDs into his hands and we stayed in touch briefly meeting up for the Manics gig at Preston Guildhall later on.

I pushed The Digger members and the Movement's vision as much as I felt I could and Huw said he would listen to the CDs and "let me know".

However, nothing tangible came from it directly - rather like putting the Pretendgirlfriend CD/DVD into Tony Wilson's hands back in 2005. On both occasions I felt that I had seized the moments to get as close as physically possible to people who had the power to change the lives of those I represented. I held a deep belief at that time that what I was doing was the best anyone could expect me to do for them. I shared the hope of all the Diggers in that their music would be listened to and the breaks and chances would follow. Maybe I should have pushed Huw and Tony further. Huw had given me his mobile number but I did not call him. I always felt the material stood on its merit and if it had been good enough he would have been in touch or contacted the bands directly. He didn't and maybe that says something about what he may have heard...but I don't know and never will! He has since gone on to have a much bigger profile today but for that occasion in 2007 he, like Sean McGinty, struck me as a genuinely knowable DJ caring for fledgling non mainstream music. Both were unlike some of the DJs on radio stations who, even today ,still talk absolute drivel and push their own celebrity status more than the musicians they are supposed to promote.

Meanwhile, my success with the International Weekender at The Attic the previous year, led Foxy to ask me to organise another one. This was on the Sunday of the Bank Holiday at the end of May and featured **Ebony Tay** (Canada), **Transport** (Australia), **Brother Big Bad** and **Flutter Effect** (both from the USA), **The Shakes** (Scotland) and **The Convulsions** – the later being a band based around Lancaster and fronted by Ben Ruth. Ben is a gifted singer and harmonica player and he helped form and organise international bands to play in England. On the day he brought all those above except **The Shakes** who Julian Clayton had recommended to me and I suppose Scotland does count as another country. The Digger bands called into support were **Exit State** and **The Freespirits**. I invited **Seamus McLoughlin** (Whittle Le Woods) and **San Froyd** (Preston) to play too. It was a free event and doors were scheduled to open at 1pm. However, it was a slow start as no one turned up by that time and the coach carrying most of the bands was late arriving. Then there was a lack of urgency on the part of some of Ben's entourage when they came in. It was indebted to Seamus going on earlier than planned to ease the tension. From then on the day gained momentum, the bands were brilliant and it was packed by the end of the night. However, it was an unnecessarily stressful gig for me as there were too many variables outside my control. While everyone else did enjoy its eventual success it left a mental scar on me.

Coping with the competition

Paul Wright had started as a web based promoter. He set up a dot com business featuring North West bands and tried his hand at running his own nights too. Paul organised the Oxjam event in Accrington that year. This was a national initiative sponsored by the Charity, Oxfam presented as music festivals and Paul asked for my help by way of attending his meetings, drawing up shortlists and schedules of acts and venues committed to the fund raising events over several days. Paul, like me and the growing numbers of other local promoters, was firmly established by 2007. Most had not been around or active when I began. In fact apart from Glaswerk Media, Russ Carlton, Ben Greenaway, Phil Baker, Damian "Cheesepress", Noize Anoize, Alex Martindale and Kerry McGregor (*Burn Out* fanzine), I did not know anyone who was not a venue owner, part of a collective or a musician in a band or acting for themselves who was doing any promotion for anyone other than themselves up to 2006. If there were I apologise but I was not aware of your activities or whatever you were doing did not impact on me directly. By 2007 there were more people who were having a go which did reduce my potential work and income. Initially, I hoped to replace this by exploring other sources. It also released more time for me to work on the Digger Movement objectives and help some of newer members.

I was contacted by Martin Bedford (Dog Day Promotion) who is a respected promoter with a long association to the Lead Mill (Sheffield) and many of the successful bands/musicians from thereabouts. I invited him over to show him the venues in the area and discuss a tour support for Hard Rock band, **Crowley's Dead**, who he was helping. This band fitted **Elcho's** style and we met up with **Elcho**'s manager (Lance Rawlinson) at the Mad Ferret, Preston. Lance was enthusiastic for **Elcho** to do the tour too as the band were about to launch a single. We struck a deal for a 10 date tour from 13th -23rd June inclusive. The costs were shared between Dog Day Promotions and The Digger Movement which was, in the main, the publicity. This included double sided post card size hand bills. One side in black, red and white featured the tour dates, the latest single from **Crowley's Dead** (*In the Eyes/Stripped*), photos of the band and on the back the Digger Movement CD and the list of all Digger members at that time. It was a professional package and I oversaw the gigs this side of the Pennines. The tour was well received but it took its toll on **Elcho** who split up for a while directly after it. It taught me that until a band get in a van and are in each other's pockets for 24/7, several days/weeks then they do not know if they can cut it and deal with the downsides to life on the road!

Sometime in early June I got a call from Steve Birch – manager and father to two members of **New Breed of Monkey** (NBOM). The band had entered the battle of the Bands competition which started at the beginning of that month at the Good Night Club (GNC), Nelson. The Landlord there needed help organising some of the heats and the final. He was keen to keep the momentum from the BOTB after the final by running regular band nights and Steve had put my name forward to help. As things progressed I saw the place getting busier each week and the final was packed out. In July I had an idea to build a tour circuit along the M65. Most of The Digger Movement members were based in the towns on this motorway which also had at least one established music venue. Preston is at one end with, Darwen, Blackburn, Accrington, Burnley, Nelson and Colne stretching through to the other. If the Digger Movement used this circuit it could attract signed bands/soloists to play 3- 4 nights or any night as a one off as part of a national tour. The Digger bands would act as support(s) and door charges could cover expenses for all.

I floated this concept to Steve and a few of the bands and it got encouraging support. Steve committed **NBOM** to join the Movement and booked the GNC for 18th November with **Sprungloaded** and **Rayne** (a North East based band that were keen to provide gig swaps). I booked gigs at the GNC in August: **Red Badge of Courage** - the GNC's BOTB winners (from Warrington), **Costello** (from Preston, who had been put on BBC Radio One's play list by Steve Lamaque during the One Big Weekend, Preston), **Avalon Way** and **Sprungloade**d.

September's would feature Kill Casino whose agent had contacted me. This band was launching their debut LP on Nothing Stays Golden/ Cargo records and wanted a tour date. I liked the band and their LP had good reviews. I thought they would be ideal for Digger support and the gig would embody all that the M65 Tour Circuit could be. October's date was filled with **Stupid Little Cars, Brother Bastion** and **Sprungloaded. The Wheel Jacks, Small Amp** and **Sprungloaded** were down for December. Despite the distance to Nelson I visited the GNC regularly to check that the place was being run to the standards I expected and to see the attendances on other nights. All appeared fine and, having agreed terms with the Landlord for the Sunday gigs, I set about doing my usual publicity – i.e. posters, flyers, press etc; making sure that everything was sorted before my two weeks holiday returning 5th August. Things were looking up once more at last!

Stand up you Diggers

This is where the Digger Movement storey ends. Abruptly! I cover the reasons in more details in the next chapter. For now, let's just say that it had very little to do with the Movement or any of the musicians or others involved with it. Like Gerard Winstanley and the Diggers in 1650 – things happened and it all fell apart. But, unlike those Diggers there weren't villains but there were elements of skulduggery and a sequence of events that lead to an inevitable fade out. Hence, in honour of those who did join the Movement that existed for an equally short space of 18 months or so, I have singled out their finest moments in a summary below. It is not definitive and you can search the usual avenues to track them down. What follows is my own tribute to their place on my journey as well as to put it in print for others to know that they tried and did leave their mark on the local subculture. I owe them more than the memories of what we did achieve together and I take this opportunity to acknowledge the trust they placed in me. Thank you everyone!

Ad Nauseum

Did not survive long enough to become members of the Movement but did ask for my help after their gig with Pretendgirlfriend at the Kierby. At that time they were Tony Harris (Drums/lead guitar/backing vocals), Chris "Tiddy" Child (Bass) and Craig Atkinson (lead vocals/guitar) based around Blackburn/Burnley. They paid A3H £10 per month and I did as much as I could to help as covered elsewhere. I felt they were like The Cure when they started out and had an idea of promoting them as such. The live recording I got for them playing the Late Rooms is one of my favourite live recordings. When Chris left Tony and Craig formed **The Scarlet Marshalls** and I put them on the Vibes CD. Not sure what they are doing now and would love to catch up with them. Included here as they did support what I was trying to do and their faith in me did inspire the Digger idea.

Aurota

This band formed from the ashes of Dumpstar – Rob Foster and guitarist Matt and were supporters of The Movement. They came to a Pretendgirlfriend gig at the life Cafe and always spoke positively about what the Digger ideals represented. I did not see many of their gigs but wanted to acknowledge their encouragement for the cause. I have a 5 track recording (without a song listing) and the stand out track has the line "I put my face on the sun". Hope you all made it work for you?

Avalon Way

One night in the autumn of 2002 I was in the Cellar bar on King Street (Blackburn), having a drink with Mark Mckeown (The Reserved) who introduced Rik Holden to me. He was friendly, unassuming and his band was called If All Else Fails a four piece Indie Rock band from Darwen. He gave me a business card it was the first any unsigned band gave me. A little later on I received a copy of *Pick a Number* – their debut CD. I am equally whelmed or underwhelmed by how much or how little effort musicians put into their CD package. At that early stage this CD did impressed me a lot as it was meticulous presented compared to others I had received by then.

If all else fails.... Pick a number, Pick a colour [This way up] EP. 2002

This CD is packaged in a predominantly white card case rather than a plastic box. The front art work is of the band members stencilled in a performing position – Rik in the centre leaning back, flanked by Ric and James. Their equipment and guitar leads are in heavier black outline and they are set against an inverted triangle of white which is on top of the point of another triangle giving an hour glass effect. The whole scene or picture is to the bottom left in and each character is shaded in pastel violet, mustard yellow, lime green and rouge. Across the top of the white triangle is If all else fails...followed underneath this, starting at the centre, Pick a number Pick a colour. Bottom right is an arrow with THIS WAY UP stamped in black.

The back has all the following slanted left to right. The band name has "if", " a" and the final "s in white set against a black background while the rest of the letters are in black against a darker violet back ground. The track listing is:

1. Pick a number,
2. Life We Planned
3. Superman [live recording]

The photos of the four band members are in two cm square frames caught in live performance from the shoulders up. Rik Holden (Vocals, Guitar) is in light brown, James McNeil (Bass guitar) is in red, Ric Roberts (Lead Guitar) is blue and Matt Dearden (Drums) in green.

To the right of Matt's picture is a bar code- iaef band. Finally, on the opposite left side is:

Written, arranged and performed by If All Else Fails....

Art work By Rik Holden. Original logo concept by Rik Holden and Matt Dearden.

Tracks 1 & 2 produced & mixed by Peter Lawrence at 72 Oakley Sq, Camden Town.

Track 3 a one take live recording at Zag Zag studios, Winter Hill Cottage, Darwen.

The disc itself is a paper circle – on body printing which was a rarity back then when most discs were hand written. The artwork is a swirl of circles in the same pastel shades with the EP title left of the centred hole and the track listing to the right. At the very top is written, arranged and performed by If All Else fails.... Artwork by Rik Holden original logo concept by Rik Holden and Matt Dearden All songs/artwork copyrighted to If All Else Fails...copyright logo. All rights reserved. At the bottom is the front cover artwork picture.

This demonstrated how the band wanted to present a professional image and an awareness of protecting every aspect of their brand and music.

My first sight of them live was on one of the gigs I put at the North Bar in the summer of 2003. They were polished, powering a metal edge to Indie Pop tunes and exceeded the promised quality of their recordings. They had stage craft, presence and confidence way ahead of most of their peers. They performed an explosive set fired with expertise that glued me to them. I was an instant fan and came to respect them as people whose personalities were as appealing as their professionalism was impressive.

The name changed to Avalon Way which I think was in homage to the road where one of them lived and where they rehearsed in a tiny garden shed at the back. My collection also includes what I take to be "official" releases:

Avalon Way 2005 EP - *Had enough, Moment of inertia, Hit the kerb, Beautiful strange*

Avalon Way 2007 EP We Are....2007 We Are..., *See What I see, Transparency, Now, We're Both Falling.*

The last CD came by post with a letter from Ric dated 3rd April 2007. It's on Avalon Way logo headed A4 white paper – again a first! I have other discs with other recordings but would direct anyone to the members of the band for copies.

Avalon Way was consistently excellent when it came to their product and as a live band they never gave a duff performance. The post card flyers quoted my assessment of them as *"Tighter than a Dirk Diggler condom" (A3H Promotion)"*. On joining the Digger Movement their self assessment form (which I issued to all the bands), lists the key players as above; but I should point out that Simon Howarth was the bass player during their If All Else business card days and I will be ear bashed if I fail to mention that Maureen (Mo) Holden was listed as Manager too. Amongst the band's "best achievements" they listed "supporting China Crisis" and being runners up to the national winners of the Emergenza competition, as well as a "publishing deal with State of Independence". They singled out "poor stage image" as a weakness but I disagree with them as they were generally co-ordinated in black attire. But I did agree that they "talked too much between songs" and that their strengths included being "well practiced, hard working, punctual/reliable" and "social".

The band also gigged as "**The Duvettes**" which was (get this...) a COVERS band – clever! I have a press cutting from an interview with Jenny Scott that mentions they were "equally at home singing the Beatles of Britney Spears" – they knew that by doing a wide range of covers they could make money which helped subsidise the unsigned work. More bands should have done this in my opinion but did not for reasons best known to themselves and the credibility factor amongst their peers I guess.

I was invited to the band's last gig at the Millstone in Darwen on 5th September 2008. They played two sets to represent both incarnations of the band. It was a glorious farewell that moved me to say a few word of thanks on behalf of their many fans. I knew that I was witnessing the death of one of local area's brightest stars. I got asked to a few last gigs by bands after that one but didn't attend as I found the experience sinister, unnatural and morbid. I took no comfort in "celebrating" the end! However, I feel intensely privileged to have witnessed IAEF and Avalon Way and, like too many bands, I have to content myself with that – a private knowledge I share with a few others and a memory that the rest of the world will never know.

We helped each other on many occasions over the years and I am so glad that there are three of their tracks on the Digger Movement CD - *The Other Side of Me, Had Enough* and *Moment of Inertia*. I have to single out *"Had Enough"* as my favourite track which also appears on *Vibes from the Attic*, what's yours?

Colorpool

I first met Ritchie, John and Liam at the Casbah, Sheffield in 2003. They were one of four bands that included The Commies and it was Ritchie who I bonded with most as we just seemed to be on each other's wave length and ever since. Unfortunately, they were based in Sheffield/ Lincolnshire which meant that when I arranged gigs for them I tried to set up a few so it was worth their journey over. In truth I was more impressed with their live performances than anything they recorded after the *Drift Away* EP as the title track, *D – Minus* and *Suite*

Barraca embodied what they said of themselves – *"...energetic...tight aggressive guitar driven pop/rock, with funky bass lines, rock steady beats and melodies you'll be humming all week whilst our stage antics have often been described as organised insanity, chaos and general mayhem"*. However, that opinion did change after they recorded *Yield Monkey* which was/is a killer track and far ahead of its time. In April 2006, after their gig at The Railway, Chorley, we had a meeting to discuss what they needed from The Movement. In my notes I say that their material is like their personalities – "imaginative, intelligent and fun". I could not understand why they were not at a higher level to what they were as they had courted attention from people associated to Dinosaur Junior and the Inspiral Carpets as well as producer Chris Sheldon (who had worked with the Foo Fighters, Biffy Clyro and Feeder). My fondest memory is a gig they did for me in 2004 - Liam wore a Russian military head warmer – even on the hottest day of that year in the open yard area of the Cellar Bar, Blackburn. Ritchie was one of those rare breed of drummers who did lead vocals while John did amazing guitar lead licks whilst adding backing vocals. The day was glorious and Colorpool's set raised the temperature of the crowd even more. Their likability as people and the warm appreciation they showed me made me want to help them more. They were one of the few bands who played most of the venue's I was involved with – probably because I knew them the longest. Like **Avalon Way** – always professional, positive and willing to help with any of the arrangements as best they could. I tried to cover expenses when I could and they camped in my back garden once and we talked shit to the dawn. *Dark Harvest, Get Out* and *Yield Monkey* made it onto the Digger Movement CD.

Where are they now? Visit www.tripdown.co.uk.

Daniel Rossall

I met Daniel at The Marquee club, Preston when he was playing lead guitar in 3 piece experimental rock band **Gaheena Paradise**. I interviewed them after the gig and Dan didn't say much but when he did it was measured and perceptive. He stood out as a self assured understated young lad. Although I did not know much about guitar playing back then I could tell that he had a high technical ability. Later on he appeared at CCC in **Sterling Rose** and their "Cock Rock" performance is captured on the MACY DVD. Dan made a point of staying in touch with me and responded to my mail shot in 2007 to join the Movement. I met him at his parents' in Brinscal and he told me his ambitions and how I could help him. He paid me perhaps the biggest compliment of all the bands by saying *"you're an inspiration to the community and I am happy that you're still hungry for it it's amazing – I take my hat off to you"*.

With soloists I tried to do more one to one mentoring. I took him to Manchester to watch Giant Sand at The Roadhouse to show him Howe Gelb who I held in high regard at the time as a singer songwriter. This was polls apart from the reference points he had and I was opening him up to the craft of the acoustic performance. I like to feel this may have rubbed off on him as I next saw him play an acoustic set at The Cavern and he nailed it. The only material I have of Dan's solo work is a CD of 14 tracks titles *"Through My Mind"*. He went to London to try his luck and I sense the frustrations he endured from the titles of the songs on the collection *"Beware the Giant"*, *"What I Give"* and *"Lost and Alone"*. I last saw Daniel in 2012 in Withnell when he said he was going to give it another twelve months and then.....he shrugged his shoulders and we both knew that that would be a waste of his considerable talent! I hope he didn't give up and doubt he would be able to, maybe, like me he has found some comfort in tempering down his expectations?

Elcho

Date: Thu, 22 Mar 2007 21:40 email

Hi john

Just a quick thank you for all the effort you have put in for us this week, its much appreciated. There's a real buzz around us right now, MySpace is going crackers, and the gigs are piling up! All is good. We also have a 5 day UK tour in October, we've been asked to support a band called Tolerance, it will take in London and Manchester, other dates not confirmed yet, but this is all between me and you at the moment so keep under your hat for a while please..........Crowley's dead are just the dogs bs, Dead Legacy has been playing constantly since I heard it, if you wanna know what kinda music floats my boat, that's it!, not much impresses me, as you know! But this does. Also been listening to a band called Kill Kenada who seem too roughly fit into the same mould as Elcho and Crowley's but maybe more punky, and are having some minor success right now and have a song in a similar vein called In Your Throat which I just love, is this the year of the power trio ????? !!! Who knows ....Lance (Rawlinson aka "the boss")?

I find it up setting to write about Elcho knowing that Lance is no longer with us as he died suddenly in October 2007. He was a true enthusiast for the unsigned music scene and shared my passion for promoting the undiscovered talents within it. I miss him now as I am sure he would have reminded me of many points I have probably missed out here's to you mate!

Gaz Evans (G/vox), Chris Rawlinson (bass/vox) and Ric Nicholson (drums) branded themselves as "English Emo Alternative Power Rock" during our meeting at their rehearsal space at Coppull Mill in March 2006. I tended to deal with Ric most as the representative of the band when Lance was not available. I described his drumming as "The butcher of Leon at work on a carcass", unrelenting and precise! Chris also helped organise the Bad Apple gigs at the Adelphi (Preston) and Gaz told me how he wanted to capture the sound **Fi-Lo Radio** had. I got them several gigs as Elcho was a highly respected band – especially in Preston and Chorley. The best and worst thing I did for this band was getting them the tour support slot with **Crowley's Dead** for the reasons described above. However, my best memory is of the last gig on this tour at Riffs, Blackpool. Gaz gave a movingly intense performance as a man possessed by his own demons using the occasion to perform his own exorcism. Chris, probably the tallest bass man about back then, confidently swinging his axe hung low making his arms appear unnaturally long. He stabbed the air swotting an imaginary fly to accent the harmonies he provided. All the while Ric kept the onslaught of Indie grunge rock together tighter than the grip around his sticks. They were one of the most intense performers on the local landscape. *"Always"* is a classic that no one has equalled.

Dead Honchos

Formed in early 2003 by likeminded musicians and friends Kai Silva (guitar/vocals) and Craig Hall who wanted to write original songs based on their mutual influences – Lead Zeppelin, Radiohead, Long Pigs, Jeff Buckley and Blind Mellon. After the successful feedback from their first gig – an acoustic one in Bacup, the duo decided to form a band. Early 2004 Craig's brother Dave provided Bass with Dave Morely taking up duties on the drums. They self produced six tracks on what they described as a "prehistoric 8 track recorder" just before Dave had to leave the band due to personal commitments in February 2005. From that session three tunes made it onto *Rough Cuts* which they thought represented the quality of their live sound. About this time the trio introduced themselves to me at The Attic one night and set me a challenge to review the recording. It was the only time a band took up my offer to do so for a £10 fee. In return I typed up a one page review noting:

"Burning Sun" - is ambitious as it aspires to stadium proportions in loudness but the vocal harmony could do with being stronger. Lyrically, and this is a general statement running through all three songs, there is no story being told. There are statements and nothing/nowhere lines – a style that is double edged. On the one hand it allows the listener to put his/her own slant on the interpretation but on the other it does not make you stand apart from everyone else doing the same thing. This is why there is a backlash against Keane, Cold Play and Dido. It is wall paper MOR pop that happens to be fashionable

for everyday consumption. Hence, "down the line where you think it goes" and "you could bring shelter to everyone" have little relevance to me as I don't know what they are about. If the melody gets my attention then I hope the words do too, as this is a winning combination....The solo guitar work and musicianship is a high quality but there is nothing that makes it unique. *Honey* ...opening guitar hook has a hint of the "Personal Jesus (Depeche Mode) twang to it "Honey make me an offer...one I can't refuse" comes over American (even the name infers south of the border but all members of the band are from deepest Lancashire by the way).... but if it is not about sex then I can interpret it as a homage to drugs. "Just keep digging on it" fuels this thought as we launch into a Nirvana grunge mosh pit fodder chorus. The breaks between sections are refreshing allowing the highs of volume and vocal range to be fully effective during the lows. This movement is often over looked making tunes flat by being on one level all the way through. In short there is talented song writing skill at work. *Radio*...loose the Hi-Hat intro, it does not need it - go straight into the song. This is lay back on a sunny day and watch the world go by tune with a lovely "Lucy In the Sky with Diamonds" feel about it. Lilting acoustic guitar has that familiarity I can't put my finger on it. If I were pushed I'd have to say it is my least favourite track as the emphasis on "line" and "hide" as a rhyme in the chorus is too forced and annoying. But as part of a three song sampler it works....showing a difference in style and balance...

I did another page of comments on the packaging of the CD. It details exactly what impression I had of the band just from the gatefold cover, covering letter/note and the words used. Little points that indicate their confidence "crafting", "set about", "armed", "focused|" and "determined". It all adds up to that vital first impression that even now has not tarnished. I summarised by saying that it was a "good demo" but "good isn't enough you have to be brilliant to blow people away. These tacks don't do that for me...I don't dislike your material I just don't like it enough to get excited. Yes, I am curious to see you live in the hope that there are other tunes or the aspect of hearing the songs live may take on a completely different relevance....in short, some potential but plenty of work to do to make me go wow!"

I've said it elsewhere, that a god critic is one who makes comments that points to and balances both the good, bad and ugly in an attempt that the writers/musicians take away something that they can use. I have an email from Craig dated 4th July *2005 "...I'd like to thank you for the review of our demo; it was good for us to have a measured outside view of our material and good advice on how to present it. We've taken on board some of your pointers on packaging etc."*

Shortly after they found a replacement drummer – John Kirby, and, apart from lining them up with a few gigs, I introduced then to Red Cat Studios (Standish), owner Alan had an offer for free recording time which they took up in the August. I do not know what happened to the band as such, but I stayed in touch with Kai for a while and tried to promote him by featuring his solo recordings on my website for a while. Another band that supported the Digger Movement aims and took up my offer of help when/where I could provide it. Such things gave me confidence at the time and, are of comfort to me now as it vindicates what I did.

Exit State

See chapter 8 for the background to when I met leader (Roy Bright) of this 4 piece Burney based Indie/ Metal band. I asked the band to play the Attic early on in my involvement with the venue and, if I remember rightly, it was a last minute favour as a band had pulled out and I needed a band to supply the back line. Roy told me not to worry and from that moment on I never doubted his or his band's dependability. I returned the favour by inviting them onto the *Vibes* CD and *Tick Tock* is still my favourite track of theirs. They came to the first Digger meeting in 2007 with a two page hand out. This consisted of "opportunities and nice to know's for the Digger Movement members" comprising a series of articles on "Great uses of MySpace" "Good Studios to use" and a request from a film project looking for a rock band with at least 3 girls in it. This was precisely what I wanted the Movement to do as part of its activities – sharing information and helping each other in any way possible. Ultimately, my help for this band was a gig I organised and invited Steve Fenton to. He brought some bands over from Yorkshire that he was involved with to play at the Attic. I invited loads of musicians to the gig to talk to Steve about his recording experience. That night I introduced Roy to Steve and.....the rest is history as they say. Steve invited Exit State to record with him and from then on Exit State went from strength to strength. They are now on their third LP and have toured extensively in the UK and abroad. There is little more to add that cannot be found out on the internet other than to say that drummer "Texas" Pete was in The Freespirits and it was a quick and shrewd move on Roy's part to recruit him when that band split up (see below). Guitarist, Adam was in 3 Ways West who I promoted at CCC and are featured on the BOTBs DVD for MACY.

Finally, I asked the Digger bands for a half year assessment in June 2007 and Exit State responded with the following email:

As with all things that involve parting with money, you wonder whether you will ever truly get value for the funds relived from your pocket. Like anyone, we at Exit State HQ were sceptical what the Digger Movement could do for us but joined up with the notion that if we just get 1 contact or gig then at least it's something. What we can say is that this has been one of the best things that we have decided to become involved in. We feel we have embraced the spirit of the Movement by identifying and working with bands that we feel sit within our genre. Gigs with Avalon Way, Elcho, Crowley's Dead, Freespirits (R.I.P), Small Amp and Morning Call have all resulted in Exit State not only making friends and fans but some awesome contacts......Thanks for the effort you stick in John its appreciated mate.

The Freespirits

This band appeared at the Attic one night by way of an invitation from Three White Sisters joining Exit State and Leaf. I did not know what to expect from this "Rock'n' roll Royalty" trio of Lemo (vocals & lead guitar), Leonard Matthews (bass & backing vocals) and Texas Pete (drums/backing vocals/strings/organ). They played to a half empty room as if it was the Isle of Wight festival circa 1970's. They melted my face off with the purest form of R&R you want to have programmed into your unborn children's DNA. One of the few instances I turned round to anyone in sight and said "Fuck me!" I took a giant swallow dive in love with them! They had it all and their recordings speak louder than anything I can hope to shout out in type set. A *"Rock revolution sent here...to save music from the boring, passionless crap out there....to be part of the future today..."* – is how they summed themselves up in their press release email to me and others at the start of 2006. Contemporaries were Wolfmother and now it would be The Virginmarys but if they had been born in the fifties even Led Zep would have tipped their denim collars to these boys. I felt so strongly about their potential I contemplated managing them full time around the time I set up their interview with Sean McGinty (BBC Radio). Their blistering songs *Free Your Spirits, Shame My Soul* and *Rock 'n'Roll Royalty* are the opening tracks on the Digger Movement CD. Stefano Millanese (Riot Act Promotions and Management Ltd, based in Rawtenstall) was also a big fan of theirs who helped them and who I know would not forgive me if I did not mention in any reference to this band. They supported Gringo Star on their tour and we discussed a gig swap in the USA for them but it did not happen, John moved on, the band broke up and I found out by text. I salute you as sometimes it is better to burn bright and go out in an instant than be a light that fades away...time will not wither them eh!

317

Green Quarter

Formed from three bands this trio comprised Curtis McKenna on bass from Blackburn trio **Hope**: Chris "Buster" Kay (David Kay's younger brother) from **Free Falling Camels** who I think were Blackburn based too and Chris Unsworth, G/V from Adlington's **Helico**. On paper it should not have worked but somehow it did and *"I want you to know"*, made it onto *The Vibes from the Attic* release and was the only live recording on it. Their output was like the band's characters – dynamic, unpredictable and thoughtful in that order. Curtis started to do sound tech work at the Attic and progressed to doing it for some well know bands. He was a really good guy to have around as I never had any concerns when he was in charge of the mixing desk. Quiet, steady and very good at getting the best of whatever showed up. Buster loved to perform - Keith Moon like – and you never knew if he would pull off all the fills he managed to pack into every song. Chris was a very well respected guitar/singer/songwriter who had a dry sense of humour and a disarming smile. I only caught them twice which was at the Attic and once at a rehearsal in Brightmet, Bolton. I do not have any material for the band save the Vibes track and an untitled song with the hook line "just want you to be free"- recorded live and all the better for it- impressive in its raw simplicity just like they were. They left the Movement when the band separated just as the Digger CD was being put together otherwise I am sure they would have been on that too.

Leaf

My introduction to twins Jay and Ben Shepherd and drummer Adam Grills is covered in chapter 8 but, what I do not emphasise is how impressive this trio were on first sighting and just got better every time watched them. Not sure who wrote the following-

Leaf – *"Burn Out"*. *Fortune smiled on us the evening Pretendgirlfriend got invited to a billing with this trio from Bolton as guests of This Product's (Retro Bar, Manchester) gig back at the end of February (2004). This 5 track does show their immense talent to the full as best any recording can. From the Bass battery and downright dirty grunge on Trash Compacter and Smack. Hole moves to the slower moodiness of Goth cranking drums saved by an Ash like chorus. While 4eva & Andy is a fair album filler if somewhat self indulgent- it is Burnout we find the most appealing in its diversity from acoustic start and precise two part harmonies that plunge back to the octave roving guitars that amplifies all the characteristics of the finest band seen this year. Contact and book this band (email address) you will not be disappointed.*

At that time they had *a dedicated band manager in Dave Collins (of* ex-Team HiFi Records indie label fame), a homemade recording studio and rehearsal room, a seemingly never-ending list of gig offers all over the Northwest, and a development company (Pioneer Production Development, or PPD Music) interested in them that had good contacts at several record labels (including Sanctuary). I admired them from afar and they, and the **Minions of Jeffrey**, were the only bands I rated who were from the Bolton area. The brothers confessed to me that after their manager left Manchester to join the R.A.F. they were: *selling our souls trying to make a dent on the Manchester scene for promoters who constantly promised better gigs next time in exchange for bringing shed loads of people down to crap ones.* Sometime in the middle of all this chaos they invited me over to Bolton on a few occasions but the one that sticks out was at the Number 15 in the centre. The gig was organised for a bit of themed fun amongst the local bands as a tribute to a local wrestler, 'Rick Flair' who was a WWF wrestler. Everyone that played that night, and some of the audience, dressed in mock wrestling attire. The gigs I could offer them were mainly in Lancashire and *a refreshing change from the Manchester scene; the audiences were more appreciative and the gigs were usually well attended AND more reasonable drinks prices at the bar, hurrah! John used to introduce the bands himself, a practice that we thought at the time was a bit old fashioned but it was a welcome change to the Omni-absent Manchester promoters who practically hid during the gig in case there were any problems. John was proud of being there and we remember thinking he actually gave a shit about the bands, so much so that he decided to set up a sort of collective of bands. "The Digger Movement" was born, the idea being that a group of 20+ bands could easily support each other and provide an audience for gigs and share ideas and experiences.*

John wanted to work closer with Leaf and get us more involved with the scene, but the carrot was still being dangled by PPD Music and we were still convinced that playing Manchester gigs was more important and would eventually lead to us getting signed. I guess our mentality was that there was more prestige about the Manchester venues, everyone in bands knew Dry Bar, Night and Day, Band on the Wall, The Roadhouse etc. and knew the bands that had played there and eventually reached stardom, who ever talked about The Attic in Accrington?! However, the industry interest turned out to be all piss and wind from those who promise everything and deliver nothing. *PPD were showcasing 3 other artists on the Hard Rock Café gig and our set was being downgraded to an acoustic slot. Apparently we were too heavy for Hard Rock Café, what utter bullshit. We were an energetic 3-piece playing riff-based songs on acoustic guitars and some congas for a kit; we weren't showcasing anything at all. Then there was the Slunt* gig, we played to a practically empty Music Box and the realisation was finally sinking in, we were back to square one.

For a while it was fun just rocking out again, without the pressure of trying to get signed we used gigs to blow off some steam and have a few drinks. Some of the Digger bands were great, and they were all good company too and we'd not been part of a gang since Team HiFi Records. But spending all our time chasing the dream of being rock stars had taken its toll, and Leaf was running out of steam. We carried on playing around the Bolton scene, and with plenty of gig offers at our doorstep and, without transport; the Digger Movement became less attractive. Gigs were now more like nights out and almost always involved heavy drinking prior to playing, which affected the band's performances. After our bass guitar broke after only a couple of songs in during a performance at The Alma (Bolton) we had just had enough of it. We called it a day, coincidentally at the venue where it all began! Three of us continued to play in other bands together until we got Leaf back together early 2013.

The Making
Previously known as Re:verb (sic) are one of the most easy to listen to bands I had the pleasure of knowing. Their line up went through a few changes by the time they joined the Movement. Their 2006 EP contains *Times like These* and *Tell Me Everything* which along with the other Digger Track *I Feel Love* still gets regularly plays on my iPod. I tended to talk to Mark Smith (g/Vox) and John Maelor (lead singer) the most – two of the most enthusiastic musicians I have met who are still playing locally. Live, the line up reproduced their carefully crafted songs perfectly no matter the size of the audience when I saw them, most notably in front of loads of fans at The Late Rooms, Manchester (as Re:verb) and then, with zero fans, at The Attic (as The Making). I had many words of encouragement for The Movement from the band and they stuck with me to the end. Mark sent me the following text when I announced my retirement *"hi John, sorry to hear that you really are a fantastic influence to the local music scene"* (20.14 21/8/07).

The Neon Trees
I was invited by Sean McGinty to review the opening night of Riffs Night club in South Shore, Blackpool as he knew I was looking for venues beyond Lancashire to promote the bands I was helping. I watched The Neon Trees there and was struck by the delicate songs from singer songwriter Joanna Byrne. She had a beautiful voice and the band backed the tunes perfectly. I saw her support Seamus McLoughlin at one of his gigs at Worden Arts Centre, Leyland and she played solo and absolutely nailed it. Regrettably I have few

recordings of the band but if I could have done a follow up Digger Movement CD then Jo or a Neon Trees track would have made it.

New Breed of Monkey (NBOM)

I have probably spent more hours listening to this band since I stopped my involvement with unsigned music than I did when they were still together. This has to do with divided loyalties to Pretendgirlfriend as I felt NBOM were their closest rival when it came to song writing. The standard of all their output never failed to impress me and some of their tunes were, arguably better than Pretendgirlfriend's especially tracks like *Cradle to the Grave, Mannequin* and *Greater Than Thee. Can't Stop Thinking of You* was a must for the Vibes CD and, like some of the other Digger bands, I would have trouble choosing what songs to include on a second Movement CD but my personal favourite *Trapped under The Smog of the Industrial Blanket* would be top of the short list. Managed by Steve Burke they pushed themselves further than most of the bands I knew at that time but called it a day in July 2012 filming their last gig for DVD at Colne Municipal. Steve did try his hardest to stop me from retiring as he felt the Movement could work if I had more help which he was offering to provide. Had I met Steve a few years previously it may have turned out different as I am sure he would have been a great asset to the Movement and taken the Diggers further than I did.

Pretendgirlfriend (see Chapter 8)

Small Amp

This four piece band was based around Blackburn that made a big sound, thanks to their front man, who had a huge voice and personality to match. They joined in the second wave of Digger bands and appeared many times at the Attic where Julian Clayton eventually took them on as their manager. Aways explosive in their delivery of forceful Indie songs like *Cinematic* and had a subtler side too as evidenced in *Boy's Brigade* – both being the only tunes of theirs I have copies of today. Their gig for me at the Queen's in Chorley with **Brother Bastion** was blistering but totally unappreciated by the resident tenants who refused to pay me, but I paid them both out of my own pocket. Best gig I saw them play was at The Academy 3 (Manchester) in July 2008 and they were excited about a tour shortly afterwards.

Sprungloaded

We met John when we had a stall on Chorley market in 2006 selling sprung loaded glasses. Steve was strumming his guitar and John introduced himself and the Digger Movement concept for promoting local bands. He put us on at The

Attic in Accrington, which was our first ever gig – it was nerve-racking but we enjoyed every bit of it- so much so, we decided to continue to write and perform music as a duo in the Digger Movement.

Anthony at this time was under chemotherapy and this restricted the amount of times Sprungloaded were able to play. John helped us find gigs and gave us the confidence to play with other bands which supported each other. We couldn't find a genre for our music and John thought our genre was Americana at the time; this was at the start of our writing, which seemed a fitting genre for our music, especially as a duo. We continued to write and introduce new band members, which began a continuous change to our music. We really enjoyed being part of the Digger Movement, as we felt supported by John and all the bands involved. Unfortunately the Digger Movement finished but the experience gave us the confidence and the drive to continue alone.

We had many gigs in the North West before deciding to try our luck in London, where we ended up losing our drummer and bassist. Nevertheless, we started from scratch and looked for new players but the down side was that London was too expensive to live and we found ourselves destitute and sleeping on Hyde Park benches. Our story of London is a book in itself but it did not put us off playing. However, eventually we had to admit defeat and returned home, leaving us back at square one with no drummer or bassist and boxes of our first LP. After 8 months of auditioning we finally found Joel (bass) and Bobby (Drums) who fitted in perfectly. We met up with John at our first gig at The Imperial in Chorley (June 2013) and we really appreciate the suggestions he continues to offer us on how to promote Sprungloaded in the future.

Stupid little Cars (see Chapter 9)

This Product

This was the first band I interviewed at one of my first gigs away from anywhere "local" back in 2002. David Naylor, who ran 1000 Watt Recordings, put regular showcase nights on at Bury Met – a larger venue than I was use to. Unfortunately, that evening I went was poorly attended, being on the same night the Foo Fighters played Manchester. After This Product's set I spoke to front man Gus Fairbairn who was engaging both on and off stage. Articulate and precise in what he was doing, his demeanour was welcoming and we remained in contact all through the years.

When I imported all these CDs to my iPod, they all had track listings, band name and titles –a welcome feature and an indication of how techno savvy these guys were even back then. Their music stands out in terms of style, lyrics and delivery. I never saw a band like them as every performance differed and trying to describe their uniqueness in words does not do them justice. Or does it? I have listed all the CDs I have below in detail as an exercise to see if that old adage "judging a book by its cover" *does* work. It is my attempt to demonstrate the complexity and humour of their output which I hope gives you sufficient hints to check them out for yourselves.

Ape 2001

1.   Hammers and Nails [5.06] Ballard of Every Ignorant [5.54] That [6.53] In the Black [7.35]

The disc is on body printed CD in black. The following in white- THIS PRODUCT at the top APE all in capital to the left of centre hole and the copyright logo 2001 on the right of the hole. The above tracks listed underneath at the bottom.

The insert cover has a picture of a cross in black slightly off centre to the right at an angle. The back ground looks like skin so that the cross could be a crucifix tattoo or branding or just a shadow. Top right is THIS PRODUCT in black and bottom right APE in white. The inside left page is a collection of photos – mixing desk, Gus in long black coat and white shirt leaning his back on a wall, bass player in profile while playing, Joe standing facing the camera with his back leaning against a wall and in the centre is the cross in black this time against a yellow and grainy brick red and black surface. To the right a car dash board at the top but the majority of the page is a picture of the sky taken from the car window with the frame off to the right and the tops of a row of houses and telegraph pole to the left just in shot. In between is contact details for Gus, Manchester land line number with his postal address , Winsor Rd, Prestwich, and http// address and thisproduct @hotmail email. The back cover lists the tracks and the on line address for a copy of the lyrics. Recorded at Blue Moon Studios, Manchester Produced by Phil Green and this Product. This Product may contain Joe Fairbain [drums], Myles [?] Modder [bass/vocals] Gus guitar/? Vocals. All music by this product, lyrics by Gus. This product thanks all those who helped in one way or another – you know who you are and we know you don't need your name on an inlay to prove it. Thanks.

On the box cover is a sticker with the following information " this product next gig 27th Oct 2001 Rawshack Radcliffe. For tickets or information call Gus – [0161 tel number] http://thisproduct.tripod.com great site – see for yourself C D available at Vibes in Bury, and other small music shops around Manchester.

The back cover is the three photographed looking to their left on a road with a white wall. Band name, ape and track listing against the wall to the far right –i.e. as if they are looking at it.

We're sorry this product has sold out Stereotype! Cr S'ecrit April 2003

The picture is a painting in browns two figures lean with their backs to a bell like central feature but the bottom of the bell shape is open and has a rim of metal teeth that should fit into cogs but at a glance you'd mistake it as a ships control gearing consol. The dimples in the bell end could be eye sockets so combined it feels like the mechanical device is open mouthed like a dog's muzzle as there are two ear like flaps at the top to the left and right of the bell. The reverse is packed with details in relief is pictures of the three band members playing live. Tracks are listed along the very top edge: 1.Experiment 2. MP 3. Limerik. 4 Buggerdichaggerda.

The left edge inverted bottom left to top by Chris Evans for fatrob records, April 2003. Right edge inverted top to bottom all music by Alan Scott Hodder, Joe Fairbairn and Alabaster. Bottom edge upside down De Plume. Recorded by Mike Harries at Hope Studios, produced by – i.e. the whole edge is meant to be read from the top clock wise. The Fat Bob logo is in the top left in blue and This Product logo Warning and to avoid suffocation keep this product away from babies and children. Type from a fifth of the way down from the top is the following as it appears:

It's so obvious it SPELLS ITSELF. Dripping, pink, repugnant....just what IS that he's hiding behind his back?...Did you see me cry? Gritted teeth, then the smile.....You thought nothing could be worse than an asshole with five monkeys, well you guessed wrong. Pallid, sugary, there's a good grill, Hitler. Why won't you do what I say? Oh please – I wish I was real, but it's not up to me to DECIDE, they know the deal, they're coming to get you whilst you sleep. It's never happened, but I@M scared and it's only shit if you can tell....besides, we all need a bit of Hell, sometimes....

Disc is silver with band name at the top and below the hole the tracks.

I hope you're ready asshole/retarded single 2004

I bought this at HMV as the bar code label is on the top right of the slim disc cover. The picture is of a sky line clouds for four fifths of it in fire orange the bottom fifth is the silhouette of a city with traffic lights and street lamps that may not be English. There is a continental traffic light suspended on an arch over a road that you cannot make out. There are oriental [Chinese?] symbols [in white] below the yellow this product typed against a black boarder in the top fifth of the frame. Similar but different symbols and at the top of a red circle in the circle that has BONUS TRACK "Buggerdichaggerda" Re-recorded "Howling " version!

Inside cover has a picture of an alien face top left looking down on a trail winding from the bottom centre to the right and a black trees and white clouds at the top is the single title and tracks;

I Hope You're Ready. Asshole. Retarded. Soul-Gristle Intersection. It was A head. BONUS Buggerdichaggerda ("howling" version)

Under the alien creature to the bottom left is THIS PRIDUCT.Com tracks 1 and 2 taken from the forthcoming 1000 Watt release "Magic Bull" a small picture below it is a fish lens photo of three faces more Chinese symbols and magic bull in purple. 1000 Watt PO Box address and www.1000watt. com [the black disc is on body printed again the band name at the top] and title [below the centre hole] is in yellow. The rest is in white. To the left of the centre hole 1000 Watt recordings CD0013 copyright C 1000 Watt recordings 2004 All Rights Reserved. To the left of the centre hole is the band logo with more Chinese symbols. Below the title are the tracks.

Chicken Beak and feet 2005

Box CD case front cover top frame band name on black with Chinese symbols underneath and logo to right. The picture is two sperm like objects – a black eye centred in a round head with a white tail that is straight set against a black back ground. The title in the bottom frame with yet more Chinese symbols. In lay which is the back of the front cover has Stay away from me, you're ugly Ugly! Ugly! *It's not what you look at, boy, it's what you see.... Well, it was a long time ago! And the fins don't grow back, you know! Anyway, why do you ask? Yes, you are! O, no I ain't Yes, you are! O, no I ain't Stay away from me, I'm ugly! Ugly! If you don't like me looking at you, Close your eyes!.* Alabaster De Plume, Alan Scott Hodder Joe Fairbairn this product.com. The back ground is in colour with the three band members photographed playing live.

Disc is silver on body printed band name at top, logo to the left of centre hole and Chinese symbols to the left of centre hole. Bottom of hole is the single title and 5 tracks numbered. The back cover has in the bottom right Copyright 2005 1000 Watt CD0014 www.thisproduct.com with the PO Box address and www one for 1000 Watt.. The picture is what looks like a fish eye/head for the first half but it could equally be a snake or turtle it does not look like any recognisable chicken head I've ever seen if it is meant to be. Half way down to the left of centre is the 5 tracks listed against a black stripe that stops two thirds of the way across cut at 45 degrees with a mottle green stripe? Below is a third stripe of white followed by a purple line that has the scale like features that are on the eye/face picture at the top. The final stripe is a small purple section and a longer green line.

The other CDs are plain in fact the Red Eyes copy is just a white plain label – Gus may have just burnt it off to bring to me at the time of a gig end of 2006 or it may have been a gig which he compared for me once. That may have been the last time I saw him? Or was it when he was doing a solo sax performance art piece at a pub in Bolton near the bus station one night I went over to take Holly trampoline lessons and popped in to see him and the Leaf brothers perform as The Management –a 12 piece band -at the same venue.

3 Men Gone Mad

I saw this trio at The North Bar and didn't know about lead man Woody's prior history on the Manchester circuit in the punk and post punk days. He soon brought me up to speed when we talked about The Digger Movement. He was sceptical given all that he had seen and been through over the years but did join. Unfortunately, we had a difference of opinion following the incident I describe above and I never recovered from that to provide the band anything worthwhile. We must have left on good terms as I had a text from him on 2/1/08 at 16.56 in response to my New Year well wishing – *"Keep it in there jonny...be in touch soon...all the best, Woody.*

*NB. For more information on Gerrard Winstanley and The Digger Movement please refer to **John Gurney**'s books-

"Gerrard Winstanley The Digger's Life and Legacy" (Pluto Press).

"Brave Community: The Digger Movement In The English Revolution" (Manchester: Manchester University Press)

The Attic, Warner Street, Accrington, Lancashire BB5THN.

1. Avalon Way* - Had Enough
2. Exit State- Tick Tock
3. Buck Brothers- Manish Girl
4. Colorpool* - Yield Monkey
5. Green Quarter* - Can You Hear Me
6. Litterbug - Laugh Out Loud
7. Pretendgirlfriend - Green & Alcohol
8. Leaf*- I'm Not Emo, I Just Forgot My Belt
9. Free Spirits- Two Good Reasons
10. The Colonial Movement Company- Doodlebugs
[Courtesy of Spiral Scope Records]

11. Elcho* - Always
12. Architect- Pillars on a Broken World
13. Uncle Jeff- Beggin'for a Metorite
14. The Making* - Tell Me Everything
15. New Breed of Monkey- Can't Stop Thinking of You
16. The Sleaze- Modern People
17. Scarlet Marshals- Speculative Effort
18. No AV on The Tv- Cops'n' Shops
19. Little Girl Screaming- Breathe
20. The Reserved- Girl On The Internet

This CD is dedicated to audiences everywhere who go out and support unsigned bands and local venues, least we never forget music is nothing without you! Thanks to members of Failsafe, Capulet, Pretendgirlfriend and the Digger Bands* for their trust, Paul Fox for the opportunities and his brilliant staff at The Attic. Recognition to others on the local scene –

Sean Mcginty/BBC Radio Lancashire, John Anson/Lancashire Evening Telegraph, www.northwestbands.co.uk, www.cheesepress.co.uk and the independent people at. www.joinourfaction.com,Simon Brierly/www.thebee.co.uk, Alex & Kerry -Burn Out fanzine. Pictures by Dave Gilmour. Art work by Pikeman Mick. CD production at www. digital-reproductions.co.uk. To all those bands not on this CD but made it possible sorry I could not fit you on this one, cheers - John Winstanley www.a3hpromotion.co.uk

Contact: John Winstanley www.a3hpromotion.co.uk
19 Thirlmere Drive, Withnell, Chorley, PR6 8AY tel 07812 577 987

PROMOTION LTD.

Vibes from The Attic

A Promotional CD of bands from near and far who have played

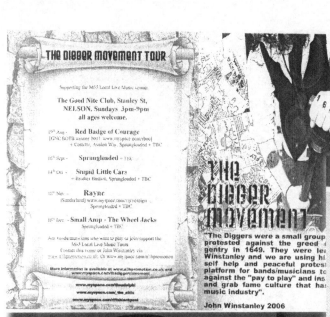

THE DIGGER MOVEMENT TOUR

Supporting the M65 Local Live Music venue.

**The Good Nite Club, Stanley St,
NELSON, Sundays 3pm-9pm
all ages welcome.**

19th Aug - **Red Badge of Courage**
[GNC BOTB winner 1007] www.myspace.com/rboc]
+ Cassette, Avalon Way, Springloaded + TBC

16th Sept - **Springloaded** + TBC

14th Oct - **Stupid Little Cars**
+ Brother Bastion, Springloaded + TBC

12th Nov - **Rayne**
[Sunderland] www.myspace.com/rynereign
Springloaded + TBC

16th Dec - **Small Amp + The Wheel Jacks**
Springloaded + TBC

Any bands/musicians who want to play or join/support the
M65 Local Live Music Tours
Contact this venue or John Winstanley via
www.a3hpromotion.co.uk. Or www.myspace.com/a3hpromotion

More information is available at www.a3hpromotion.co.uk and
www.myspace.com/thediggermovement

www.myspace.com/theadelphi
www.myspace.com/the_attic
www.myspace.com/ifthisblackpool

"The Diggers were a small group
protested against the greed
gentry in 1649. They were lea
Winstanley and we are using hi
self help and peaceful protest
platform for bands/musicians to
against the "pay to play" and ins
and grab fame culture that has
music industry".

John Winstanley 2006

**The Digger
Movement Tour**

**The Attic
Accrington**

**24th Nov
8pm**

£2 / 3

125

THE
DIGGER
MOVEMENT
1649-2006

www.a3hpromotion.co.uk
Is proud to present
The Digger Movement Tour
At the Attic, Warner Street, Accrington
24th November - doors at 8pm
Featuring The Neon Trees
+ support
Entry £2(with this ticket) £3 on door

130

12 The privilege of hearing what I've learned

Lives in the balance

I was exhausted by the time I got to our place in Spain and was ready for a rest. It was the end of July 2007 and we had two weeks at our apartment with glorious weather – all I had to do was relax. This was perfect for me to do a lot of thinking, reflecting and eventually I concluded that I was ready to quit from the intensity of my "hobby". I can only explain it as a deep down sense of not having the heart for it anymore. When I faced up to facts that I had weighed up, down and sideways in reaching this point it hit me in an instant. The only logical thing to do was to stop. I hear about couples splitting up because one of them says that they are no longer in love with the other. The feelings fade; the flame of love no longer burns or the desires have dissolved – whatever it once was is no more and the end has come. How sad! In the same way the passion I had for what I had been doing was gone. I thought about the happier times when the unknown was new, exciting, and how it had all made me feel a lot younger. I sense it now in the earlier chapters when I refer to falling in love with the bands, the thrill of arranging gigs or going to events arranged by others. Then there was the intoxication of the live performances and the musical high that swallowed you whole like a warm bath. In a strange way the atmosphere in the venues changed as the nicotine fumes got extinguished in that summer when England enforced the smoking ban in public places. My passion evaporated like the purple fumes. The A3H post bag accepted redundancy as did many ash trays and the tar stains ghosts of the best moments banished under an urgent need for fresh coasts of paint. It was time for me to put my own house in order too.

In the early days I did not let the financial setbacks, broken dreams and time wasters get to me. I took them on the chin believing that that was what you did and it was how you reacted that made you stronger and relevant. Gradually during the events over the last twelve months some scars were too deep and I was not prepared to take the knocks anymore. I felt I had done my apprenticeship and earned the right to step up a level. What I saw as that next level meant investing more time and money, both of which I could not afford. I had done a draft summary of the accounts before the holiday and the figures gnawed at me. The current year ended with a loss of over £800 and A3H's total losses for the five years of trading since 2002 totalled £10,000 all funded by my Director's loan to the company. I knew I would not recoup that any day soon and I was tilting the wrong side of the work: life balance. Holly and Hannah, as young teenagers then, would need more of my attention. Helen never once complained but, our savings were depleted and I could not expect her to keep quiet any longer if I tried to justify the costs of my hobby. The long hours and "habits" the music life style encourages had taken their toll. I was fatter and less fit than I once was as regular exercise had stopped. All things considered, I had let the music take precedent on many fronts and it was time to change, redress the scales and think about what was best for me.

The final flyer

I had booked the Attic for 20th September as part of a block of monthly A3H nights running up to the end of the year. It was to be a celebration of A3H Promotion Ltd's 5th anniversary since being formed. I had asked **Stupid Little Cars** to headline, with **Red Badge of Courage** as support and use it as a platform for **Beth Swain** (ex **Bed, Stolen Ponies**) and **Costello** to be better known in the area. It was free entry with a raffle to cover any costs. When I came back from Spain I called into King Print, Chorley, to do the double sided A3's that had the title "John Winstanley's last night in the music biz". To the side of the band roster I declared:

"Regrettably, I have to halt what I have been doing as a full time "hobby" since Sept 2002. There are all sorts of reasons why, which I won't bore you with, hence this gig will be a celebration for everyone who I have had the good fortune to meet during the last five years. I doubt I will stop being involved in the local music scene in one way or another – so you will still see me about and The Digger Movement lives on too – there are gigs at the Good Nite Club, Nelson –listed overleaf that equally deserve your support...."

There was a collage of some of A3H's key achievements and on the reverse The Digger Movement CD cover, GNC dates and a full add for Kill Casino, quoting their own press release. Peter at the shop took pity on me and did the run in colour for the cost of what he would have charged for black and white. Mick Guy had put it on the websites. I texted everyone in my phone book and sighed with relief when I pressed the send button on the last one.

The final nail

The BOTBs at The Good Nite Club, Nelson and been running during Sunday afternoons/ early evenings – when there was nothing going on elsewhere and I thought, like everyone else, that this was the key for the high attendance. However, come our first date on 19th August it was absolutely dead. I was bitterly disappointed and felt the same for the bands who played short sets to each other. I could not understand it but the next week I could not get hold of the landlord and I think it was Steve Birch who phoned me one day to say the place was shut and no one knew when it would re-open.

With the perspective of time I can see that what I thought was the start of the next stage was in fact the beginning of the end for both the Digger Movement and my involvement. I had taken on too much, yet again! I had off loaded the management of a single band and replaced it with an increasing number of other bands and soloists. The shared responsibility I expected did not happen and I had swapped the hassle/complications/personalities of one band for a multiple of others. I could not favour one above the other and it was a constant balancing act. I was more alone than I had ever been. Those nine months were the best of times and the worst of times.

I had never felt that there was, or I was part of, a race amongst promoters I knew back then. I always wanted to push the boundaries and be imaginative in whatever I did. But, I did not feel there was any rivalry that was obvious or serious in threatening me or what I was doing. The unsigned scene back then was not like that and I doubt it is now from what I see as an observer today. I believe that competition is good – it inspires standards, encourages achievement and progression. The lack of it keeps the status quo at best and at worst it leads to decline and failure. Had I been in a race or competition maybe I would have been more successful than I was and, more importantly, perhaps more of the people I represented would have been better known. This could be why The Digger Movement never went beyond 2007.

I did a lot of work in Preston for example but always regarded it as Russ Carlton's turf and tried to include him on anything I was planning in that city and, to an extent, so did Russ when he needed help with the BOTB or accepting my gig offer for **Star 27** (e.g. Little Man Tate support at The Attic). But, new people moved in and I helped where I could like Rob Clarke who approached me and I was invited to seek out Fraser Boon (Mad Ferret) by Phil Moss and I like to feel we did try and help each other. Preston is a student city so there is an ebb and flow of new promoters and bands across the life span of any three year degree course. New blood is oozing in and draining out with equal vacillation at any given moment. The problem that this creates is the lack of consistency and an understanding of proportions.

I do know that the BBC One Big Weekend was an example of what happens when the pedigree is lost. The organisers of the three day fringe event presided over a closed shop affair of nearly people. You only have to read the interviews and gig list in the *One Big Fanzine* they produced to see that. The radio one brief to them was quoted in an article by Lynn Chadwick for free magazine *Revolution*. It reads: *"Jason Carter, editor of live music and events told us "Radio 1 decided on Preston because as well as bringing a stellar line-up to the city it'll be an opportunity for R1 to put a national focus on the North West and all that people are proud of there".* That to me meant having Preston as a focal point for musicians from across the <u>North West</u> not just one town at one end of the M65. There was no one on the committee I knew representing venues in or promoters from other towns like Accrington, Blackburn, Blackpool, Bolton, Burnley, Chorley, Clitheroe, Colne, Crewe, Darwen, Lancaster, Southport or Wigan. Oh! And by the way there are some significant areas like the Lake District (Barrow In Furness, Ulvesrston, Carlisle, Kendal) and some pretty important music centres like Liverpool and Manchester that are also in the <u>North West</u> – at least they are when featured in BBC North West TV then and now. They may have realised their mistake and a page toward the end of the *One Big Fanzine* condescendingly states *"while there is a lot going on in the city centre, seems like the suburbs are catching onto the Rock N Roll vibe within Preston ...in the suburbs, live music is making a comeback...venues in Chorley, Southport, Blackburn...Leyland are holding regular live band nights"*....excuse me but these towns had never stopped hosting bands since I started in 2002! The only reference to the fact that these towns even exist is on the same page of this article in a small box stating that they are *"worth checking out.... Harry's Bar and The Railway Chorley, Evolution Lounge, Blackburn, Ronnie's, Southport and Attic Accrington"*- wow thanks a lot! It was a classic case of a minority of self interested people directing the money the BBC provided to the bands that committee wanted who were over 90% Preston based – how sad!

Preston was packed with visitors in these three days leading up to the Saturday and Sunday so the venues would all be guaranteed to be full. Hence I do not accept the argument that the selection ensured a good turnout for the gigs. Neither do I like the editorial *"...the line ups reflect the bands who gig around Preston (and elsewhere) regularly and have generally created a buzz about themselves over the last 2 years"*. I think my chapters on Pretendgirlfriend and Shaun Maxwell as well my background on most of the Digger bands and many more who are not Preston based but still from the North West - highlights that fact that there was plenty of a "buzz" elsewhere that didn't get a look in!

I am not bitter about not being asked to help by this committee- which is how this could be interpreted by the guilty -but I am deeply and genuinely disappointed for a lot of musicians who did not get the chance to feature in the line up and the impression given to the nation that Preston was the epicentre of North West music –hey news flash - it wasn't then and it still isn't today!

It all added to the rust gathering from a lot of other factors that corroded my energy and enthusiasm for the Unsigned Scene. In the end the machine that turned me on could not work for me anymore and I decided to switch it off and let others have their go.

Epilogue

We are approaching the end of my journey and I thought you may want to know what conclusions I have reached. By putting what happened to me into perspective has helped me understand my younger self better and eased my acceptance of who I am now and what I have to look forward to. The rest of this chapter is written with the hope that some of it will be of assistance to others. I offer them up to scrutiny by anyone who is starting out or wondering why they are not getting where they want to be. If it serves for you to avoid the mistakes I made then we have both gained. A lot of what follows is peppered with comments from those around at the time who have got back in touch and given their thoughts on what I did or did not do for them.

Before I begin my list I feel I should mention **Sprungloaded** again. They joined the Digger Movement in 2006 and you can read their story in that context. On 21st June 2013 I watched them play at the Imperial, Chorley and they were brilliant. It was their first gig after several months of rehearing with new bassist Joel and drummer Bobby. They were tight, powerful and full of confidence. I'd not seen an unsigned band play with such a high level of professionalism and passion since watching **Red Badge of Courage** or **Gringo Star** for the first time. Later, when we were chatting, I couldn't help myself fall back into my old ways, spinning ideas about and making suggestions on what they could do next. I was back where I had left off because I had been bitten by that gig bug again and was having the same reaction I had had when I first set out on this adventure. I had a few drinks with the brothers' parents (Karen & Paul) who offered to give me ride home. As I got out their car I promised Karen that I would write down some of the suggestions as she was certain the lads would have forgotten what I had been talking about. Hence, what follow is as relevant now as it was all those years ago.

Why form a band or decide to play to an audience? Musicians can sing or take up an instrument for a range of reasons and at any age. As with any art form, there are no rules other than those they put on themselves or have imposed on them by others. The majority of the most exciting music ever written has been created by people below the age of twenty seven. Apart from being the age when some of the most talented have died (Jim Morrison, Kurt Cobain, Amy Winehouse and many other notable musicians) it is also the turning point away from the previous ten years. Mid to late age teenagers have both the ability to dream and turn those imaginings into reality. For them anything is within reach because the future is Weller's "oyster", or, as the Stone Roses declared "ours". Their hormones are fermenting and bursting with endless possibilities. Most of the successful and enduring artists have grafted and forged their skills before the age of twenty. The Beatles did it as kids amongst the strip bars of Hamburg, The Sex Pistol at dingy rehearsal rooms in London and doubtless countless others worldwide did/do the same at a similar age. However, during the time I spent with musicians there were very few that I met who recognised their potential and understood how to express it. This is because the rest made the decision to start doing what they do for reasons that are not exclusively about the music. These include: something to do: to make new friends; get members of the opposite gender to have sex with; be invited to parties: drinking loads of alcohol: do the drugs: seek fame and fortune etc. etc Nothing in that list says "I make music because I have to".

The true musicians I have met took up a guitar, started to sing or scribbled down a lyric because they had to let out something that comes from deep within them.

I do not have to like what a musician produces, but I do appreciate that which drives them to do it. I did what I did in and around musicians because I felt I had to as no one else seemed interested. I fell in love with what I was doing. It was and still is about emotions. Art stirs emotions and writing this book has enabled me to face up to the fact that I did let my emotions run away with my common sense on many occasions. That is what love does and in the same way teenagers are inspired to make music and express it in anyway and style they want. I was following that path too, choosing directions and getting lost at will and making it up as I went. We all make mistakes and that's the way most of us learn just as a musician does to master an instrument or perform. They carry on becoming increasingly more skilful at letting out what it is that drives them. They do it and keep going because they have something inside of them that will not let them go until they let it out. For some it is relentless, an addiction and never ending. I see it in everything Shaun Maxwell has written or will write – he will never stop until the day he dies and he is not unique. But, he is one of the very few truly talented people I should have focused on more when I was involved.

I would not deny anyone the right to play music for any reason – freedom of expression and all that. The key question I would ask any musician or others

334

in the business is "why do you do what you do?" The response is what singles out the wheat from the chaff. Having fun, a laugh and all those non musical replies I understand and accept. "I do it because I have to" is the reply that tells me they are driven with those endless possibilities and that means they are open to ideas, help and support. If that applies to you then you will attract attention and those people willing to invest in you – providing of course you have talent!

Are you honest about your talent factor? To assume makes and "ass" of "u" and "me"! Constructive criticism is lacking at the grass roots level– somewhere it went out of fashion or never existed on the unsigned scene while I was involved. When I got asked "what did you think?" after a gig or the play of a tune, I always gave a balance of the good and the bad without being ugly about it. I know this is what the people generally say about me.

"John, we may not have agreed with what you told us all the time, but we knew what you said is what you felt and it was always honest and fair". (Simmy - Pretendgirlfriend).

Anyone can offer their opinion – "...it was good or it was crap!" Very few have the experience to back up the statement with why they feel that way and, in particular, how to make it better if it was the later. Simon Cowell is a popular because he tells the TV show contestants what they need to hear to affirm how good or bad they are, and he has the track record to back up what he says. There is a need to seek out the people who can provide this type of critique. Journalists, promoters, record shop owners, their staff and other musicians should be the best source.

Every musician needs a degree of courage at any level of competency. Courage, like talent, is something you either have or need help to develop. Generally, anyone who has never performed on a stage is the audience – they are the people who cannot do it themselves but have an opinion on what they see and hear. Like teachers – most have never done it in the real world or they have and now have a vocational drive to pass on the theory or their experience to others. They should be a reliable source of education. If, what is produced from any art form, stirs emotions, the audience it is aimed at, will communicate their feelings about it. It is that simple. But is it honest? Sometimes, as a parent, I know you have to be economical with the truth when your child seeks out your opinions as truth can/does hurt! Hence, family and friends are not the best critics as they will balance factors that deflect and confuse the honesty – losing the integrity of what you want to know.

Putting down an animal that is suffering pain and unlikely to recover is a merciful thing we humans do. No one likes to do it when it has to be done but it happens. We get over it or we let it fester and never recover. Being told you don't have what it takes has the same effect. How do we agree on what we consider to be "talent"? Perhaps that depends largely on taste and we know that our tastes change as we get older. Look at your record collection and see how it varies from your earliest to latest acquisition. If you have got rid of the ones that you dislike as you went along then you have culled the suffering and been your own judge on what you liked or disliked at that moment. Can you do the same to someone face to face? Shouting at the TV or to others watching the same show is not the same as going up to a stranger and saying what you felt about their performance. Gushing with adulation is easy, but negative feelings should be kept to yourself unless you have both the bottle and experience to deliver a balance.

Simultaneously, we are all both the audience and judge for any musician. We can be the best and the worst at both and a talented musician will know which naturally or with the passing of time. Their success or failure will be determined by their own honesty to themselves. You know deep down whether you are the driver or a passenger in your own destiny.

What is your definition of success? I've talked about this in other chapters and summarise it here to those of you who feel you have got passed the questions above and want to go further. It applies to everyone – not just musicians or those in the music industry. When will you know you have succeeded and what are the bench marks you are working towards to achieve it? Too many people I worked with didn't have the answer to this question and I didn't apply this question to a lot of what I did myself. You have read my successes and failures and it reminds me of the maxim *if you fail to plan you plan to fail!* Common sense! I was trained to ask this question to my own business customers and provide guidance on how to achieve it in the day job. However, I did not follow my own advice and sometimes you have to act spontaneously and deviate but someone should be there to remind you to ask the question on a regular basis to get you back on course. Have that "go to" person you can rely on to be your independent sounding board and keeper of your goals.

How do you help yourself? (For musicians). Gigs get booked and a successful one is measured on different levels. After a period of public performances in front of an audience usually comprising friends and relations you feel ready to play out of your comfort zones/venues. A definition of success could be to play a big city gig. I've talked about the pay to play trap and it demonstrates how you get exploited because of your ignorance or plain stupidity. Who do you want to come and see you perform? Family, friends and local fans....? No! You can play to them closer to home so why drag them to a city to line the pockets of that venue and their promoter! Gigs in big towns and cities away from home should have a plan. Will the gig attract new fans and other musicians, promoters, journalists and anyone you want to target to achieve what you've put into your definition of success?

What are you going to do to ensure they come? Will you contact the venue in advance to check the publicity for the event? Who is sorting this out and what do they need from you? Do you need to supply advance material like posters, art work, press cuttings and give aways (CD samplers of your songs, pin badges and flyers) etc? Will you think to contact a local journalist to do a feature on you that will get printed in advance and another write up after the gig that you can use in future publicity? Now you have the social net work medium and all the online possibilities which I did not have but the principles apply to that too.

How many tickets are you expected to sell? Is this a reasonable number and can you exceed it? You should never expect to just do the minimum number of ticket sales. That's a given for the promoter to break even and provide a profit – the business end of things! Exceeding your quota will usually bring you extra income off the sales deal and, more importantly, it will demonstrate to the promoter that you can exceed expectations. That, aside from the money, will be impressive enough for him/her to offer you a return gig. If you end up saving the day by making up for another band's failure to supply their quota then the promoter will be in your debt and gives you an edge. You can use this to build a reputation. Word gets around and the unsigned scene is usually a small community so it spreads quickly. Equally, if you fail to deliver your minimum, a bad reputation gets talked about too - even faster and more loudly!

What value do you place on your talent? I do not advocate giving music away for free. How many people would spend weeks, months or years, painting a picture, sculpting a work of art or writing a book and then give it away? So why do musicians put their music on line and hand out CDs for free at gigs? If you do not value what you create why would you expect others to?

I do advocate you put out a sampler – 30 to 60 seconds of the best parts of your songs. They should be part of your pre gig publicity material, printed with the dates of your gigs, contact details etc – this will lead to true fans coming to the gig or going on line to buy the rest of the songs. That way you generate income and record companies take note of that – selling units is what they do, that's their business and they want you to help them to stay in business. Keep a ledger of what you sell. It will be a measure of your financial viability/success to them and to yourself. If you had to rely on the income could you?

Build a team around you and delegate duties them. A band should focus on writing songs, rehearsing and doing interviews. Their image, publicity, gigs and logistic should be managed by others. However, at the unsigned level they have to do everything themselves until they can attract others to help. That takes time and they usually expect a manager to do all of this for them.

The manager should co-ordinate all the above but not be expected to do it all but often has to until a team is built up. In time, the manager would then "manage" the team. The manager is the prime representative and as such must understand exactly what he/she is expected to do on behalf of who they manage. They should always act with the best interest of those they represent and have this in mind at all times. The manager needs to be objective and not, necessarily, a fan of the band's music. It is a fact some of the most successful managers didn't like the music their artists produce. That way they stay focus on everything else and leave producers and A&R people to do their job in making others love the music. I know that in the manager role I was too in love with the music that it clouded my perspective in how to perform the job efficiently. If success does not happen for a football team the manager gets the sack. Any manager is the hero when success is abundant but the villain is left to share failures on their own.

Merchandise and other representative(s) is an image thing. At the gig or on line – apart from your songs/CDs, what else can you sell? Here is where you generate more income and future publicity. Clothing, badges, posters and the array of key rings, pens etc are vast and they all serve to advertise your name. The buyers become your walking bill boards – in effect you gain more than an instant sale.

The stall you set up at a gig has to be professional and reflect how serious you are about what you are selling. It is the business end – your shop window and demands that you ask your self would you buy from it? Make it eye catching and have plenty of stock, price labelled and set out so it draws people in. Have flyers for future gigs/release dates available to hand out and put with any purchases made. The person you get to look after your stall should be professional too. Someone who knows the band and can answer questions any punter may ask. Ideally, the age and appearance of the stall holder should be in keeping with the band's image. Parents and anyone a lot older than the members of the band does not look right. Fans want to relate to someone who they can relate to them. They don't want to talk to someone's mum or dad or anyone too far beyond their own age, it's not cool!

You do need to build a team of people who could include your parents and family just so long as they know their place. The place for older people in your team is somewhere out of sight particularly at live gigs – ideally they should not go to gigs unless they are part of the transport/road crew and need to hump heavy gear about. To the public a band should appear self sufficient and have a team who set the stage up, make sure the equipment works, instruments are tuned and everything else you may need is to hand −set lists, drinks and towels etc. Very few bands have such a team but those I dealt with that did said a lot about the respect and enthusiasm the team had for the band. They were there because they want to help the band and are usually driven with the same desire the members of the band have to want to see them succeed.

What's your style and stage presence? The internet has moved a long way since 2007 and this window to the world is truly global now. It is a saturated environment too and in order to stand out you have to be conscious of what you want others to see and hear. Your image and output can either match what you want or can act against you if it is not done correctly. The musicians have to understand this and agree on image from the moment they form and decide on a name. Ritchie Edwards did this for the Manic Street Preachers and Stuart Sutcliffe for The Beatles. They understood the other members of the band and had a clear and unique idea about image on and off stage. They were both band members too until someone else came along and developed what they had started i.e. Phillip Hall and Brian Epstein respectively. Even they had to adapt their talents to suite their charges and fight vigorously for the bands' success.

I think it was Bruce McKenzie who told me that you can tell if someone has "it" (X Factor etc) by the way they walk on stage. I agree with that and for the rest that occurs up to the moment the show ends. It is a performance. A piece of art to the performers but, fundamentally, it is a moment of entertainment for the audience. The audience has an expectation and the right to be entertained. They need and demand satisfaction. What is their tolerance of anything that is not perfection? Taken it to the extreme - a fan adores their idol and worships aspects of what they are or do. They say what they want to hear, struts about in a way they want to see and the live act consummates the bond. Beware! The wrong comment or act contrary to the religion and the follower is dissolute, betrayed and fickle. They find another God.

Take notice of your appearance and pay equal attention to rehearse and consider every moment you are in public. This starts at any point you deal with anyone involved in what you do. You are being judged all the time. The attention you attract is your own doing as you chose to work in the entertainment business.

Press – essential! The circulation of the local papers reaches tens to hundreds of thousands of people and a feature in it will profile you, and your business. It is required reading you must stay up to speed with who, what, where and when. Get to know the journalists as it is in their interest to report on what is happening too. Feed them information and ask them to share what they know is happening before it gets printed so you are ahead of the action. Offer to meet and take them for a coffee, lunch/drink or suggest when you are available for a telephone interview if they prefer – let them set the agenda and be interested in what they report on. Find out what recent articles they wrote and mention that you have read them. Offer to make free copies of what you are selling as a prize for a phone in/competition and always send them free tickets to the events you play/organise/promote/host etc. In return, ask them for a review and to pass their (positive) views on to anyone who may be interested in what you did/do.

Radio – equally important and do the same as the above but offer to perform or do an interview live if they can accommodate this – you may need to do a striped down acoustic set/spiel but let them decide.

Promoters, venue owners and sound technicians. These people may be limited to the venue you use and could be all the same person. Either way they are vital to your success. They want your event to go well - so help them to help you by using the points above. Listen to what they tell you about their customers and others connected to what they do in their area of expertise or what knowledge they have of others they know or have worked with recently elsewhere. Taking an interest in them should lead to them taking more of an interest in you.

(Musicians) - Secure a regular venue you can use as a base and consider the "gig swap". This is about building your local fan base – hopefully in your home town or close by. Having the support of a good venue that you play regularly (and pack out) means that the owner is more likely to let you have your own gig night. You can use this opportunity to promote yourself and negotiate a deal with the owner in your favour financially. Usually, the owner takes the bar and you take whatever you want to charge on the door. This is another source of revenue and a measure of success too.

The "gig swap" is to help you play out of town to a crowd that like your music. You find a band or musicians who play in a similar genre to your own. You suggest that you will put them on at your own night (as explained above) and cover their expenses. They are more likely to agree as they want to play out of their home town and to a crowd to where they will gain new fans and be able to sell their merchandise to, just like you. The gain for you is when they do the same for you. When you get a few of these under your belt you get an appreciation of what is involved in the work that others do – the promoting and logistics of a gig – especially what can go wrong. Being able to anticipate and have a plan B, C and even a D for disasters becomes second nature. For example if a band's transport breaks down and they have to turn back have you got another band that can fill the space at short notice?

(Musicians) Put on a gig for a band or musician who is at the next level to you. Small record labels that put one of their acts on tour may need a gig between gigs. They may offer a lower deal in return for feeding the band and giving them some money to cover costs to get to the next gig. If you do this well and, you get on with the act you put on, they will be grateful and are usually willing to share their experiences, how they got signed and would have a favourable opinion of you that may help you in time. Keep in contact and build this until you get signed and others take care of it for you.

Know everything you can in your area. Go out and visit venues on a regular basis. Get your face known and offer to share information. Don't be put off if the venue and musicians are not conducive to what you are into. You would be surprised where some of my breaks came from – often the most unexpected sources and occasions. Just because a venue, promoter or other musician does not like or deal in your genre/style/business you all have the same interest in keeping music live and share a common bond with the art medium. A chance conversation or being at the right place at the right time can make the difference - being as knowledgeable about everything gives the impression that you have a grasp on the pulse of the local scene and are the "go to" person for information and contacts.

Independent Record and instrument shops. Find out if they champion local bands/ musicians/ events and for the former, do they sell local music. Will they stock yours or let you put posters up and flyers for your event? Owners of these places tend to love music like you – it's finding one that will help promote what you want that's key. They usually know music representative and other industry related people who could be useful. You won't know until you hang around, listen and ask questions.

Time wasters – having a built in bull shit detector is essential. Just as you want to promote yourselves so does everyone else. Promoters and venue owners get musicians bigging themselves up all the time. People lie to get what they want – some will be polite about it and say they may have exaggerated when they said they could pack the place out and in the end only bring 4 people. Or they have to cancel playing as the drummers granddad has just died – when in fact they have either double booked your gig or got what they think is a better gig somewhere else or they just can't be arsed to be honest and say they are hung over from playing the night before. You will have to exaggerate the truth too so don't be too hard on them it is what the business thrives on –Hype! Cutting through the crap and finding the diamonds in the rough is what will make you stand out and survive.

Conclusion and final words – this list is not exhaustive and only reflects what I experienced and that was over a decade ago. I have written about what I know. There may be new obstacles and pitfalls or help and support now that I do not know about but that's for you to discover and write about in your own book. Hence, the contribution of others may be more relevant than my own – take it the best way you can or ignore it as you please. I still offer my opinion and this book is partly for those of you who may want what I say in writing and partly to others from the past who want to put me or them in some kind of perspective. Anyway, I hope it has been a good read to them and anyone else I don't know.

Final word of advice?: Have fun! It is so obvious you have to be reminded of it. Yes it is "work" a business and you have to put a lot of time and effort into it. But, you have to enjoy it or find aspects of it that make it all worthwhile. Not having fun is partly why I stopped. Getting out while you are enjoying it is better than carrying on to a point when you no longer get the pleasures you once did. You'll end up despising it- it will become a downwards spiral and I could see myself becoming bitter and I'm sure it ruins a lot of once very happy people. I have had my turn and for 95% of the time it was brilliant. Yes I would change a lot of what I did or didn't do but the past is history. I am not bitter and I am not sad. I cannot go back to it now as I am a different person and have other things I want to do. Perhaps I'll write about them too one day. Take care as it is a beautiful distraction....

PS. What's my all time favourite song.......? Spearmint – "Sweeping the Nation" (Hitback records) – see the back cover as to why. I was in a reflective mood when I sent that email as a couple of hours earlier I responded to a Facebook pole of favourite LPs and I replied with the following:

09.30 21/12/13 FACE BOOK to Shaun Maxwell's request for our top 10s I was on an economy drive so ended up with those shit sounds like LPs "Hot Hits" or "Top of the Pops" compilations on Pickwick records - sad thing is some of the cover bands/singers were better than the originals! I asked for the greatest hits of Cliff Richards one Xmas (yeah no one said this is a "cool" list) and it did influence me though - much underrated singer in his prime - so what if he was copying what others were doing -*uck me the rest of R&R is full of copyists (i.e. Rolling Stones, Beatles, Sex Pistols etc) Pushed at a moment's notice I'd have to say 1,40 Greatest hits form 50/60s on Arcade records (first time I heard Paul Anka, Neil Sedaka, The Troggs, Dusty Springfield etc) 2,Collection of Beatles Oldies,3, In The City (Jam)4,

342

999's first LP (because Nasty Nasty was the first Punk song I ever heard at a disco at Chorley Cricket Club), 5,Unknown Pleasures, 6,Smith first LP, 7 Systems of Romance (Ultravox with John Foxx -who was born in Chorley if you didn't know),8, Hearts & Bones (Paul Simon's LP before equally influential Gracelands),9 On The Beach (Chris Rea), 10 Live at The Attic (my own LP compilation of 20 bands I booked to play this venue in Accrington 2005/6). What influences you is not something you can control. For better or worst I felt, thought, behaved, shagged and believed differently after hearing these LPs.

THE ATTIC
Accrington
Over 18's, no sportsware

Thursday
20th September

FREE entry from 7.30pm

A3H Proudly Presents..

John Winstanleys
Last night in the music biz

Regrettably, I have to halt what I have been doing as a full time "hobby" since Sept 2002. There are all sorts of reasons why, which I won't bore you with, hence, this gig will be a celebration for everyone who I have had the good fortune to meet during the last 5 years. I doubt I will stop being involved in the local music scene in one way or another - so you'll still see me about and The Digger Movement lives on too - there are gigs at The Good Nite Club, Nelson - listed overleaf that equally deserve your support.

Please make a date to join me and many of our friends in welcoming 2 talented bands and a truly gifted soloist for their Attic debut. Also my favourite Chorley band - SLC-headline for a much anticipated return.
It's a FREE gig from 7.30ish so you can spend your money on raffle prizes, drinking and a having party!

John

Stupid Little Cars
(Chorleys most handsome)

Red Badge of Courage
(Battle of the band winners from wellington)

Beth Swain
(Unique GV from Salford)

Costello
(Steve Latham)

The Digger Movement Tour

The Diggers were a small group of people who protested against the greed of the landed gentry in 1649. They were led by Gerrard Winstanley and we are using his principles of self help and peaceful protest to create a platform for bands/musicians to stand united against the 'pay to play' and instant TV smash and grab fame culture that has infected our music industry

SPRUNGLOADED

Live
14th July
@ The Retro Bar
5:50pm

Upcoming Shows

17th Aug	Barca live	Manchester
29th Aug	The Thirsty Scholar	manchester
13th Sept	Lock91	Manchester
18th Sept	Antwerp Mansion	Manchester
23rd Nov	The Railway	Chorley

www.sprungloadedofficial.com
info@sprungloadedofficial.com

The Good Nite Club
Stanley Street Nelson

Sundays 3pm - 9pm
all ages welcome

19th Aug	Red Badge of Courage good night club battle of the bands winner 2007 www.myspace.com/rboc + Costello + Avalon Way + sprungloaded
16th Sep	Spungloaded + Kill Cassino + more TBC
14th Oct	Stupid Little Cars + Brother Bastion + Sprungloaded + more TBC
18th Nov	New Breed of monkey + Rayne www.myspace.com/raynereign + Sprungloaded +Limousine + more TBC
16th Dec	Small Amp + The Wheel Jacks + Sprungloaded + more TBC

Any bands/musicians who want to play or join support the M65 Local Live Music Tours contact the Good Night Club or John Winstanley at WWW.A3Hpromotion.co.uk (www.myspace.com/a3hpromotion)

13 OUTAKES from "A beautiful distraction" – which was the working title for the book

<u>Chapter 2.</u> (Cut at 3rd edit: *Re The Punk Wars: I felt I'd made my point by this stage :)*

We know that there have always been talent scouts and a short cut to becoming a star as long as there has been music or an entertainment business. The BBC created Radio 1 and Top of The Pops – which became the barometers of what, was hip or cool in Pop. The arrival of the hit parade in the 1950's and the 45 single speeded up the race to find the next hit maker and TOTPs, for my generation, was essential viewing. We spotty teenagers wanted to see the latest stars performing in our living rooms. The music industry was, and still is, big business and there are massive sums of money to be made either behind or on the backs of the talented and good looking. Society has permitted it and there are courses to testify to how a bit of grooming goes a long way.

(**Moments of inspiration....**) Like an antennae you had to tune it in and then await for whatever signals it picked up. Sorting out the static you eventually received clarity – it seemed all I had to do was to apply the interpretation.

(**The) Burn.** Daniel Davidson, Michael Spencer, Graham, Lee and....After a gig at The Night & Day Café, Manchester, seen by Badly Drawn Boy, they were invited to use his studios to record their early demos. Signed to Hut Records, they went on to open up on tour supports for Oasis, Ian Brown and Paul Weller, "The Smiling Face" debut single on Hut Records 2002. I bought this but wasn't that impressed. Other singles "Drunken Fool" (31/12/2002) and "Big Blue Sky" followed by the LP "Sally O'Mattress" before Hut records got shut down by owners Virgin records in 2004.

The Iinviisiibles – My first interview with a "proper" band, 4/7/02, North Bar and then after their support gig to The Fall at King George's Hall 26/11/02 – both in Blackburn. Comprising of Dave Stirrup (LG & Vocals) from Northampton with relatives in Preston: Van Campbell (drums) from Louisville, Kentucky, USA and "Professor" Jason Bootle (Bass & Vocals) from Adelaide, Australia. Formed in London and had a short burst of recordings. My interview appeared in issue 3 of PTID, in which Dave told me how his father was "...Killed not divorced ...and two members of my family have mental illness....nothing is trivial or meaningless. We don't want to be taken too seriously but at the same time we're not writing jokes...we're writing about what happened to us...sorry if its offensive but we don't sit contriving these things...who the fuck would want to...it's all too real! I'm talking about subjects that you don't deal with but that's part of my life...It's not just about the music it never is there's more to it than that!" I mention one of their songs being about peeking inside a sex shop and how it leaves you with a sense of how fascination embellishes the embarrassment. I met Brian Malcolm who was a sort of road manager and fan but didn't hear from him or the band after that.

The Jamm - The first interview I did for Pogo'til I die 3/06/2002. At that time it consisted of Paul Weller look a-like guitarist John Southorn (founding member), bassist Ray Begg and drummer Andy Cartwright. Based in Burton-on-Trent the band was originally a covers band when they started out in December 1997. Soon the demand for the Jam material in the set lead them to become a tribute act and their reputation had got them gigging constantly from Butlins themed weekends to venues all over the UK, Ireland, Japan and Italy. I saw them some month's later at the Mill, Preston and last time at The Witchwood, Ashton-Under-line, by which time they had a new drummer.

Chapter 3. (Cut at 3rd edit: This *over egged the point on my new sense of freedom from the rat race :)*

When I made that "vow to myself to get the balance right" it was a work life one I was referring to. I now had self determination. I was in charge of time. I could plan a day the way I wanted to, rather than have the constrictions of the 9 to 5 Mon-Fri. I saw this as the biggest gain to being self employed. The time to do what I wanted, when I wanted, gave me more control to fit in with what Hannah and Holly needed too.

Chapter 5 (*Cut at second edit as it was not essential to The Commies story. It is the last gig instructions I drew up and an example of my meticulous attention to detail, name checks others it is only of nostalgia for those who were there*).

All equipment should arrive at 3.45pm

All members of all bands should be at the venue before 4pm ready for

Sound check. Unless special arrangements have been made with me. The line up for that night is

6.30 till 7.00 – **Dead Jim** 7.15 till 7.45 – **Duckhunt** (or Let's Not Lose Mars to the Commies) 8.00- till 8.30 – **Idiom Lifeline** 8.45 till 9.15 - **Echo Freddy** 9.30 till 10pm - **Let's Not Lose Mars to the Commies** (or Duckhunt) (All times are approximate)

With the Duckhunt and Commies times we've left it up to you to decide who plays when, though with it being the Commies last gig maybe it would be nice for them to play last. I know there's gonna be some pissing about drum kit wise but there isn't really a way round that as far as I can see. Your set should be 25 minutes long.

Equipment FULL PA WILL BE SUPPLIED. BANDS ARE EXPECTED TO PROVIDE AND SHARE BACKLINE. (DRUMS AND AMP) ALL drummers are expected to bring their own snare, cymbals and foot pedals.

ALL band members should bring any straps, cables, tuners or accessories they may need.

Please contact the other bands playing to who will bring what equipment contact details are;

Guests

Any non-official band persons should not arrive with the bands and should come as customers and pay to get in at 7pm. However we accept that some bands have managers, merchandise people, or press. If you have anybody like this please contact *guests@hyper-value.com* ASAP with names and reasons why they should be allowed in with you. If we do not have their names at least 48 hours before the gig then they will not be allowed entry to the venue until after 7pm and they will have to pay for entry.

Chapter 8
(Third edit as their chapter was running into 85 pages)

....What hooked me into Pretendgirlfriend was a combination of their live performance, meeting and interviewing them and hearing their recorded material all in the space of a few weeks.

...I had lost touch with Pete Buttle and it would have been handy to have him to talk to at that time. Pete set up Way Cool Records and signed other bands like **Bleach** and **Basti.** He had invited me on a trip to Europe in 1986 to watch the Alarm. He lived in Acton, London back then and would have been full of industry contacts had I been able to hook up with him again. Like me, back in the 1980's, he was watching all the up and coming bands, recording most of the gigs he went to and it was through his selling of these recordings on cassettes, that I got to know him.

Chapter 9 (Cut at Shaun's request at the second edit as he was. *not keen on this bit really makes me sound like I really think I'm somebody .. I think I'm popular with other musicians n people who have an inclin of my past).*

Where do you stand on bands reforming?

I feel the need to deviate slightly at this point to put what Shaun did/is doing into context, to explain his appeal and why he is so popular amongst those of us "who get it" i.e. who he is and his professional pedigree.

Punk Rock as a concept does not encourage longevity. The Sex Pistols, X

347

– Ray Spex, The Adverts and many others only lasted a few years either through design or circumstances. Arguably, by default, they are better preserved in an embalmed/ mummified like state compared to some of their contemporaries who went on too long ending up like pickled onion to stretch the simile. It was like The Beatles in Hamburg (their formative period), when it was all young, fresh, dangerously enticing and limited to the small troop of followers – before the trappings of fame and predictability soured its integrity. The urge to want to go back to those times and the wish to revive the memories could be a sad mistake like digging up the corpse of an old friend.

Revivals do have an appeal to the reunion tours of countless bands. Most do it for the money and the fans turn up to relive their past and is there anything wrong with either? Purists and even my own experience show it is not something to be encouraged blindly. For a Punk Rock band it is a double damming as the act of reforming is a betrayal of its principles – the originality and spontaneity that gave it its raison d'être first time round. How ironic the *hope I die before I get old* philosophy of The Who has proved to be when sung today by pensioners Daltry and Townsend or is it to be expected as Mod, for some, was/is more about style than substance? The Rolling Stones Glastonbury set in 2013 divides opinions. Some regard it as their finest moment. While others feel The Stones have pulled off the Greatest Rock'n Roll Swindle of them all. A bunch of strung out wrinklies who continue to snigger up their sleeves for how long they have duped the world into stretching out their careers based on their initial shock value and a handful of R&B standards!

Is reforming acceptable on any level and especially a Punk Rock one without it being a novelty act? Perhaps, as a jolt to other generations of what it was to be Punk Rock or any genre for that matter as a "back in the day" experience....well maybe. For example, I saw The Things at The Kings Arms (Bloom Street, Salford) in August 2013 and was astounded by a band I had never known of before recently tempted out of retirement. The Bill Nighy look alike lead singer had stage presence and a vocal delivery that was a master class to any generation. It got me thinking whether it is better to have had a moment of fame, even if one single's worth or be it as a bit player in an iconic band, than to be part of the "also rans"? Do those moments of fame hang like a lead weight fixing you to a given point or song that you will never be free of? Will whatever you do from then on never be good enough if you are always compared to it. Do the hangers on sustain the legends to provide themselves with equal sustenance or by association to them wear this as badges of credibility for the existence of both themselves and their idols? I have concluded that this form of reformation can be patronisingly referred to as a history lesson – acted out for what was and never "as is"- but it is not reality – never. Shaun Maxwell is reality; he is and always has been his own man. He has never needed the adoration of others to do what he has done and whatever his fans and friends feel to the contrary they cannot argue with that and we are all better people for it.

(*Edited out by myself toward the end of the Shorn period*):

What I do not know, until I get the opinions from other members of the bands, is what influences they had on each song. When I present the song lyrics this is often the first time some members have seen them written down and this can have a curious response of being the first time some members knew what was being sung or the meaning the composer intended to get across!

My observations on song writing which were unnecessary to Shaun's story:

From the songwriters I have known the development of a song can start and end in a very different place from when it was originally conceived. Sometimes the words are written in readiness of presenting it as a complete song to the rest of the band. Or the music is put together first from a riff, solo configuration/melody or a mash up from a strumming session. A structure is then agreed with the lyrics being added later. At other times a song writer will write a lyric as a complete whole at one sitting that may never get amended. At other times the lines are formed in stages as parts put together from other scribbling, notes, observations, one liners etc. The song is rehearsed and the lyrics may get altered again. When played live, due to any numbers of factors – feedback from fans or other band members and then they can get changed yet again.

<u>**Chapter 10**</u>

I have many regrets and while searching through the several storage boxes of files, CDs, Photos, DVDs, press cuttings, magazines and fanzines etc I became conscious of many bands and musicians that I have not mentioned up to this point. Those that are still going or who were or became more successful will probably come back to haunt me with criticisms of "Why did you not mention me/us?" or you should have wrote more about X or Y/venue/scene etc!" To make amends I have listed bands in a separate list and try and use this moment to explain their relevance. I have to draw a line somewhere and that is at the point that I asked myself – did I "know" enough of them to write anything meaningful or did any of them have any impact on me or what I was involved with through A3H. For everyone I have listed there are another 20% that I have not as I have either forgotten or I only ever got a CD or email from them. So for everyone offended by this book I say "Apologies" maybe we can talk and consider inclusion on another edit or my next book?

But....if I could write about bands who I did not know as well as perhaps I should have then and now it would include: In no particular order-

Northwest bands – you know who you are – and you may have been in the listing with nothing else in the book but it is my way of saying I did not forget you and some I may cover below?

Outside the Northwest – as above!

Torrents – I have a short news paper article (Lancashire telegraph) 4th July 2006. It informs that this four piece Blackburn band had two songs recorded by The Enemy's producer Matt Terry. It adds that Ska icon Pauline Black (The Selector) sang on one of the tracks. Their manager – Pete Eastwood is quoted as saying "Torrents don't plan to slow down any time soon". While writing this book I was briefly in contact with Pete and it reminded me of the one gig I did see the band play at the Mad Ferret, Preston. I have to admit that on that occasion they did not make the earth shake for me. The tunes were shouted rather than sung, par for the course but the Bass (Josh Croasdale) player did stand out. His stage presence was emphatic – like Bruce Foxton, he stabbed the strings and moved with purpose.

How's My Pop? – I saw at The Mill, Preston and liked. About that time Sean McGinty took an interest in them and I backed off. Then I saw them play the Dukes in Lancaster sometime after 2007 billed as *Glastonbury Festival featured Indie "exciting stuff"* XFM. I went to this BARNBOX showcase gig at the invitation of Steve Hodson from Uncle Jeff who were playing alongside Kriss Foster *Catchy comedy song - Kriss has appeared on Granada Tonight and performed at the Latitude Festival* and Jo Gillot *"An astonishing new voice"* BBC Radio 2. Uncle Jeff were a band I wanted to do more for apart from putting them on the Vibes CD but it didn't happen and Steve did some solo work around the time of the Oxjam, Accrington in 2007. HMP? Yes good and I can see what Sean saw in them.

Mad Ferret, formerly Time Square a pub venue opposite 53 Degrees, Fylde Rd Preston. Ran by Fraser Boon at that time and he was introduced to me by The Underdogs. Fraser gave me the opportunity to put some gigs on and we got on at first as these included The Purpose and Gringo Star. Then I had a disaster gig when I had book MOCO to play and they had to pull out at short notice. One of the bands I let play did not impress him and that was the end of that. I did take Huw Stephens to the pub and introduced him to some of the people I knew but I was still pissed off at not being involved in the organisation of the Big Weekend event – hence I have let my pent up steam out in chapter 12. Out of respect to Fraser and some of the bands not mentioned elsewhere I may have space for a copy of a flyer to make it to the final edit.

In case it doesn't is has Jelly's Last Jam, Wave Machines (from Liverpool), Onions (from Manchester) and Thee Neerlymen in black and white with a picture of peanuts, a boy wearing spectacles with In association with Aubrey Lyth underneath.

Fi-Lo Radio – One of the most successful and popular bands to have come out of Chorley/Preston in the naughties. I knew of them via The Commies as Jon-Lee Martin (G/V) was from Chorley and good friends to the band. Chris Jopson, the drummer, lived in Hutton, and bassist, Jude Pratt, was from Penwortham. The band formed at Cardinal Newman College, Preston in 1998, when they were teenagers studying Music Technology at A Level. One news article I have from 2004, quotes Chris as saying "New York was a real eye opener. We went into a night club and Marilyn Manson and Elijah Wood from Lord of the Rings were there. You don't get that in the Adelphi in Preston". This was at a time when they did not have a record contract but did have a publishing deal with Universal and were singled out as *one to watch* by The Big Issue. I saw them while managing The Commies and felt that they were the complete package and am equally frustrated it did not work out for them. Perhaps there is an untold story there for someone to write about?

Matt Bury (snot sure how it is spelt) and his brother **Dave**– were music promoters who did a lot of club nights at the Cellar Bar, Blackburn under the name of *Currupted*. They were very popular and I envied the art work on his posters and leaflets – eye catching and appealed directly to hard core metal heads. Pleasant guys but I didn't have a lot in common with them so that may explained why they do not figure much in my story. Matt did send the following text when I announced my retirement *"Sorry to hear that john, where's the do then?"* (18.41 21/8/07)

India Mill – I did watch them once but cannot remember where – may have been FJ Nicholls, Blackburn? A good band that impressed a lot of people and still going at time of printing, as my face Book invites confirm. I have no explanation as to why I did not have anything to do with them other than they seemed to do well enough without my help. They were not alone!

Sam Hammond – Blues singer song writer/guitarist who did support The Commies once at the North Bar. He originated from Chorley, I did not know Sam at all but he was popular with those I knew. Referring to an interview he did at the time it records that his dad played bass in 1960s beat semi-legends The Troles for anyone who remembers them. I am sure that if someone writes a more comprehensive book about all musicians/bands associated with Chorley I suspect it would have to include Sam.

Morning Call (MCUK)– Anthony Sharples (vocals/bass), Chris ("Kip)

Dickinson (G), Andrew Maculey (Keys, synth, samples & backing vocals) and Carl Elmer (Drums and backing vocals) – one of the first bands to approach me for a gig at The Attic, Accrington. Very pleasant lads who supported a lot of what I did. Did a lot for themselves and, in time, with help from Amy Fenton who I always associate with the band and will be equally grateful to for organising the acoustic guitar gift at my retirement.

Cropduster – I felt the CD they sent me for an Attic gig had potential but the band split and I've included them here in tribute to a lot of bands that were ones that fell through the cracks. I singled them out too as they wanted to gig with the likes of Uncle Jeff and "Andy" use to write complimentary letters to me from Lancaster.

Quotations I didn't use: All by text unless indicated* in which case they were in person.

Pretendgirlfriend are a meeting of the Arctics and Oasis in a street, with moderate violence. Certificate 15.' Sean McGinty BBC Radio Lancashire

"YEAH JOHN IM KINDA GOING THAT WAY TOO. (David Hall, on the news of my retirement 18.13. 21/8/07)

"Well matey music will always be in you! (Ray Ferguson 18.12.21/8/07)

"Hey John this is sad news. Hope u won't disappear completely!" (Fiona and Martin, Riffs Live Music Venue, Blackpool 18.32 .21/8/07)

"John! don't want you to leave but of course I want an invite x" (Amy Fenton 16.07 21/8/07).

"Hi Jon, don't blame u-it's a hard and expensive sometimes thankless graft. Thx again thoug 4 helping us out last spring. Peace!" (Ben Ruth 17.20 21/8/07)

"Gosh, what on earth will u do with yourself?" (Kerry McGregor 18.31. 21/9/07)

"Sorry 2 hear that John....I rekon u don a lot of gd in yr time doin music" (Sean McGinty, date/time not recorded).

"I'm sure y'll be back John, yu helped too many bands!" (Steve Fenton 17.39. 21/8/07)

"Like the music your parents hate"*

"Start off with zero expectations and you won't be disappointed"*

"You didn't really make any money u made history" (Sam Flanagan 19.45. 21/8/07)

Index and abbreviations

This is not a definitive list only a guide to those who have expressed interest while I have been writing the book and *indicates name only as an acknowledgement of some people who I may have only met briefly but have not forgotten. I apologise to a lot more of you not listed as I may only have had a first names or nicknames /email addresses in my old contact books so you may want to refer to the band listing instead.

venues in East Lancashire (Ch 11)

Boardman, Tom– member of Onset/Idiom Lifeline/Elohymn at some stage - mentioned throughout the book (Ch various).

Blue Bird Club, Barrow in Furness where I saw Primal Scream, PWEI, Weather Prophets and many other bands

Bohemia – (Contact name "Elouise") the name The Attic, Accrington was known as for a while before changing back to The Attic.

Bondage, Beki – G/V Vice Squad (Ch 2).

Boon, Fraser – ran the Mad Ferret, Preston (Ch 12,Out takes).

Booth, Bruno – original drummer with Let's Not Lose Mars to the Commies (Ch 5).

BOTBs – Battle of The bands.

Bright, Roy – founding member of Exit State (ex Depon Eye) (Ch 8,10, 11)

Bromley, Michael – Kinesis (Ch 2)

Brookes, Tony – sound engineer at CCC in the early days after the 2002 BOTBs (Ch 7).

Brown, Ronnie – owner of The North Bar, that use to be on Town Hall Street, Blackburn. Great music fan and vital in helping me and a lot of others on the local scene. Use to promote bands at Clouds (Church St, Preston) in 1980s and married to Joy – who both came to my retirement party and two of the nicest people I ever met who supported me all the way through– thank you both (Ch various).

Buckley, Stephen James*– Baby Bitch front man "sound of metal wearing a feather boa with slick riffs and dirty grooves" (Ch 7)

Bullard, Ian – set up Jambeezi, played bass in Digby, The Usuals and one of the nicest people I met in the early days (see Jambeezi).

Bury, Matt &his brother **Dave** – Music Promoters in Blackburn e.g. Currupted Nights at The cellar Bar (Ch 11,Out takes)

Buttle, Peter – manger of Way Cool records, involved with Senseless Things, Basti and Bleach.

Byrne, Robbie – ex Scots Guardsman who played the Uilleann Pipes (Ch 4)

Cardwell, Chris – ex Boddah, Doublethink and Ronin went out as a G/V (Ch 7,10)

Carlton, Russ – co-founder of first Chorley BOTBs and Hype Nights! Set up hyper-value.com and promoted many club nights in Preston like Where's Mavis, Club Fuzzy as well as running BOTBs at Aquellenium in conjunction with the LEP. Bass player in bands (eg, Digby and Star 27) – supported a lot of what I got involved with and active in a lot of what happened in Preston (Ch various).

Canny, Gaz – bassist in Rebekah and Capulet (various).

Cardy, Fin*– appear in an old address book under King Rolo but may have been a CCC regular as his address was in Brinscal.

Carr, Mike* – my contact at Bacup FC who helped me set up and run a couple of successful gigs there.

Carteret, Cliff De – co-presenter on Live and Let Live Radio (Ch 4,6)

Catlowe, Rob – Drummer – played in Day's End, Let's Not Lose Mars to the Commies, Duckhunt/Failsafe (Ch various)

Cawood, Mike – ex swimming instructor to my kids at Brinscal Baths (Ch 4)

C.C.C. – Chorley Community Centre – featured throughout the book.

C.C.M.C. – Chorley Community Music Consortium – run by those who put gigs on at CCC and which I became Chairman of at one point.

Chadwick, Lynn – see article in Revolution magazine - BBC One Big Weekend, Preston (Ch 12)

Chlond, Stephanie – Co-presenter on the RSL for Chorley FM (Ch 4)

Chorley Citizen – free weekly newspaper whose journalists include Chris Gee who did many features for me and Chorley musicians.

Chorley Guardian – weekly paper and some of its journalists who helped me include Malcolm Wyatt, Tracy Bruce and others.

Clarke, Rob – former landlord of The Mitre Tavern, Preston. Lead guitarist and singer in Shot Gun Fairies and Phlegm Fatales. Involved with Preston Music Collective (Chapters 7,8,11,12).

Clayton, Julian – promoter at the Attic, Accrington, ex manager of Small Amp who set up the Live Lounge, Blackburn (Ch 11).

Cleverly, Rachel – Dance teacher to my kids at Anita Murray's Dance School (Ch 4).

Cliffe, Pete* – fan of Pretendgirlfriend.

Clough, Dave - Preston Music Collective (chapter 11)

Cogley, Matthew – member of Let's Not Lose Mars To The Commies, Duckhunt/Failsafe and now performs solo G/v. (Ch various).

Cohurst, Mark – involved with Pail and who invited The Commies to his home to see his recording studio (Ch 5)

Collins, Dave – former manager of LEAF.

(The) Commies – shorter name for Let's Not Lose Mars to The Commies (CH 5 & various).

"Connolly"* – door man at The Attic.

Cornwell, Tony* – member of Perfect Strangers (Ch 1).

Coxhead, Sandra* – Hand Prints, Croston -who did my T Shirts for A3H's launch party and The Commies (Ch 5,10)

Craig, Lesley – long time friend who introduced me to Latin Quarter and friend to Elizabeth Voskamp (Chapter 1).

Croasdale, Joss – bassist in The Torrents (Ch Out takes)

Crosby, Pat – G/v in Rebekah and Capulet (Ch - various).

Dewhurst, Christopher – long time friend who introduced me to The Alarm, Roy Harper and Peter Buttle (Ch 1).

Digman, Adam "Diggy" – lead singer of Onset/Idiom Lifeline/Elohym (Ch various).

Dobson, Steve – author of "The Man Who Killed the Hamsters" (Ian Moss) who recommended Intoprint to for publishing this book.

Duckworth, Mark – member of Rocket Dog (no hard feelings Mark Re Ch 2) but liked you better in Sterling Rose (Ch 7)

Durrigan, Peter – former Chairman of the CCC Board of Trustees (CH 7).

Eastwood, Pete – manager of Torrents

Entwistle, Nathan* – member of the CCMC and founding member of MACY.

Evans, Colin – CCC board of trustee member (Ch 7)

Evans, Gaz – guitar vocalist in Elcho (Ch various).

Fairburn, Gus – street performer musician. Former guitarist and singer in The Product (Chapters 8 & 11).

Fairholme, Steve and Mona – friend from Otley who introduced me to folk music (Ch1)

Farnham – Jonathan – younger brother of Anthony (ex member of Boddah) whose mother, (Julie) sent me the first fan mail letter I got for The Commies, in Feb 2003 requesting copies of the band's CDs.

Farrington, Tom – CCC regular, guitarist in Drop In The Ocean and first Chairman of MACY 9Ch 7).

Faud, Bryan – Drummer with Pretendgirlfriend after Daniel Spinks left, connected with Abacus Studios & ex Spitfire (Ch 8).

Fenton, Amy – music promoter from Darwen who helped with Morning Call and took loads of photos at my retirement and arranged for all the bands to sign an acoustic guitar that was presented to me on behalf of everyone I knew. (Ch Out takes)

Fenton, Steve – owner of Calder recordings and friend to Pretendgirlfriend who went into the Revel's joint venture with A3H Ch 8 & 11.

Flanagan, Sam – Blackburn based DJ and promoter (Ch Out takes)

Fogg, Ally – journalist for Big Issue In The North who gave me encouragement at the very start (Ch 10)

Ford, Lee & Wayne – brothers in Burnley based four piece Spitfire. Played at

A3H launch party and other gigs (Ch 8,10).

Forte, Simon – drummer in The Reserve and regular on the Blackburn scene (Ch 2)

Foster, Rob - singer songwriter ex Dumpstar and Auorta (Ch 4,11)

Foulds, Andy – set up Blackburn Punk label Noize Anoize, put on bands and went to work with The Buzzcocks (Ch 10)

Foxx, John – musician whose real name is Dennis Leigh, born in Chorley–formed Ultravox after Tiger Lily (Ch 4)

Fuller, Ben* – DJ at my launch part y for A3H at The Marquee Club, Preston (Ch 10).

Fox, Paul – entrepreneur and owner of The Attic, Warner Street, Accrington. Big help to me and many local bands (Ch 8, 11).

Fullalove, Dave – involved in organising the Sound festivals in Accrington (Ch 10).

Garner, Steven – member of CCMC and singer in Geoffrey Bungle (Ch 6,7)

Gee, Chris – the last journalist to interview me before my retirement – thanks Chris for all you help with features in The Chorley Citizen!

Gibson, Gordon – owner of Action Records, Preston and probably, like Ronnie Brown , someone who knows more about local music than most of us will ever know (Ch various).

Gillett, Damion* – from Darwen set up and ran Cheesepress.co.uk which provided me with a few good reviews when there were few others doing it.

Gilmour, Dave – Chorley based photographer (www.digitalman.co.uk) who provided a lot of the images I used (Ch various).

Goodwin, Robin – best man at my wedding and my oldest friend (Ch 1)

Graham, Michelle – employee of South Lancashire Arts Partnership (chapter 7).

Green, Paddy – see Jambeezi, ex Digby and Bikini Black Special*, and another

one of the nicest guys in the early days (Ch various).

Greenaway, Ben – co-organiser of the first Chorley BOTBs and Hype Nights! Ex manager of Dumpstar who introduced me to Chorley Radio and a prime mover in the early days of Chorley's local music scene (Ch 4).

Griswood, Andrew – member of The Dangerfields (Ch 2).

Gurney, John – author of Gerrard Winstanley The Digger's Life and Legacy (Pluto Press) and Brave Community: The Digger Movement In The English Revolution (Manchester: Manchester University Press)

Guy, Michael – next door neighbour, supported me in many ways especially art work for the CD s, DVDs, posters and leaflets (Ch various).

Guy, Peter – Journalist with Ormskirk Advertiser and involved with the Lancashire Wigan Music Collective (Ch 11).

Hartley, Adam – member of Let's Not Lose Mars to the Commies, Capulet (Ch various).

Hardman, Peter – school friend (Ch 1)

Hall, David – Music promoter – use to talk about The KBC – a band from Preston. (Out takes)

Henderson, Steve – music promoter in Chorley under "Mr Kite presents…" (Ch 4).

Hammond, Sam – blues singer song writer from Chorley (Ch Out takes).

Harry's Bar – St George's St, Chorley. Use to be The Reform Club in 1970s but was run as a music venue in the naughties by Ivan Lynas.

Hatfield, Mike – singer with Tessem (Ch 4,8)

Hesketh, Roy – journalist for Pogo 'til I Die – the Punk fanzine he set up (Ch 2).

Higgins, Andy – "Minister of Order and Reason" and part of his www.jsntgm.com journalist for Blackpool Rox fanzine (Ch 2).

Higson, Paul * – Facebook friend who I occasionally meet to watch Shaun Maxwell in with The Taser Puppets or Sinister Chuckles.

Hill, Bert – organist at Chorley Labour Club in the 1970s – gave me my first job as a drummer (Ch 1)

Hingley, Tom – Ex Inspiral Carpets singer, who I promoted in Chorley playing in Too Much Texas (chapter 8).

Hodge, Carol – AKA Crystal Grenade lead singer in Sadie Hawkins Dance and Synko who I got to know via Stuart Taylor (Ch 2)

Hodson, Steve – ex Starkey's Walk, Let's Not Lose Mars to the Commies, Capulet, Oceansize, Kong and other bands (Ch various).

Holden, Barry – Chorley based Ju-Jitsu black belt and instructor (Ch 4).

Holding, Julie* – fan of Rebekah and possibly a CCC regular.

Hope, Chris – Guitarist in many bands including Elohymn (Ch 7)

Horrocks, David- booking agent of Independent Sound 9chapters 9 & 8).

Howarth, Ben* – drummer in Hope (Ch 11).

Howarth, Craig* - a contact name for Numpti – a band who did the first cover version I ever heard live of Green Day's *Basket Case* (at BOTB at Aquellenium).

Hughes, Chris – Sound technician for Studio-Nyne (chapter 8).

Hughes, Paul – guitar vocalist with The Passion – did a few gigs together, I thought he was talented too.

Humphries, Simon "Si" – guitarist with Duckhunt (Ch various)

Hunter, Kevin – lead singer with Wire Train (Ch 1).

Imperial – pub on Union Street, Chorley., which caters for live music at date of printing.

I-Profile – a Bolton based website business I used to run my website that did art work for Live In Hope CD/DVD (Ch 8).

Jambeezi – 18 tracks compilation CD put together by Paddy Green and Ian Bullard featuring local bands in 2002 (Ch 2).

Jennings, Michael – Ex Holy Cross pupil and Chorley based boxer (former British Welterweight champion) and drummer in the Shoks (chapter 8).

Johnston, Peter & Lorraine – Landlord at the Dudley Arms, Rhyl (Ch 8).

Jones, Graham – author of Last Shop Standing (chapter 1).

Jopson, Chris – drummer in Fi Lo Radio (Ch various & Out takes)

Kapur, Vuz – Manchester promoter as V Man Events.

Kay, Chris – brother of David, ex drummer in Free Falling Camels and Green Quarter (Ch 11).

Kay, David – Brother of Chris, Film maker and founder of Red Brick Productions who provided music videos for Let's Not Lose Mars to The Commies, Pretendgirlfriend and many famous bands and musicians (Chapters 11).

Kelly, Fred & John – bought a drum kit off the former and use to admire the later playing drums at The Tiger, Leyland in 1970s (Ch 1).

Kershaw, Dom – member of Tin Gods from Preston who only ever saw once but thought were good for what it's worth now Dom!

Kings Arms, pub/music/theatre venue close to Salford Central Railway Station – and where I saw the 2012 Wigan Digger Festival poster.

Kirkman, Oliver – Guitarist in The Reserved and regular on the Blackburn scene (Ch 2).

Lawrence House Preparatory School – Former boarding school in St Annes – and some friends there are mentioned in chapter one.

Leigh, Dennis – see John Foxx above.

Lawrence, Clive – journalist for Burnley Express (chapter 8).

LEP - Lancashire Evening Post – Preston based newspaper, whose journalists included Phil Widdows, Naomi Smith, Claire Wright

LET - Lancashire (Evening) Telegraph – Blackburn based newspaper whose journalists included Jon Anson (see above), Gail Atkinson, and Caroline Innes, Martin Cooper. I may have referred to it as (Evening) in parts when it is just Lancashire Telegraph – apologies.

Loat, Alan – organist at Trade Hall, Bamber Bridge where I drummed for a while in the early 1980s (Ch 1)

Long, George – promoter of a BOTBs competition at The Dungeon Club, Skelmersadale (Ch 8).

Lynas, Ivan – use to run Harry's Bar and now runs The Imperial Pub on Union Street in Chorley.

Lynch, Richard – Manchester promoter through Charabanc Promotions who put bands on at The Late Rooms, Peter Street (Ch 8)

Lyth, Andy & Vicky – Preston Music Collective (Ch 11).

Lyth, Aubrey – Ch Out takes.

M.A.C.Y. - Music & Art for Chorley Youth (chapter 7).

Mad Ferret – Pub venue in Preston – (Ch various and Out takes).

Malcolm, Brian – helped secure the interviews I did with the Iinviisiibles (Ch Out takes).

Mansfield, Paul* – original lead vocalist with Duckhunt (Ch various).

Marsh, Andy – member of Helico (Ch 6)

Martin, Jon-Lee – Ex Fi-Lo Radio lead singer and guitarist. Also in Kong and Then Thickens (Various & Out takes)

Martindale, Alex – ex Turgid, Blackburn based promoter and long term partner of Kerry McGregor (see below). (Ch 2,8, 11).

Mason – Michael – childhood neighbour and friend (Ch 1)

Matlock, Glen – Sex Pistols bassist, ex Rich Kids, song writer and author (Ch 2, 3).

Maxwell, Jake – Son of Shaun (Ch 9). "Maxi" was a CCC regular and played in many Chorley bands including Geoffrey Bungle. Is now a successful sound technician to many more famous bands and is a member of The Ligaments (Ch 4,8).

McKenna, Curtis – sound technicians at The Attic, Accrington and ex member of Hope and Green Quarter (Ch various)

McKeown, Marc – "Quzi" bassist in The Reserved and regular on the Blackburn scene (Ch 2,11)

McDonald, Rachel – member of Wowzer and a CCC regular.

McGinty, Sean – BBC Radio Lancashire presenter and actively involved with promoting bands and musicians on the Fylde Coast. His shows provided exposure to local music via interviews and air play. Introduced me to Radio One's Big Weekend in Preston (Ch 8, 11).

McGregor, Kerry – journalist and founder of Blackburn based fanzine Burn Out – long time partner to Alex Martindale (Ch 2,8, 11).

McKenzie, Bruce – Worked at Townsend Records shop in Chorley in 2002 and introduced me to Glen Matlock. He has helped many bands and solo artists including Malibu Stacy and Icicle Works front man Ian McNabb. He has helped develop Townsend Records mail order business and at the time of writing is managing Macclesfield's Rock trio the Virginmarys.

McLoughlin, Seamus – singer song writer from Chorley (Ch11).

McNulty, Kristy* - use to be a regular gig attendee around Blackburn – see I didn't forget to mention you in my book!

Mellor, Chris – Cultural Development Manager for Chorley Borough Council when I started (Ch 7).

Millanese, Stefano – set up Riot Act Promotions & Management Ltd, based in Rawtenstall. Fan of Freespirits (Ch11).

Moonan, Dusty* – singer songwriter from Colwyn Bay and Facebook friend who I have seen at the Railway, Chorley on many occasions

Morgan, Alasdair and Gareth - (brothers)– childhood neighbours and friends (Ch 1)

Moss, Christian – AKA "Fish"- part of the RSLs for Chorley FM (Ch 4).

Moss, Ian – founder of The Hamsters and various bands based around

Manchester up to his current band Kill Pretty. His biography "The Man Who Killed The Hamsters" (Paragon Publishing) was written by Stephen Dobson.

Moss, Phil – singer with The Message, Supa Nova and Underdogs (Ch 6,8,12)

Murray, Conrad – Manchester Journalist who gave Let's Not Lose Mars to the Commies a favourable review (Ch 5,10)

Norman, Giselle – co-worker and friend in Barrow-in-Furness whose husband Kym played in local bands (Ch1)

Naylor, David – G/V with David R Black, promoter of gigs at Bury Met and set up 1000 Watt Recordings (Ch various)

Murrell, Allan* – Met him at BOTBS, Preston. He set up Red Cat Studios in Standish and I passed his name on to a few bands.

Nicholson, Ric – drummer in Elcho (Ch 11)

Noblet, Peter – Judo buddy of mine from Mill Hill Club, Blackburn (Ch 4).

O'Brien, Liam* - bassist in Hope (Ch 11).

O'Neil, Gary- my contact at Euxton Cricket Club (Ch 6)

PA – Public Address – i.e. sound speakers used at venues.

Parker, Alan – journalist from Blackburn who wrote books about Sid Vicious, The Clash and Stiff Little Fingers (Ch 2).

Parker, Susan* – contact name for the band SCAR – a band who were popular in Darwen

Parker, Joe* - member of Geoffrey Bungle (Ch 6)

Patrick, Oliver – lead singer with Farse – the band that The Commies supported who were on Moon Ska records (Ch 5)

Peters, Mike – Alarm front man and played with Dead Men Walking (Ch 2, 8).

Pikemanmick – on line identity of Michael Guy see above.

Platt, Alex* - member of Gehenna Paradise and Sterling Rose.

Porter, Joseph – drummer and singer for Blyth Power, raconteur and thoroughly nice chap (Ch 2).

PTID – Pogo'til I Die – punk fanzine – see chapter 2 and refer to Roy Hesketh above.

Quinney, Andrew – ex Faultline (Ch 6).

Railway, The – Pub on Steely lance, Chorley that caters for live music at time of printing.

Ramsbottom, Andrew 8 – vocalist in Three Ways West (Ch 7).

Rawcliffe, Martin *– ex The Flares, who I tried to help as a solo G/vocalist during some live recording sessions at The Attic.

Rawlinson, Lance – manager of Elcho, father to Chris – bassist in this Preston trio (Ch11).

Reid, Kris – booker and promoter of The Roadhouse, Manchester (Ch6).

Richardson, Matt – Guitar and vocals in Missed-Her-Bliss (Ch 6)

Riffs – Live Music Venue, Blackpool (Ch Out takes)

Riley, James – student and founder of Flea Pit Films (Ch 8).

Ripman, Paul *– Manchester on Line radio DJ who I met while transporting Shaun Maxwell to his interview with him.

Roberts, Lynda & Steve – couple who recommended Stephen Dobson to me and Lynda has an excellent blog Echo Stains.

Robinson, Michael – ex Head boy at Balshaws High School, Leyland who introduced me to The Jam (Ch1)

Robb, John – journalist and member of Goldblade and The Membranes (Ch2)

Rossall, Daniel – guitarist in Gahena Paradise and Sterling Rose before going solo (Ch 11).

Runshaw Sixth Form College*, Leyland – attended 1979-1981. Here **Helen Tozer** (English Teacher) inspired my appreciation of poetry and acting. (Ch 1)

Ruth, Ben – singer and harmonica player in R&B band The Convulsions (based in Lancaster) helped overseas bands play in the UK (Ch 11, Out takes)

Savage, Peter – player of the Uilleann pipes

and ex owner of the Post Office on Bury Lane, Withnell, (Ch 4).

Scarisbrick, Phil – bassist in The Message, Supa Nova and The Underdogs (Ch 6,8,12)

Seal Films, Based in Higher Wheelton when I started and did some excellent work for me and MACY (Ch 6,7)

Seward, Charlotte-Jane -founding member of MACY and use to introduce bands on Saturdays nights at CCC (Ch 7).

Sharp, Sam* – contact name for Nana's revenge Ch 5)

Sharpe, Dave – ex Alarm guitarist (Ch 2).

Shooman, Joe*– Good journalist based in Liverpool who I knew briefly at the start who recommended The Relatives to me.

Shorthouse, Alex – relation of Dave Gilmour's who is the model on the Digger Movement CD (Ch11).

Smith, Simon* – member of Geoffrey Bungle (Ch 6)

Stanley, Karl – co-presenter on second set of my Chorley Radio sessions and responsible for me seeking out Bruce McKenzie (Ch 3).

Stephens, Huw – Radio One DJ (Ch 11 & Out takes).

Sticky Tapes Studios* -popular recording studio with a lot of bands when I first started out.

Stokes, Michael – Guitar vocalist in Pike and member of Dumb Down (Ch, 3, 6, 10)

Sullivan, Justin – G/v with New Model Army (Ch 2).

Sumner, Mike* – member of "Ji" – pronounced "Gee" from Great Crosby.

Swain, Beth – ex BED and Stolen Ponies (Ch 12)

Taylor, Jay – former promoter at the Night & Day Cafe, Manchester (Ch 8, 11).

Taylor, Stuart – Punk promoter who was the first person I knew who used CD compilations to promote the bands he helped. Gave me encouragement, introduced me to Vice Squad and bands that Carol Hodge fronted – see above and Ch 2.

Thomas, Gareth – writer for Audience magazine (Ch10).

Thorpe, Dave AKA Brother Bastion – East Lancashire singer song writer ex Fetish (Bass & Vox) – (Ch 11).

Thwaites, Chris – Bassist ex Spitfire and best man to Noel Duffy at his wedding (Ch 8).

Townsend, Darren *– Landlord at The Adelphi, Accrington who helped me put some bands on there for a while.

Townsend Records, Market Street, Chorley & other shops in Clitheroe, Great Harwood, Leyland and on line providers of music (Ch 10)

Turley, Liz – sound engineer and CCC regular and voice of "Chorley Girl" radio show (Ch 2).

Turner, Andrew – Presenter on 2BR radio (Chapter 8).

Timms, Jonathan – AKA "Timsy" sound tech who provided PAs to many venues.

Troughton, Pete – engineer and producer at Studio Studio where Pretendgirlfriend recorded.

UK Nige – stage name for front man of Sick 56 (Ch 2).

Upton, Robert – member of Rhythmic Intent (Ch 6)

Unsworth, Chris – guitarist vocalist – member of Helico and Green Quarter (Ch 6, 11).

V Man Events – I associated Vuz Kapur with this music promotion company (Ch 8)

Walsh, James* – singer songwriter in Starsailor, grew up in Chorley and attended St Michael's School (Ch 7)

Ward, Gary – Darwen Music Festival (Ch 8).

Watt, Martin* – ex member of In Car Stereo who looked me up when his new band Dana Walker played in Blackburn.

Webster, Kyle – lead singer in Leyland based band Crazy Talk (Ch 6).

Wells, Gary*– was either a member of a recommended me to The Kiss Off when I was in Bolton once – never got to see the band but liked the CD by the way!

Wez* - sorry don't have your full name but you were a regular /bar staff at the Attic, Accrington and recommend Ground Cru to me.

Whalley, Michael – fan of The Commies and CCC regular. Last met doing sound at The Imperial and runs his own recording studios in Chorley.

Whatley, Matthew – son of Catherine –a long time family friend- who fronted Barrow-In-Furness based, The Usual Suspects (Ch 8).

Wigan Diggers – who hold a festival in the town centre in September and champion the work of Gerrard Winstanley (Ch 11).

Wheble, Daniel* - member of CMC.

Whitehead, Daniel – guitar vocalist in The Reserved and regular on the Blackburn scene (Ch 2)

Wilson, Anthony – former Granada TV presenter, set up factory Records and wrote 24 Hours Party People. (Ch 8,11)

Winstanley, Gerrard – born in Wigan, founder of The Digger Movement in 1649 & the inspiration to the Wigan Diggers Festival (Ch 11).

Winstanley, Glyn and John David – my half brothers to my father's first wife Elizabeth /"Betty (Ch 1).

Woods, Sam – lead guitar and vocals for Hyperjax (Ch various))

Wright, Amanda – CCC regular who use to take money on the door there and at few gigs I did at The Attic, Accrington.

Wright, Chris– member of Crashed Out (CH 2)

Wright, Liam – drummer with Let's Not Lose Mars to the Commies (Ch 5).

Wright, Paul – set up northwestbands.co.uk, Oxjam music promoter and half of Nashville City All-Stars.

Wylie, Pete – Liverpool musician in Wah (and its variations), Dead Men Walking (Ch 2, 9).

X – Ray Spex – Fronted by Poly Styrene who was the first female in Punk I respected for being anti glamorous in both looks and vocal style.

Yates, Jordan – Guitar vocalist with In Car Stereo (Ch 5,6,8)

"Zoltan"* – real name not listed but he was the drummer with Tessem and included in the list to complete the alpha bet.

Band listings

Key: Those in Speech marks or with Chapter numbers by them mean that there is more than a name check in the main part of the book - See Index & abbreviations too.

A is For Ape
10 Days
12ft Machette
13 Amp (Ch 10)
13th Conspiracy
22 Drop Out
3 Men Gone Mad (Ch 11)
3 Yards Of Susage
36C
4 Day Hombre
4 Past Midnight (Ch 2)
5th Element
76 Seconds
"999 (Ch 1,2)"
A.D.I.
Abiosis
Acacia
Act of Abortion
"Ad Nauseum (Ch 8,11)"
Adequate 7 (Ch 2)
Adesire (Ch 9)
Adnayseam
Aftercast
Age of Consent
AK Riot
AK47
"Alarm (Ch 1,8)"
Alfa 9
All Rights Rejected
Ambush UK
Amy Costello
"Anamosa (Ch 4,6)"
Anderson Shelter
Anodize (Ch 6)
Anti Placid
Arc Delta
Architect
Armrug
As Night Falls Upon Us

Ascudos
Asmiov (Ch 6)
Asylum
Atonal Perkie
Audio Rush
"Aurota (Ch 7,11)"
Automatic Hound Dog (ch 6)
Avalon Way (Ch 11)
Baby Bitch
Backwash
Basti (Ch 8)
Bed (Ch 6)
Belief System
Bikini Black Special
"Billy Bragg (Ch 1,11)"
Billy Club
Bingo Bay
Birdman
Black Jackals
Black Lines
Black Tie & Straight Jacket
Bleach (Ch 8)
Blimp
Blind Inside
Blue Hobo
Blue Tile Lounge
Blueprints (Ch 1)
Bluntfoot
"Blythe Power (Ch 1,2)"
Bobby Dazzlers
Boddah (Ch 10)
Boredom
Bourgie Bourgie (Ch 1)
Bret Classical
Broke ?n? English
Brother Big Bad (USA Ch 11)
BSI
Buck Brothers
Bunny

Burn (Ch Out takes)
Burn Machina
Bushbabies
Cacophony
Cadium
Cameron
Captain Everything
Captive Audio
Capulet (Ch 11)
Cassidy
Catcher
Censa Feye
Chapel 10
Chase
Cherries
Chevrons
Chompo-Pompo
Circle
"Citizen Band (Ch 8,10)"
Clerks
CMC
Colonial Movement Company
Colorpool (Ch 11)
Columbia
Container Drivers
Convulsions (Ch 11)
Cornerstone
"Costello (Ch 11,12)"
Cotton Scourge (Ch 1)
Counteract
Crashed Out (Ch 2)
Crazy Talk
Crimson Rise
Cropduster (Out takes)
Crosbi
Crouch Mog
Crowley's Dead (Ch 11)
Dana Walker
Dance Troop
Dangerfields (Ch 2)
Daniel Rossall (Ch 11)
Dash Rip Rock (Ch 9)
David R Black
Days End
Dead Clowns
Dead Girls Don't Say
Dead Honchos (Ch 11)

Dead Jim
Ded Mole Cricket
Deplorable Word
Depon Eye
Derrin Nauendorf
Desire (Ch 9)
Destructive Issue
Die Haut (Ch 1)
Digby
Dislocation Dance (Ch 1)
Displacement
Dog Food (Ch 1)
Dog Toffee
Double Ended
Doublethink
Douglas
"Duckhunt (Ch 2,3,10)"
Duffle
"Dumpstar (Ch 4,11)"
Duvettes
Dyenisis
Easy Street
Ebony Tay (Canada Ch 11)
"Echo Freddy (Ch 4,10)"
Efferescent
Effigy
Elcho (Ch 11)
Electric Circus Band
Elia's Last Day
Ellis
Elohymn (Ch 7)
Elpileptics
Eneurysm
Enima
Ernest
Ethergy
Everydays
Excels
Exit State (Ch 11)
Exorsisters
Failsafe (Ch 10)
Failure By Designed
Fairmount Park
Fallout Theory
False Resolutions
Fashionable Wino?s
Fast Eddys

Fat Cat
Faultline
Fetish (Ch 10)
Fi Lo Radio (various & Out takes)
Fire In The Empire
Flamingo 50
Flares
Flutter Effect (USA Ch 11)
For My Anger
Forced Entry
Former Bullies (Ch 11)
Four Day Autumn
Four Kings (Ch 8)
Freaky Kojack
Free Falling Camels
Freespirits (Ch 11)
Frencheryck
Fresh Dropped Mites
Fried (?Wigan)
Friend of Foe
Froyd Egg (Ch 9)
Funding Emo
Fyst
Gahenna Paradise (Ch 11)
Garland Green
Generic Nothing
Genocides
Geoffrey Bungle
Gift
Girls (Israel)
Glyn Bailey
God Botherer
Gone Beggin
Gone to Earth
Gotukola
Grand Cru
Grechin Falls
Green Quarter (Ch 11)
Grim Beavers
Gringo Star (Ch 11)
Ground Crew (Ch 10)
Guilty Pleasures
Gun Powder Plot
Hair
Hamiltons
"Hangman (Ch 2, 9)"
Hara Kiri

Harrison
Hawthorns
"Helico (Ch5,11)"
Hello Mother Fucker
Hit and Run Holiday
HMF
Hollis Brown (Ch 4)
Home Made Memory
Hoover Dams
Hope
Howard's Alias
How's My Pop? (Ch Out takes)
Hug Lorenzo (Ch 6)
Hyer-Value
"Hyperjax (Ch 2, 10)"
Ianio
Icemen
Idanos
Idiom Lifeline
If All Else Fails (Ch 11)
III On Speed
"In Car Stereo (Ch 8,10)"
In The Way
India Mill (Ch Out takes)
Inertia Rise
Infalable Heroes
Inspiral Carpets
Interface
Jack In The Green
Jackpot Golden Boys
Jahooli
Jelly's Last Jam
Jethro
Ji
Joe's Steakhouse
Johnny 5
Johnny No Stars
"Joseph Porter (Ch 1, 2)"
Kai Silva (Ch 11)
Karma
KBC
Kenesis (Ch 2)
"Kid Conspiracy (Ch 2,)"
Kill Casino (Ch 12)
Kill Pretty
King Casanova
King Genius

Quarters
Rage
Rarebird (Ch 1)
Raynes (Ch 11)
Re:Verb (Ch 11)
Rebecca
Rebekah
Rebound
Reemer
Relatives
Remedies
Remedy
Remote Inca School
Renton (Ch 8)
Resent
Reserved (Ch2 and 11)
Resin
Riot to Us
Riptons
Rise to Ruin
Ritzi
Riverside Happy
"Rocket Dog (Ch 2, 8)"
Ronin
Runs
Rythmic Coughing
Rythmic Intent
Sadie Hawkins Dance (Ch 2)
Sam Salon
San Froyd (Ch 11)
Say Jansfield (Ch 9)
Scar
"Scarlet Marshalls (Ch 8,11)"
Scary Billy Bob
Schism
Schismatic
Scribes
Seamus McLoughlin (Ch 11)
Sell Out Flaw
Semi Smalls
Seven Years Dead
Seventeen (who became The Alarm)
Sex Pistols (Various)
Shakes (Scotland Ch 11)
Shoks
Shorn (Ch 9)
Shot Gun Fairies

Shoulders (Ch 1)
Shyler Jansen
Sick 56 (Ch 2)
Sighing Gaia
Silvertones
Sinsiter Chuckles (Ch 9)
Sirclus
Skys Came Tropic
Slash Monkeys
Sleaze
Sleeper Cell
Slick Fifty
Slideshow
Small Amp (Ch 11)
Smear
Smudge
Soma
Someone Famous
Sonnetts (USA)
Southpaw
Spanglefish
Sparehed3
Spaz The Apple Core
Spiral Rocks
"Spitfire (Ch 8, 10)"
Spitting Dummies
"Sprungloaded (Ch 11,12)"
Stabilisers
Stalker
Star 27
Starkey?s Walk
Steranko
Sterling Rose (Ch 11)
Still Life
Stolen
Stolen Ponies
Stone Devils
Strange Days
Stringybark MacDowell
Stunt Face
Stupid Little Cars (Ch 9)
Sudden Death
Sugarrush (Finland)
Super Nova
Superkings
Sures
Suspicious Stains

SWF
Synko (Ch 2)
Tango Brigade (Ch 1)
"Tansads (Ch 1,4)"
Taser Pupets (Ch 9)
Terza-Rimar
Tessem
Thee Neerlymen
Things (Ch Out takes)
This Product (Ch 11)
Three Man Amp
Three Minute Warning
Three Ways West
Three White Sisters (Ch 11)
Tier Garden (Ch 1)
Tin Gods
Titan
Titus Gein
Tompaulin (Ch 10)
Too Much Texas (Ch 8)
Torrents (Ch Out takes)
Transport (Australia Ch 11)
Turgid
Twinky
Unchosen
Uncle Jeff
Underdogs
Underground Mongs (Ch 9)
Unfinnsied Business (Ch 8)
Usual Suspects
Usuals
Valley Forge (Ch 1)
Venus Star
Vinyls
Virginmarys
Virtues (Sweden)
Volume 12 (Ch 8)
Waltones (Ch 1)
Wasted Earth
Wave Machines
What the...? (USA)
Wheel Jacks (Ch 11)
White Haze
White Rod
Window Right
Wire Train (ch 1)
Wires

Witches of Elswick
Wormwood Scrubs
Wowzer
X Rippers
Your Mum
Yr Impossible (Ch 11)
Yumi Yumi
Zeroscape
Ziv
Zombina & The Skelatons

Lightning Source UK Ltd.
Milton Keynes UK
UKOW04f1445280814

237663UK00002B/190/P